SO-AWB-724

Crisis and

ity

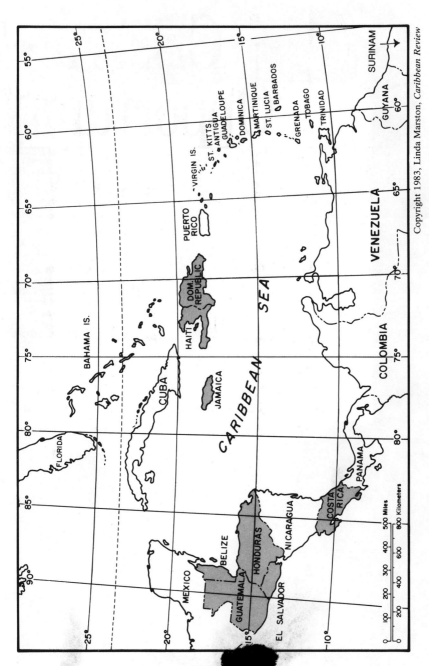

CENTRAL AMERICA AND THE CARIBBEAN

Crisis and Opportunity

U.S. Policy in Central America and the Caribbean

Thirty Essays by Statesmen, Scholars,
Religious Leaders, and Journalists

Edited by Mark Falcoff
and Robert Royal

Ethics and Public Policy Center
Washington, D.C.

Library of Congress Cataloging in Publication Data
Main entry under title:
Crisis and opportunity.
Bibliography: p.
Includes index.
1. Central America — Politics and government — 1979-
— Addresses, essays, lectures. 2. Caribbean Area —
Politics and government — 1945-   — Addresses, essays,
lectures. 3. Central America — Relations — United States
— Addresses, essays, lectures. 4. United States —
Relations — Central America — Addresses, essays, lectures.
5. Caribbean Area — Relations — United States — Addresses,
essays, lectures. 6. United States — Relations — Carib-
bean Area — Addresses, essays, lectures. I. Falcoff,
Mark. II. Royal, Robert, 1949-
F1439.5.C73 1984   972.8'052   84-1660
ISBN 0-89633-081-8
ISBN 0-89633-082-6 (pbk.)

$19 cloth, $12 paper   Second printing 1984

Contents

Introduction

THE CONTINUING CRISIS in Central America and the Caribbean raises three questions that are crucial to U.S. foreign policy: What is the proper role of our military power in world politics? What are the causes of political insurgency? And what is the moral and political character of regimes in the Third World?

These are large questions, but—as in the Vietnam era—the countries that have given them a new currency are small and not well known. It is hardly surprising that the debate has been clouded by ignorance and misunderstanding.

The Caribbean Basin, however, is far closer to us spatially and spiritually than Southeast Asia. Informed observers may disagree sharply on what occurs there and what it means, but all of them, from Fidel Castro to Ronald Reagan, agree that the relation between the United States and that region is of vital importance to the Caribbean countries, to U.S. interests, and to the world at large.

In the absence of adequate knowledge of Central America and the Caribbean, the discussion about U.S. policy there has been prey to false dilemmas, deceptive caricatures, and, not infrequently, hidden agendas. A common error is to separate domestic and international factors by citing either poverty alone, or Cuban and Soviet subversion alone, as the cause of violence and instability. The causes are more complex. Revolution cannot simply be exported from one country to another; it can establish itself only in a society ripe for radical exploitation. But support from external sources is a crucial factor. Foreign-backed revolutionaries have the means to aggravate social or economic problems, which in turn can precipitate a grave political crisis.

When this happens, collapse becomes almost inevitable. As the Kissinger Commission observed, "once an insurgency is fully under way and once the lines of external support are in place, it has a momentum which reforms alone cannot stop. Unchecked, the insurgents can destroy faster than the reformers can build."

Great inequalities and injustices exist in Central American societies; yet there is no simple relationship between them and the fortunes of a revolutionary movement. Modern history provides many examples of revolutions produced more by rising expectations than by abject despair.

The current economic situation in the Caribbean Basin certainly gives cause for profound concern. The rising expectations produced by a decade of economic growth have been suddenly frustrated by sharp increases in oil prices, the collapse of commodity markets, high interest rates, and a worldwide recession. Foreign investment has decreased abruptly in the face of increasing political uncertainty. Unless greater political stability can be achieved, economic recovery may be impossible.

Contributing to the political instability are the activities of the Soviet Union, Cuba, and Nicaragua, as well as an odd assortment of "outlaw states." Documents captured in El Salvador in 1980 and published early in 1981 made it clear that the international support network of the Salvadoran guerrillas included not only Eastern-bloc countries but also Soviet-backed Ethiopia and North Vietnam. Documents discovered after the rescue mission in Grenada revealed plans to export the instruments of revolution to the entire Caribbean Basin. Large numbers of weapons and advisors from the Soviet Union, Cuba, Bulgaria, and East Germany have given Nicaragua greater military forces than those of all the other Central American countries combined. Arms travel from Nicaragua to El Salvador's rebels, who maintain headquarters in Managua and regularly consult with Fidel Castro in Havana. All this is clearly a threat to U.S. interests as well as to the security and economic well-being of the small and vulnerable countries of the region.

This collection of essays seeks to add depth and texture to an often superficial policy debate by providing some essential facts, historical perspective, and a sharper look at current conditions. The reader should bear in mind that the situation in this region is changing rapidly. Major events have occurred since many of these articles were written, most notably the U.S. action in Grenada.

Part One examines the region in a broad framework that takes into account the uniqueness of particular states, long-term U.S. interests, and the global context. The problems of the Caribbean Basin stem in part from conditions that have existed for decades. Their solutions are certain to require time and a sustained U.S. commitment.

Part Two analyzes the struggle for power, land, and justice in El Salvador. In some respects the drama in this tiny republic is a microcosm of the struggle throughout the region, but it also has unique national elements. This section looks at the forces for change and what each represents; the relationship between rising popular expectations, the economic crisis, and the guerrilla movements; and how the United States can combine its strategic goals with its commitment to human rights and to the long-term interests of the peoples of the region.

Part Three focuses on Nicaragua. In many ways the debate over Central American policy is really about the significance of that country's revolution. On one side, the U.S. government regards the Sandinista regime in Managua as a tragic example of what might happen in El Salvador and, ultimately, in other nearby countries. On the other side, a small but highly influential group of Americans in the universities, the prestige media, and the churches regards the Nicaraguan experiment not merely as the inevitable outcome of more than three decades of "right-wing tyranny" but as a model to be emulated.

The Sandinista regime has evoked passionate reactions across the political spectrum, as this section shows. The regime has been winning advocates abroad even as it has been alienating many former supporters at home, including several key figures who helped overthrow Somoza. Although some sympathizers assert that the Nicaraguan revolution has gone sour because of U.S. provocations, many other observers, including several major intellectuals of the American left, see events in Nicaragua unfolding with a sinister logic of their own.

As in an earlier volume published by the Ethics and Public Policy Center, *The Apocalyptic Premise: Nuclear Arms Debated,* each essay in this collection is preceded by a brief introduction, called "Focus," that points out main themes and relates complementary and opposing selections to one another. Each of the three parts of the book opens with a chronology, and parts two and three also have a country map. The map of the entire region is on page ii. Four official documents referred to in the text are printed as appendixes. The index of proper names will help the reader sort out the complex web of political coalitions and guerrilla movements.

The amount of published material on Central America and the Caribbean is large, growing rapidly, and of highly uneven quality. The editors have provided a short bibliography as a reliable guide for further study.

The editors would like to thank Daniel James for his help at an early stage in the production of this volume. Georges Fauriol and Juan Carlos Weiss of the Georgetown Center for Strategic and International Studies made several important suggestions. Thanks are due also to the embassies of Mexico and Jamaica, which provided documents and other information.

At every step, the editors benefited from the wise counsel and patient encouragement of Ernest W. Lefever, president of the Ethics and Public Policy Center. The Center's editor, Carol Friedley Griffith, did her usual masterly job in transforming a pile of manuscript pages into a well-constructed book.

We are grateful to the authors and publishers for permission to reprint these essays. The editors alone are responsible for the selection of the pieces and for the introductions.

MARK FALCOFF
ROBERT ROYAL

Washington, D.C.
February 15, 1984

MARK FALCOFF is a resident fellow at the American Enterprise Institute for Public Policy Research in Washington, D.C. He received his M.A. and Ph.D. from Princeton University and has taught at the universities of Illinois, Oregon, and California (Los Angeles), as well as at the U.S. Foreign Service Institute. His books include (with Ronald H. Dolkart) *Prologue to Perón: Argentina in Depression and War, 1930-43* (1976) and (with Frederick B. Pike) *The Spanish Civil War, 1936-39: American Hemispheric Perspectives* (1982).

ROBERT ROYAL, a research associate at the Ethics and Public Policy Center, was formerly editor-in-chief of *Prospect* magazine, published in Princeton, New Jersey. He holds an M.A. from Brown University, where he also taught. He spent 1979 in Italy as a Fulbright Fellow, has done extensive research in Latin languages, literatures, and cultures, and has written essays and reviews for several publications.

PART ONE

Regional and Global Perspectives

Chronology

1812–1899

1812	Constitutional monarchy established in Spain; colonial rule liberalized. Election of town councils in Central America marks beginning of national political life.
1814	Fernando VII restored to Spanish throne; annuls 1812 constitution and all its outgrowths in the New World.
1821	Guatemala and other provinces of Central America declare independence from Spain, but differ on subsequent course of action.
1822	Central American provinces annex themselves to independent Mexican Empire under General Augustín de Iturbide, later Emperor Augustín I.
1823-24	Augustín I overthrown; Mexico becomes a republic. Costa Rica, Guatemala, Honduras, Nicaragua, and El Salvador form Central American Federation, with capital in Guatemala City (later, briefly, San Salvador).
1825	United States and Central American Federation sign treaty of friendship, ratified following year.
1829-38	Political conflict between federation members and the capital increases. In 1838, Central American Congress allows states to leave federation; Nicaragua, Honduras, and Costa Rica secede.
1847	Guatemala declares itself a "republic" rather than a "state," foreclosing possibility of reunion. Other Central American states follow suit.
1850-55	Trans-Panama railway built. Most Central American commerce moved from Caribbean to Pacific ports.
1895-99	Major efforts to restore Central American Federation fail.

1900 – 1983

1903	**Panama** declares independence from Colombia; United States quickly recognizes it and negotiates favorable treaty to build interoceanic canal.
1914	**Panama Canal** opened.
1917	**Attempted union** of five Central American states, on Honduran initiative, fails when Nicaragua refuses to cooperate.
1927	Peace accord among fighting factions in **Nicaragua** provides basis for U.S. occupation and subsequent elections.
1927-34	General Augusto C. **Sandino** leads Nicaraguan guerrillas against U.S. occupation.
1934	**Sandino** murdered by members of Nicaraguan National Guard; Guard chief Anastasio **Somoza** dominates country until 1956.
1936	U.S.-**Panama** Canal Treaty abrogated; United States abandons protectorate powers over Panama and agrees to nonintervention.
1944	Dictator Jorge Ubico in **Guatemala** resigns under pressure of violence and protests.
1944-50	"Spiritual socialist" Juan José Arévalo heads reformist administration in **Guatemala.**
1948	Fraudulent conservative government in **Costa Rica** overthrown by José Figueres and his Army of National Liberation; start of long period of democratic institutions and dominance of Figueres in Costa Rican politics.
1948	**Organization of American States** (OAS) created.
1950-54	Jacobo Arbenz elected president of **Guatemala.** Revolutionary reforms intensify; Communist infiltration of government increases.
1952	Fulgencio Batista seizes power in **Cuba** and establishes repressive dictatorship.
1953	Cuban revolutionary leader Fidel **Castro** imprisoned after unsuccessful attack on army post in Santiago de Cuba.

1954	OAS "Declaration of Solidarity" against intervention of International Communism is directed against Arbenz government in **Guatemala.** After Eastern European arms arrive, Colonel Carlos Castillo Armas overthrows Arbenz with aid of Honduras, Nicaragua, and U.S.
1955	Fidel **Castro** released from Cuban prison; goes to Mexico.
1956	Anastasio **Somoza** assassinated. His sons, Luis and Anastasio, Jr., continue family domination of Nicaragua to 1979.
1956	Fidel **Castro** and several dozen companions arrive in Cuba from Mexico to begin guerrilla struggle.
1957	Castillo Armas assassinated. Period of instability and violence begins in **Guatemala.**
1958-63	Conservative Miguel Ydígoras Fuentes elected president of **Guatemala.**
1959	**Castro** overthrows Cuban dictator Batista; establishes totalitarian regime.
1961	U.S.-sponsored exile invasion of **Cuba** fails to establish beachhead at Bay of Pigs; Castro declares himself Marxist-Leninist and ally of Soviet Union.
1962	U.S.-Soviet crisis over placement of strategic missiles in **Cuba** resolved by compromise: Soviet Union agrees to remove the weapons; U.S. promises not to invade the island.
1964	Riots in **Panama Canal Zone** lead to new canal treaty negotiations.
1965	U.S. intervention in **Dominican Republic** restores order after left-wing insurgency.
1972	Earthquake devastates Managua, **Nicaragua.** Poor handling of crisis and mishandling of international relief aid by Anastasio Somoza Debayle increase opposition to his dictatorship.
1972	Michael Manley of pro-socialist People's National Party begins first term as prime minister of **Jamaica.**
1972	Christian Democrat José Napoleón Duarte wins plurality in **El Salvador** election. Legislature, however, acting

	within constitution, chooses Colonel Arturo Armando Molina as president. Duarte charges fraud, is arrested and exiled.
1974	Election fraud in **Nicaragua** ensures Somoza's reelection to six-year term.
1977	New Panama Canal treaties establishing means for eventually ceding canal to **Panama** ratified by U.S. Senate after long fight.
1979	Somoza overthrown in **Nicaragua;** new governing coalition dominated by Marxist FSLN (Sandinista National Liberation Front) assumes power.
1979	Young military officers overthrow **El Salvador** dictator General Carlos Humberto Romero.
1979	Maurice Bishop seizes control of **Grenada** while elected prime minister Eric Gairy is out of country.
1980	New government of **El Salvador** declares land, tax, and banking reforms. Carter administration suspends U.S. aid to Nicaragua because of evidence that FSLN is arming Salvadoran insurgents. In December, José Napoleón Duarte becomes president of military-civilian junta.
1980	Anti-Communist **Jamaica** Labor Party defeats Michael Manley; Edward Seaga becomes prime minister.
1981	Guerrillas in **El Salvador** launch unsuccessful "final offensive" early in year. Carter administration resumes arms sale to Salvadoran government.
1981	U.S. Congress requires semi-annual certification of progress in human rights in **El Salvador** as condition for military aid.
1982	Elections for constituent assembly in **El Salvador** draw record turnout despite guerrilla threats. Alvaro Magaña named provisional president.
1982	President Reagan launches **Caribbean Basin Initiative.**
1983	Marxist dictator Maurice Bishop and other government officials in **Grenada** murdered in October by hard-line Marxists led by Bernard Coard. U.S. forces restore peace and parliamentary democracy; Coard imprisoned, Cuban "advisors" expelled.

1. U.S. Responsibility in Central America

By RONALD REAGAN

Focus The President's address before a joint session of Congress on April 28, 1983, is the keystone of the Reagan administration's policy on Central America. It related the political and economic problems in that region to specific proposals for a responsible U.S. role towards our allies and friends.

The President emphasized that he was acting not to resolve a crisis but to prevent one. Central America, he said, is vital to the United States because two-thirds of our foreign trade and petroleum pass through the Panama Canal and the Caribbean. If in a crisis we needed to supply our NATO allies, at least half of our sea cargo would transit this region.

Furthermore, he added, we have a duty to defend our ally, El Salvador, against armed aggression masquerading as a "people's movement." The President quoted Secretary of State George P. Shultz: "Unable to win the free loyalty of El Salvador's people, the guerrillas are deliberately and systematically depriving them of food, water, transportation, light, sanitation, and jobs. And these are the people who claim they want to help the common people." (For an estimate of the magnitude of this damage see appendix C.)

This "revolution" is being aided, said the President, by Nicaragua, Cuba, and ultimately the Soviet Union. To defend the imperfect but partly free regime in El Salvador, we must stop this flow of arms and assistance to the insurrectionists.

President Reagan acknowledged the severe economic problems and human rights difficulties of the Central American governments. Both military support and economic aid are necessary to our policy of encouraging peace with freedom, he said. The President pledged twice as much economic as military aid to El Salvador and promised to encourage progress toward greater respect for human rights, but he emphasized that substantial reform and development are impossible while guerrillas continue to cause widespread social and economic disruption. For an opposing overview of the U.S. role in the region, see Fidel Castro's speech delivered three months later (selection 2).

Ronald Reagan was elected fortieth President of the United States in 1980.

A NUMBER OF TIMES in past years, members of Congress and a president have come together in meetings like this to resolve a crisis. I have asked for this meeting in the hope that we can *prevent* one.

It would be hard to find many Americans who are not aware of our stake in the Middle East, the Persian Gulf, or the NATO line dividing the free world from the Communist bloc. The same could be said for Asia.

But in spite of, or maybe because of, a flurry of stories about places like Nicaragua and El Salvador and, yes, some concerted propaganda, many of us find it hard to believe we have a stake in problems involving those countries. Too many have thought of Central America as just that place way down below Mexico that cannot possibly constitute a threat to our well-being.

That is why I have asked for this session. Central America's problems do directly affect the security and well-being of our own people. And Central America is much closer to the United States than many of the world trouble spots that concern us. As we work to restore our own economy, we cannot afford to lose sight of our neighbors to the south.

El Salvador is nearer to Texas than Texas is to Massachusetts. Nicaragua is just as close to Miami, San Antonio, San Diego, and Tucson as those cities are to Washington, where we are gathered tonight.

But nearness on the map does not even begin to tell the strategic importance of Central America, bordering as it does on the Caribbean—our lifeline to the outside world. Two-thirds of all our foreign trade and petroleum pass through the Panama Canal and the Caribbean. In a European crisis, at least half of our supplies for NATO would go through these areas by sea. It is well to remember that in early 1942 a handful of Hitler's submarines sank more tonnage there than in all of the Atlantic Ocean. And they did this without a single naval base anywhere in the area.

9

Today, the situation is different. Cuba is host to a Soviet combat brigade, a submarine base capable of servicing Soviet submarines, and military air bases that are visited regularly by Soviet military aircraft.

Because of its importance, the Caribbean Basin is a magnet for adventurism. We are all aware of the Libyan cargo planes refueling in Brazil a few days ago on their way to deliver medical supplies to Nicaragua. Brazilian authorities discovered the so-called medical supplies were actually munitions and prevented their delivery.

You may remember that last month [March 1983], speaking on national television, I showed an aerial photo of an airfield being built on the island of Grenada. Well, if that airfield had been completed, those planes could have refueled there and completed their journey.

If the Nazis during World War II and the Soviets today could recognize the Caribbean and Central America as vital to our interests, should not we also?

For several years now, under two administrations, the United States has been increasing its defense of freedom in the Caribbean Basin. And I can tell you that democracy is beginning to take root in El Salvador, which until a short time ago knew only dictatorship. The new government is now delivering on its promises of democracy, reforms, and free elections. It was not easy, and there was resistance to many of the attempted reforms, with assassinations of the reformers. Guerrilla bands and urban terrorists were portrayed in a worldwide propaganda campaign as freedom-fighters representative of the people.

Ten days before I came into office, the guerrillas launched what they called a "final offensive" to overthrow the government. Their radio boasted that our new administration would be too late to prevent their victory. They learned democracy cannot be so easily defeated.

President Carter did not hesitate. He authorized arms and ammunition to El Salvador. The guerrilla offensive failed, but not America's will. Every president since this country assumed global responsibilities has known that those responsibilities could be met only if we pursued a bipartisan foreign policy.

As I said a moment ago, the government of El Salvador has been keeping its promises, like the land-reform program, which is making thousands of farm tenants farm owners. In a little over three years, 20 per cent of the arable land in El Salvador has been redistributed to more than 450,000 people. That is one in ten Salvadorans who has directly benefited from this program.

Elections in El Salvador

El Salvador has continued to strive toward an orderly and democratic society. The government promised free elections. On March 28 [1982], little more than a year ago, after months of campaigning by a variety of candidates, the people of El Salvador were offered a chance to vote, to choose the kind of government they wanted.

Suddenly, the so-called freedom-fighters in the hills were exposed for what they really are—a small minority who want power for themselves and their backers, not democracy for the people. The guerrillas threatened death to anyone who voted. They destroyed hundreds of buses and trucks to keep the people from getting to the polling places. Their slogan was brutal: "Vote today, die tonight."

But on election day, an unprecedented 80 per cent of the electorate braved ambush and gunfire and trudged for miles, many of them to vote for freedom. That is truly fighting for freedom. We can never turn our backs on that.

Members of this Congress who went there as observers told me of a woman who was wounded by rifle fire on the way to the polls, who refused to leave the line to have her wound treated until after she had voted. Another woman had been told by the guerrillas she would be killed when she returned from the polls, and she told the guerrillas, "You can kill me, you can kill my family, kill my neighbors, you can't kill us all."

The real freedom-fighters of El Salvador turned out to be the people of that country—the young, the old, the in-between, more than one million of them out of a population of less than five million. The world should respect this courage, not allow it to be belittled or forgotten. Again, I say in good conscience, we can never turn our backs on that.

The democratic political parties and factions in El Salvador are coming together around the common goal of seeking a political solution to their country's problems. New national elections will be held this year [later postponed to March 1984], and they will be open to all political parties. The government has invited the guerrillas to participate in the election and is preparing an amnesty law. The people of El Salvador are earning their freedom, and they deserve our moral and material support to protect it.

Yes, there are still major problems regarding human rights, the criminal justice system, and violence against noncombatants. And, like the rest of Central America, El Salvador also faces severe economic problems.

But, in addition to recession-depressed prices for major agricultural exports, El Salvador's economy is being deliberately sabotaged. Tonight in El Salvador, because of ruthless guerrilla attacks, much of the fertile land cannot be cultivated; less than half the rolling stock of the railways remains operational; bridges, water facilities, telephone and electric systems have been destroyed and damaged. In one twenty-two-month period, there were 5,000 interruptions of electrical power. One region was without electricity for a third of a year.

I think Secretary of State [George P.] Shultz put it very well the other day: "Unable to win the free loyalty of El Salvador's people, the guerrillas are deliberately and systematically depriving them of food, water, transportation, light, sanitation, and jobs. And these are the people who claim they want to help the common people."

They do not want elections because they know they would be defeated. But, as the previous election showed, the Salvadoran people's desire for democracy will not be defeated.

The guerrillas are not embattled peasants armed with muskets. They are professionals, sometimes with better training and weaponry than the government's soldiers.

The Salvadoran battalions that have received U.S. training have been conducting themselves well on the battlefield and with the civilian population. But, so far, we have provided only enough money to train one Salvadoran soldier out of ten, fewer than the number of guerrillas trained by Nicaragua and Cuba.

And let me set the record straight on Nicaragua, a country next to El Salvador. In 1979, when the new government took over in Nicaragua, after a revolution which overthrew the authoritarian rule of Somoza, everyone hoped for the growth of democracy. We in the United States did, too. By January of 1981, our emergency relief and recovery aid to Nicaragua totaled $118 million, more than provided by any other developed country. In fact, in the first two years of Sandinista rule, the United States directly or indirectly sent five times more aid to Nicaragua than it had in the two years prior to the revolution. Can anyone doubt the generosity and good faith of the American people?

These were hardly the actions of a nation implacably hostile to Nicaragua. Yet the government of Nicaragua has treated us as an enemy. It has rejected our repeated peace efforts. It has broken its promises to us, to the Organization of American States, and, most important of all, to the people of Nicaragua.

No sooner was victory achieved than a small clique ousted others who had been part of the revolution from having any voice in government. Humberto Ortega, the minister of defense, declared Marxism-Leninism would be their guide, and so it is.

New Dictatorship in Nicaragua

The government of Nicaragua has imposed a new dictatorship; it has refused to hold the elections it promised; it has seized control of most media and subjects all media to heavy prior censorship; it denied the bishops and priests of the Roman Catholic Church the right to say Mass on radio during Holy Week; it insulted and mocked the Pope; it has driven the Miskito Indians from their homelands—burning their villages, destroying their crops, and forcing them into involuntary internment camps far from home; it has moved against the private sector and free labor unions; it condoned mob action against Nicaragua's independent human rights commission and drove the director of that commission into exile.

In short, after all these acts of repression by the government, is it any wonder that opposition has formed?

Contrary to propaganda, the opponents of the Sandinistas are not diehard supporters of the previous Somoza regime. In fact, many are anti-Somoza heroes who fought beside the Sandinistas to bring down the Somoza government; now they have been denied any part in the new government because they truly wanted democracy for Nicaragua and still do. Others are Miskito Indians fighting for their homes, lands, and lives.

The Sandinista revolution in Nicaragua turned out to be just an exchange of one set of autocratic rulers for another, and the people still have no freedom, no democratic rights, and more poverty. Even worse than its predecessor, it is helping Cuba and the Soviets to destabilize our hemisphere.

Meanwhile, the government of El Salvador, making every effort to guarantee democracy, free labor unions, freedom of religion, and a free press, is under attack by guerrillas dedicated to the same philosophy that prevails in Nicaragua, Cuba, and, yes, the Soviet Union.

Violence has been Nicaragua's most important export to the world. It is the ultimate in hypocrisy for the unelected Nicaraguan government to charge that we seek their overthrow when they are doing everything they can to bring down the elected government of El Salvador. The Salvadoran guerrilla attacks are directed from a headquarters in Managua, the capital of Nicaragua.

But let us be clear as to the American attitude toward the government of Nicaragua. We do not seek its overthrow. Our interest is to ensure that it does not infect its neighbors through the export of subversion and violence. Our purpose, in conformity with American and international law, is to prevent the flow of arms to El Salvador, Honduras, Guatemala, and Costa Rica. We have attempted to have a dialogue with the government of Nicaragua, but it persists in its efforts to spread violence.

We should not, and we will not, protect the Nicaraguan government from the anger of its own people. But we should, through diplomacy, offer an alternative. And, as Nicaragua ponders its options, we can and will—with all the resources of diplomacy— protect each country of Central America from the danger of war.

Even Costa Rica, Central America's oldest and strongest democracy, a government so peaceful it does not even have an army, is the object of bullying and threats from Nicaragua's dictators.

Nicaragua's neighbors know that Sandinista promises of peace, nonalliance, and nonintervention have not been kept. Some thirty-six new military bases have been built—there were only thirteen during the Somoza years.

Nicaragua's new army numbers 25,000 men supported by a militia of 50,000. It is the largest army in Central America, supplemented by 2,000 Cuban military and security advisors. It is equipped with the most modern weapons, dozens of Soviet-made tanks, 800 Soviet-bloc trucks, Soviet 152 mm howitzers, 100 anti-aircraft guns, plus planes and helicopters. There are additional thousands of civilian advisors from Cuba, the Soviet Union, East Germany, Libya, and the Palestine Liberation Organization. And we are attacked because we have fifty-five military trainers in El Salvador.

Guerrilla Goal: Destabilization

The goal of the professional guerrilla movements in Central America is as simple as it is sinister: to destabilize the entire region from the Panama Canal to Mexico. If you doubt me on this point, just consider what Cayetano Carpio, the now-deceased Salvadoran guerrilla leader, said earlier this month. Carpio said that after El Salvador falls, El Salvador and Nicaragua would be "arm in arm and struggling for the total liberation of Central America."

Nicaragua's dictatorial junta, who themselves made war and won power operating from bases in Honduras and Costa Rica, like to pretend they are today being attacked by forces based in Honduras. The fact is, it is Nicaragua's government that threatens Honduras, not the reverse.

It is Nicaragua that has moved heavy tanks close to the border and Nicaragua that speaks of war. It was Nicaraguan radio that announced on April 8 the creation of a revolutionary coordinating board to push forward the Marxist struggle in Honduras.

Nicaragua, supported by weapons and military resources provided by the Communist bloc, represses its own people, refuses to make peace, and sponsors a guerrilla war against El Salvador.

President Truman's words are as apt today as they were in 1947, when he, too, spoke before a joint session of the Congress:

At the present moment in world history, nearly every nation must choose between alternative ways of life. The choice is too often not a free one.

One way of life is based upon the will of the majority and is distinguished by free institutions, representative government, free elections, guarantees of individual liberty, freedom of speech and religion, and freedom from political oppression.

The second way of life is based upon the will of a minority forcibly imposed upon the majority. It relies upon terror and oppression, a controlled press and radio, fixed elections, and the suppression of personal freedoms.

I believe that it must be the policy of the United States to support free peoples who are resisting attempted subjugation by armed minorities or by outside pressures. I believe that we must assist free peoples to work out their own destinies in their own way.

I believe that our help should be primarily through economic and financial aid, which is essential to economic stability and orderly political processes.

. . . Collapse of free institutions and loss of independence would be disastrous not only for them but for the world. Discouragement and possibly failure would quickly be the lot of neighboring peoples striving to maintain their freedom and independence.

The countries of Central America are smaller than the nations that prompted President Truman's message. But the political and strategic stakes are the same. Will our response—economic, social, military—be as appropriate and successful as Mr. Truman's bold solutions to the problems of post-war Europe?

Some people have forgotten the successes of those years and the decades of peace, prosperity, and freedom they secured. Some people talk as though the United States were incapable of acting effectively in international affairs without risking war or damaging those we seek to help.

The Fruits of Passivity

Are democracies required to remain passive while threats to their security and prosperity accumulate? Must we just *accept* the destabilization of an entire region from the Panama Canal to Mexico on our southern border? Must we sit by while independent nations of this hemisphere are integrated into the most aggressive empire the modern world has seen?

Must we wait while Central Americans are driven from their homes, like the more than a million who have sought refuge out of

Afghanistan or the 1.5 million who have fled Indochina or the more than one million Cubans who have fled Castro's Caribbean utopia? Must we, by default, leave the people of El Salvador no choice but to flee their homes, creating another tragic exodus?

I do not believe there is a majority in the Congress or the country that counsels passivity, resignation, defeatism in the face of this challenge to freedom and security in our hemisphere. I do not believe that a majority of the Congress or the country is prepared to stand by passively while the people of Central America are delivered to totalitarianism and we ourselves are left vulnerable to new dangers.

Only last week, an official of the Soviet Union reiterated [the late Soviet leader Leonid I.] Brezhnev's threat to station nuclear missiles in this hemisphere, five minutes from the United States. Like an echo, Nicaraguan *comandante* Daniel Ortega confirmed that, if asked, his country would consider accepting those missiles. I understand that today they may be having second thoughts.

Now, before I go any further, let me say to those who invoke the memory of Vietnam: There is no thought of sending American combat troops to Central America. They are not needed—indeed, they have not been requested there. All our neighbors ask of us is assistance in training and arms to protect themselves while they build a better, freer life.

We must continue to encourage peace among the nations of Central America. We must support the regional efforts now under way to promote solutions to regional problems.

We cannot be certain that the Marxist-Leninist bands that believe war is an instrument of politics will be readily discouraged. It is crucial that we not become discouraged before they do. Otherwise, the region's freedom will be lost and our security damaged in ways that can hardly be calculated.

If Central America were to fall, what would the consequences be for our position in Asia and Europe, and for alliances such as NATO?

If the United States cannot respond to a threat near our own borders, why should Europeans or Asians believe we are seriously concerned about threats to them?

If the Soviets can assume that nothing short of an actual attack on the United States will provoke an American response, which ally, which friend will trust us then?

The Congress shares both the power and the responsibility for our foreign policy. Tonight, I ask you, the Congress, to join me in a bold, generous approach to the problems of peace and poverty, democracy and dictatorship in the region. Join me in a program that prevents Communist victory in the short run but goes beyond to produce, for the deprived people of the area, the reality of present progress and the promise of more to come.

Let us lay the foundation for a bipartisan approach to sustain the independence and freedom of the countries of Central America. We in the administration reach out to you in this spirit.

Four Goals in the Region

We will pursue four basic goals in Central America:

• First, in response to decades of inequity and indifference, we will support democracy, reform, and human freedom. This means using our assistance, our powers of persuasion, and our legitimate leverage to bolster humane democratic systems where they already exist and to help countries on their way to that goal complete the process as quickly as human institutions can be changed.

Elections in El Salvador and also in Nicaragua must be open to all, fair, and safe. The international community must help. We will work at human rights problems, not walk away from them.

• Second, in response to the challenge of world recession and, in the case of El Salvador, to the unrelenting campaign of economic sabotage by the guerrillas, we will support economic development. By a margin of two to one, our aid is economic now, not military. Seventy-seven cents out of every dollar we will spend in the area this year goes for food, fertilizers, and other essentials for economic growth and development.

And our economic program goes beyond traditional aid. The Caribbean Initiative introduced in the House earlier today will provide powerful trade and investment incentives to help these countries achieve self-sustaining economic growth without exporting U.S. jobs.

Our goal must be to focus our immense and growing technology to enhance health care, agriculture, and industry and to ensure that we who inhabit this interdependent region come to know and understand one another better, retaining our diverse identities, respecting our diverse traditions and institutions.

• Third, in response to the military challenge from Cuba and Nicaragua, to their deliberate use of force to spread tyranny, we will support the security of the region's threatened nations.

We do not view security assistance as an end in itself but as a shield for democratization, economic development, and diplomacy. No amount of reform will bring peace so long as guerrillas believe they will win by force. No amount of economic help will suffice if guerrilla units can destroy roads, bridges, power stations, and crops again and again with impunity. But, with better training and material help, our neighbors can hold off the guerrillas and give democratic reform time to take root.

• Fourth, we will support dialogue and negotiations both among the countries of the region and within each country. The terms and conditions of participation in elections are negotiable.

Costa Rica is a shining example of democracy. Honduras has made the move from military rule to democratic government. Guatemala is pledged to the same course.

In Support of Political Solutions

The United States will work toward a political solutions in Central America which will serve the interests of the democratic process. To support these diplomatic goals, I offer these assurances:

• The United States will support any agreement among Central American countries for the withdrawal under fully verifiable and reciprocal conditions of all foreign military and security advisors and troops.

• We want to help opposition groups join the political process in all countries and compete by ballots instead of bullets.

• We will support any verifiable, reciprocal agreement among Central American countries on the renunciation of support for insurgencies on neighbors' territory.

• And, finally, we desire to help Central America end its costly arm race and will support any verifiable, reciprocal agreements on the nonimportation of offensive weapons.

To move us toward these goals more rapidly, I am tonight announcing my intention to name an ambassador at large as my special envoy to Central America. He or she will report to me through the Secretary of State. The ambassador's responsibilities will be to lend U.S. support to the efforts of regional governments to bring peace to this troubled area and to work closely with the Congress to assure the fullest possible bipartisan coordination of our policies toward the region.

What I am asking for is prompt congressional approval for the full reprogramming of funds for key current economic and security programs so that the people of Central America can hold the line against externally supported aggression. In addition, I am asking for prompt action on the supplemental request in these same areas to carry us through the current fiscal year and for early and favorable congressional action on my requests for fiscal year 1984. Finally, I am asking that the bipartisan consensus which last year acted on the trade and tax provisions of the Caribbean Basin Initiative in the House again take the lead to move this vital proposal to the floor of both chambers. And, as I said before, the greatest share of these requests is targeted toward economic and humanitarian aid, not military.

What the Administration is asking for on behalf of freedom in Central America is so small, so minimal—considering what is at stake. The total amount requested for aid to all of Central America in 1984 is about $600 million; that is less than one-tenth of what Americans will spend this year on coin-operated video games.

In summation, I say to you that tonight there can be no question: The national security of all the Americas is at stake in Central America. If we cannot defend ourselves there, we cannot expect to prevail elsewhere. Our credibility would collapse, our alliances would crumble, and the safety of our homeland would be put at jeopardy.

We have a vital interest, a moral duty, and a solemn responsibility. This is not a partisan issue. It is a question of our meeting our moral responsibility to ourselves, our friends, and our posterity. It is a duty that falls to all of us—the President, the Congress, and the people. We must perform it together. Who among us would wish to bear responsibility for failing to meet our shared obligation?

2. On the Caribbean Revolution

By FIDEL CASTRO

Focus On July 26, 1983, in the city of Santiago de Cuba, Fidel Castro celebrated the thirtieth anniversary of the beginning of the Cuban Revolution with a lengthy account of the heroes and glories of that revolution. His speech concluded with the section printed below, which places Cuba in its Central American and Caribbean context.

For Castro, the United States threatens Cuba as well as the rest of the region—indeed, the whole world—with its "demented policy of aggression." In his view, the several revolutionary movements in the Caribbean Basin form part of the worldwide people's revolution against "imperialism." Among the fellow revolutionaries he salutes are the comrades of the Palestinian Liberation Organization, the "fraternal peoples" of Ethiopia, Angola, and Mozambique, and people in all parts of the world fighting to end the nuclear arms race. The arms race, according to Castro, is fueled by the United States, whose planned installation of Pershing II missiles in Europe he describes as "an unusual, unprecedented provocation against the socialist countries."

Like President Reagan (selection 1), Castro endorses the proposals of the Contadora group—Mexico, Panama, Venezuela, and Colombia (see appendix B). These countries call for a halt to all foreign interference and a negotiated solution of

the conflicts in Central America. But Castro sees
the President's speeches and U.S. military maneuvers as deliberate threats to Nicaragua, threats that
cannot succeed against the popular forces that have
come to power. An open, armed struggle against
Nicaragua could lead only to "another Vietnam in
the very heart of Latin America."

Castro's view of the Caribbean Basin contrasts
sharply with that of the many Latin American and
U.S. analysts who deny that conflict in the region is
a part of the East-West confrontation. Further, he
blames the United States and its traditional allies
for the problems that exist there—an effective rallying cry but hardly a realistic account of Latin
American history. For more balanced views of the
history of the region, see Mark Falcoff (selection
22) and John Kurzweil (selection 13).

The editors' notes for this selection are on page
29.

Fidel Castro has been the ruler of Cuba since he
seized power in 1959 after three years of guerrilla
warfare against the government of Fulgencio
Batista.

I N THIS AREA, OUR COUNTRY is not alone in suffering threats and facing risks. Nicaragua and indeed all of Central America are seriously threatened by the same demented policy of aggression.

The fact is that the United States is intervening in Nicaragua through thousands of former members of Somoza's National Guard—based, trained, and supplied on Honduran territory. Imperialism openly proclaims its support for the counterrevolution, which in any event it has been unable to hide in the form (to use the language of the CIA) of covert action.

Hundreds of humble Nicaraguan patriots have already lost their lives as the result of these crimes by the government of the United States. The same story of Escambray and the Bay of Pigs is being retold with unheard-of cynicism, at the cost of our brothers in Nicaragua.

The United States intervenes in the same fashion in El Salvador, supplying, training, and advising the army of a genocidal regime, which has already murdered more than 40,000 Salvadorans.

The United States is also intervening in Honduras, installing land and air bases, crushing the authority of the civilian government there, and openly transforming it into an instrument of aggression against Nicaragua.

The historical causes of the problems of Central America are well known. They originate in a long and brutal history of internal oppression and exploitation, and a series of armed interventions by the United States. The struggles of Sandino in Nicaragua against North American occupation, the peasant insurrection in El Salvador during the 1930s, and the Guatemalan Revolution crushed by the United States in 1954 were events that preceded by many years the Cuban Revolution, the Sandinista victory in Nicaragua, and the current revolutionary situation in El Salvador.

The situation in the tormented Central American region has provoked profound concern worldwide, even among European governments allied to the United States. In our part of the world,

Mexico, Panama, Venezuela, and Colombia some months ago took the initiative in the search for a negotiated political solution to the serious problems of the area. At a summit meeting in Cancún, Mexico, last July 17 [1983], these nations, known as the Contadora Group, made a broad plea to all of the Central American countries, and also to the United States and Cuba, to assist in seeking a political solution.

Nicaragua responded on July 19 by agreeing to begin immediate multilateral negotiations under Contadora auspices with a six-point program that included its willingness to sign a non-aggression pact with Honduras, and its willingness to reach an agreement with El Salvador on the basis of a cessation of arms supplies to both sides. The responsible, dignified position of Nicaragua excludes any type of unilateral concession, capitulation, or surrender to the pressures and aggressions of the United States. But it does clearly express its willingness to discuss and resolve—in an honorable and principled fashion—the points mentioned, as well as any other that figure in the declaration of the Contadora presidents.

The Cuban reply was equally clear and rapid: we support unhesitatingly the Contadora efforts to reach a dignified and proper negotiated solution to the problems of Central America. We are in full solidarity with the sentiments raised in Nicaragua's statement of July 19, and we indicated our desire to assist that country in its proposal to achieve a negotiated political solution to the problems of the area.

An Aggressive U.S. Response

The reply of the United States—quite apart from its formal statement—was a highly aggressive speech by President Reagan against Nicaragua on July 18, in which he practically demanded the resignation of the Sandinista government; the precipitous dispatch of an aircraft carrier and numerous armed craft to the Pacific coast of Nicaragua; the announcement that another aircraft carrier, currently stationed in the Mediterranean, also escorted by armed patrols, would be sent to the Atlantic coast of that country; and the decision to stage military maneuvers with the participation of thousands of American soldiers on Honduran territory at the beginning of the month of August. We understand that the maneuvers include blockade exercises and will last for six months. This type of maneuver, for so extended a period of time, is truly unusual. What is obviously happening is a massive deployment of American troops in Central America. Nicaragua is already surrounded by Yankee soldiers and naval attack craft. The threats and pressures could not be cruder or more worthy of condemnation.

Nonetheless, we must not panic. We have no doubt that the government of the United States has been trying deliberately to surround Nicaragua with an atmosphere of terror and insecurity during the last few weeks, elevating pressure to the maximum. Nonetheless, such measures are dangerous, because the space between this type of psychological warfare and military action has been greatly reduced; the irresponsible personalities who advise Reagan are doubtless tempted to take the next steps, which will make the situation irreversible.

We are thus particularly privileged witnesses to the form in which the United States is moving towards an extremely serious error of incalculable consequences. The Nicaragua of 1983 is not the Nicaragua of 1926: a heroic and victorious people's revolution has drawn the entire nation into a struggle contrary to the wishes of a tiny minority tarnished by association with Somoza and the counterrevolution. The patriotic and revolutionary fervor has increased as a consequence of foreign aggression, and the people are united as never before in their valiant history. Nicaragua does not possess a modern air force, nor abundant armor, nor the kind of artillery necessary to resist a large-scale invasion by the United States, but it does possess the means to arm its people—that is to say, the thousands of patriotic combatants who already have experience in struggle, and who are capable of making life impossible for any aggressor, however powerful he may be. Imperialism also underestimates the peoples of Central America.

We are convinced that the Nicaraguan and Salvadoran revolutionaries will never be conquered by force. The attempt to crush the revolutions in Nicaragua and El Salvador by armed intervention would be like trying to extract a cancerous tumor that is already spreading rapidly throughout the cancerous body of Central America.

Barely a year has passed since a war was unleashed by a NATO country (with the support of the United States) against a Latin American nation, which constituted an insult and a humiliation for all of the peoples of our continent; the United States now threatens another people of Latin America with its squadrons and its soldiers. A new Vietnam in the very heart of Latin America? May this never happen! There is still time to avoid it! The peoples of Latin America and the world would not sit idly by while such a crime was consummated.

The same aggressive policies of the new American administration find expression in every corner of the earth: in the Middle East, in South Africa, in the Indian Ocean, and in Europe itself, where the United States proposes to install 572 medium-range nuclear missiles, an unusual, unprecedented provocation against the socialist countries.

In the midst of a terrifying economic crisis, a new arms race is being unleashed with uncommon force.

We live in difficult and dangerous times. The risk of confrontation is not only local—it is international. If we wish to confront the aggressor successfully, if we wish to keep the peace—if we wish, indeed, to survive—we require nerves of steel, the greatest firmness, the maximum mobilization of peoples, and the absolute refusal to knuckle under to blackmail.

Homage to Bolívar

Two days ago we celebrated the bicentenary of the birth of Simón Bolívar, the father of Latin American liberty. To him we owe a special homage.

Our America is still far from achieving Bolívar's dream. It still is not the community of solidly united peoples that he sought to forge. The revolting, brutal empire of the North has succeeded in perpetuating us in a state at once balkanized and divided; many of our peoples live under brutal fascist systems or are subject to fierce repression; in greater or lesser measure nearly all are affected by illiteracy, disease, poverty, merciless exploitation by multinational corporations, and reactionary local oligarchies. Even those of us who in the last few years have been undergoing profound revolutions are obligated to struggle against a centuries-old legacy of foreign domination. Notwithstanding, a Latin American consciousness is beginning to manifest itself. The Malvinas war demonstrated for all to see the opportunistic cynicism of the government of the United States; it exposed the crude form in which imperialism is capable of avoiding the fulfillment of its own commitments. Fascism is in crisis, and progressive and democratic ideas are gaining the hearts and minds of people everywhere.

In the struggle for that awakening of the collective Latin American consciousness, this time the peoples of Central America have placed themselves in the vanguard. We can properly repeat today the words of José Martí concerning the Liberator, written on October 28, 1893:

> There you will find Bolívar, still on watch in the heavens of the Americas . . . still shod in the same campaign boots, for what he left uncompleted remains still to be accomplished—in effect, Bolívar still has work to do in Latin America!

Saluting Other Heroes

From this rostrum I salute the indomitable sons of Sandino, who tore to shreds Somoza and his cohorts, and do not tremble before the crudest Yankee aggressions or threats to blockade and invade that country; the admirable Salvadoran fighters, who have shown themselves capable of countering imperialist domination of their tiny country, and as such have astounded the world with their heroic exploits in combat; the tenacious, self-sacrificing Guatemalan patriots, who for more than twenty years have been struggling against the genocidal regime imposed upon it by the United States in 1954; the valiant, decisive people of Grenada, who broke the chains of oppression and are constructing a just society; the valiant Chilean people who have risen up as one man to confront fascist tyranny; the peoples of the Southern Cone of South America, who struggle for democratic freedoms and an end to oppression and repression.

I salute all the peoples in other continents who also struggle against the same imperialism: the brave combatants of the Sahara;[1] our unshakable Palestinian friends; the valiant patriots of Namibia; the stoic and unconquered fighters of South Africa; the fraternal peoples of Ethiopia, Angola, Mozambique, and other front-line African states who courageously resist the pressures, threats, and attacks of racism and imperialism; the Arab countries, permanent victims of imperialist and Zionist aggression; all the peoples of Asia and Africa who are confronting underdevelopment, colonial exploitation, and abysmal poverty, the legacy of centuries of exploitation past and present.

I salute with particular affection the Soviet Union and all fraternal socialist countries, with the profoundest gratitude for the solidarity they have offered us in crucial and difficult moments, and for their continued support.

I salute the workers of the world and those who struggle for peace on all continents and in the very heart of Europe, in Japan, even in the United States, all working with determination to put an end to the ridiculous arms race and avoid an international holocaust which could put an end to the human race.

I offer special regards here for those who suffered persecution and unjust punishment for their revolutionary struggles; for those who share our ideals while incarcerated in the prisons of tyranny; for those who went into exile with us and organized the *Granma* expedition; for those unforgettable combatants in the Sierra Maestra and on the plains;[2] for the tenacious defenders of the Cuban Revolution in Escambray and at the Bay of Pigs; for those who confronted and defeated the conspiracies, the terrorist plans, the sabotages and crimes of the United States against our revolution; for those who raised up with honor the internationalist banner in Angola, Ethiopia, and other lands; for those who, with their blood or labor, express their solidarity—insofar as their resources permit—with many other peoples; for the selfless families of those who died in combat, and families who suffered for the absence of their loved ones during these long and glorious years of struggle.

We offer a profound and eternal vote of thanks to our own working class, which with sacrifice, perseverance, and heroism clasped to its bosom the ideas and program of Moncada,[3] and carried those ideas forward to culminate in the most radical revolution in our history and the establishment in Cuba of the first socialist state in the Western hemisphere—and which not only achieved this but defends it and is willing to continue defending it to its last drop of blood.

Eternal glory to the Cuban people and its heroic sons!

Eternal glory to those fallen for the Fatherland and the Revolution!

Eternal glory to the ideas that made us revolutionaries, that gave us freedom, justice, honor, and victory!

Fatherland or death!

We shall triumph!

NOTES BY THE EDITORS

1. Castro refers here to the Polisario guerrilla movement in what was formerly the Spanish Sahara, ceded by Spain to Morocco in a 1976 agreement and now called the Western Sahara. The Polisario disputes Moroccan claims to the territory and continues sporadic resistance.

2. References to events in the history of the Cuban Revolution: *Granma* was the name of a yacht that brought Castro and several dozen Cuban exiles from Mexico in 1956 to mount a guerrilla offensive against the dictator Fulgencio Batista. Most of Castro's campaign took place in the Sierra Maestra range of the Oriente province, far from Havana, but by referring to those who struggled "on the plains," he tacitly admits that there was also a significant urban resistance movement in the Cuban cities. Although official historiography in Cuba sometimes admits the existence of this urban movement, it generally plays down its significance and never admits that it was largely independent of Castro.

3. The Moncada fortress in Santiago de Cuba was the site of a putsch by Castro and some revolutionary comrades in 1953 after Fulgencio Batista seized power. Generally speaking, Castro dates his revolution from this event.

3. The Crisis and Our Opportunity

By the KISSINGER COMMISSION

Focus In July 1983, President Reagan set up a bipartisan commission under the chairmanship of former secretary of state Henry Kissinger to draw up a plan for U.S. policy in Central America. After a half year of research, hearings, and visits to the key Central American countries, the six Democratic and six Republican commissioners released a 132-page report in early January 1984.

The report emphasized the threat to the region and to U.S. security posed by Soviet, Cuban, and Nicaraguan support for Marxist insurgents. In response to this threat the commission recommended sharp increases in both development and security assistance. More than $8 billion in economic aid alone would be earmarked for the region over the next five years. At a news conference, Henry Kissinger defended the increases: "If present levels of expenditures are continued, we will fail both in economic and social progress and in the security field. There will be lingering deterioration with very grave consequences."

An Emergency Stabilization Program should be adopted immediately, said the report, as a multi-faceted response to the severe economic crisis. Continued pressure should be applied to the Sandinista government of Nicaragua, including U.S. aid to the rebel *contras*. Concerning the stalemate in El Salvador the commission said: "There might be an argument for doing nothing to help the government of El Salvador. There might be an argument for doing a great deal more. There is, however, no logical argument for giving some aid but not enough. The worst possible policy for El Salvador is to provide just enough aid to keep the war going, but too little to wage it successfully."

The commission proposed that large increases in military aid to El Salvador be dependent upon continuing reforms in the government, the military, and the judiciary. Dr. Kissinger and two other members of the commission noted, however, that this recommendation should not be taken to the extreme of allowing a Marxist-Leninist takeover, which would abolish the human rights of a whole people.

For humanitarian reasons as well as for reasons of U.S. self-interest, concludes the report, we cannot turn away: "Central America's crisis is our crisis."

President Reagan immediately made known his strong support for the general recommendations of the commission, which in important respects coincide with announced initiatives and objectives of the Reagan administration (compare selection 1).

The chairman of the commission, **Henry A. Kissinger,** was secretary of state from 1973 to 1977. Other members were: Nicholas F. Brady, Henry G. Cisneros, William P. Clements, Jr., Carlos F. Díaz-Alejandro, Wilson F. Johnson, Lane Kirkland, Richard M. Scammon, John Silber, Potter Stewart, Robert S. Strauss, and Dr. William B. Walsh.

M OST MEMBERS OF this commission began with what we now see as an extremely limited understanding of the region, its needs and its importance. The more we learned, the more convinced we became that the crisis there is real, and acute; that the United States must act to meet it, and act boldly; that the stakes are large, for the United States, for the hemisphere, and, most poignantly, for the people of Central America.

In this report, we propose significant attention and help to a previously neglected area of the hemisphere. Some who have not studied the area as we have may think this disproportionate, dismissing it as the natural reaction of a commission created to deal with a single subject. We think any such judgment would be a grave mistake.

TOWARD DEMOCRACY AND ECONOMIC PROSPERITY

Most past U.S. development programs have been predominantly economic. We argue here that the crisis in Central America cannot be considered in solely economic or political or social or security terms. The actions we recommend represent an attempt to address this complex interrelationship in its totality, not just in its parts.

We envision, in the short term, an emergency stabilization program and, in the medium and long term, a new multilateral regional organization to measure performance across the entire political, social, economic, and security spectrum, and to target external aid resources where they can provide the most significant impetus. In support of these efforts, we urge a five-year commitment by the United States to a substantially increased level of economic assistance.

We recognize that it is unlikely that the social inequities and distortions that have accumulated over the last five centuries will be corrected during the next five years. But the groundwork for recovery should be laid as soon as possible. The costs of not

Excerpts from the report of the National Bipartisan Commission on Central America.

meeting the challenge in Central America would be too great, today and for generations to come.

For their part, other countries are also contributing to Central America's economic recuperation. Mexico and Venezuela have established a major facility to provide oil on concessional terms.

But the outlook, even under optimistic assumptions, is not very promising. Even if economic stabilization policies are consistently implemented, if official capital flows remain at roughly current levels through the rest of the decade, if private capital flows eventually recover, if the international stability returns, unless more is done the economies of Central America will only gradually begin to recover. Without a significant increase in the levels of foreign assistance, improvement in the ways those resources are managed and used, and the introduction of growth-oriented economic policies, economic activity in the region, measured on a per capita basis, would probably reach no more than three-quarters of the 1980 level by 1990. This would mean more unemployment and continued widespread poverty.

An Emergency Stabilization Program

The commission urges the immediate adoption of an emergency stabilization program combining public and private efforts to halt the deterioration. The program includes eight key elements:

• We urge that the leaders of the United States and the Central American countries meet to initiate a comprehensive approach to the economic development of the region and the reinvigoration of the Central American Common Market.

• We encourage the greatest possible involvement of the private sector in the stabilization effort.

• We recommend that the United States actively address the external debt problems of the region.

• We recommend that the United States provide an immediate increase in bilateral economic assistance.

• We recommend that a major thrust of expanded aid should be in labor-intensive infrastructure and housing projects.

• We recommend that new official trade credit guarantees be made available to the Central American countries.

- We recommend that the United States provide an emergency credit to the Central American Common Market Fund (CACMF).

The Central American countries have asked for a credit to refinance part of the accumulated trade deficits among themselves which have contributed to the contraction of intra-regional trade. The United States should use part of the increased economic aid for this purpose; the Central American countries that have been in surplus would be expected to transform the remainder of the deficits into long-term local currency credits. As the Central American countries have proposed, CACMF regulations should then be adjusted to avoid future buildups of large unsettled balances. Since the debts that would be refinanced under this proposal are among central banks, there should be no adverse implications for other rescheduling efforts.

We recognize that support for Common Market institutions benefits all members of the Common Market, regardless of their political orientation or social and economic performance. There is no way to isolate one or two member countries. However, support for the Common Market would be one of the quickest ways to revive intra-regional trade and economic activity. The Common Market continues to enjoy strong support among Central Americans.

We have concluded that the benefits of an infusion of capital into the CACMF outweigh the disadvantages. However, we are convinced that the Common Market will have to change toward a more open trading posture. This will require a basic reorientation of regional trade and industrial policies.

- We recommend that the United States join the Central American Bank for Economic Integration (CABEI).

The Central American countries are opening membership in CABEI to countries outside the region. We urge the United States to join this institution and to encourage other creditor countries to seek membership. The infusion of new resources would help reinvigorate the bank, which could channel much-needed funds to small-scale entrepreneurs and farmers, provide working capital to existing private-sector companies, and encouraging the development of new industries.

U.S. Development Support

We urge a major increase in U.S. and other-country financial and economic assistance for Central America.

Reaching that goal will require a significant effort. External financing needs between now and 1990 have been estimated at as much as $24 billion for the seven countries [Belize, Costa Rica, El Salvador, Guatemala, Honduras, Nicaragua, and Panama] as a group. The World Bank, the International Monetary Fund, the Inter-American Development Bank, other official creditors, private investors, and commercial banks are likely to provide at least half of these funds—especially if each Central American country follows prudent economic policies, if there is steady social and political progress, and if outside aggression is eliminated. The balance, as much as $12 billion, would have to be supplied by the United States.

We now propose that economic assistance over the five-year period beginning in 1985 total $8 billion.

This global figure would include direct appropriations as well as contingent liabilities such as guarantees and insurance. In effect, this would represent a rough doubling of U.S. economic assistance from the 1983 level.

We recognize that such a proposal may be viewed with skepticism. However, we firmly believe that without such large-scale assistance, economic recovery, social progress, and the development of democratic institutions in Central America will be set back.

Ultimately, the effectiveness of increased economic assistance will turn on the economic policies of the Central American countries themselves. We agree with what many experts have told us: that unless these reforms are extended, economic performance will not significantly improve, regardless of the money foreign donors and creditors provide. In too many other countries, increased availability of financial resources has undermined reform by relieving the immediate pressure on policy-makers. This must be avoided in Central America.

What is now required is a firm commitment by the Central American countries to economic policies, including reforms in tax systems, to encourage private enterprise and individual initiative, to create favorable investment climates, to curb corruption where it exists, and to spur balanced trade.

We recommend that the United States expand economic assistance for democratic institutions and leadership training.

Key initiatives which either are already under way or should be developed include:

- The encouragement of neighborhood groups, community improvement organizations, and producer cooperatives which provide a training ground for democratic participation and help make governments more responsive to citizen demands.
- The United States Information Service's binational centers provide valuable insight into the advantages of personal freedoms in the United States. Significantly expanded funding would allow the centers to expand their library holdings, courses, and programs.
- Exchange and training programs for leaders of democratic institutions. The International Visitors Program of USIA and AFL-CIO's George Meany Institute are both examples of effective programs that bring leaders from Central America, as well as from other regions, to the United States for training programs. Additional programs should be established to bring leaders of such democratic institutions as labor unions, local governments, legislatures, and professional associations to work and study in counterpart U.S. organizations.

Expanded Trade Opportunities

Rapid Central American economic growth requires increased foreign-exchange earnings. In the short run the region will continue to rely largely on the earnings which come from the export of commodities.

The solution to this problem will necessarily be a slow one. Over the medium term, the Central American countries should try to broaden their export bases in both the agricultural and manufactured-good sectors. More diversified exports would help to insulate the region from some of the swings in the international economy.

Central American export-promoting policies will come to naught, however, if the rest of the world fails to open its markets. The United States has taken the lead in this respect, and the

Caribbean Basin Initiative (CBI) will provide additional encouragement for the development of new export industries.

We encourage the extension of duty-free trade to Central America by other major trading countries.

We urge the European Community to extend trade preferences to Central America under the Lomé Agreement, since the United States is extending CBI benefits to Lomé beneficiaries in the Caribbean. Other countries of Latin America should also be encouraged to offer special trade benefits to the Central American countries as their own economic recovery progresses.

We urge the United States to review nontariff barriers to imports from Central America.

We recognize that this issue—which principally applies to products like textiles, sugar, and meat—is highly contentious, both internationally and domestically. All of these products are affected by multilateral agreements which partly determine the degree of access to the United States market. We encourage the President to use whatever flexibility exists in such agreements in favor of Central American producers.

Several initiatives could be undertaken by the United States to encourage U.S. investors to consider projects in Central America.

We encourage the formation of a privately owned venture capital company for Central America.

We recommend that a venture capital company—which might be called the Central American Development Corporation (CADC)—be established for Central America. The CADC, capitalized by private-sector investors, would use its capital to raise funds which, in turn, would be lent to private companies active in Central America. It would be managed and directed by experienced entrepreneurs. Its loans would be made to commercially viable projects in high priority economic sectors for working capital or investment purposes. The U.S. government could support the CADC initiative through a long-term loan as it has for similar initiatives in other areas of the world.

Agricultural Development

Integrated programs of rural development targeted at the food-producing sector have enormous potential for improving the welfare of large numbers of people while increasing and diversifying agricultural production and lessening dependence on food imports. Such programs require a variety of coordinated measures which would have to be undertaken by the Central Americans themselves.

We recommend that the financial underpinnings of the efforts to broaden land ownership be strengthened and reformed.

In programs of land reform, ways should be found to insure that the redistribution of land provides the new owners with a valid title, that governments promptly allocate resources as they become available to insure that former owners are effectively compensated, and that in the end the system enhances incentives to expand the nation's total agricultural output.

Organizing for Development

We have developed the outline of a structure which we have called the Central American Development Organization, or CADO. We put it forward not as the only design, but as a means of illustrating how the concept could be implemented.

Membership in CADO, as we envision it, would initially be open to the seven countries of Central America—Belize, Costa Rica, El Salvador, Guatemala, Honduras, Nicaragua, and Panama—and to the United States. Associate member status would be available to any democracy willing to contribute significant resources to promote regional development. We would hope that the other Contadora countries would participate actively, as well as the nations of Europe, Canada, and Japan. The organization's chairman should be from the United States with an executive secretary from Central America.

Central American participation in the program should turn on acceptance of and continued progress toward political pluralism, and a process of recurrent elections with competing political parties. Only nations prepared to base their governments on the free choice of their people should be eligible. This does not necessarily mean that each country would institutionalize its political process in the same way as the United States, but it does mean that each would adopt democratic forms appropriate to its own conditions.

We recommend that an economic reconstruction fund be established with CADO and that the United States channel one-quarter of its economic assistance through such a fund. Loans to countries would be in support of development programs and policies including the implementation of growth-oriented economic policies, the establishment of genuine democratic institutions, and the adoption of programs to improve social conditions. They would be quick-disbursing, balance-of-payments support loans.

Governments, including that of the United States, would not be bound to accept the judgments of CADO. The United States would be free to maintain a bilateral economic assistance program in a particular country, regardless of performance. But the present purely bilateral process has its drawbacks. It factors political assessments directly into economic aid decisions. This makes the United States the prosecutor, judge, and jury. It leads to rancorous debate, sometimes poorly informed. This commission's proposal is an effort to explore a new process. The responsibility for assessing development performance would be assumed in the first instance by a respected multilateral body, with donors retaining effective final control of their financial resources. The process should be more effective, more acceptable to Central America, and more compatible with present-day views of how sovereign nations should deal with one another.

CENTRAL AMERICAN SECURITY ISSUES

Cuba and Nicaragua did not invent the grievances that made insurrection possible in El Salvador and elsewhere. Those grievances are real and acute. But it is important to bear in mind three facts about the kind of insurgencies we confront;

• They depend on external support, which is substantially more effective when it includes the provision of privileged sanctuaries for the insurgents.

• They develop their own momentum, independent of the conditions on which they feed.

• The insurgents, if they win, will create a totalitarian regime in the image of their sponsors' ideology and their own.

Propaganda support, money, sanctuary, arms, supplies, training, communications, intelligence, logistics, all are important in both morale and operational terms. Without such support from Cuba, Nicaragua, and the Soviet Union, neither in El Salvador nor elsewhere in Central America would such an insurgency pose so severe a threat to the government.

Therefore, curbing the insurgents' violence in El Salvador requires, in part, cutting them off from their sources of foreign support.

If reforms had been undertaken earlier, there would almost surely have been no fertile ground for revolution, and thus no effectively developed insurgency. But once an insurgency is fully under way and once the lines of external support are in place, it has a momentum which reforms alone cannot stop. Unchecked, the insurgents can destroy faster than the reformers can build.

One reason for this is that an explicit purpose of guerrilla violence is to make matters worse.

None of this legitimizes the use of arbitrary violence by the right in El Salvador or elsewhere. Indeed, the grim reality is that many of the excesses we have condemned would be present even if there were no guerrilla war supported by outside forces.

Beyond the issue of U.S. security interests in the Central American–Caribbean region, our credibility worldwide is engaged. The triumph of hostile forces in what the Soviets call the "strategic rear" of the United States would be read as a sign of U.S. impotence.

Thus, even in terms of the direct national security interests of the United States, this country has large stakes in the present conflict in Central America.

The fundamental dilemma is as follows: both the national interests of the United States and a genuine concern for the long-term welfare of Central America create powerful incentives to provide all necessary assistance to defeat totalitarian guerrillas. At the same time one of the principal objectives of the guerrilla forces is to destroy the morale and efficiency of the government's administration and programs.

Much attention has been paid—correctly—to the shortcomings of the El Salvador government. But it is important—and only fair—to recall the many demands that have been made upon it and the progress that has been made in many fields. It carried out impressive elections in 1982, despite severe intimidations by the guerrillas, and will conduct another one this March. It has been going forward with an extensive land reform program. It allows debate, freedom of assembly, opposition, and other aspects of democracy, however imperfect. Albeit belatedly and because of U.S. pressure, it is beginning to address the problem of right-wing violence.

There is, of course, a darker side as well in El Salvador. The United States obviously cannot accept, let alone support, the brutal methods practiced by certain reactionary forces in Central America. Some of these actions are related to counterinsurgency. Other violence has, in fact, nothing to do with insurgency at all. It is designed to terrorize opponents, fight democracy, protect entrenched interests, and restore reactionary regimes.

Whatever their aims, these methods are totally repugnant to the values of the United States. The methods of counterinsurgency developed over the last generation by the armed forces of the United States are consistent with such models. They depend upon gaining the confidence and support of the people and specifically exclude the use of violence against innocent civilians.

The present level of U.S. military assistance to El Salvador is far too low to enable the armed forces of El Salvador to use these modern methods of counterinsurgency effectively. At the same time, the tendency in some quarters of the Salvadoran military towards brutality magnifies congressional and executive pressures for further cuts in aid. A vicious cycle results in which violence and denial of human rights spawn reductions in aid, and reductions in aid make more difficult the pursuit of an enlightened counterinsurgency effort.

In the commission's view it is imperative to settle on a level of aid related to the operational requirements of a humane anti-guerrilla strategy and to stick with it for the requisite period of time.

Another obstacle to the effective pursuit of anti-guerrilla strategy is a provision of current U.S. law under which no assistance can be provided to law-enforcement agencies. This dates back to a previous period when it was believed that such aid was sometimes helping groups guilty of serious human rights abuses. The purpose of the legislation was to prevent the United States and its personnel from being associated with unacceptable practices. That concern is valid, but, however laudable its intentions, the blanket legal prohibition against the provision of training and aid to police organizations has the paradoxical effect, in certain cases, of inhibiting our efforts to improve human rights performance.

We therefore suggest that Congress examine this question thoroughly and consider whether Section 660 of the Foreign Assistance Act should be amended so as to permit—under carefully defined conditions—the allocation of funds to the training and support of law-enforcement agencies in Central America.

Stalemate in El Salvador

The war is at a stalemate—a condition that in the long term favors the guerrillas. They have relatively little popular support in El Salvador, but they can probably continue the war as long as they receive the sort of external support they are now getting.

In part, the Salvadoran military's difficulties in containing the guerrilla threat are related to manpower problems—their training, their retention, their equipment, and their development.

The Salvadoran armed forces have also suffered from inadequate command and control, coordination, and leadership. A recent major reorganization of the military command structure is designed to achieve needed improvements in command and control and coordination, and to lead to a more aggressive prosecution of the war. But to end the stalemate will require much more in equipment and trained manpower.

Insurgency in Guatemala

The insurgency in Guatemala is at a much lower level. There are about 2,500 guerrillas in four groups loosely organized under an umbrella organization. The guerrillas lost critical ground in the fall of 1982 and have not yet recovered. The guerrillas engage in harassment and terrorism but make no attempt to hold ground or to engage military units in sustained combat.

But an even more serious obstacle in terms of the ultimate containment of armed revolt in Guatemala is the brutal behavior of the security forces. In the cities they have murdered those even suspected of dissent. In the countryside, they have at times killed indiscriminately to repress any sign of support for the guerrillas. Such actions are morally unacceptable. They are also self-defeating—as long as they persist, the conditions in which insurgency can appear and reappear will continue.

Military Aid to El Salvador

While important U.S. interests are engaged in El Salvador, and while we pay a high political price at home and abroad for assisting the armed forces there, the United States has not provided enough military aid to support the methods of counterinsurgency we have urged. At the same time, the United States cannot countenance the brutal alternative methods of counterinsurgency which wreak intolerable violence upon the civilian population. In our judgment, the current levels of military aid are not sufficient to preserve even the existing military stalemate over a period of time. Given the increasing damage—both physical and political—being inflicted on the economy and government of El Salvador by the guerrillas, who are maintaining their strength, a collapse is not inconceivable.

The Salvadoran government's National Campaign Plan combines military operations with follow-up civic actions to restore agriculture and commerce. The plan is designed to provide secure areas within which the Salvadoran *campesino* can grow, harvest, and market his crops, and where industry can again operate. The plan assumes that sufficient security can be established countrywide to reduce the insurgency at least to a low level within two years. But the government's forces must be significantly and quickly strengthened if the plan is to succeed.

There might be an argument for doing nothing to help the government of El Salvador. There might be an argument for doing a great deal more. There is, however, no logical argument for giving some aid but not enough. The worst possible policy for El Salvador is to provide just enough aid to keep the war going, but too little to wage it successfully.

The commission has concluded that present levels of U.S. military assistance are inadequate.

We are not in a position to judge the precise amounts and types of increased aid needed. We note that the U.S. Department of Defense estimates that it would take approximately $400 million in U.S. military assistance in 1984 and 1985 to break the military stalemate and allow the National Campaign Plan to be carried out.

The department believes that thereafter assistance levels could be brought down to considerably more modest levels.

The commission recommends that the United States provide to El Salvador—subject to the conditions we specify later in this chapter—significantly increased levels of military aid as quickly as possible so that the Salvadoran authorities can act on the assurance that needed aid will be forthcoming.

To be effective, U.S. military assistance programs require greater continuity and predictability. As we have seen, local commanders are now uncertain whether an adequate supply of such critical support items as ammunition will be on hand. The result in El Salvador has all too often been a less than vigorous prosecution of the war. The commission believes the Administration and the Congress should work together to achieve greater predictability. That could be most effectively achieved through multi-year funding.

Military Aid and Human Rights

The question of the relationship between military aid and human rights abuses is both extremely difficult and extremely important. It involves the potential clash of two basic U.S. objectives. On the one hand, we seek to promote justice and find it repugnant to support forces that violate—or tolerate the violation of— fundamental U.S. values. On the other hand, we are engaged in El Salvador and Central America because we are serving fundamental interests of the United States that transcend any particular government.

The commission believes that vigorous, concurrent policies on both the military and human rights fronts are needed to break out of the demoralizing cycle of deterioration on the one hand and abuses on the other. We believe policies of increased aid and increased pressure to safeguard human rights would improve both security and justice. A slackening on one front would undermine our objective on the other. El Salvador must succeed on both or it will not succeed on either.

The United States government has a right to demand certain minimum standards of respect for human rights as a condition for providing military aid to any country.

With respect to El Salvador, military aid should, through legislation requiring periodic reports, be made contingent upon demonstrated progress toward free elections, freedom of association, the establishment of the rule of law and an effective judicial system, and the termination of the activities of the so-called death squads, as well as vigorous action against those guilty of crimes and the prosecution to the extent possible of past offenders. These conditions should be seriously enforced.

Implementation of this approach would be greatly facilitated through the device of an independent monitoring body, such as the Central American Development Organization.

As an additional measure, the United States should impose sanctions, including the denial of visas, deportation, and the investigation of financial dealings, against foreign nationals in the United States who are connected with death-squad activities in El Salvador or anywhere else.

THE SEARCH FOR PEACE

Americans yearn for an end to the bloodshed in Central America. On no issue in the region is there a stronger consensus than on the hope for a diplomatic solution that will stop the killing and nourish freedom and progress. The commission shares this deeply felt goal.

We believe that there is a chance for a political solution in Central America if the diplomacy of the United States is strategic in conception, purposeful in approach, and steadfast in execution. Our broad objectives should be:

- To stop the war and the killing in El Salvador.
- To create conditions under which Nicaragua can take its place as a peaceful and democratic member of the Central American community.
- To open the way to democratic development throughout the isthmus.

El Salvador

The commission has concluded that power-sharing as proposed by the insurgents is not a sensible or fair political solution for El Salvador. There is no historical precedent suggesting that such a procedure would reconcile contending parties which entertain such deeply held beliefs and political goals and which have been killing each other for years. Indeed, precedent argues that it would be only a prelude to a takeover by the insurgent forces.

We believe that a true political solution in El Salvador can be reached only through free elections in which all significant groups have a right to participate.

Thus the El Salvador government must take all appropriate measures to make the March 25 [1984] elections as safe and open as possible. This should include the introduction of outside observers to help insure the security and fairness of the process.

We understand that El Salvador contemplates holding municipal and legislative assembly elections in 1985. The elements of the following approach could be applied to that process.

1. The Salvadoran government would invite the FDR-FMLN [Democratic Revolutionary Front–Farabundo Martí National Liberation Front] to negotiate mutually acceptable procedures to establish a framework for future elections.

2. As part of this framework a broadly representative Elections Commission would be established, including representatives of the FDR-FMLN.

3. Violence should be ended by all parties so that mutually satisfactory arrangements can be developed among the government, pro-government parties, the different opposition groups, and insurgent groups for the period of campaigning and elections.

4. A system of international observation should be established to enhance the faith and confidence of all parties in the probity and equity of arrangements for elections. This might include senior advisors to the Elections Commission drawn from the OAS, Contadora nations, or third countries agreed upon by all parties to the conflict.

Nicaragua

Though the commission believes that the Sandinista regime will pose a continuing threat to stability in the region, we do not advocate a policy of static containment.

Instead, we recommend, first, an effort to arrange a comprehensive regional settlement. This would elaborate and build upon the

twenty-one objectives of the Contadora group [see Appendix B].
Within the framework of basic principles, it would:

- Recognize linkage between democratization and security in
the region.
- Relate the incentives of increased development aid and trade
concessions to acceptance of mutual security guarantees.
- Engage the United States and other developed nations in the
regional peace system.
- Establish an institutional mechanism in the region to implement that system.

The commission believes that whatever the prospects seem to be
for productive negotiations, the United States must spare no effort
to pursue the diplomatic route. Nicaragua's willingness to enter
into a general agreement should be thoroughly tested through
negotiations and actions.

As a broad generality, we do not believe that it would be wise to
dismantle existing incentives and pressures on the Managua regime except in conjunction with demonstrable progress on the
negotiating front. With specific reference to the highly controversial question of whether the United States should provide support
for the Nicaraguan insurgent forces opposed to the Sandinistas
now in authority in Managua, the commission recognized that an
adequate examination of this issue would require treatment of
sensitive information not appropriate to a public report. However,
the majority of the members of the commission, in their respective
individual judgments, believe that the efforts of the Nicaraguan
insurgents represent one of the incentives working in favor of a
negotiated settlement and that the future role of the United States
in those efforts must therefore be considered in the context of the
negotiating process. The commission has not, however, attempted
to come to a collective judgment on whether, and how, the United
States should provide support for these insurgent forces.

CONCLUSION

We have concluded this exercise persuaded that Central America
is both vital and vulnerable and that whatever other crises may
arise to claim the nation's attention, the United States cannot

afford to turn away from that threatened region. Central America's crisis is our crisis.

All too frequently, wars and threats of wars are what draw attention to one part of the world or another. So it has been in Central America. The military crisis here captured our attention, but it has also wakened us to many other needs of the region.

As we have studied these nations, we have become sharply aware of how great a mistake it would be to view them in one-dimensional terms. An exceptionally complex interplay of forces has shaped their history and continues to define their identities and to affect their destinies.

We have developed a great sympathy for those in Central America who are struggling to control those forces and to bring their countries successfully through this period of political and social transformation. As a region Central America is in midpassage from the predominantly authoritarian patterns of the past to what can, with determination, with help, with luck, and with peace, become the predominantly democratic pluralism of the future. That transformation has been troubled, seldom smooth and sometimes violent. In Nicaragua, we have seen the tragedy of a revolution betrayed; the same forces that stamped out the beginnings of democracy in Nicaragua now threaten El Salvador. In El Salvador itself, those seeking to establish democratic institutions are beset by violence from the extremists on both sides. But the spirit of freedom is strong throughout the region, and the determination persists to strengthen it where it exists and to achieve it where it does not.

The use of Nicaragua as a base for Soviet and Cuban efforts to penetrate the rest of the Central American isthmus, with El Salvador the target of first opportunity, gives the conflict there a major strategic dimension. The direct involvement of aggressive external forces makes it a challenge to the system of hemispheric security and, quite specifically, to the security interests of the United States. This is a challenge to which the United States must respond.

But beyond this, we are challenged to respond to the urgent human needs of the people of Central America. Central America is a region in crisis economically, socially, and politically. Its nations are our neighbors, and they need our help.

Our task now, as a nation, is to transform the crisis in Central America into an opportunity: to seize the impetus it provides and to use this to help our neighbors not only to secure their freedom from aggression and violence but also to set in place the policies, processes, and institutions that will make them both prosperous and free. If, together, we succeed in this, then the sponsors of violence will have done the opposite of what they intended: they will have roused us not only to turn back the tide of totalitarianism but to bring a new birth of hope and of opportunity to the people of Central America.

Because this is our opportunity, in conscience it is also our responsibility.

4. The Cuban and Soviet Dimension

By R. BRUCE MCCOLM

Focus According to R. Bruce McColm, urgent events in El Salvador and Nicaragua have diverted our attention from the "larger scenario" in Central America and the Caribbean. The most important U.S. interests in that area are "the maintenance of stable, trouble-free national borders and unhampered access to the vital sea lanes that flow into the Caribbean Sea," he says. Moscow, he argues, also has long-term objectives in the region: "to create through a Soviet naval and air presence and enhanced Cuban forces" an offensive capacity able to block U.S. economic traffic and disrupt U.S. military movements, particularly in the event of a large-scale conflict. While the United States has held sway unchallenged for decades, McColm believes that the Soviet-Cuban convergence strategy following the Sandinista triumph in Nicaragua has resulted in a fundamental strategic transformation in the area that threatens vital U.S. security and economic interests.

To effect this transformation, the Russians and the Cubans have been actively aiding revolutionary movements in the Caribbean Basin since the mid-1970s and especially since the Sandinistas came to power in 1979. They have expanded their network of arms support and guerrilla training. In Cuba, Nicaragua, El Salvador, Grenada (until the October 1983 invasion by U.S. forces), and elsewhere, the signs of their advance have been clear.

How has all this happened without a vigorous American response? McColm attributes our relative inaction to the ignorance and misconceptions of the American public and the media and to the traditional American reluctance to view international events in a broad geopolitical framework. Further, many Americans refuse to look upon Cuba as a direct threat to the United States or U.S. interests.

For a different interpretation of the larger scenario in the Caribbean Basin, see Abraham Lowenthal (selection 5).

The notes for this essay begin on page 76.

R. Bruce McColm is a resident scholar and director of the Caribbean Basin Program at Freedom House in New York. He is also a widely published journalist.

L EONID BREZHNEV, SPEAKING before the Congress of Soviet Trade Unions in Moscow on March 16, 1982, warned that NATO's deployment of Pershing II missiles in Europe "would compel us to take retaliatory steps that would put the other side, *including the United States itself, its own territory,* in an analogous position."[1] A year and a day later, Georgi A. Arbatov, director of the Institute for the Study of the U.S.A. and Canada, reiterated the threat and was seconded by Defense Minister Dimitri Ustinov and by the commander-in-chief of the Warsaw Pact, Marshal Kulikov. Asked where such threatened Soviet missile deployments would occur, a member of the Soviet negotiating team in Geneva told the Spanish news agency EFE that the site could be either Cuba or Nicaragua.[2]

In the spring of 1983, both Costa Rica's foreign minister, Fernando Volio Jiménez, and the American ambassador to the United Nations, Jeane Kirkpatrick, reported that the Sandinista government in Nicaragua had signed a secret agreement with the Soviet Union for the construction of a sea-level, interoceanic canal across the San Juan River and Lake Nicaragua. America's sovereignty over the Panama Canal is due to expire in the year 2000. Against this background, politically the reported project would become the Soviets' Latin American version of the Aswan Dam. Geopolitically, it would have the effect of severing the hemisphere, clamping a vise of Soviet naval power projection around the Caribbean.[3]

Such are the harbingers of a fundamental geostrategic transformation—at a time when the American public debate is fixed almost obsessively on narrower currents of events in El Salvador, on human rights issues, on analogies with Vietnam, and on the comforting notion that the trends we are witnessing are reflecting factors and forces "indigenous" to the region that will

Reprinted by permission from the Summer 1983 issue of *Strategic Review* (© 1983 by the United States Strategic Institute). Original title: "Central America and the Caribbean: The Larger Scenario."

eventually right themselves into a new stability. For a variety of reasons lodged in their history and traditions, Americans tend to shy away from a geopolitical framework of analysis. The danger is that the geopolitical lessons relevant to the Caribbean Basin, Central America, and Latin America generally will sink in only when it will be too late to act upon them.

The Geopolitical Stakes

From the vantage point of the United States, the geopolitical contours of the Caribbean Basin are clear enough—or should be clear enough. By virtue of its sovereignty over Puerto Rico and the U.S. Virgin Islands, the United States is a Caribbean nation. A host of vital U.S. interests intersect in this area. Prominent among these are the maintenance of stable, trouble-free national borders and unhampered access to the vital sea lanes that flow into the Caribbean Sea. The Soviet Union understands the price of maintaining a standing army on its borders. We do not. Yet, if our southern borders should become unstable, we would be forced to divert American defensive strength from Europe and Asia in order to mount an immediate defensive shield where today there is none.

The primary thrust of long-term Soviet strategic objectives in the region seems equally clear: namely, to create through a Soviet naval and air presence and enhanced Cuban forces an offensive interdiction capability effective enough to block sea lanes and disrupt NATO's "swing strategy." This strategy calls for the airlift, in the event of war, of three reinforcing U.S. divisions to Europe, where some of their equipment is prepositioned. Other equipment and five or more additional divisions would be moved aboard Military Sealift Command vessels and merchant ships of the National Defense Reserve Fleet and NATO countries. The optimal embarkation port for three of those U.S. army divisions—the Second Armored, First Mechanized, and Fifth Infantry—is Beaumont, Texas, on the Gulf of Mexico. Three others—the Seventh, Ninth, and Twenty-fifth Infantry Divisions, based in Hawaii, Washington, and California—would normally be moved by sea through the Panama Canal, thence eastward south of Cuba.[4]

Modernized Soviet naval and air forces operating from bases in Cuba, Nicaragua, and Grenada could effectively harass such reinforcements. Soviet surface and submarine fleets could close the four major choke-points in the region's sea lanes. The Soviet Backfire bomber fleet, with a 4,000-kilometer range, can now be accommodated on at least three—and perhaps as many as ten—bases in Cuba, thence to threaten mid-Atlantic sea routes. It should be recalled that during World War II, German U-boats operating in the Caribbean without the benefit of friendly regional ports or aircover managed within six months to sink 260 merchant ships, half of them oil tankers.

To counter such an interdiction threat, the United States would have to invade Cuba. Defense planners suggest that this operation alone would require 100,000 troops—in other words, the strength of our reinforcements for NATO—and more aircraft carriers than are currently available.

Even short of such worst-case scenarios, the strategic significance of the Caribbean Basin is patent. The region hosts critical links in the network of American listening posts monitoring ship and submarine activities in the Atlantic Ocean and the approaches to the Caribbean, as well as other vital communications, tracking, and navigational facilities. The Navy's Atlantic Underseas Test and Evaluation Center in the Bahamas and the Virgin Islands is critical to the development of U.S. anti-submarine capabilities.

The Panama Canal, although termed obsolete by some defense planners, during the Korean War funneled 22 per cent of all troops and matériel for that conflict, and currently remains the key to allowing a three-ocean presence for the one-and-a-half-ocean fleet of the U.S. Navy. Only 13 of the navy's 475 ships are too large to transit the canal. It is also vital, of course, to the economies of Australia, New Zealand, and Japan in their trade with Western Europe.

America's economic health is increasingly at stake also in the mounting traffic of strategic and raw materials through the thirteen maritime routes of the Caribbean. The U.S. Department of Commerce has calculated that imported raw materials will rise from the present 20 per cent of total U.S. consumption to nearly 50 per cent by the year 2000. The bulk of these materials are and will continue to be transshipped through the Caribbean Sea.

Most of the supertanker traffic from the Middle East and Africa requires the lightering facilities in the Bahamas, the Virgin Islands, Trinidad, Curaçao, and Aruba for the transfer of crude oil to standard craft. These routes carry more than 50 per cent of U.S. oil imports to domestic markets, and refinery facilities in the area account for 12.5 per cent of our total processed oil. Oil from Alaska and Ecuador passes through the trans-Panamanian pipeline, augmenting the tanker routes through the canal. Add to this some proven 45 billion barrels of oil in Mexico, and 6 billion or more in Guatemala and the Venezuelan reserves, and the aggregate importance of the Caribbean for American oil imports can be said to rival that of the Persian Gulf area.[5]

The Caribbean Basin itself is a principal source of U.S. raw material imports. After Canada, Mexico is the second most important supplier of critical raw materials to the United States, and the principal supplier of silver, zinc, gypsum, antimony, mercury, bismuth, selenium, barium, rhenium, and lead. Over 50 per cent of U.S. bauxite imports have traditionally come from Surinam, Guyana, Haiti, and Jamaica, and iron ore from Brazil and Venezuela is important to our industrial requirements. The availability of these mineral imports represents an important economic convenience for the United States today; in the event of a major global conflict, their availability would be crucial.

Strategic Shifts in the 1970s

There is not the space here to detail the interplay of Soviet-Cuban and American strategies in Central and Latin America since the advent of Fidel Castro in Cuba in 1960 and the establishment of that country as the Soviet Union's first strategic foothold in the Western Hemisphere. Suffice it to say that the stage for the currently unfolding and possibly climactic clash of those strategies was set in the early 1970s. It was then that the United States shifted from a previously active policy in the Southern Hemisphere to one of "benign neglect," screened by U.S.-Soviet détente and the so-called Nixon Doctrine.

In 1974 the United States tacitly abandoned its policy of economic denial against Cuba and, indeed, made ostensible tries at normalizing relations with Havana, even after the onset of the Cuban intervention in Angola. This encouraged Latin American and Caribbean Basin countries to enter into expanding relations with both Cuba and the Soviet Union.

Soviet theoreticians, such as Central Committee member Boris Ponomarev, waxed enthusiastic about Soviet opportunities in the region in the early 1970s. Writing in 1971, Ponomarev argued:

Seemingly quite reliable rear lines of American imperialism are becoming a tremendous hotbed of anti-imperialist revolution. A tremendous revolutionary movement is developing by the side of the main citadel of imperialism, the United States. These changes are having and, unquestionably, will continue to have a strong impact on further changes in the correlation of world forces in favor of the international working class and socialism.[6]

Under Brezhnev the Soviet Union encouraged local Communist parties to join broad electoral fronts and to infiltrate the trade unions, while Moscow put its emphasis on the pursuit of diplomatic and commercial ties with the countries in the region.[7] From 1964 to 1975, the Soviet Union expanded trade relations with Latin America to include twenty countries and through its Council for Mutual Economic Assistance (CMEA) entered into several multilateral economic agreements with organizations such as SELA (Latin American Economic System). Meanwhile populist military coups in Ecuador, Bolivia, Panama, and Peru gave Moscow inroads into the Latin American military, an institution which had previously been relatively immune to Communist influences. The military, according to Soviet theoreticians, was the only stable institution in an often chaotic political environment that could serve as the likely generator of change toward socialism.

By the mid-1970s, the Soviets had large diplomatic, economic, cultural, and scientific missions throughout the Caribbean and Central America, such as in Costa Rica, Venezuela, Trinidad and Tobago, Guatemala, Nicaragua, and Jamaica. These missions, besides cultivating indigenous cadres through an extensive KGB infrastructure, sought on a more practical level to encourage the governments in the area to play a more active role in the politics of the Third World at large, with particular attention to coordinating commodity export prices, influencing policies toward multinational corporations and Third World debt, and advocating "anti-imperialist" and "anti-colonial" positions in various international organizations.

Before the 1970s, Soviet theoreticians had believed that the region must first pass through a "popular democratic" revolutionary phase before reaching the portals of "scientific socialism." This strategy was now modified. Local Communist parties were urged to play a prominent role in left-wing coalitions, even within so-called progressive military regimes.

The defeat of the Broad Front in Uruguay in 1971, the military coup that toppled Salvador Allende in Chile in 1973, and the small turnout for the leftist alliance in the 1973 Venezuelan elections forced Moscow to reconsider the merits of the electoral path to power. The year 1975 brought a watershed for Soviet strategy in Latin America. The pro-Soviet Velasco government in Peru fell, and a spate of right-wing takeovers took place in Uruguay, Bolivia, and Argentina in what the Soviets called "a reactionary counterof-fensive unprecedented in Latin American history."

Thereafter, Moscow discreetly financed through Cuba and East European countries urban terrorist groups such as the Tupamaros and Montoneros in the Southern Cone countries [Argentina, Chile, Uruguay]—more in an effort to foster political insecurity and to isolate the governments internationally than actually to topple them. The urban terrorist campaigns of the mid- and late 1970s throughout the Southern Cone were simply well-orchestrated reminders that the revolutionary spirit was still alive.

The Bolder Cuban Connection

Meanwhile, encouraged by the passiveness of the successive Nixon, Ford, and Carter administrations in Washington, Cuba began to break out of its diplomatic and economic isolation and to knot stronger ties with regional countries, particularly in the English-speaking Caribbean. With American influence waning throughout the Caribbean Basin during the 1970s, Havana estab-lished relations with a growing number of left-leaning gov-ernments in the Caribbean. Primarily through the good offices of Michael Manley, the leftist prime minister of Jamaica, the Cubans forged links with the small, Marxist-leaning Black Power parties in the eastern Caribbean.

This political offensive by Castro reaped some early practical benefits. During the Angolan conflict, Cuba was able to refuel its Africa-bound aircraft in Guyana, with which it had established relations in the early 1970s. Cuba's participation in regional organizations helped shape more strongly anti-American positions, and through its program of scholarships and guerrilla training Havana gained a great deal of credibility among younger political elites in the region. At one point, 500 Cuban advisors were assigned to Jamaica to train its security forces, and in the bitter Jamaican electoral campaign in 1980 the Cuban ambassador, Ulises Estrada, was implicated in an arms-smuggling plot to destabilize the island. During this period Havana also gained influence with the governments of Saint Lucia, through former Deputy Prime Minister George Odlum and the Progressive Labor Party, and Grenada, after the March 1979 coup that brought Maurice Bishop and his New Jewel Party to power.

The 1970s featured not only a quickening of the Soviet-Cuban political and clandestine offensive in the Southern Hemisphere but also a busy learning period. By dint of their growing presence, Soviet analysts were able to study the inter-American defense system and maritime navigation. Cuban and Soviet trawler fleets gathered intelligence and mapped the geology and topography of the area in a systematic way. Moscow thus was preparing its eventual challenge to America's "hegemonic presumption" in its strategic back yard.

The Socio-Economic Backdrop

The Soviet Union and its Cuban surrogates, in casting their strategy toward the Caribbean Basin, no doubt were keenly sensitive to the pull of socio-economic forces that were opening opportunities for wedges of influence. Central America in particular beckoned as a prime target area. By and large, the "city-states" in this region are in the process of capital formation, in contrast with their South American counterparts which generally boast relatively sophisticated, if inequitable, capitalist systems. This process means that the small but growing middle class in most Central American states can be divided because of competing aspirations within it vis-à-vis the traditional agrarian producers, and that a large number of marginal and, for the most part, culturally homogeneous farm workers are ripe for radicalization.

During their modernization throes, these small nations cannot sustain rapid changes in the social dynamics of the traditional society without suffering political upheaval. And, more often than not, the countries of the Central American isthmus have depended on the military to protect national security and order. But, as this institution is traditionally minuscule in these countries and represents more a political than a fighting force, it is hard put to cope with a war of attrition waged by urban and rural guerrillas.

Moreover, the year 1978 brought about a rapid deterioration in the economics of the region. The prices of export commodities such as coffee, cotton, and bananas plummeted. At the same time, the costs of imported oil and borrowed capital escalated, while the slowed economic growth in the industrial countries reduced tourism in the region, a major generator of capital. Widening credit deficits turned inexorably into severe foreign-exchange shortages and national bankruptcies. The elites created during the previous periods of rapid economic growth still expected participation within the political structures of the society but were, by and large, excluded from the decision-making spheres.

Political instability exacerbated the economic decline. The Central American Common Market had been crippled by the brief 1969 Soccer War between Honduras and El Salvador. But this episode proved minor when compared to the economic consequences of increased political terrorism in the 1970s. After the Nicaraguan civil war ended, the expanding guerrilla strategy of economic warfare canceled the large strides toward industrialization made by El Salvador, Guatemala, and Honduras.

The cumulative effect of the late 1970s on the Caribbean Basin is a persistent and generalized economic depression. Since 1980 economic growth in the Caribbean has fallen far behind population growth. Unemployment and underemployment throughout the region stand between 25 and 50 per cent, with the major impact falling on the young people who make up the majorities of the populations. In some cases, inflation rates have soared over 100 per cent, and import quotas have seriously squeezed the once-growing middle class. This has resulted in a full-scale flight of capital and the middle class from the Caribbean Basin.

On the Caribbean island-states, the newly emergent leftist forces, which still view Cuba as a viable economic model, have profited from the social problems that come from population growth and increased urbanization. Over 50 per cent of the island populations are young—below the age of eighteen—and associate the economic depression in the Caribbean with an overdependence on the economies of the Western industrialized countries and with the legacy of colonialism.

The Caribbean, in addition to suffering economic depression, is also experiencing a transition from the old labor-based, populist governments modeled after the British Labor Party. The generation of such leaders as Eric Williams of Trinidad, Vere Bird of Antigua, Milton Cato of St. Vincent and the Grenadines, and "Skipper" Barrow of Barbados, who combined a Fabian socialism with a pro-Western orientation, is rapidly disappearing from the political landscape.

The micro-Marxist parties, once independent outgrowths of the New Left and Black Power movements in the local universities, have gained additional legitimacy since the success of Maurice Bishop in overthrowing the regime of Eric Gairy in Grenada in March 1979. With Cuban assistance to the Grenada regime and its close ties with intellectual-based parties on other islands, groups such as the Dominica Liberation Movement, the Antigua Caribbean Liberation Movement, and splinter factions of local labor parties have gained legitimacy and strength by dint of military training in Libya and Cuba, even if they have not scored heavily in democratic elections. In the future, these political forces will represent destabilizing factors throughout the eastern Caribbean.[8]

The Expanding Soviet Military Presence

In a 1975 article, General I. Shavrov, then superintendent of the Soviet General Staff Academy, wrote that regional conflicts in the developing world were "epicenters" of the global struggle between East and West.[9] In the aftermath of the Communist victory in Vietnam, Shavrov and other Soviet strategists noted a definite relationship between the strategic nuclear balance and the incidence of local wars. He observed that by the mid-1970s the West was experiencing a crisis at the hands of irregular warfare and had not succeeded in gaining one major victory through the use of military force. Shavrov went on to suggest that Soviet aid now was the most important factor in determining the outcome of such a conflict and remarked that the Soviet Union's bluewater navy and growing airlift capability permitted it to inhibit Western influence in regional conflicts while supporting those forces and regimes allied with the Soviet Union.

Beginning in 1975, the Soviet Union embarked on an aggressive policy addressed to the peripheral theaters of the developing world—in Angola, South Yemen, Ethiopia, Kampuchea, Laos, Zaire, and Afghanistan. The general offensive grew bolder against the background of passive and confused reaction from the United States to the accelerating tempo of conflicts in the Third World, climaxed by the image of American powerlessness in the Iranian Revolution. The successful use of Soviet military intervention evidently convinced Moscow to downgrade economic ties with the developing world in favor of the more successful and quicker-results policy of military assistance.

This policy of military assistance has entailed the expanding muscles of Soviet power in a "screening" mode while the local surrogates of that power are being strengthened. Both prongs of this strategy have been clearly in evidence in the Caribbean.[10]

Since early July 1969, when a seven-ship Soviet squadron entered the Caribbean, a new chapter has unfolded in the political evolution of the hemisphere. For the first time since the destruction of the Spanish fleet off Santiago de Cuba on July 3, 1898, the naval force of a rival great power entered the Caribbean. The construction of a nuclear submarine docking facility in Cienfuegos on the southern shore of Cuba in the summer and fall of 1970 signaled a permanence of the Soviet naval presence in the region, plus a logistical capability of servicing nuclear submarines which would operate within striking range of half the United States.

Arms Buildup in Cuba

At the same time, since the Cuban combat intervention in Angola in 1975 the Soviet Union has engaged in a remarkable effort to strengthen the Cuban armed forces.[11] From 1980 to 1981 alone, Soviet arms shipments to the island tripled, totaling about $2.5 billion worth of military matériel. Some 63,000 metric tons of Soviet arms were shipped to Cuba in 1981, more than in any year since the 1962 Cuban Missile Crisis. Some of these arms were to replace equipment used by Cuban forces deployed in various missions throughout Africa. But they were clearly aimed as well at upgrading and enhancing the island's offensive military capabilities.

During the past decade the Cuban military has been steadily professionalized, with estimates of some 120,000 men in the regular standing forces, 60,000 ready reserves, 175,000 to 200,000 second-line reserves, and about 100,000 members of the Army of Working Youth. In addition, since 1981 the Cuban government has created a 500,000-man Territorial Militia to guard the island against attack.

The Cuban military has modeled its organization, strategy, and tactics on those of the Soviet military. Ready reserves can be called up on four hours' notice; they train at least forty-five days a year. Half of the Cuban troops sent to Angola and Ethiopia were reserves, and the Cuban military thus has recourse to a large pool of personnel with combat experience. In addition, the Cubans have developed a dual command structure, which allows them to rotate high-ranking members of the armed forces between Angola and Cuba.

We may recall the revelation in September 1979 that a Soviet combined arms combat brigade of between 2,000 and 3,000 men had been spotted in Cuba. The obvious role of such a force would be implanting a tangible Soviet deterrent against any possible American strikes on Cuba in reprisal for Cuban actions elsewhere in the region. In the larger scheme of things, therefore, the Soviet brigade carries clear offensive connotations.

The upgrading of Cuba's air and naval forces now gives Havana the capability of quick strikes from the island into the Caribbean. Previously dependent on the Soviets for their logistical lines of support to Africa, Cuba now possesses the capacity to transport medium to heavy weaponry off the island and can rapidly deploy some 5,000 special forces within twenty-four hours anywhere in the Caribbean Basin. In a low-level conflict such a force could mean the margin of victory.

Part of the Soviet aid package to Cuba in recent years has included fifteen to twenty MiG-23 Floggers (bringing the combined Cuban MiG force to between 200 and 225), Mi-8 helicopter gunships, An-26 medium-range transports, Foxtrot diesel-powered attack submarines, T-62 tanks, and a number of BM-21 multiple rocket launchers. Counting fixed-wing combat airplanes and helicopters, Cuba deploys an air force of 555 aircraft. Besides the aforementioned submarines and Koni-class frigate, the Cuban navy has ten large patrol boats and twenty-six fast-attack craft armed with Styx surface-to-surface missiles. The navy also deploys another forty fast-attack craft of the Turya and Zhuk classes, which are ideal for amphibious landings.

In late May 1983, Cuba began practicing amphibious assaults around Mariel, deploying a contingent of 400 marines, four light tanks, and eight armored personnel carriers. Using Soviet-made Polnocny-class ships capable of carrying six tanks, the Cubans demonstrated a capability of projecting force particularly against vulnerable eastern Caribbean states.[12]

The Soviets also supplied Cuba in 1979 with batteries of modified SA-2 anti-aircraft missiles, as well as mobile SA-6 missiles with launchers. These large missiles, which in the Soviet inventory are often equipped with nuclear weapons, can be employed quickly in a surface-to-surface mode by the simple addition of a booster.

Since 1978, the Soviet Union has provided Cuba also with MiG-27s, which are frequently flown by Soviet pilots and have a range of 1,500 miles and the capability of carrying either conventional or nuclear payloads. At least three and possibly as many as nine Cuban airfields have recently been upgraded to handle the Soviet Tu-95 Bear heavy intercontinental bombers, capable of carrying nuclear air-to-surface missiles. Since 1970, these long-range bombers have been traveling from the Kola Peninsula to the Cuban airfields without any U.S. protests. This past spring, nearly ten Tu-95s were sighted in Cuba, at least two of them with operational bomb bays.[13]

A Protective Shield for Revolution

The military buildup of Cuba has served not only the creation of a platform for extending a conventional military threat to NATO's "swing strategy" and other American vital interests in the area. Clearly, an equally important—and more immediate—purpose behind the buildup has been the establishment of a staging area for support of guerrilla movements in Central America and the Caribbean and the creation of a protective shield for the revolutionary governments in Grenada, Nicaragua, Surinam, and others still to follow. Indeed, the acceleration of Moscow's arms supplies to Cuba during the past several years may well reflect also the Soviet leaders' recognition of the revolutionary potential in the region that was expressed in the leftist coup in Grenada in March 1979 and even more dramatically in the July 1979 Sandinista overthrow of the Somoza regime in Nicaragua.[14]

It should be noted that in previous years the Soviet Union had been more skeptical of the success of guerrilla attack in the region—a skepticism that was expressed in contemptuous Soviet references to the failure of the Ché Guevara mission in Bolivia in 1967. Castro in the early years had felt shackled by Soviet reluctance to countenance Cuban adventures in Latin America. To be sure, in December 1964, at the Havana Conference of Communist Parties, Moscow had relented somewhat, allowing Cuban support of armed struggle in Venezuela, Colombia, Guatemala, Honduras, Paraguay, and Haiti in return for Castro's promise to pursue peaceful change elsewhere in the hemisphere. At the 1966 Tricontinental Conference in Havana, which was conceived and coordinated by Moscow to undercut Communist China's inroads in the Third World, an elaborate network was established among national liberation movements in Africa, Asia, and Latin America. The Latin American Solidarity Organization (OLAS) headquartered in Havana cultivated revolutionaries who recognized Cuba as "the vanguard of the Latin American revolution." Yet the failures of Castroite guerrilla movements during the late 1960s further convinced Moscow of the unproductiveness of this approach.[15]

This Soviet view changed sharply in the late 1970s with the Sandinistas' success in Nicaragua. Soviet theoreticians who previously had heaped scorn on Cuban concepts of revolution now indulged in revisionist payments of respect to Guevara's theory of guerrilla warfare and declared that armed struggle was the only option in the hemisphere. Local pro-Moscow Communist parties from Uruguay to Guatemala ritualistically endorsed such a strategy and formed alliances with Castroite guerrilla movements and the broad political fronts opposing the standing governments in the region. The formula of a diverse political front combined with factional guerrilla forces now was considered capable of substituting as the "revolutionary vanguard" for Communist parties.[16]

The Nicaraguan revolution produced a sophisticated synthesis of popular-front techniques previously used by the Soviets in Latin America and guerrilla tactics. Since 1978 the key Soviet-Cuban tactics have included the unification of traditionally splintered radical groups behind a commitment to armed struggle in return for promises of training and material assistance; the placement of ideologically committed cadres, trained since the 1960s, in pivotal positions of the guerrilla command structure; the development of secure logistical supply lines; and the insertion of Cuban advisors in the strategy-planning sessions of the guerrilla movements to ensure control of the movements—and of their governments once they have achieved power. This process, aided by a huge intelligence and political infrastructure built up since the late 1960s, tightens Soviet-Cuban control over insurgencies.[17]

Significantly from the American vantage point, the strategy of unifying the democratic left with the guerrillas increases pressures on those center-left forces that traditionally have been aided covertly by the United States to counter insurgencies in the area. This strategy was reflected in Nicaragua in the formation of the Broad Opposition Front, a coalition of democratic political parties and representatives of labor and the private sector, and it is also evident in El Salvador in the presence of certain democratic elements in the FDR [Democratic Revolutionary Front] . The inclusion of Social Democratic and Christian Democratic forces in the guerrilla-controlled opposition creates a Spanish Civil War scenario in which substantial outside support is attracted to the guerrilla cause.

Salient targets of this popular-front mobilization have been the Catholic Church and elements of the Christian Democrats, traditionally bulwarks against Communism in the hemisphere. Jesús Montane Oropesa, a member of Cuba's Politbureau Secretariat and the director of the General Department of Foreign Relations of the Cuban Communist Party, summarized the new strategy at the International Theoretical Conference in Havana on April 3, 1981:

The fruits and knowledge we gain from the temporary strategic unity achieved by Marxist-Leninists and Christians are of profound importance. We must exploit the possibilities of this interesting and promising opportunity. Using this intelligent policy of *temporary strategic unity,* we must reach out to patriotic elements within the armed forces, the intellectuals of different political backgrounds, the middle class, and include sectors of the bourgeoisie. It has been demonstrated that without *undermining* or *impairing* the firmness of our purpose and convictions, we can cooperate on the basis of similar concrete objectives with Social Democrats, and we can reach even to Christian Democrats (Social Christians notwithstanding) and their reactionary bureaucratic hierarchy. . . . This is only a temporary strategy. We cannot always advance as rapidly as we want. We have to consider not only national but international factors as well. Sometimes this advance can be fast; in other instances, to ensure a strategy that would allow us eventually to be more expeditious, we opted to move cautiously and slowly.[18]

The unification of the guerrilla movements began in earnest in 1978 when Castro spent forty-eight hours welding together the diverse groups that constituted the Sandinista forces. In the following year, the first of many unity pacts between the rival guerrilla forces in El Salvador were signed in Havana, and eventually the Farabundo Martí Liberation Front was established in 1980, coordinating four guerrilla forces and the Salvadoran Communist Party. The same process was applied to the Guatemalan guerrillas in 1980 and to the minuscule Honduran terrorist squads this past spring [1983] in Managua.

Coordinating Cuban Support

Most of these operations are planned and coordinated by the Americas Department of the Cuban Communist Party headed by Manuel Pineiro Losada. After a purge of the General Directorate of Intelligence (DGI) by the Soviets in the early 1970s, the Americas Department emerged in 1974 to coordinate and centralize all operational control of Cuban support for guerrilla movements. The operation brings together the expertise of the Cuban special forces and the DGI into a network of training camps and the covert movement of personnel and matériel between Cuba and abroad, while sponsoring propaganda support for the insurgents.

By and large the cadres of these insurgencies are veterans of the 1966 Tricontinental Conference and the Junta de Coordinación Revolucionaria (JCR) established in 1974 in Paris to coordinate Latin American terrorist organizations. This network of organizations such as the Sandinistas, the Argentinian Montoneros, the Colombian M-19, and the Uruguayan Tupamaros has, in turn, established links with European ʼand Arab terrorist organizations.[19]

Military training is conducted in far-flung areas from Cuba to the Middle East. Several camps in Cuba are dedicated exclusively to military training, including one in Pinar del Río and another near Guanabaco, east of Havana. In the past three years alone, groups from nearly every country of the Caribbean Basin have been trained there in military strategy, sabotage, explosives, and special commando operations. From the late 1960s, the Sandinistas received training from the Libyans and the PLO in Lebanon, Syria, South Yemen, Libya, and Algeria. Various Central American guerrilla cadres, according to Palestinian sources, fought with the PLO against Israel in past Middle Eastern wars and joined with West European terrorists in the early 1970s in acts of terrorism in Europe. An example of this international cooperation can be found in Tomás Borge Martínez, the current minister of interior of the Nicaraguan government, who in the 1970s acted as Castro's emissary to the PLO. Documents captured by Israeli forces during the invasion of Lebanon record training for Salvadoran and Haitian guerrillas as late as 1982.[20]

The Nicaraguan Funnel

With the triumph of the Sandinistas in Nicaragua, camps for the training of Central American guerrillas, as well as terrorist groups such as the Basque ETA, have been established in Estelí, Montlimar, Somotillo, Ocotal, Tamarindo, Puerto Cabezas, the island of Soletiname in Lake Nicaragua, and several others in the Punta Cosequina area immediately across the Gulf of Fonseca from El Salvador.

Today Nicaragua has become a solid base for insurgencies in neighboring countries. An elaborate supply network extends from Nicaragua to the Salvadoran and Guatemalan guerrillas. The logistical support systems are arranged by a trusted Communist Party leader such as Shafik Handal, the secretary-general of the Communist Party of El Salvador, from a variety of arms depots. To hide their hand, the Soviets encourage the use of the surplus American arms stockpiled in Libya, Vietnam, and Ethiopia, and reconditioned weapons from World War II available in Eastern Europe. At the initial stage of the insurgency these arms are channeled through an elaborate and flexible network of routes that crisscross Central America.

In the case of El Salvador, the arms, once deposited in Nicaragua or Cuba, are broken down into small lots and transported over land in trucks or on vessels down the estuaries of the coastal regions in Belize and Guatemala and directly into the Usulután Department of El Salvador. The acquisition by Nicaragua of some 100 planes from Vietnam enhances the ability of the Sandinistas to maintain airdrops to the Salvadoran guerrillas on small bush strips in the remote rural areas of the country. As was demonstrated in North Korea and Vietnam, interdiction of such arms flows is an almost impossible task. Currently the Salvadoran guerrillas receive supplies nearly every night, including heavy artillery by overland routes through Honduras. According to the Department of Defense, the Salvadoran guerrillas are reinforced every forty-eight to seventy-two hours.[21]

Footholds in Grenada and Surinam

Immediately after the 1979 coup in Grenada by Maurice Bishop and his New Jewel Party, the Cubans under the guidance of Ambassador Julian Rizo, a DGI agent whose previous experience included cooperating with the New Left in the United States, offered assistance in creating a 2,000-man Grenadan army, along with a popular militia to protect Bishop in the model of previous praetorian guards surrounding African leaders favorable to the Soviets and Cubans. With a population of 100,000, this Windward Island is now the most militarized country on earth. Notwithstanding Bishop's denials, the airport being constructed with Cuban help at Point Salines provides Havana with the secure airfield needed for the reinforcement of troops in Africa and an ability to extend airpower over much of mainland South America.

In 1982, Maurice Bishop visited Eastern Europe, Libya, and the Soviet Union. Agreements between Grenada and the Communist countries have in effect integrated the island into the military communications system of the Soviet bloc, and plans to construct a harbor on Grenada lead to speculation that a Soviet base threatening the deep-water trench in the Caribbean is in the offing. Plans for developing the harbor came after a 1980 visit by Admiral Sergei Gorshkov to the island. Subsequently, General Gennediy Sazhenev was appointed permanent ambassador of the Soviet Union to Grenada. Since then, Grenada has served as a transit point for Caribbean radicals destined for guerrilla training in Libya and Cuba.

A subsidiary target of the Soviet Union has been Surinam, the former Dutch colony on the northeast coast of South America. Since a group of sergeants toppled the democratic government in February 1980, the strongman, Lieutenant Colonel Daysi Bouterse, a thirty-eight-year-old former physical education instructor, has been steadily courted by the Cubans and the Soviets.

By 1981, Bouterse in a secret meeting with Fidel Castro received promises of Cuban military and economic assistance. There are reports that Cuban and Nicaraguan advisors entered Surinam to help create a popular militia to protect Bouterse's regime against possible threats from Surinam's 2,000-man army. This first pro-Soviet government on the mainland of South America since the fall of Allende in Chile has publicly pledged to send an international brigade to fight in Nicaragua. The Cubans immediately introduced Oswaldo Oscar Cárdenas, a confidant of Castro, as ambassador to aid in the training of the militia and the police. After the Dutch government terminated its aid, Surinam signed a friendship treaty with Libya and pledged to defend "Cuba, Nicaragua, and Grenada." The Cubans maintain their influence through the small Cuban-trained group of intellectuals of the Revolutionary People's Party who determine policy.[22]

The Soviets after reaching an agreement to establish an embassy in Surinam finally sent Igor Bubnov, an ideologue from the Washington embassy, to supervise the adoption of the "correct ideology" of the government.

Nicaragua as a Mainland Platform

After the Sandinistas' triumph in Nicaragua, Cuba took effective control of Nicaragua's military and security forces. The number of military and security advisors to the new regime increased steadily after 1979, doubling in 1981 to some 2,000 within a total Cuban presence that may have reached as high as 11,000.[23]

The Nicaraguan military buildup and the consolidation of Sandinista control over that society clearly is aimed at creating an extension of Cuba's military shield in support of guerrilla struggles in neighboring countries. During the 1979-82 period, the Managua government received an estimated $125 million of military equipment and supplies from the Soviet Union alone. According to the Department of Defense, the Nicaraguans have some fifty to sixty Soviet T-54/55 tanks, 1,000 East German trucks and armored personnel carriers, and 7,000 French surface-to-air missiles. The buildup has been fed from Libya's huge stockpile of arms purchased from the Soviet Union in the 1970s and from the equally large supply of weapons left behind by the United States in Vietnam. In addition to the $100 million of economic assistance provided Managua by the Libyan government in 1980, another $200 million of weapons from Qaddafi's stockpiles has been pledged for use in Central America.

Responsibility for the control of certain institutions in Nicaragua has been assigned according to a division of labor among Communist-bloc personnel. Between 100 and 200 East German advisors are said to be reorganizing the country's internal-security apparatus and intelligence system, as well as developing the elaborate military communications network linking Managua, Havana, and Moscow. Fifty or more Soviet advisors supervise the reorganization and Sovietization of the economy under Moscow-trained economic planner Henry Ruíz as well as overseeing the whole control effort. Some seventy Nicaraguan pilots have been trained in Bulgaria, and Bulgarian techniques are helping to organize the trade-union movement. Training and instruction at the guerrilla camps is apportioned according to specialty and function among the Cubans, the PLO, Libyans, Vietnamese, North Koreans, and Latin American revolutionaries.

The Nicaraguan Army has already grown to a combined force of 75,000 regulars and reservists. In addition, a force of unknown size is attached to the Ministry of Interior: it is believed to include specialized border troops and an elite commando detachment. Nicaragua's goal is to fashion a 200,000-man army, which would be roughly three times the military forces of the other Central American countries combined. The Nicaraguan military, with Cuban and Soviet techniques, has added thirty-six new military installations to the thirteen remaining from the Somoza years and has extended the airfields at Puerto Cabezas and Bluefields on the Atlantic Coast and Montilimar on the Pacific to handle MiGs. The smaller airfields such as Papalonal, twenty-three miles northwest of Managua, were extended to facilitate the shuttle of arms to the Salvadoran guerrillas.

While the current Nicaraguan Air Force reveals a dependence on small, mobile gunships such as retrofitted Cessna-185s, T-33 jets, and several reconverted trainers, South Yemen apparently has sold ten Soviet-built MiG-17s to the Sandinistas, the addition of which would neutralize neighboring Honduras's present air superiority.

The Soviet-Cuban Strategy in El Salvador

It is against this larger background that the guerrilla wars in neighboring countries should be assessed, particularly the conflict in El Salvador. The inability of the Salvadoran guerrillas in 1981 and 1982 to mount a decisive offensive and their lack of popular support should not obscure basic trends in that war.

The Salvadoran guerrillas now have recourse to a reliable base next door in Nicaragua, where Cuban advisors in a command headquarters outside Managua can map strategy and provide consistent and reliable logistical support.[24] Operating from rural base areas near this logistical support line, the Salvadoran guerrillas, numbering between 7,000 and 8,000—plus a popular militia of around 12,000 and the "internationalist brigades"—have moved from a traditional hit-and-run strategy to one of coordination of brigades in semi-regular fighting. As of January 1983, certain guerrilla units have made the transition to a classical positional war, with the ability to pin down and hold regular army forces, while mobile units have encircled and in many cases destroyed the government formations. The strategy of a "continuous offensive" by the guerrillas compels the government troops to act in dispersement, unable to consolidate control over war-torn areas.

Unlike the Nicaraguan conflict, the Salvadoran battle is a classic war of attrition. The Soviet-Cuban strategy in this war is based on the premise that the Salvadoran government cannot sustain a lengthy internal war financially, psychologically, or politically. The Salvadoran military, as has been increasingly evidenced, is not capable of waging a successful counterinsurgency campaign without substantial American training and assistance, and must increasingly depend on inexperienced and generally inadequate young conscripts.

Since the initiative in the Salvadoran fighting continues to be on the side of the guerrillas, the government is under constant and growing pressure, exacerbated by economic sabotage and sinking popular morale. Moreover, the perceived stalemate tightens the government's isolation in international forums and, as we have seen, furthers the erosion of support from the United States.

While the Vietnamese model has conventional forces sweeping into the capital for the final victory, neither Havana nor Moscow wants to tempt the United States with such a blatant pretext for possible military intervention. Instead, the drum-beat for negotiations by the guerrilla forces becomes an effective, if slower, road to victory. The ultimate goal of engaging in negotiations is to (1) allow the guerrilla forces to secure their military positions, (2) split the democratic elements in El Salvador by disagreements over tactics and the desire to end domestic violence, and (3) lead to a coalition government that will pave the way for a guerrilla victory and/or control of the government.

A Matrix of Developments

The foregoing have been at best strokes on a broad canvas. But that is precisely one of the main points of the preceding pages: namely, the breadth of the phenomenon that has been unfolding at the very strategic doorstep of the United States. It is a phenomenon, moreover, that has barely made an imprint on U.S. media reporting, let alone on U.S. public opinion.

How did it come about? We have tried to sketch the major causes and circumstances. Perhaps the best way to summarize them is in the form of a rough matrix.

On one side of the matrix stands the relative neglect by successive U.S. administrations of the areas, peoples, and problems south of our borders. Notwithstanding occasional, usually belated, and often myopic "initiatives," we have tended to take the region for granted in terms of our strategic priorities. We have been preoccupied by conflicts and crises elsewhere on the globe and by problems at home.

On the opposite side of the matrix is the extensive operational groundwork laid in the area by the Soviet Union and Cuba over the past two decades. Although their admixture has varied, there has been nothing really new in the techniques that have been applied: the careful creation of an expanding infrastructure of intelligence, recruitment, and subversion; the nurturing of radical splinter groups; the cooption of key political figures; the schooling and training of revolutionaries; the infusions of weapons; and so on. If there has been a novel touch to the combination of these time-honored techniques in the Southern Hemisphere, this has been the success of the Soviets and the Cubans in welding a "popular front" model that links guerrillas and terrorists with a broad diversity of democratic elements, including even those of the traditionally conservative Catholic Church and Christian Democracy. And while the perspectives in Havana and Moscow have not always been harmonious, the latest phase has featured a triumph of Soviet-Cuban unity of action over synthesis of doctrine.

On the third side of the matrix are the revolutionary opportunities in the region. They vary from sub-region to sub-region, but a common denominator relates to the disruptive effects of economic modernization upon societies whose frail political institutions have been largely incapable of accommodating to or even cushioning these effects. And although the Marxist-Leninist model has not, in demonstrated practice, offered the promised land, nevertheless it is particularly seductive to a youthful majority of the area's population who feel estranged from the established political processes of their societies.

The final side of the matrix represents the shifts in the global environment, notably the changes in what the Soviets call the "correlation of global forces." The trends in the overall balance of military power in favor of the Soviet Union—at the strategic and tactical nuclear levels, in the conventional arena, and in the wider realm of power-projection—have been amply described and need not be repeated here. The relevance of the changing "correlation of forces" to our hemispheric scenario is that not only has it provided the Soviet Union with vastly improved means of projecting power over long distances and with a greater willingness for risk-taking: it has also clothed the expanding Soviet intervention in remote places with a contrived "legitimacy" that supposedly attaches to the global presence of a global superpower. This is reflected, in part, in the signal lack of support the Reagan administration has been receiving in its Central American policies from our European allies. Furthermore, this "legitimacy" theme, which is persistently invoked by Soviet propaganda to cover their global adventures, also creeps into some American attitudes toward the unfolding hemispheric scenario.

This returns us to the more general subject of prevalent American attitudes toward the developments in Central America and the Caribbean. We noted at the outset that the larger picture of what is transpiring has been neglected partly because of the concentration of the U.S. media, and of the public debate, on events in El Salvador. Yet one suspects that the failure to grasp the larger picture has to do also with a reluctance to contemplate that picture and with some lingering myths from the past. One of these involves the image of a "tiny Cuba" that is able to foment mischief in neighboring countries but, in the final analysis and despite Soviet help, will be incapable of mounting a direct threat against the overwhelming power of the United States.

It is this myth that obscures the realities. The current focus on guerrilla warfare in El Salvador distracts from an understanding of the remarkable qualitative escalation of the regional arsenals and conflict potential—of an accelerated buildup of modern, conventional forces and armaments that are directed ultimately against vital American lifelines and interests. The developments trace the prospective scenario of America's global strategy becoming hostage to its own back yard. As was suggested, this may be precisely the central objective of the Soviet Union, abetted by its willing surrogates who are looking for their own regional spoils.

NOTES

1. *Pravda,* March 17, 1982.

2. Associated Press, March 17, 1983, and April 14, 1983, and *New York Times,* April 26, 1983.

3. The Nicaraguan canal plans were first disclosed by Volio in *La Prensa Libre* (San Jose, Costa Rica) on March 25, 1983. This report came after the pro-government newspaper *El Nuevo Diario* of Managua announced on March 10, 1983, that the Soviets were establishing a floating dock at the southern Nicaraguan port of San Juan del Sur. It is believed that Soviet technicians assigned to this project are also involved in the canal planning. Ambassador Kirkpatrick at a press conference claimed that the canal was part of the Soviet plan to accelerate its power projection into the Western Hemisphere. Only the *Washington Times,* on April 29, 1983, reported the Ambassador's remarks.

4. Much has recently been written about NATO's contingency plans in the area. The specifics of the "swing strategy" were outlined by John Cooley, *Christian Science Monitor,* October 11, 1979.

5. For a short overview of the oil traffic in the Caribbean Basin, see Lewis Tambs's testimony before the House Subcommittee on Inter-American Affairs, "Guatemala, Central America and the Caribbean: A Geopolitical Glance," July 30, 1981.

6. Boris Ponomarev, "Topical Problems of the Theory of the Revolutionary Process," *Kommunist,* October 1971, p. 75.

7. The détentist line of local Communist parties is best exemplified by the Declaration of the Conference of Communist Parties of Latin America and the Caribbean, Havana, June 1975 (reprinted as "Latin America in the Struggle Against Imperialism," *New Outlook,* December 1975). The short analysis of conditions in Latin America recommends close cooperation with "progressive elements" within the church and tactical alliances with other political parties. Despite the overthrow of Salvador Allende in 1973, the Conference still held that the Chilean model was valid. Armed struggle was reserved for Haiti, Nicaragua, Guatemala, and Paraguay. This followed the line in defense of peaceful coexistence established by Leonid Brezhnev in Havana on January 30, 1974, where he proclaimed Cuba to be in the "socialist" camp and its revolution irreversible. Yet Brezhnev praised the peaceful road to power and the warming of relations with the United States. James D. Theberge, *The Soviet Presence in Latin America* (New York: National Strategy Information Center, 1974), presents the best overview of Soviet policy toward the region during the détente era.

8. A good summary of the diversity of Caribbean socialist parties is W. Raymond Duncan, "Caribbean Leftism," *Problems of Communism,* May-June 1978, pp. 37-57. This article, however, was written before local parties received military and financial assistance from Havana and other radical states.

9. A lengthy analysis of I. Shavrov's article, "Local Wars and Their Place in the Global Strategy of Imperialism," is contained in David Holloway, *The Soviet Union and the Arms Race* (New Haven: Yale University, 1983), pp. 83-94.

10. Soviet strategists in the late 1970s began a reevaluation of the role of the Soviet Army in Third World conflicts. Admiral Sergei Gorshkov, the architect of the Soviet bluewater navy, in *Naval Power in Soviet Policy* (Moscow: Voyenizdat, 1979) stressed the strategic importance of creating capabilities to paralyze or deter the West in secondary theaters—in other words, a policy of strategic denial. *War and Army,* by D. A. Volkogonov (Moscow: Voyenizdat, 1977), pp. 354-55, stressed the new role of the Soviet military in deterring aggression against and strengthening the "progressive forces" in the developing world.

11. Rand Corporation analysts Stephen Hosmer and Thomas Wolfe in *Soviet Policy and Practice Toward Third World Conflicts* (Rand Corporation, Lexington, Mass.: Lexington Books, 1983), pp. 79-109, have outlined the strategy behind the Soviet-Cuban alliance since Angola, terming the Soviet use of a proxy "cooperative intervention." The authors stress that there are convergent, but not identical, interests between the Soviet Union and Cuba to intervene directly in the Third World. In *A Strategy for Dealing with Cuba in the 1980s* (Rand Corporation, September 1982), Edward Gonzalez emphasizes the heightened strategic importance of the militarization of the island and the conventional threat it poses to the Caribbean Basin nations. Although the author takes the position that the Cuban military buildup is simply a defensive measure, Carla Anne Robbins in the chapter "Cuba" in *Security Policies of Developing Countries* (Lexington Books, 1982), edited by Edward Kolodziej and Robert E. Harkavy, details the professionalization and modernization of the Cuban military and the government's sensitivity to the change in the "correlation of forces."

Details about the recent improvements in weaponry can be found in Christopher Whalen's "The Soviet Military Buildup in Cuba," *Backgrounder* (Washington, D.C.: Heritage Foundation, June 11, 1982); U.S. Department of State, "Cuban Armed Forces and the Soviet Military Presence," *Special Report*, No. 103, August 1982; and *New York Times*, March 28, 1983. The Soviets' conventional capabilities and their large intelligence operation at Lordes, Cuba, are reviewed by Jay Mallin and Ralph Konney Bennett in *Washington Times*, July 13 and 26, 1983.

12. *Washington Post*, May 27, 1983.

13. The possible presence of nuclear weapons on the island of Cuba and questions about Soviet compliance with the series of agreements over such matters has provoked a controversy between the U.S. Senate and the Department of State. For documentation by Senators Helms and Symms of Tu-95 and Soviet missile installations on the island, see *Congressional Record—Senate*, Vol. 129, No. 53, S5233-37.

14. Soviet theoreticians overhauled much of their doctrine on guerrilla warfare and the revolutionary potential of the Caribbean Basin with the triumph of the Sandinistas in Nicaragua and of the New Jewel Party in Grenada. For samples of this new Soviet enthusiasm for revolution, see O. Ignat'yev, "The Victory of the People of Nicaragua," *Kommunist*, No. 13 (September 1979), p. 95ff.; Boris Koval, "La Revolución, Largo Proceso Histórico," *América Latina*, No. 3, 1980; Sukhostat et al., "A Continent in Struggle," *World Marxist Review*, March 1981, p. 47ff.; and the article by the leading Soviet Latin Americanist, Sergei Mikoyan, "Las Particularidades de la Revolución en Nicaragua," *América Latina*, No. 3, 1980.

15. Several accounts exist of the Tricontinental Conference and early Castroite efforts at spawning guerrilla warfare in the Western Hemisphere. The latest are Carla Anne Robbins, *The Cuban Threat* (New York: McGraw-Hill, 1983), pp. 29-33, Maurice Halperin, *The Taming of Fidel Castro* (Los Angeles: University of California, 1981), p. 185ff., and Claire Sterling, *The Terror Network* (New York: Holt, Rinehart and Winston, 1981), p. 14ff.

16. The major treatise on the theory of vanguard parties and the creation of Third World armies modeled after the Soviet Union is Yu. V. Irkin, "Revolutionary Vanguard Parties of Working People in Liberated Countries," *Voprosy Istorii*, No. 4, April 1982, pp. 55-67.

17. The combination of a unified guerrilla structure and a political front composed of diverse, sometimes democratic elements is not peculiar to Central America. In Haiti, the pro-Moscow Communist Party PUCH in a 1981 Panama

meeting sought to unify Christian Democrats, Social Democrats, and the Haitian Fathers, a Catholic order, for armed struggle against the Duvalier regime. After the meeting, a terrorist group, the Hector Riobe Brigade, named after a guerrilla killed in the Communist-sponsored uprising in 1969, was created and is supported by Libyan funds ("International Outlook," *Business Week*, April 18, 1983). This policy has recently failed in the Dominican Republic and Colombia, where the left is more divided.

18. *Granma*, April 4, 1981.

19. Claire Sterling, op. cit., p. 247ff.

20. Training camps and their curricula are detailed by the Department of State in "Cuba's Renewed Support for Violence in Latin America," *Special Report*, No. 90, December 14, 1981, and in "Cuban and Nicaraguan Support for Salvadoran Insurgency," *Congressional Record—Senate*, May 6, 1982.

Radical Arab support of the international terrorist network and the Central American guerrillas is extensively documented. A review of Arab and Southern Cone support for Central American revolutionaries is contained in "The PLO in Central America" by Shoshana Bryen, *Newsletter*, Jewish Institute for National Security Affairs, Vol. III, No. 21, June 1983. Libyan and Cuban cooperation in providing logistical support for revolutionaries and terrorists is discussed in John K. Cooley's account of the Libyan revolution in *Libyan Sandstorm* (New York: Holt, Rinehart and Winston, 1982), p. 227ff., and Claire Sterling, op. cit., p. 267ff. Israel's invasion of Lebanon produced a wealth of documents from the PLO's library. A selection of these have been presented in *PLO in Lebanon*, edited by Raphaeli Israeli (London: Weidenfeld and Nicolson, 1983). Pertinent documents on the Latin American and Caribbean connections are on pages 144-58 and 169-70.

21. The use of Nicaragua as an arms depot has been documented by the Department of State's *Special Report*, No. 80 and No. 90. The most detailed view of the flexibility and complexity of the logistical supply-lines to the Salvadoran guerrillas is George Russell's article in *Time*, May 9, 1983.

22. Author's interviews with former Surinamese prime minister Chin-A-Sen and "International Outlook," *Business Week*, February 14 and April 25, 1983. The degree of Cuban and Soviet involvement in consolidating the Bouterse regime was confirmed by *Time*, May 30, 1983.

23. The Nicaraguan military buildup has been documented in the *New York Times*, March 10, 1982, which ran the transcript of the press briefing by John Hughes, deputy director for intelligence and external affairs in the Defense Intelligence Agency. In the briefing, Hughes showed satellite photographs of base enlargements and the extension of runways to accommodate MiGs. The Department of State in a White Paper entitled "Nicaragua: Threat to Peace in Central America," April 12, 1983, documented the arms buildup within the country and Managua's assistance to the guerrillas in neighboring countries. Independent assessments of the Nicaraguan arms buildup and the sources of supplies appeared in the *New York Times* on March 29 and April 27, 1983. Libyan supplies to the Nicaraguan regime were reported by the *Washington Post*, April 25, 1983.

24. For a detailed analysis of the makeup of the Salvadoran guerrillas, see the author's "El Salvador's Guerrillas—The Winning Side?," *Freedom at Issue*, Sept.-Oct. 1983.

5. *The Development Alternative*

By ABRAHAM F. LOWENTHAL

Focus "Caribbeans of whatever race, religion, or nationality want economic growth, more equity, full employment, political participation, enhanced national autonomy, and more self-respect," says Abraham F. Lowenthal. The problem is that these goals are not necessarily compatible. Cuba, for instance, "has achieved full employment at the cost of underemployment and severe limits on political freedom. Martinique is prosperous in large part because it is not autonomous" and is dependent on France. No simple solution presents itself for the complex problems of the Caribbean region.

In this essay written shortly after President Reagan's speech to the Organization of American States in February 1982 (see appendix A), Lowenthal describes in detail some of the more salient problems of particular Caribbean nations. Most of them stem more from economic underdevelopment than from political conflicts. He sees massive American aid, probably at twice the currently budgeted level, as the only likely way to improve the lot of the average person in the region.

Military security, argues Lowenthal, is not as important as it once was. Furthermore, the strategic situation has changed drastically; even the Panama Canal is no longer "essential in the old

80

sense." Consequently, he discerns no major need for U.S. military aid.

Convincing the Congress and the American people of the need for large economic stimulants in the Caribbean will not be easy, he admits. But Americans should also realize that "doing nothing has its costs."

The Kissinger Commission (selection 3) agrees with Lowenthal that economic assistance must be greatly increased, but also argues that increased military aid is vital.

R. Bruce McColm (selection 4) examines some of the same problems from a quite different perspective. The Reagan administration's plans for aid to the region, known as the Caribbean Basin Initiative (appendix A), and the analysis of it by Richard Feinberg and others (selection 6) should be compared with Lowenthal's recommendations.

The notes for this essay are on page 100.

Abraham F. Lowenthal is professor of international relations at the University of Southern California. He was formerly secretary of the Latin American Program of the Woodrow Wilson Center for Scholars in Washington, D.C.

THE CARIBBEAN NOW COMPRISES no fewer than thirty-two political entities with a population totaling some 30 million people.[1] Fifteen of these entities are now independent countries, twelve having achieved independence since 1960. The natives in several British territories (including Montserrat, Anguilla, and St. Kitts-Nevis) are actively seeking independence. Residents of other "dependent" islands (France's Guadeloupe and Martinique, for example) seem happy with the status quo. Puerto Rico's future, perennially under discussion, is less clear than ever, after the nearly equal vote registered in the 1980 gubernatorial election by the pro-statehood and pro-commonwealth forces—with the *independentistas* getting less than 6 per cent of the vote.

The Caribbean territories are remarkably diverse, yet they are also surprisingly alike in important ways. As historian Franklin Knight has noted, the people of the region "have more in common than the Texan and the New Yorker, or the Mayan Indian and the cosmopolite of Mexico City."

To begin with, most of the territories are tiny. Two-thirds of the islands of the Caribbean could fit together into the King Ranch in Texas, or inside the Everglades. Cuba is by far the largest island, 745 miles long, but even Cuba is smaller in area than the state of Ohio. Trinidad is smaller than Rhode Island; Grenada is not much larger than the District of Columbia.

None of the territories is ethnically or culturally homogeneous. Five different racial groups (black, white, Oriental, native Indian, and East Indian) and their numerous subgroups and combinations mingle with varying degrees of integration and hostility. A certain color- and shade-consciousness persists. Numerous languages and dialects are spoken within the region, including Dutch, Spanish, French, and English and their derivatives, plus the Creole mixtures

Reprinted by permission of the author from the Spring 1982 issue of the *Wilson Quarterly*.

with African and Indian tongues. The result is at once a linguist's feast and nightmare. In Barbados, Antigua, and elsewhere, many archaic English words are still in use, augmented by local inventions—*birdspeed* (for "very fast"), for example, or *dontcarish* ("indifferent").

Caribbean religious sects include mixtures of the borrowed and the invented, the traditional and the ultramodern. A blending of West African religions with French or Spanish Catholicism produced voodoo in Haiti and *Santería* and *Nañiquísmo* in Cuba, Puerto Rico, and the Dominican Republic. In the English and Dutch Caribbean, there are Moravians, Anglicans, Catholics, and Pentecostals; in Trinidad and Guyana, large communities of Muslims and Hindus flourish. Rastafarians, "black Israelites," wear their long hair in braided "dreadlocks" and look to Ethiopia as the Promised Land.

CARIBBEAN ECONOMICS

The economic organization of the Caribbean runs the gamut from the tax havens of the Bahamas, reportedly the largest single Eurocurrency market outside London, to Cuba's brand of socialism (where free market transactions are beginning to be permitted again), with all manner of hybrids in between.

In the Dominican Republic, because dictator Rafael Trujillo's vast personal fiefdom passed to government ownership after his assassination in 1961, a big share of the economy is now in the public sector; the government tries through generous incentives to encourage private investment, domestic and foreign. Jamaica and Guyana, whose leaders chose to build various forms of socialist-oriented "mixed" economies, are now concerned about how to re-attract and stimulate private investment. Grenada, whose principal exports are bananas and nutmeg and whose main economic potential lies in tourism, is apparently opting for Cuban-style "socialism" in a mini-state where no form of economic organization can much alter the obvious constraints on growth: scant resources, a small island, a tiny population.

Economic productivity ranges from the abysmal showing by Haiti—"the land of unlimited impossibilities," whose chief local growth industry may be the smuggling of refugees to the United States (at up to $1,500 a head)—to the uneven but impressive performances of Martinique and Guadeloupe, the Bahamas, Puerto Rico, Trinidad and Tobago, and Barbados. The region includes four out of six of the countries with the lowest GNP per capita in the Western Hemisphere (Haiti, Dominica, Grenada, and Guyana). But it also boasts eight territories with GNP per capita among the highest (Martinique, Trinidad and Tobago, the Netherlands Antilles, Guadeloupe, Puerto Rico, Surinam, the Bahamas, and Barbados). Trinidad and Tobago has been lucky. It is the only Caribbean nation to have struck oil and today produces 200,000 barrels per day.

Although per capita incomes in the region are high by Third World standards, bitter poverty is still widespread. Two-thirds of Haiti's rural population were reported in 1978 to have annual incomes below $40; 50 per cent of Haiti's children under five suffer from protein-calorie malnutrition, with 17 per cent classified as severely undernourished. Seventy-five per cent of pre-school children in the Dominican Republic suffer from malnutrition, 4 per cent severely. One-third of Jamaica's people have annual incomes under $200, barely enough to cover a tourist's stay for a single night at one of Montego Bay's fancy hotels. In the slums of West Kingston, writes Trinidadian V. S. Naipaul, "hovels of board and cardboard and canvas and tin lie choked together on damp rubbish dumps behind which the sun sets in mocking splendor."

The poverty of the region is highlighted, and its psychological effects aggravated, by the juxtaposition—through migration, tourism, the media—with American affluence. Between 60 and 80 per cent of the programs shown on Caribbean television are U.S. imports—"Sesame Street, "Peyton Place," "Marcus Welby." At the Mallard's Beach Hyatt in Jamaica, a Canadian Club on the rocks costs $4.75, about three times the hourly wage of a local security guard. Shop windows taunt the poor with duty-free items they cannot afford but which tourists perceive as bargains.

Overall, the island economies are in deep trouble. Caribbean shares of world production of sugar and of bauxite are falling, and even absolute levels are declining in many cases. (This is true of sugar in Barbados, Guadeloupe, Guyana, Haiti, Jamaica, Trinidad and Tobago, and Puerto Rico, and of bauxite in Guyana, Surinam, and the Dominican Republic.) The region's share of world tourism revenues is also dropping.

At the same time, higher prices for oil and other imports burden economies in the Caribbean as elsewhere in the Third World.[2] Jamaica has had seven consecutive years of negative growth. Cuba's economic growth, even by Castro's own account, is not much more impressive. The Dominican Republic's significant progress counters regional trends, but the Dominicans have been hard hit by the price of oil. In 1973, the Dominican Republic earned almost twice as much from sugar exports as it spent on oil imports; by 1979, oil imports cost about $75 million more than the country's total income from sugar.

The Caribbean islands share other painful characteristics. They are densely populated and heavily dependent on exporting a few primary products. They are extremely susceptible to international market fluctuations and the vagaries of disease and weather. The epidemic of dengue fever in Cuba last summer (infecting 100,000 people) and the erratic path of Hurricane David in 1978 (sparing Barbados at the last moment and devastating Dominica instead) vividly illustrate this point.

Most islands have few known resources beyond the sun and sea, and this fact will never change; "the pencil of God has no eraser" is an old Haitian proverb. Those places with a broader resource base—Jamaica, for example, with its bauxite (used in aluminum) and the Dominican Republic with its nickel and gold—have seldom been able to exploit these assets fully. Christopher Columbus's assessment of the Arawak Indians on Hispaniola in 1492 remains valid when applied to Caribbeans today: "They very willingly traded everything they had. But they seemed to me a people very short of everything."

All of the islands have limited domestic markets, insubstantial local savings, and inadequate financing capacity. Agriculture is weak and declining through most of the region. "King Sugar" is now, at best, a princely pretender, its dominance undercut during the twentieth century by large cane growers in Louisiana and Brazil and by the thriving European sugar-beet industry. Most of the islands have deliberately sought to diversify their economies, moving toward manufacturing (Puerto Rico, for example), textiles (Barbados), petroleum refining (Aruba and Curaçao), financial services (the Cayman Islands), mining (many places), and tourism (everywhere). As they did elsewhere, people moved off the farm and into the towns. The result: Food production per capita—of pineapples, bananas, beans—has fallen during the past fifteen years in Jamaica, Guyana, Haiti, and Trinidad and Tobago. The region as a whole now imports more than $1 billion worth of food annually, costing the equivalent of at least 10 per cent of total exports.

While agriculture is declining, so is the push toward industrialization. The region-wide burst of industrialization-by-invitation begun during the 1960s has run out of steam. Most of the islands have found that it is easier to "take off" than stay aloft. Constrained by small size, they cannot generate enough power, in the form of capital, local markets, and so on, to sustain altitude. And capital must generally be imported, with much of the profits—from the making of watches or socks, the retreading of tires, the refining of oil—therefore exported. Few Caribbean islands show any growth since the mid-1970s in the share of GNP accounted for by manufacturing. Industrial stagnation, combined with a rural exodus and populations that are growing by 2 and 3 per cent a year (versus 0.7 per cent in the United States), have produced unemployment rates exceeding 30 per cent in some countries—according to *official* statistics.

POLITICS IN THE CARIBBEAN

All of the Caribbean countries—including Haiti, which has been independent since 1804—bear the mark of centuries of colonial rule and of plantation societies. Ninety per cent of the region's population are descendants of the four million slaves imported from West Africa, beginning in 1506. The history of the Caribbean has always been largely shaped, and even written, from outside. A few outstanding Caribbean intellectuals—V. S. Naipaul, Frantz Fanon, Aimé Césaire, C. L. R. James, Eric Williams, Juan Bosch, William Demas, and Arthur Lewis among them—have projected the Caribbean condition onto a much broader canvas. Their work,

and the common experiences of Caribbean peoples, have reinforced the outsider's notion of this as a region. As Demas, president of the Caribbean Development Bank, has written, "The
[Caribbean] countries have a common historical legacy: the sugar
plantation, slavery, indentured labor, monocultural economies
producing what they did not consume and consuming what they did
not produce . . . and perhaps the longest period of external political dependence in any part of the Third World."

Most Caribbean societies are still not well integrated internally.
Many, indeed, are more fragmented socially and politically now
than they were a generation ago. The Dominican Republic's civil
war in 1965; Trinidad's 1970 Black Power uprising; Bermuda's
1977 race riots; the 1980 general strike in Martinique; Jamaica's
recurrent urban violence—all exemplify this trend. Cuba is not
immune. Recall the 10,800 Cubans who sought asylum within the
garden walls of the Peruvian embassy in Havana in April 1980, and
the subsequent sea lift that brought 125,000 Cuban refugees into
the United States.

The Caribbean islands are even less well integrated
"horizontally"—with one another, that is. Although a sense of
regional identity is slowly emerging—enhanced by the creation of
certain regional institutions, such as the University of the West
Indies—local efforts to forge a "common market" have come to
naught. The West Indies Federation of ten territories established
in 1958 lasted only until 1961; it could not survive inter-island
rivalries, especially between Jamaica and Trinidad. The eastern
Caribbean, the last portion of the Americas to shed colonial rule, is
shattering into mini-states so small as to raise the possibility that
one or another could be taken over by international criminal
elements, such as those involved in the narcotics trade.[3] Inter-
change between the British Commonwealth Caribbean countries
and the Spanish-, Dutch-, and French-speaking countries is still
minimal.

The Trend Toward Polarization

Politically, the Caribbean territories face contradictory currents.
All but four of the fifteen independent countries are formal democracies. "Nowhere else in the world," Jamaica's Edward Seaga has

said, "does a conglomeration of parliamentary democracies exist as it does in the Caribbean." But democracy is not always deeply rooted. For every Barbados, there is a potential Grenada or Surinam. Grenada's prime minister, the eccentric Sir Eric Gairy, was ousted in a 1979 coup while he was in New York to address the United Nations General Assembly on the subject of flying saucers. In 1980, sixteen Surinamese army sergeants occupied several public buildings in a bid for higher pay—and accidentally toppled the government. "We only wanted a union," one of them said, "but ended up with a country."

While Grenada and Surinam have joined Haiti and Cuba as the Caribbean's only nondemocratic sovereign states, an extended period of deceptive political "stability" elsewhere may be coming to an end. Many long-standing practitioners of "doctor politics"—Lloyd Best's unimprovable phrase to describe the role of Caribbean scholar-statesmen such as Eric Williams (Trinidad and Tobago), Juan Bosch (Dominican Republic), and Luis Muñoz Marín (Puerto Rico)—are either dead or out of power. Their passing has ushered in an era of uncertainty.

Jamaica, once considered highly developed politically, verged on chaos as the 1980 election approached; some 600 persons were killed in pre-election violence. In the Dominican Republic, the first peaceful transition from one elected president to another came in 1978 only after the Carter administration "jawboned" the local military and thereby made sure the ballots were fairly counted. Even Barbadians, who "consider that they and their institutions are perfect," as one nineteenth-century British governor put it, are nervous about the influence of leftist activists on small neighboring islands. Haiti, long ruled by "Papa Doc" Duvalier, is now ruled by his son "Baby Doc"; no one knows when or how this dynasty will end. And in Cuba, where Fidel Castro has directed a highly authoritarian regime for twenty-two years, overt dissidence is increasingly evident.

Indeed, polarization seems to be the prevailing political trend. Grenada's leftist coup and the quasi-leftist coup in Surinam have been matched by a rightward swing (albeit through elections) in the politics of Dominica, St. Vincent, St. Kitts-Nevis, and Antigua, and especially by the decisive election in 1980 of Edward Seaga as prime minister in Jamaica after eight years of Michael M. Manley's "democratic socialism." The prospects for some sort of "pan-Caribbean" consensus grow dim as the islands' politicians move in diverging directions.

In Search of an Orbit

On the world scene, most of the Caribbean countries are satellites in search of an orbit, or perhaps of multiple orbits, in the sense of regular and predictable relationships with Big Powers. The United States acts increasingly as the principal *métropole*; France and Britain have been slowly withdrawing from the area. Mexico and Venezuela have shown some interest in expanding their relations with the Caribbean, an interest that reached its most concrete expression in mid-1980 with a Venezuelan-Mexican commitment to sell oil to nine Caribbean and Central American states on extremely favorable terms. The Soviet Union's close relationship with Cuba makes the Kremlin a Caribbean actor, although direct Soviet influence has so far been slim outside of Cuba itself, where Moscow underwrites the island economy with some $3.4 billion annually and equips Havana's military.[4]

Cuba's situation is not the most extreme case of dependence on a foreign power, contrary to popular belief. Almost all of the island states have special trade and aid agreements with various powers. Martinique, Guadeloupe, and French Guiana, for example, are juridically part of metropolitan France; their citizens participate in French elections and send voting delegates to the National Assembly in Paris. These three territories (combined population: 702,000) receive some $570 per capita a year from France, making their economies, in William Demas's words, "the most highly artificial in an area in which there is considerable artificiality." The residents of the Netherlands Antilles receive about $200 per capita, courtesy of The Hague. The U.S. subsidy to Puerto Rico, in the form of transfer payments, amounts to more in per capita terms than the U.S.S.R.'s subsidy to Cuba. The Caribbean islands receive more foreign aid per capita than any other group of countries.

The volume of trade with the United States—$12 billion in 1980—reflects one characteristic shared by most of the Caribbean: a high degree of dependence on the U.S. mainland. Not counting

Puerto Rico, the United States has more than $4.7 billion in direct private investment in the Caribbean. Some 75 per cent of the bauxite that the United States imports (more than half of our total consumption) comes from the Caribbean, as does about $4.5 billion worth of refined petroleum products.

The most significant ties between the United States and the Caribbean involve people. As I have noted, Caribbean economies depend heavily on tourism and cater primarily to U.S. travelers. Thousands of young Americans attend "last chance" medical schools in the Dominican Republic, Grenada, and Dominica. U.S.-based criminal syndicates find in the Caribbean congenial bases for narcotics and gambling operations, more lucrative than the rum and slave traffic of old. And American culture and technology—high and low—pervade the islands, at all levels and in all classes, from top-forty music and college T-shirts to Ford Mustangs and illegal arms shipments.

The most dramatic link of all is the stream of Caribbean migrants to the United States. Migration has long been a fact of life in the region, beginning with the arrival of the Indians from the South American rain forest and augmented, after 1492, by an influx of Europeans, of slaves, and, during the late nineteenth century, of indentured laborers from India, China, and Java. Up until the 1930s, however, Caribbean migration was essentially migration *into* the Caribbean or *within* the Caribbean. Today, the primary trend is migration *out* of the Caribbean.

Since World War II, some 4.5 million Caribbeans have left the islands and entered the United States. (Many others have gravitated toward France, Britain, the Netherlands, and Venezuela.) Puerto Rico has exported 40 per cent of its total population to the mainland since 1945, primarily to New York, Chicago, and other northern cities. More than one million Cubans have come to stay since 1960, more than 400,000 Dominicans, at least 300,000 Haitians, and about one million West Indians—all of this over and above the continuing shift of populations from island to island in the Caribbean itself. These movements of people are not unrelated events. They reflect a fundamental, continuous, and probably irreversible response to regional overpopulation and the magnetic attraction that any stronger economy exerts on any weaker one.

Haitian peasants flock to the Dominican Republic, where they can earn up to $1.50 for every ton of sugar cane cut, stripped, carried, stacked, and loaded—a princely wage compared to the thirty to seventy-five cents offered back home. Dominicans, meanwhile, head for more prosperous Puerto Rico. Citizens of all Caribbean countries seek opportunity in the United States, where jobs that native Americans, black or white, will not accept go begging. The flow of people back and forth between the Caribbean and the United States is today the most salient feature of U.S.-Caribbean relations.

In sum, much of the Caribbean is in turmoil as a new decade begins. Underlying the contemporary uneasiness is a conflict among goals. Caribbeans of whatever race, religion, or nationality all want economic growth, more equity, full employment, political participation, enhanced national autonomy, and more self-respect. These goals are not necessarily compatible. Cuba has achieved full employment at the cost of underemployment and severe limits on political freedom. Martinique is prosperous in large part because it is not autonomous. Barbados has grown "birdspeed," but not equitably.

The truth is, no single development strategy in the Caribbean has really worked. As Lloyd Best summed up the post-war experience: "We hoped for economic transformation by borrowing capital, by borrowing management, by borrowing technology, by borrowing this and borrowing that, and by kowtowing before every manner of alien expert we could find." Yet sustained progress has been elusive, and high expectations have turned, here and there, to frustration and violence.

DEFINING U.S. INTERESTS

What is at stake for the United States in the Caribbean? What are U.S. interests? How are they changing?

Most discussions of U.S. interests in the Caribbean emphasize our military security and economic ties. The security interest has usually been seen in terms of keeping hostile political and military influences away from this country's "soft underbelly." That was the aim of both the Monroe Doctrine (1823) and the so-called

Roosevelt Corollary of 1904. (Theodore Roosevelt stated then that the United States, in the face of "wrongdoing" in Latin America, would act, "however reluctantly," as an "international police force.")

U.S. military installations dot the region, from the Roosevelt Roads naval base in Puerto Rico to Guantánamo Bay in Cuba. The Caribbean provides access to the Panama Canal, long considered vital to U.S. commerce and defense. The sea lanes on which much U.S. trade depends (including one-half of our imported oil) pass through or near the Caribbean. The economic interest, as traditionally conceived, turns on protecting American commerce in the region, as well as U.S. access to various local strategic minerals and raw materials. For all these reasons, it has long seemed crucial that, if nothing else, the United States maintain what Secretary of State Cordell Hull once called "orderly and stable governments" in the Caribbean.

Many U.S. diplomats and scholars continue to think in these terms. They cite the presence of Soviet fleets in the Caribbean (since 1969, twenty-one Soviet naval deployments, varying in size from two to five ships, have visited the Caribbean); the possible construction of a submarine base capable of handling Soviet vessels at Cienfuegos on the southern coast of Cuba; and the KGB's electronic intelligence-gathering installations, also based in Cuba. In addition, they say, U.S. commercial interests in the Caribbean are being threatened by political instability.

Ray Cline, former deputy director of the Central Intelligence Agency, and now on the staff of Georgetown University's Center for Strategic and International Studies, has urged the White House to "reproclaim" the Monroe Doctrine. To support their views, Cline and others have drawn on the writings of Admiral Alfred Thayer Mahan and Sir Halford John Mackinder, leading geopolitical theorists of the nineteenth century.

Other observers, mostly in academe, ask whether the Caribbean is really still so important to the United States.

Changing technology—jet aircraft, long-range missiles—have reduced both the military significance of the Caribbean and the feasibility of excluding foreign influence. U.S. naval bases and other outposts in the region are no longer vital; U.S. power can easily be brought to bear from the mainland. Indeed, most of the remaining U.S. military installations in the Caribbean are currently due for phase-out by the mid-1980s, primarily for budget reasons. The Panama Canal, although still useful, is no longer *essential* in the old sense. A shrinking share of U.S. trade passes through the canal; many of the world's new oil supertankers are too big to negotiate it, as are almost all of the aircraft carriers around which U.S. fleets are organized.

In practical terms, the United States can no longer exert the total control over this region it once enjoyed. From 1898 to 1969, no hostile naval force (aside from German submarines during World War II) entered Caribbean waters. But, as noted, Soviet surface ships and submarines have been visiting regularly to "show the flag." The primary means for protecting U.S. strategic interests now lies in great-power agreements, exemplified by the apparent U.S.-U.S.S.R. "understandings" of 1962, 1970, and 1979, which, seriatim, are said to have banned from Cuba land-based nuclear missiles, Soviet submarines carrying nuclear missiles, and further deployments of Soviet combat troops.

In economic terms, too, the relative significance of the Caribbean for the United States has waned. Before World War II, the region accounted for more than 11 per cent of direct U.S. foreign investment and an even higher share of overseas trade. By 1978, U.S. investment in the Caribbean (excluding Puerto Rico) amounted to only 2.5 per cent of direct U.S. foreign investment, and considerably less if the $2 billion in "paper" investment in the Bahamas is excluded. The share of U.S. petroleum imports coming from or passing through the Caribbean, though still significant, has been declining in recent years, as imports from the Middle East, Nigeria, and Mexico have risen. Today, the United States depends on no commodity imported from the Caribbean. Bauxite, the principal strategic import, is available from many other countries.

Yet there are other reasons why Washington should keep its eye on the Caribbean.

First, the sovereign Caribbean nations constitute a significant bloc of votes at the U.N. and in other international bodies. That puts them in a position to help or hurt. The Caribbean democracies have voted, en bloc, to condemn the Soviet invasion of Afghanistan; they have consistently supported the U.S. position on Israel. Caribbean hostility could prove to be a considerable irritant. One can imagine, for example, the trouble that might ensue if the island nations went on record in the U.N. in favor of Puerto Rican independence.

Second, the Caribbean has become, by reason of its proximity to the United States and the increasing international prominence of the region's leaders, a kind of litmus test of the attitudes and policies that Washington will adopt toward Third World countries generally.

Third, and most important, there remains the sheer scale of the human interpenetration between the Caribbean and the United States. The United States and the Caribbean import from each other music, dance, crime, literature, and political ideas and techniques. Grenada's radical New Jewel movement is led primarily by men who were influenced, as students in U.S. universities during the 1960s, by the Black Power movement. Jamaica's prime minister, Edward Seaga, was born in Boston and educated at Harvard. People of Caribbean descent are making their presence felt in America, as they have, indeed, been doing since the 1920s, when the arrival in New York of some 40,000 black West Indians helped touch off what is now called the "Harlem Renaissance." The large, active, and growing Caribbean communities in this country are already a fact of political life in Florida, New York, and New Jersey, just as the Mexican influence grows in the U.S. Southwest.

In short, an intimate relationship exists between the Caribbean and the United States, whether either party likes it or not. What remains to be determined are its nature and consequences.

FOUR POLICY APPROACHES

In pursuing its relationship with the Caribbean region, the United States has, in essence, four policies to choose from.

The *first* of these, not now in vogue, is what may be called the "traditional" policy, its chief principle well expressed by Assistant Secretary of State Francis Butler Loomis in 1904: "No picture of our future is complete which does not contemplate and comprehend the United States as the dominant power in the Caribbean

Sea." The traditional policy combines studied indifference to the Caribbean's underlying economic and social realities with keen sensitivity to potential threats to the military security of the United States. At its crudest, it appears as the "gunboat diplomacy" of Roosevelt, Taft, and the Republican presidents of the 1920s—or of Democrat Lyndon Johnson during the Dominican civil war in 1965. This is a deceptively attractive policy because it seems cheap and simple. But it is also shortsighted. It amounts, indeed, to putting out the fires while doing nothing to remove the flammable material.

A *second* approach would be for the United States to "disengage" itself from the Caribbean altogether. The assumption here is that the region is economically and strategically irrelevant—and would perhaps fare better if left alone. This policy, too, has a certain appeal. Given all the other issues with which Washington must deal, how tempting to let the Caribbean stew in its own juices, to lavish upon each of these thirty-two struggling entities the "benign neglect" customarily reserved for Burma or Sri Lanka.

Again, such a policy is not really feasible. The United States cannot withdraw from involvement in its border region by a unilateral act of will. Even if the U.S. government tried to tighten restrictions on immigration, the movement of people to the mainland would continue. American businessmen operating in the Caribbean would still demand protection. American tourists would still migrate south in winter.

A *third* Caribbean policy—the "activist" approach—is essentially the one pursued (in different ways) by the Carter and Reagan administrations. Its tenets are two: The United States must retain its special concern for the region's military security and political stability, and it must, at the same time, increase economic and technical aid to the Caribbean.

The activist approach, which underlies the Reagan administration's "Caribbean Basin Initiative" [see appendix A], calls for beefing up the U.S. presence throughout the area: politically, militarily, economically, culturally, through both the public and private sectors. Its proponents favor adjustments in trade and tariff policy (rather than outright injections of money) to facilitate the transfer of capital and technology to the islands. When money changes hands, activists think it should be done via *bilateral* agreements to emphasize the American "partnership."

The activists also hope to turn the Caribbean away from Cuba. From its very first days, the Reagan administration moved to counter Cuban diplomatic efforts and tighten restrictions on commerce and exchange. It is currently planning to establish a Radio Free Cuba. Secretary of State Alexander Haig has threatened repeatedly to "go to the source" to stop Cuban arms shipments to guerrillas in Central America.[5]

The activist policy has some obvious plusses. Focusing more attention—and aid—on the Caribbean gives Washington a certain leverage in the region. Most Caribbean states are so small that even limited American assistance would go a long way. The timing is also good: Cuba's internal difficulties are growing, while general Caribbean trends are toward greater cooperation with the United States.

But there are also risks. One danger is creation of unrealistic expectations. Jamaica's Prime Minister Seaga hopes for a U.S. commitment of $3 billion annually to the region—perhaps ten to fifteen times what is likely to be forthcoming. (The *total* U.S. foreign economic aid budget is currently $7.5 billion.) Moreover, the preoccupation of the State Department and the White House with Fidel Castro's Cuba does not sit well with most Caribbean leaders, who perceive Castro as only one of many Caribbean actors rather than as a Cold War instrument. Indeed, most of them are not above "playing the Cuba card" to please domestic voters or curry favor in Third World meetings. Washington's obsession with Cuba diminishes the chances of cooperating with Canada, Mexico, and Venezuela—all of which maintain diplomatic (if not cordial) relations with Castro's government—to develop the Caribbean. This issue, more than any other, helped to dampen enthusiasm for any "mini-Marshall Plan" that depended on close U.S. cooperation with the three.

More generally, the activist approach to the Caribbean carries the risk that Washington will become too "interventionist." Even assuming benign intent, active or covert U.S. pursuit of political goals could stifle local initiative or provoke nationalist reactions. And, to the extent that U.S. interest in the Caribbean appears to be merely expedient—not really concerned with the region's people but rather only with potential threats to the United States—the chances increase that an active U.S. presence in the Caribbean will backfire.

The *fourth* possible U.S. approach—one favored, not surprisingly, by many Caribbean leaders—is the adoption by Washington (and others) of a sustained commitment to Caribbean development. Such a commitment would emphasize underlying economic progress rather than immediate military security; concentrate on the long-term rather than the short-term; and tolerate diverse political and economic approaches.

This "developmentalist" policy would involve large sums of money, channeled primarily through multilateral rather than bilateral channels; imaginative efforts to provide "non-aid" concessions to help Caribbean development; and a scaling down by Washington of its efforts to contain or reverse the Cuban revolution. Rather than building up U.S. visibility, Washington would downplay its own role and lay the foundations for a healthier future U.S.-Caribbean relationship by focusing on the region's economic stagnation, extreme inequities, malnutrition, illiteracy, and poor social and health services.

The developmentalist approach responds to a fundamental U.S. interest—"security," in a broader sense than the strictly military—in having stable, working societies on our third border. It reflects both a moral concern (that one *is*, to an extent, one's brother's keeper) and a practical realization that festering problems in societies so intertwined with our own will eventually affect this country.

Three drawbacks are apparent, however.

One problem is, again, the danger of exaggerated expectations. It is not likely that the high aspirations of Caribbean peoples can all be achieved, even with substantial foreign aid. Some of the obstacles to sustained, equitable growth—meager resources (material and human), insufficient size, extreme vulnerability to bad weather and world market slumps—cannot be wished away.

Second, there is an inevitable tension between accepting any form of economic and social organization—even Cuba's—and reassuring domestic and foreign investors about the region's prospects. Stanching the flow of capital from the Caribbean (not to mention attracting more investment) depends in part on giving businessmen confidence that their role will be valued and their assets protected. The prospect of nationalization or outright expropriation undermines that confidence, to say the least.

Finally, the developmental approach would be hard to sell at home. Congress is not likely to go along with what would be portrayed as a "no strings" commitment to aid a bewildering cluster of small countries—at least not until Americans come to realize that their own future well-being depends, in some measure, on that of their neighbors. No administration so far has been willing to make that case, and it may be that none can.

Some Positive U.S. Steps

Whether Washington maintains its current policy toward the region or adopts a longer-term developmentalist approach, several steps could be taken to better the Caribbean's lot:

• Strengthen Caribbean agriculture by earmarking aid funds for research and development, improving access to farm credit, and encouraging private U.S. investment in rural areas.

• Improve access to U.S. markets for both farm products and manufactured goods. Tariff barriers could be lowered or even eliminated (as the Reagan administration has suggested). Indeed, Washington has already done this for one Caribbean country by granting duty-free status to twenty-seven Jamaican products, including peppers and tomatoes. Reduction or elimination of the U.S. tariff on rum and cigars would have a more positive short-term effect on several Caribbean countries than almost anything else Washington could do.

• Stabilize the export earnings of Caribbean countries that depend on the export of one or two major products by bolstering international commodity and stockpiling arrangements.

• Set up regular procedures to help Caribbean territories cope with hurricanes and other natural disasters, as chronic as they are unexpected.

• Expand tourism—and make it more "efficient." Shared air transport facilities, jointly agreed routings, and other measures would help Caribbean countries divide the annual revenue from tourism more equitably—which would be far preferable to the current cut-throat island rivalry. A decision by the United States to increase the dollar value of duty-free imports permitted to returning tourists would be hailed by island merchants. So would a revision of U.S. income tax codes to allow expenses for business-related conventions held in the Caribbean to be treated as are conventions in Canada and Mexico.

• Promote the transfer of U.S. capital and technology. For example, American companies could be induced, via tax and other incentives, to "export" many of their operations to the Caribbean.

• Expand the existing "guest worker" programs and raise current immigration quotas for the Caribbean. (U.S. quotas are now 20,000 annually from any sovereign nation, 600 from any dependency.) This would enlarge the "safety valve" for the many islands plagued by overpopulation and unemployment.

• Help the Caribbean cope with its energy problem. No other region of the world has been harder hit by the rise in the price of oil since 1973. A breakthrough in solar energy, if it ever comes, might do more for Caribbean development than all other steps combined. But a solar collector that is both practical and economical does not yet exist. Because of the research costs involved, developing one is something only the United States and other industrialized nations can hope to achieve.

These steps, taken together, would cost money and stir much opposition. Letting in more agricultural produce would anger growers of winter fruits and vegetables in Florida and California. Lowering the tariff on rum would hurt Puerto Rican firms. A tax deduction for Caribbean conventions would raise the hackles of U.S. innkeepers. Encouraging added American investment in island industries would be labeled "exporting jobs" by the AFL-CIO and could hurt marginal businesses in the United States (although manufacturers in Asia may, in fact, sustain the biggest loss from Caribbean competition). Permitting more migration from the Caribbean would contribute to social tensions and the demand for public services.

What is more, the American taxpayer would certainly have a larger bill to foot. To implement *all* of these measures, the current

$600 million aid package to the Caribbean (not including U.S. payments to Puerto Rico) from all non-Communist countries would, I estimate, have to be doubled; as usual, a large share of that increase would have to come from Washington.

The costs are undeniable. On the other hand, because the Caribbean countries are so tiny, the benefit to their economies from these measures would be greatly disproportionate to any expense the United States might incur. And one should not forget that doing nothing also has its costs: unregulated and illegal immigration, regional instability, and the quality of 30 million lives—not to mention the strains put on the health of democracy and free enterprise by the persistent failure of democratic societies to "make it" in the shadow of the United States.

Taking a special interest in the economic and social health of the Caribbean countries is the right thing for the United States to do. At the same time, Washington should refrain from proclaiming a "special relationship" and from promising "regional preferences" that significantly contradict basic U.S. policies on trade, finance, immigration, and the like. U.S. stakes in the Caribbean are fairly high, but there is even more at stake *outside* the Caribbean. On a practical level, history suggests that American interests in the Caribbean, however important they may appear from time to time, would not long sustain the adoption of policies and practices that contravene universal rules. Preferential policies that substantially hurt some other region important to the United States simply would not last.

For their part, local leaders in the Caribbean are uneasy about the idea of a special relationship. Historically, U.S. promises of "special treatment" have meant singling out the Caribbean for rhetorical or military attention: the approach either of Arpège ("Promise her anything . . .") or of Hallmark Cards ("When you care enough to send the very best"—the Marines).

The Caribbean is too near the United States to take for granted, yet too far—historically and politically—to integrate comfortably into a U.S. "sphere." The challenge for policy-makers in Washington is to keep that in mind. It is up to U.S. officials to understand how sensitive the Caribbean is to the impact of the United States and how much our country is affected by the Caribbean. It is important for them to understand the Caribbean for what it was, for what it is, and for what it could become. And it is essential to focus on the realistic possibilities that exist for the United States to affect the region positively—for our sake as much as for the Caribbean's.

NOTES

1. Analysts differ about how to define the Caribbean. For the purposes of formulating U.S. policy, it is helpful to conceive of the Caribbean region as that set of territories, in or bordered by the Caribbean Sea, concerning which the United States has historically felt a special security interest, arising primarily from their proximity and their perceived vulnerability to external penetration. All the Caribbean islands, together with Belize on the Central American isthmus and Guyana, Surinam, and French Guiana on the South American mainland, would fit this definition of the region. While there has been much fashionable talk of late about the larger "Caribbean Basin," the experiences of Venezuela, Colombia, Mexico, and most Central American nations differ in significant ways from those of the Caribbean territories I deal with in this essay.

2. Only Trinidad and Tobago is self-sufficient in oil, but many other nations—Surinam, Cuba, Barbados, Guyana, Jamaica, the Dominican Republic—are exploring. Because Caribbean countries are small, even modest discoveries could be of major importance.

3. In 1980, the FBI arrested ten men in New Orleans who were allegedly planning to overthrow the government of Dominica (population: 77,000) using mercenaries drawn from the ranks of the Ku Klux Klan. The plot was reportedly bankrolled by a Texas millionaire (who hoped to establish a free port in · Dominica), supposedly with the blessing of a former Dominican prime minister.

4. Cuba has the best air force in the Caribbean and a modern "gunboat navy." The Soviets have supplied the island with MiG-23 "Floggers" and missile attack boats. Russian pilots reportedly help patrol Cuban skies to free Cubans for duty in Angola, Ethiopia, and elsewhere in Africa.

5. Fidel Castro charged in July 1981 that the United States had also employed germ warfare in Cuba, accounting for the dengue epidemic as well as for the appearance of blue mold tobacco blight and roya rust, which attacks sugar cane. I have no evidence to support this, and I do not believe it, but one U.S. official's observation that Castro is "now as paranoid as he was at the time of the Bay of Pigs" was not unambiguously reassuring.

6. *Caribbean Basin Initiative: Pros and Cons*

By RICHARD E. FEINBERG, RICHARD NEWFARMER, *and* BERNADETTE ORR

Focus The controversial Caribbean Basin Initiative (CBI) proposed by the Reagan administration (appendix A) seeks to promote economic growth and political stability on the Caribbean islands and the Central American mainland. In the Caribbean, some people feel it will benefit only U.S. companies and larger American interests; in the United States, organized labor and certain manufacturers fear that the CBI will export jobs and profit-making opportunities badly needed for full economic recovery at home.

In July 1983 Congress passed the CBI legislation specifying January 1984 as the date of implementation. It promises twenty-eight nations economic assistance and duty-free access to U.S. markets for twelve years. The three authors of this article, writing before the legislation was passed, examine the details of the CBI and the arguments of both its supporters and its opponents. Their main conclusion: "In the coming years, even if the CBI is tremendously successful, economic growth in the United States based upon a sound monetary and fiscal policy will probably have a far greater impact on the region's welfare."

They conclude, however, that several of the proposals are valuable. Trade incentives such as the Free Trade Area and Investment Tax Credits hold

101

out the possibility of genuine economic growth. Economic assistance, though needed—especially given the debt burden of many of these nations— may otherwise, they say, only contribute to further dependency.

On the Central American mainland, where needs are different from those of the islands, say the authors, President Reagan's policies have sharpened political conflict and have worked at crosspurposes to the economic goals of his CBI. Only political stability will enable these countries to profit from the economic initiatives already under way.

This analysis differs widely from that of Abraham Lowenthal (selection 5), who views massive economic assistance as the principal means for development in the region.

Richard E. Feinberg is director of the Foreign Policy Program at the Overseas Development Council (ODC). **Richard Newfarmer** is director of the Trade and Industrial Policy Program at ODC. **Bernadette Orr** is a free-lance journalist.

PRESIDENT REAGAN UNVEILED HIS PLAN for the economic recovery of Central America and the Caribbean, the Caribbean Basin Initiative [see appendix A], in a speech before the Organization of American States on February 24, 1982. Economic progress in the Caribbean Basin was "vital to the security interests of this nation and this hemisphere," the President said. He argued that economic growth was a necessary condition for democracy, and warned that "economic disaster has provided a fresh opening to the enemies of freedom."

Since the first presentation of the plan, the CBI has faced strong criticism as well as praise in its long and frustrating journey through Congress. This spring [1983] the new 98th Congress reopened debate on the economic and foreign policy rationale of the measure, its probable impact both domestically and within the beneficiary nations, and its merit at a time of continued economic recession and high unemployment here at home.

As originally proposed by the President, the CBI was to have three legs—trade, investment, and concessional aid—to generate foreign exchange, create new employment, and raise production levels. In brief, the CBI would:

1. Provide $350 million in supplemental assistance to meet balance-of-payments shortfalls in key countries, notably El Salvador (which was scheduled to receive $128 million).

2. Establish one-way, duty-free access to U.S. markets for Caribbean Basin exports for a twelve-year-period—the so-called Free Trade Area.

3. Create an investment tax credit of 10 per cent for U.S. businesses investing in the Caribbean Basin.

Let us examine each component in greater detail.

Reprinted by permission from the Spring 1983 issue of *Caribbean Review* (© 1983 by Caribbean Review, Incorporated, Florida International University, Miami, Florida).

1. ECONOMIC ASSISTANCE

The Administration proposed $350 million in quick-disbursing funds to help Caribbean Basin countries meet pressing balance-of-payments needs. Shortages of foreign exchange are a major cause of the profound economic crisis gripping the region. The cost of imported energy has risen, whereas prices of such key commodities as sugar, coffee, bauxite, and nickel have declined. The drop in export prices in 1981 alone reduced the region's export earnings by roughly $500 million. In addition, high market interest rates have increased the burden of a swollen foreign debt.

The aid portion of the CBI was the only measure to become law, after passing both houses in September 1982. It stirred controversy for several reasons.

First, the $350 million amount provided less than 10 per cent of the external resources needed to cover the region's balance-of-payments shortfalls. Although a substantial addition to the $474 million provided to the region in the FY 1982 budget, the CBI supplemental aid nonetheless was a small sum relative to the need—or the aid levels of other donors. For example, Venezuelan president Luis Herrera Campins pointed out that his country's aid program for the Caribbean provided an equivalent amount of money each year, despite the much smaller size of Venezuela's GNP as compared to that of the United States. Certainly, by itself, the supplemental aid was insufficient to stimulate strong growth.

A second objection to the aid portion of the bill was the emphasis on the Central American countries: El Salvador alone was scheduled to receive $128 million, or 37 per cent of the total. Two other Central American countries—Costa Rica ($70 million) and Honduras ($35 million)—were also to receive significant aid. Outside Central America, only the Dominican Republic ($40 million) and Jamaica ($50 million) were to be major beneficiaries. The evident slant toward Central America prompted human rights groups and congressional critics of U.S. policy to view the CBI as a means of financing misconceived U.S. security objectives, rather than as a true effort to promote development. The fact that the proposed aid was for general balance-of-payments support reinforced this impression. Aid that is slated for "development projects," for example, in the agriculture or health sectors, is more carefully programmed and monitored.

In its final version of the bill, therefore, Congress made several adjustments. Amounts were reallocated to give more representation to smaller Caribbean countries and to reduce controversial aid to El Salvador. The House also required—and Secretary of State George Shultz agreed—that 12.5 per cent of the total $350 million be spent for basic needs-oriented projects. A Senate proposal to convert the CBI from a bilateral to a multilateral fund administered by the World Bank—where developmental concerns would dominate—passed the Foreign Relations Committee but was eliminated in the final bill.

The second and third components of the CBI were never passed by the 97th Congress, although a revised trade bill was approved by the House in late December.

2. FREE TRADE AREA

President Reagan heralded the Free Trade Area (FTA) as the "centerpiece" of the CBI. Indeed, trade liberalization is potentially the most important development instrument at the disposal of the Administration: development economists contend that trade is a much more important stimulus to sustained growth than development assistance. Coming at a time of rising demands for protectionism, the FTA is a positive step—albeit small—in the direction of a more accessible U.S. market for developing countries.

The FTA, in reality, will affect only slightly more than 5 per cent of the region's total exports to the United States. As the President mentioned in his formal announcement of the CBI before the Organization of American States, 87 per cent of the region's exports into the United States already enter duty free. These exports include petroleum, products covered by the Generalized System of Preferences (GSP), and other goods, mainly agricultural products not produced in quantity in the United States.

Whether the original or an amended version of the FTA is adopted, it is certain that some categories of goods that are now "dutiable" will not be granted free entry under the CBI. These include textiles, products not eligible for the GSP because their value-added in the CBI country of origin is too low, and products not eligible for the GSP because the country exports more than is allowed under the legislation (most of the category is sugar exports). The exclusion of textiles from the program is particularly lamentable because this industry holds the greatest opportunity for expanding exports and creating jobs in the Caribbean.

The economic impact of the FTA upon the region will depend on two things: how much more United States consumers buy of the imported product because prices fall and goods are cheaper, and how much more consumers buy of the imported product from the region favored with a price advantage and shift away from similar imported goods produced elsewhere. The total amount of new trade generated for the CBI countries therefore depends upon how high the original tariff was prior to cutting, the responsiveness of consumers to changes in prices, and the shift of consumer purchases into CBI imports at the expense of other imports.

Our study (Richard E. Feinberg and Richard Newfarmer, "The Caribbean Basin Initiative: Bold Plan or Empty Promise" in *From Gunboats to Diplomacy: New U.S. Policies for Latin America*) of the FTA revealed that eliminating the tariffs would initially raise only about $45-90 million in foreign exchange for the beneficiary nations. The reason for this is that for many of these products, tariff levels are not high, and consumers are not particularly responsive to price changes.

The new U.S. demand created for imports from the region will amount to only $23 million. But the region will also benefit from consumers shifting from already imported products to those imported from the region. This response will vary widely. For undifferentiated products where brand names are unimportant, such as beef, handbags, and scrap tobacco, the effect could be large, limited only by the capacity of the exporting countries to expand their production. For other products, the effects are likely to be somewhat less. Even relatively large consumer shifts to CBI-country products, however, would generate additional exports of less than $100 million or 1 per cent of the region's 1980 exports.

The FTA is only one element in the trade package. A potentially more important change, at least in the short run, was the decision in

May 1982 to impose worldwide sugar quotas, a move which undermined some of the beneficial effects the CBI was intended to produce. The CBI had included a provision for sugar quotas. However, the quotas for the Caribbean's three principal sugar producers—the Dominican Republic, Guatemala, Panama—turned out to be even lower than the amounts the Administration had originally proposed.

The Caribbean Basin nations opposed even the higher quota levels originally proposed in the CBI, since this was the first time the United States had imposed quotas since 1974. Since sugar is one of the region's major foreign-exchange earners, the impact of the restrictive quotas implemented in May was severe. The Organization of American States estimated that total losses for Latin America would be about $90 million through the end of 1982. Many officials from the sugar-producing Caribbean nations expressed concern that the losses from lower sugar exports would more than offset the amount of supplemental aid to their countries.

Nonetheless, as part of the political dealing over the 1982 budget cuts, the Administration bowed to the powerful group of U.S. sugar growers and levied the new quotas, thereby supporting a higher domestic sugar price. Their imposition sent contradictory signals to friendly governments in the Caribbean, many of whom questioned the sincerity and depth of the Administration's commitment to assisting their economic growth. Said one Dominican Republic diplomat, "you can be sure" that the President lost some credibility in his country. The $41 million in supplemental aid "is certainly not enough to offset the impact of the quotas."

The emphasis on the tariff-reducing aspects of the CBI obscured one key point: the impact of all the proposed changes in trade regulations would probably be much less than that of renewed U.S. domestic growth. An acceleration in the U.S. growth rate from zero to 3 per cent per year would probably generate over $300 million in new export earnings for the region. Or consider the effects of lowered U.S. interest rates. Debt service not infrequently absorbs from 15 to 25 per cent of export earnings of CBI countries. If interest rates were to fall by five percentage points on the debt of $5.4 billion dollars owed to private creditors (as of December 31, 1980), interest payments would be reduced by more than $250 million. In the coming years, even if the CBI is tremendously successful, economic growth in the United States based upon a sound monetary and fiscal policy will probably have a far greater impact on the region's welfare.

The FTA, then, provides an opportunity for the region to increase in modest measure its domestic employment, export earnings, and growth. Its impact could be greater if it included freer trade in sugar, textiles, and other manufactured products. For this to occur, the Administration would have to reverse its stand on trade adjustment assistance, worker training, and other legitimate trade concerns of domestic labor. Without an appeal to labor, the CBI will face a continuing tough battle, since during 1982 organized labor was the most virulent and consistent opponent of the measure.

With the unemployment rate about 10 per cent nationally and even more for industries and regions competing with low-wage imports from the Caribbean, labor's reaction to proposed trade liberalization is understandable. The Administration cannot hope to enlist the support of domestic labor for freer trade in the very industry which would benefit the region if it fails to help American workers make the painful adjustment to alternative employment. In its own statement on the CBI, the AFL-CIO called for the entire trade and tax-incentives portion of the bill to "be sent back to the drawing board." Labor has not changed its position, and its strength in Congress has grown as a result of the November 1982 elections, in which the Democrats gained twenty-six new seats. It remains to be seen whether President Reagan's support for a jobs bill will be able to defuse the strong protectionist sentiments which the domestic recession has provoked.

3. INVESTMENT TAX CREDIT

The third major component in the CBI proposal was a five-year investment tax credit. A U.S. parent corporation may claim a credit against its total tax liabilities for an amount equal to 10 per cent of new investment in plant and equipment in Caribbean Basin countries. These incentives were coupled with increased protection for foreign investment offered through the Overseas Private

Investment Corporation. The U.S. private insurance sector was also encouraged to become active in the Caribbean Basin, to reduce the risk associated with investment. The U.S. Treasury Department estimated that the cost of the investment tax credit in foregone tax revenues would be $40 million. No one knows how much new investment would be generated by this $40 million. New investment is highly sensitive to swings in the business cycle, changes in the perception of risk, and changes in overall levels of profitability.

Studies of the U.S. experience with domestic tax credit, however, offer reason for skepticism. Although this experience contains no "substitution" effect, i.e., shifting among regions in response to changes in relative profitability, it does illustrate the uncertainty of this instrument. According to a study by the Office of Tax Analysis in the Department of Treasury of the effect of the 1973 investment tax credit on domestic investment, every dollar of tax expenditure generated only 76 cents of new investment. Using the 76 per cent figure, an investment tax credit in the CBI that costs the U.S. Treasury $40 million can be predicted to generate only $30 million of investment. This may be even less in the case of a foreign tax credit because of increased risks associated with doing business abroad.

Although the exact estimate of the new investment generated varies depending on the assumptions, the relatively small payback for tax expenditures can be traced back to a central weakness of this instrument: much of the new investment would occur anyway because business activity is ongoing. Yet to get an additional investment, the Treasury has to include all investors in the tax credit. Therefore, if U.S. investors in the region currently spend $400 million on new plant and equipment, and an investment tax credit creates an additional $30 million of investment, the total tax expenditures will be $43 million.

Opposition to the Investment Tax Credit

In the course of the CBI's passage through the legislative process, the investment tax-credit provision proved to be the most controversial aspect of the bill. It was unpopular with labor and with congressmen who feared job flight from their districts. Many deficit-minded congressmen were reluctant to endorse a measure reducing Treasury revenues still further. Several economists observed that it was unlikely that the tax incentives would generate a large amount of new investment as long as business conditions in the region remain precarious. Weak domestic economies, a depressed international economy (particularly in the United States), and in some countries high political risk have depressed expected profitability. Without growing markets, businessmen cannot justify new investments. In fact, capital flight now constitutes a serious drain to Caribbean Basin countries. For at least the foreseeable future, U.S. investors in many countries will probably invest only that amount which is absolutely necessary to maintain their ongoing plant and equipment. This investment will occur anyway, and the investment tax credit would be an unrequited loss to the Treasury. These arguments were responsible for the fact that the investment tax credit was never seriously considered in either house.

At the same time, however, the government has mounted an impressive surge of activity designed to promote U.S. investment and trade. At least eight federal departments or agencies have developed promotional programs focused on the Caribbean. The Department of Agriculture has established an agricultural information center for U.S. businesses interested in Caribbean markets, and is working closely with an Agribusiness Promotion Council to design appropriate investment projects for the region. USAID and the Peace Corps are devoting greater resources to small business ventures and entrepreneurial training in the region. The Department of Commerce has opened a Caribbean Basin Business Information Center, to provide comprehensive economic information to interested U.S. businesses. According to recent State Department statements, the response has been dramatic: "Literally thousands of companies have asked for guidance on trade and investment opportunities." The Center is sponsoring a series of regional seminars throughout the United States on business opportunities in the Caribbean Basin.

A key agency supporting greater investment in the Caribbean has been the Overseas Private Investment Corporation (OPIC), which provides political-risk insurance to U.S. investors operating in developing countries. Since FY 1980, OPIC has sharply stepped up its activities in the Caribbean, mainly in the politically less volatile islands. OPIC issued insurance policies on forty-seven new projects in FY 1981 and FY 1982, totaling $361 million in new investment; authorized direct loans to eighteen small and medium-sized joint ventures, also in FY 1981-82, totaling $149 million; and supported investment feasibility studies and missions. Follow-up investment missions to Haiti and Jamaica that occurred in late 1982 and early 1983 may result in new investment for those countries.

Lastly, the government has developed a program of bilateral investment treaties which provide clear rights and obligations for the host government, the U.S. government, and the foreign investor. The State Department, which strongly supports such treaties as a means of improving the investment climate in developing countries, recently concluded a treaty with Panama. Another was successfully negotiated in January 1983 with Costa Rica. Many other Central American and Caribbean nations have expressed an interest in such a treaty, which could serve to attract greater investment while guaranteeing certain rights of their countries vis-à-vis the investor. Thus, with or without the CBI, the Administration has aggressively sought to promote U.S. trade and investment linkages. If a U.S. economic recovery takes firm hold, these efforts could well produce some success at the margin, especially in the insular countries.

ECONOMIC RESPONSE TO POLITICAL PROBLEMS

But there is more to the CBI than economics. In fact, the CBI is an unabashed attempt to use economic assistance to attack the roots of unrest in the area, a foreign policy objective reminiscent of the Alliance for Progress. The concept of a "Caribbean Basin" is more geographical than economic. Central America differs from most Caribbean islands in culture, economic structure, and, most importantly, political institutions. In the Dominican Republic and much of the English-speaking Caribbean, relatively stable and democratic structures already exist. Since the negotiation of new Panama Canal treaties and the removal of this historic irritant in U.S.-

Panamanian relations, Panama too has enjoyed stability and economic prosperity. The Caribbean Basin Initiative has a better chance of success on the Caribbean islands and in Panama, where the requisite political stability exists, than in the rest of Central America, where the political status quo has been challenged by powerful insurgencies.

In Central America, the Administration's economic and political strategies have been working at cross-purposes. The Administration's economic plan aims to stimulate business, but a confrontationist diplomacy threatens to delay restoration of investor confidence. By heightening political conflict, the United States threatens to inflict deeper wounds on already badly mangled economies. Fearing that political strife will continue and even worsen, frightened Central American businessmen are stashing their savings in Florida's banks and condominium market. Because capital flight often occurs through illegal channels, it is not possible to measure its magnitude exactly. One study sponsored by AID estimated capital flight during 1979 and 1980 to have surpassed $500 million. The investment climate in Central America has certainly deteriorated since then. Informed observers believe capital flight from El Salvador alone has reached $500 million per year.

The investment climate has been so bad in Central America that even U.S. government agencies have hesitated to commit their own resources there. Although it has vastly increased its activity in the Caribbean nations, the Overseas Private Investment Corporation has been virtually closed for business in El Salvador, Guatemala, and Nicaragua, and has been considering only small projects in Honduras and Costa Rica. The proposed changes contained in the CBI will allow for a greater OPIC involvement in the region, but its activities will still be constrained by its own risk criteria.

The Export-Import Bank (Eximbank) has also been unwilling to undertake major new exposures in Central America. It is noteworthy that, according to the language in the legislative package the Administration sent to Congress, the Eximbank promises to expand its activity in the Caribbean Basin only "where its lending criteria allow."

In the absence of peaceful resolutions to conflicts within and between nations, private capital will continue to flee Central

America. Without investor confidence, two of the three prongs of the CBI—investment incentives and trade opportunities—will be irrelevant to Central America. The remaining prong—official aid—will in large measure be devoted to maintaining consumption levels and indirectly to purchasing weapons. Investment planning and implementation, whether by the public or by the private sector, cannot proceed safely and efficiently in an environment of political turmoil.

The Administration's diplomacy of confrontation has also prevented the realization of a truly multilateral Caribbean Basin Initiative. The Administration had been consulting with Canada, Mexico, Venezuela, and Colombia. It has not yet, however, been willing to make the political compromise necessary to permit the elaboration of a cooperative and integrated approach to the region's economic problems. Each donor nation is pursuing its own programs, largely as if the CBI had never been announced. As a result of its uncompromising diplomacy and divergent concepts of national interest, the Administration is actually working at cross-purposes to other donors.

There is an alternative to strictly bilateral effort. A genuinely multinational framework, based on a common political vision, would have several economic advantages. A multilateral mechanism would allow for more efficient coordination of scarce resources. It would make donors feel it was in their interests to match contributions made by others, thereby sharing the aid burden more widely. Moreover, multilateralism provides mechanisms for the transfer of aid resources without the political tensions and resentments that accompany bilateral programs. The Caribbean Group for Economic Cooperation and Development has, since 1977, provided such a multilateral vehicle for aid to the insular Caribbean. The Administration's uncompromising bilateral and hardline diplomacy has impeded the formation of a similar group for Central America.

CONGRESSIONAL INACTION ON THE CBI

With so much attention focused on it, why has the CBI languished in Congress for months? After being formally introduced in Congress on March 17, 1982, the CBI was split into its separate components and sent to the Foreign Affairs and Ways and Means committees in the House, and Foreign Relations and Finance committees in the Senate. Each portion of the bill galvanized a different set of interest groups in favor of or in opposition to the package. In addition to organized labor, which remained the most consistent opponent throughout the process, various aspects of the CBI drew criticism from U.S. sugar growers, textile and shoe manufacturers, church and development organizations, and budget-conscious citizens and congressmen.

Within the Caribbean, businessmen from Puerto Rico and the Virgin Islands sought guarantees that their export position would not be adversely affected by the CBI. CARICOM [Caribbean Common Market] objected to the selected, exclusionary aspects of the bill and the fact that the plan was developed with inadequate consultation with leaders in the affected countries. CARICOM and other nations in the basin also recognized the essential and complementary nature of the trade and investment incentives, and were confused and damaged by the sugar quotas.

Finally, some church organizations, farmers' cooperatives, and small business groups in the Caribbean concluded that the CBI would only enhance American control over local resources, open the door to increased participation of American multinationals in local economies, and increase economic dependence on the United States. At a conference sponsored by the Development Group for Alternative Policies in Jamaica in December 1982, representatives from twelve nations argued that American firms, not local interests, would be the major beneficiaries of the CBI. As Neville Linton of the Caribbean Council of Churches said, "It [the CBI] again means multinationals, large industry, and export to the United States. Do we only industrialize for the United States to meet its needs, or do we move into production and exports which are enhancing our own societies?" And former Salvadoran minister of economy Jorge Sol added, "At least the Alliance for Progress promoted a degree of social progress."

The aid section of the bill was approved in September 1982, once it was agreed to give greater emphasis to basic needs development and reduced amounts to El Salvador. The momentum of the CBI then seemed to come to a halt. The Administration insisted that the CBI remained a "top priority," but House Ways and Means Committee chairman Dan Rostenkowski (D.-Ill.) predicted the bill had virtually no chance of passage. Meanwhile, the chairman of the Senate Finance Committee, Robert Dole (R.-Kan.), awaited the results from the House before he would take action to move the bill in the Senate.

A major push came just prior to the President's trip to Latin America in early December during the 1982 lame-duck session. It seemed politically undesirable for Reagan, Secretary of State George Shultz, and Assistant Secretary of State Thomas Enders to appear in Central America without offering some encouraging news on their much-heralded and long-awaited initiative. The greatest push came in the House, and the Administration helped arrange a trip to the region for members, including Rostenkowski, to convince them of the critical need for the bill. That trip "had an enormous amount to do with [the chairman's]change of opinion," said one Ways and Means staff member.

Dropping the Investment Tax Credit

Once the members returned to Washington, Rostenkowski became one of the CBI's strongest supporters, moving the bill forward quickly and stifling several attempts to cripple it with amendments. Through his efforts, the CBI passed the full committee on December 9 by a strong 27-6 vote and was sent on to the House for a final decision. But the version passed on to the floor of the House had undergone important alterations from the initial plan. Most significantly, the five-year, 10 per cent tax credit for investment had been removed, because of the apparent ineffectiveness of the measure and the lack of a political constituency. Rostenkowski chose to delete it to give the bill a decent chance of passage by the full House. In its place, the committee voted for tax deductions for businesses holding conventions in beneficiary countries.

Although such a tax break will undoubtedly bring in greater income to the Caribbean nations, and although Special Trade Representative Bill Brock said the new measure "in the short term can be even more beneficial" than the original proposal, it is clear that its impact would be much more limited. Rather than helping to diversify the export base of the Caribbean economies and take advantage of the twelve-year duty-free trade provisions, the tax measure will result in greater income and investment only in the tourism and service sectors, and does nothing to promote new manufacturing and light industry in the basin.

More Protectionist Action

Protectionist sentiment in the House also led to the addition of petroleum and its derivatives, leather goods, and footwear to the list of products excluded from the Free Trade Area. And, in its final version, which pased the full House on December 17, tuna was also exempted. The Ways and Means Committee did manage to reverse an earlier recommendation of the trade subcommittee to place a quota on rum imports from the region. Instead, rum remained eligible for the Free Trade Area, and Puerto Rico and the Virgin Islands were granted rights to all excise tax collected on rum sold in the United States, as compensation for lower shares of the U.S. rum market.

The final measure also raised the local-content requirement to 35 per cent from Reagan's proposed 25 per cent, again in response to labor concern that a flood of imports produced in other countries could be assembled in the Caribbean and then later enter the United States duty free. Lastly, the CBI legislation gave the President the authority he requested in the original bill to exclude any country which does not sign an extradition treaty with the United States or which is "Communist."

It was the action in the Senate, or more precisely the lack of action there, that ultimately prevented the CBI from reaching the President's desk. Finance chairman Dole had been waiting to see what happened to the House before acting on it in his committee. The CBI, introduced in March, was not considered in the Senate until December 20, two days after the House adopted the measure. Despite administration pleas to hold back amendments, thereby avoiding the need for a conference with the House, two amendments were adopted.

One amendment eliminated an earlier provision exempting products produced in the Virgin Islands from meeting the local-content requirement for duty-free entry to the United States. The original measure had been intended to give Virgin Island products preferential status over products from elsewhere in the Caribbean. A second amendment also took aim at preferential treatment of the Virgin Islands by requiring Virgin Islands rum distilleries to comply with U.S. federal water pollution controls. The House had earlier voted to exempt the Virgin Islands distilleries from the requirements.

Despite all these compromises, however, the bill was never taken up by the full Senate, which adjourned on December 23. Senator Jesse Helms's (R.-N.C.) filibuster over the Administration's tax bill prevented any work from being accomplished and frustrated the exhausted senators. It was clear soon after the Finance Committee reported on the bill that it had no chance of passage by the 97th Congress.

In the 98th Congress, which opened in January 1983, the CBI must follow the same long path it nearly completed in December. The White House has continued to emphasize the high priority it places on passage of the CBI. In his January 1983 State of the Union address, President Reagan said, "Final passage of the remaining portions of our [CBI] . . . is one of this Administration's top legislative priorities for 1983."

Nonetheless, the CBI faces some tough going on Capitol Hill. Buried under labor opposition and scholarly analyses which reveal its inefficiencies, the investment tax incentive is likely to die in Congress. The remaining portion—the Free Trade Area—has already been reintroduced, but at a time of rising protectionist sentiments. On the other hand, the bill enjoys a residue of interest and support among congressmen who worked on it in the 97th Congress. The best guess is that the FTA will eventually reach the President's desk for his signature, but that labor and selective business opposition will succeed in excluding important products from the list of duty-free items.

Whatever eventually transpires in Congress, the CBI cannot begin to contribute substantially to the region's economic growth until the global economy begins to recover and, in Central America, unless peace is restored.

7. The Struggle in Jamaica

By W. RAYMOND DUNCAN

Focus Jamaica underwent a dramatic political shift when the outspoken anti-Communist Edward Seaga defeated pro-socialist Michael Manley in October 1980. Manley and his People's National Party (PNP) had controlled the government since 1972, and his defeat signaled widespread dissatisfaction with the economic and political consequences of his program.

Writing shortly after the election, W. Raymond Duncan recognizes the 1980 mandate for change but does not see it as a sharp capitalist break with earlier Communist leanings. In his view, Manley courted the Cubans and Soviets as a way to achieve some measure of independence from Jamaica's traditional ties with the United States and Britain, not to align the country with another colonial power. For Duncan, dependency, a central factor in Jamaican history, continues to plague the country. "The domestic elements in Communism's appeal," he says, "include a long and melancholy history of colonialism and slavery; a psychology of dependence on outside powers; grinding poverty, hunger, and unemployment; discontent with the status quo; and, consequently, political instability."

That the PNP has not been Marxist-Leninist either in ideology or in organization is for Duncan proof that the type of Communism attractive to Jamaicans is not of the hard, doctrinaire variety. Michael Manley, though a friend of Castro, "values democracy, social justice, and equality, not Marxism-Leninism," says the author.

Although Duncan draws a basically balanced picture of current Jamaican society, other observers see greater significance in the former Cuban and Soviet presence and influence in Jamaica and are less willing to accept Manley's claim that the 400-450 Cuban doctors, nurses, and construction workers sent to Jamaica were only technical advisors.

Since this essay was written, Edward Seaga's government, after a brief spurt of new investment and an economic upswing, has been plagued by many of the same economic difficulties that Manley faced in the 1970s.

This selection should be read in conjunction with R. Bruce McColm's observations on the larger scenario in the Caribbean Basin (selection 4).

Notes for this essay begin on page 133.

W. Raymond Duncan is a distinguished teaching professor and director of global studies at the State University of New York (SUNY) at Brockport.

C OMMUNISM, A RELATIVE NEWCOMER to the English-speaking Caribbean,[1] was a major issue in Jamaica's violence-ridden elections of late 1980, when anti-Communist Edward Seaga's Jamaica Labor Party (JLP) defeated pro-socialist Michael Manley's People's National Party (PNP).[2] Communism shapes foreign policy: Manley courted close Cuban ties; Seaga is determined to rid the island of Cuban influence. It also conditions Jamaica's role in the international relations of the Caribbean. Kingston supported an expanded Cuban presence in the Caribbean and within the Third World nonaligned movement during the 1970s. This action attracted considerable Soviet interest in this strategically important region and alarmed Washington about growing Cuban and Soviet influence. In response, the new government of Prime Minister Seaga promised to return Jamaica to a pro-American course, using opposition to the Communist threat as one means to attract international aid and private U.S. investment.

Communism's place within the Jamaican political landscape depends on its underlying ideological power and long-term political impact, factors conditioned by the perceptions of Jamaica's competing political leaders. Manley, who polled more than 40 per cent of the vote in the October 1980 elections and retains wide support despite his defeat, is convinced that "democratic socialism" is the correct path to development. Manley's vision involves alignment with Cuba, extended Soviet contacts, and widened links with other leftist Caribbean and Third World governments. These competing views of Communism make the issue a continuing source of conflict between radical Manley supporters and strongly conservative followers of Seaga.

Communism remains an issue because Jamaica is wracked by economic and social tensions, strained by an increasingly polarized political system, and clearly influenced by Fidel Castro's model ninety miles to the north.[3] Between 1975 and 1980, the country experienced food riots, strikes, and an economic crisis that left approximately 20 per cent of the island's industrial plant shut down and another 40 per cent working at only marginal capacity.[4] Inflation, spawned by petroleum price rises since 1973, is rampant; raw materials are in short supply; 50 per cent of the island's young people face unemployment; and educated Jamaicans are departing the island in exceptionally large numbers.[5] It was Seaga's promise to deal effectively with these conditions that gave his JLP fifty-one of the sixty seats in Parliament in the October 1980 elections.

The violence of the 1980 election campaign, however, adds to the difficulty of assessing the long-run ideological appeal and political impact of Communism or the extent of its presence. During the nine months preceding the 1980 elections, hundreds of urban residents were killed by feuding groups. Seaga characterized Manley's supporters as "Communists," and Manley described Seaga as a "fascist." This legacy remains. Immediately after assuming office, Seaga expelled the Cuban ambassador, requested that the incoming Reagan administration form a U.S.-backed anti-Communist alliance in the Caribbean, and appealed for a new Marshall Plan to combat the economic conditions that make Communism seem attractive.[6] Meanwhile, some Jamaicans were concerned that radical Manley supporters, many of them trained in Cuba, were preparing to wage a guerrilla war.

The domestic elements in Communism's appeal include a long and melancholy history of colonialism and slavery; a psychology of dependence on outside powers; grinding poverty, hunger, and unemployment; discontent with the status quo; and, consequently, political instability. Another factor is the presence of left-wing intellectuals within the PNP, many of whom are attracted to the Cuban model. Two Communist parties, moreover, have been formed since 1975: the Jamaican Communist Party (JCP) and the Jamaican Workers' Party (JWP). Given the heightened Soviet attention and influx of Cuban personnel during 1972-1980, a perception of a drift toward Communism was understandable.[7] The close relations between former prime minister Manley and Fidel Castro strengthened that conclusion.

Yet caution is in order regarding Communist strength in Jamaica. It is not simply that leftist tendencies in the PNP are offset by the more conservative JLP now in power. Manley's political beliefs are also a factor. Although friends with Castro, Manley values democracy, social justice, and equality, not Marxism-Leninism. As the 1980s began, he remained committed to furthering the public interest through mixed forms of economic ownership, which translated into a determined effort to prevent foreign domination but a continued interest in foreign investment and tourism. Manley did not overlook the financial strength of the West, despite his flirtation with Cuba and the Soviet Union. Moreover, not all sectors of the PNP supported Jamaica's affair with Cuba; ideological divisions within the party were strong.

Communism in Jamaica is one of several competing political ideologies, which adds to the complexity of the situation and to Jamaican instability. Jamaica's history and its current economic and social problems form the backdrop to leftism on the island, as well as to the conflict between most leftists and the JLP's more conservative position and ascendancy after October 1980.

DEPENDENCY AND ECONOMIC STRESS

Jamaica's national self-image is based on its location, ethnic-racial background, resources, production, and historic ties. The essential leitmotiv in Jamaica's legacy is one of perceived and real *dependency* that makes the island both sensitive and vulnerable to external economic and political pressures.[8] Jamaica became a British colony in 1655, gaining independence only in 1962, whereas most of Latin America's Spanish-speaking states had acquired political independence by the early nineteenth century. This colonial past, vividly imprinted in leadership perceptions, corresponds to a largely black population; about 90 to 95 per cent of Jamaicans descend from African slaves brought in during the eighteenth century. The historical forces of colonialism and slavery created a psychological dependency in the Jamaican population against which many leaders—Communist and Fabian socialists alike—wage a continuing struggle.

Sensitivity to dependency forces Jamaican leaders into economic nationalism and the urge to carve their own way in the world, to steer clear of cold war antagonisms, and to shake off past indignities of outside control.[9] This objective—the concerted effort to find a Jamaican way—inspires the moderate and radical leaders inside the PNP as much as the Marxist-Leninists outside the party. It results in an egalitarian ethic—in Marxist and non-Marxist form—within Jamaica's left wing (replicated elsewhere in the Caribbean).[10] The colonial and slave heritage also fosters a "neo-colonist" view of Jamaica's contemporary economic status among Marxist and non-Marxist politicians, but given the extensiveness of foreign ownership and control over Jamaica's economy despite political independence, this is not surprising.[11]

Owing largely to physical and economic conditions, the realities of dependency continue to plague the country. Its small size, restricted consumer markets, limited resources, diseconomies of scale, constrained domestic productivity, and insular setting force Jamaican leaders to seek outside financial, technical, and other types of support. Sources of support range from other Caribbean nations and Western lending institutions such as the International Monetary Fund (IMF) and the World Bank to Cuba and the Soviet Union. This continuing economic dependency, evolving out of an essentially single-commodity export system (from sugar in the earlier periods, to bananas, to bauxite after 1952), has created enormous development problems. Manley's attempt to reverse patterns of dependency—largely by increasing the government's control of bauxite operations and by joining other Third World countries in the call for a New International Economic Order (NIEO) to share resources, money, and power more equitably between the developed and the developing countries—still assumed that the impetus for growth must come from outside.[12]

An Economic Crisis

Despite government efforts, dependency will not go away, and Jamaica finds itself increasingly in an economic crisis. The oil price rises of 1973-74 adversely affected Jamaica, as did a decline in sugar prices and droughts that cut sugar and coffee production.[13] Bauxite production, which earns 35 per cent of the country's foreign exchange, fell 32 per cent between 1974 and 1976 for a variety of reasons. The result is a persistent balance-of-payments deficit.[14] The country's foreign debt reached a staggering $1.7 billion by early 1980.[15] External borrowing unfortunately did not improve the island's economic growth rate in the 1970s, as demonstrated by declines in the gross national product, registering −2.6 per cent in 1973, −6.9 in 1976, −4.0 in 1977, and −2.0 in 1978.[16] By early 1980, Jamaica's economy had worsened to the point where U.S. and European banks were refusing to make new loans. Meanwhile, the Manley government had decided to end its negotiations with the IMF, given the country's inability to meet IMF conditions for new loans.[17] As might be expected, the deteriorating economy led to a flight of domestic capital and professionals as well as a sharp slowdown in foreign investment—problems that the Seaga government had begun to address by November 1980.

Jamaica is plagued by high unemployment, escalating inflation, rapid urbanization, low agricultural productivity, and violent crime that further weakens the economy and political system. Unemployment, officially estimated at 24 per cent, is probably over 50 per cent in the 14-24 age group, in a country where 60 per cent of the population is under 21 years old. Inflation exceeds 20 per cent, following a period in 1978 when it reached 50 per cent. Urban growth has greatly increased the need for public services in an already overextended economic and political system. By 1980, for example, only 14 per cent of all dwellings in central Kingston had running water, 80 per cent of all households shared toilet facilities with others, and 43 per cent of all dwellings consisted of one room.[18] The average black in Kingston could expect inadequate water and sewage systems and poor police protection and recreational opportunities. Breakdowns in public transportation, public health systems, and postal facilities were a regular occurrence. Maldistribution of income is clear: per capita income is over $1,000, but 85 per cent of the population exists on less than $200 a year.[19]

Herein lies the origin of the violent crime and gang warfare that rocked Kingston before the 1980 elections.[20] Victims of Kingston's high crime rate are generally middle- and upper-middle-class individuals, who tend to be fairer skinned. They live in the suburban homes on the hills outside Kingston, where security measures have recently been increased. By 1974 violent crimes were up 50 per cent over the 1960-61 crime rate, with robberies rising from 43 to 418 cases reported per 100,000 population.[21] Accompanying the crime rate have been high rates of labor unrest and strikes, which formerly were rare in Jamaica.

RECENT POLITICAL DEVELOPMENTS

Jamaica has a functioning two-party system, which draws strongly on the liberal ideas, parliamentary institutions, and rule of law inherited from Great Britain. The political system provides representation for diverse class and sectional interests, and elections are held at least every five years. During the 1950s and 1960s neither the JLP nor the PNP seemed willing or able to address key economic issues or stimulate any radical economic transformation of the country. Manley's program of "democratic socialism," however, began to move in this direction following his election in 1972 and his re-election in 1976. Both parties today appeal to all sectors of the population, although neither has gained the support of the politically alienated, chronically frustrated, and volatile sector of unskilled laborers.

Manley's version of socialism is decidedly Fabian in origin and concept, drawing on the ideas of British socialist theoretician Harold Laski, understandably so given Manley's training at the London School of Economics in the 1940s during Laski's tenure there and his subsequent political career as a union organizer. Manley's father was a union leader and founded the PNP in 1938. The PNP is not a Marxist-Leninist association, either in ideological origins or in organization. There is no official government or party newspaper, no massive youth organization, and certainly no systematic propaganda tactics.[22] Manley has been the essential carrier of the message of democratic socialism since the early 1970s, emphasizing government control of the economy and stressing equality and social justice. And it was Manley who decided to open new avenues of diplomacy to Cuba and the Soviet Union, albeit with considerable encouragement from others within the PNP, in an effort to escape traditional U.S. and British Commonwealth ties—a direction widespread in Latin America from the 1960s.

By the late 1970s, Manley's democratic socialism was in trouble. Discernible frictions existed within the ruling PNP, with Marxist radicals opposing moderates on a number of matters, including relations with the IMF.[23] This situation was not eased by Manley's commitment to allowing opposing viewpoints within the PNP and his appointment of antagonistic ministers to party positions. These decisions not only stimulated public PNP disunity but led Jamaica's businessmen and the JLP to see the specter of Communism within the government itself and the possibility of the government's eliminating private enterprise and establishing Jamaica as a second Communist country in the Caribbean.[24] By late 1978 Manley's popularity had sunk to a new low. An opinion poll conducted by Carl Stone, a Jamaican social scientist, indicated that 29 per cent of the Jamaican people supported the JLP and only 15 per cent the PNP.[25]

As Manley's popularity waned and the economy stagnated, political violence began to rise. A number of people were killed in clashes between Manley's and Seaga's supporters. On April 13, 1980, gunmen fired on a party of 500 people accompanying Manley on a tour of a decaying section of downtown Kingston. One week later, twenty-five uniformed gunmen attacked a dance being held in the area by the opposition JLP, killing four people and wounding ten others. By May 1980 rival JLP and PNP gangs maintained roadblocks at the boundaries of their territories.[26] As elections approached in late 1980, tensions arising from deep-seated economic and social frustrations continued to increase.

Conflicting Political Trends

A number of distinct, frequently conflicting political trends operate in Jamaica. Prime Minister Seaga and the JLP seem determined to diversify the economy and produce for North American and European markets by using Jamaican labor and foreign capital, management, and technology.[27] During the 1980 election campaign, the JLP constantly hammered away at the theme of growing Communist tendencies and a "Marxist takeover" of the PNP. Manley, on the other hand, continued to flirt with Cuba, the Soviet Union, and the United States. His government invited Cuban technicians and medical personnel into Jamaica; Manley and Fidel Castro were on the best of terms and exchanged visits; and a number of agreements with the Soviet Union were signed. At the same time, Manley welcomed foreign investment. As he stated in Miami in January 1980, he encouraged the United States not to look on Jamaica as a hotbed of Communism or of "some mysterious conspiracy or adventurist plot"; rather, the United States should realize that the Caribbean

> contains a lot of very poor people who are struggling to find answers to their poverty. It has the energy to try new things when old things seem to fail. . . . I think that the United States of America will contribute toward its own stature as a great power to the extent it recognizes and respects these small, vigorous, and sometimes fractious neighbors to its south and holds out the hand of cooperation on a basis of respect offered and respect returned regardless of the size of those who shake hands.[28]

In the search for Jamaica's own special way at home and abroad, however, some policies of Manley and the PNP suggested increased radical perceptions within the government. Following a trip to Cuba in March 1980, Manley named a new, more radical finance minister after the PNP Executive Committee voted 103-45 against further negotiations with the IMF. To what extent Manley's relations with Cuba and with Grenada's new, pro-Cuban radical-leftist government under Maurice Bishop may have helped to shape these decisions is difficult to judge, especially since the IMF conditions for further loans were notably unpopular among many leading Jamaican politicians. But the decision to stop the negotiations continued to polarize the Jamaican political system among conservatives, moderates, and Marxists.[29] Ironically, the lack of foreign support could exacerbate this tension and threaten the democratic character of Jamaica's political system, thus undermining the possibilities for future loans. Prime Minister Seaga, clearly aware of this situation, began to seek new IMF loans after his election victory.

Another recent trend in Jamaica is the emergence of two Communist parties: the Jamaican Workers' Party (JWP), formed in 1978 under the leadership of Trevor Monroe, and the Jamaican Communist Party (JCP), founded in 1975 and headed by its general secretary, Chris Lawrence.[30] These parties fully supported

Manley's suspension of negotiations with the IMF in 1980 and the seeking of close ties with Cuba and the Soviet Union, as do left-wing members of the PNP itself. Both parties strongly support the PNP over Seaga's "fascist" JLP and reject the notion that Cubans are subverting the country.

Although Communist parties exert some influence on students, teachers, intellectuals, and workers, there is no probability of a cataclysmic slide toward a Marxist-Leninist Jamaica. Neither party has a large grassroots base, and opposition to them is strong. The presence of two competing Marxist parties, moreover, suggests further division in the movement, despite pro-Soviet orientation. Jamaica lies in a geographical and cultural region where most parties lack strong organizational unity and broad-based links that tie the leaders with the led through a party program. The views of intellectual leaders themselves shape party goals independent of tight party discipline and a large following. Still, the presence of Marxist parties and Marxist intellectuals inside and outside the PNP tends to polarize the Jamaican political system, making the creation of a national consensus and the mobilization of the society to carry out an agreed developmental strategy difficult. This problem troubles the Seaga government just as it plagued Manley's.

Cuban and Soviet Ties

The steady buildup of diplomatic relations between Jamaica and the Cubans and the Soviets since the mid-1970s produced a number of cultural, diplomatic, economic, and technical links. Approximately 400-450 Cubans—doctors, nurses, school-building teams, and mini-dam construction workers—came to Jamaica.[31] Jamaican youths in turn went to Cuba for cultural, educational, and athletic training. Cuban activities thus were less financial and political than technical in content, although the obvious side effects of ideology and propaganda cannot be discounted. Manley maintained that relations were based on noninterference in domestic policies, a judgment that appears to be accurate. Cuban aid and relations did not come even close to producing a centralized political system and party organization like those found in Cuba.

Manley paid his first visit to the Soviet Union in April 1979, after relations were established between the two countries. Among the economic agreements signed during Manley's trip was a contract specifying the export of 50,000 tons of alumina per year to the U.S.S.R. between 1980 and 1983 and 250,00 tons thereafter. Jamaica and the U.S.S.R. also established a joint fisheries company; and Moscow, unlike Cuba, granted a long-term loan to Jamaica to finance imports of Soviet goods.[32] Jamaica also had trade agreements with Hungary and Yugoslavia and was working toward closer ties with Bulgaria, Czechoslovakia, East Germany, Poland, and Romania. These moves were undoubtedly designed to reduce Jamaica's dependence on the IMF, but nevertheless they point up the country's enormous reliance on external support wherever it can find it. As expected, Seaga and the JLP roundly criticized Manley's visit to the U.S.S.R., his visit to Cuba in March 1980, and Castro's trip to Jamaica in 1977.

Although these events did not propel Jamaica into Communism, they clearly aroused suspicions inside the United States. Cuba's geographic proximity did nothing to ease concern, for it has facilitated increased travel to Havana by left-wing members of the PNP and other Jamaican Marxists. Nor is the perception of Communist influence in Jamaica produced strictly by Cuban-Jamaican relations. Cuba's expanded presence elsewhere in the Caribbean and Central America (Grenada, Nicaragua, El Salvador), the general rise of Soviet influence in the area, and domestic leftist trends in many other Caribbean and Central American countries also affect U.S. perceptions. These perceptions resulted in reduced aid for Jamaica, support for tariffs on Jamaican imports, such as rum and sugar, and a tendency for Congress and some members of the executive branch to couple Jamaican events with the Cuban problem. Seaga's victory in late 1980 greatly modified Washington's perceptions.

Recent events, however, could decrease Manley's willingness to associate closely with Cuba and the Soviet Union. Jamaica voted with the majority of Third World countries to condemn the Soviet move into Afghanistan. Like other developing countries, Jamaica is pressing the Kremlin for greater financial aid and not allowing it to continue to dismiss the needs of these states as the responsibility of the "imperialists."[33] Cuba's image as a Third World model, meanwhile, has been tarnished by its unabashed pressure for increased support from developing countries for the U.S.S.R. at the September 1979 meeting of nonaligned countries in Havana and especially by Cuban support for Moscow's invasion of Afghanistan. Cuba's recent economic difficulties, made so visible by Castro's public acknowledgment and the flight of refugees from April 1980 onward, do not improve its attractiveness as a role model.[34]

FACTORS IN JAMAICA'S FUTURE

Jamaican prospects turn essentially on economic development. The essential question is whether, and to what extent, the Seaga government can build a consensus on dealing with poverty and chronic unemployment, or barring consensus, whether the political system can handle the conflicting relations produced by economic stagnation.

Jamaica's capacity to cope with these issues will be conditioned by both internal and external forces. Key external elements are aid and investment responses by the United States and other developed countries and by the IMF and World Bank to Jamaica's development needs. Key internal factors are government successes and failures in agriculture, the mix of labor- versus capital-intensive investment to ease unemployment, the stimulation of capital formation, bauxite production, and a more equitable distribution of national income. Complex economic problems will challenge Prime Minister Seaga's best political skills.

The Future of Communism

The future of Jamaican Communism depends directly on economic development. Certainly its organized presence makes the building of consensus on development strategy difficult. Major questions for the future include the type of opposition mounted by ex-prime minister Manley, his ability to control his radical pro-Communist supporters during the Seaga administration, and the types of contact between Manley and Castro in the 1980s. Also important is the manner in which the United States and other developed countries react to the Seaga victory by either enhancing or decreasing his capacity to ease Jamaica's poverty. Should Seaga fail, either Communism will become more appealing or at least radical nationalism will be forthcoming. Both would destabilize the Jamaican political system.

Communism would affect Jamaican stability and instability by affecting U.S. perceptions. Given the visibility of Cuban and Soviet activities in the Caribbean and the proximity of Jamaica to Cuba, Washington during the 1970s began to see Jamaica as part of a strategically important region in a state of dislocation and increasing leftist tendencies. As the 1980s began, U.S. foreign policy responses were of a dual nature.[35] First, Washington displayed new attention to the economic problems of the Caribbean, emphasizing foreign aid and economic development. But the rise of Soviet and Cuban power projection in the area, such as the Soviet-troops-in-Cuba issue of summer 1979, produced a military response to counter a perceived Cuban-Soviet threat.[36] While the Carter administration sought to keep its dual policies separated, it nevertheless created confusion in the minds of Caribbean leaders, including the Jamaicans.[37] Moderate and Marxist leftists in Jamaica much preferred the first response; the second had the effect of giving them a common cause against U.S. military action. The second response may also have tended, in combination with the erosion of Jamaica's economic and political situation, to undermine congressional approval of economic aid.

Seaga's victory of 1980, given his pro-capitalist and anti-Communist position, may ease U.S. fears of Communism in the Caribbean, especially in light of other conservative electoral victories in Puerto Rico and the Turks and Caicos islands and in view of Jamaica's diplomatic break with Cuba. If so, increased economic aid may accompany a downplaying of military responses in the region.[38] Yet events in Central America may encourage U.S. military responses, fueling Seaga's leftist opposition in Jamaica and encouraging political instability. That scenario could in turn reduce U.S. willingness to aid or invest in Jamaica.

We are left, then, with a complicated picture. The instability is rooted in economic dislocation, which the Manley government was unable to address satisfactorily. Indeed, the government's efforts produced deep political antagonisms. What is needed is an economic breakthrough to help mute the social and political turmoil. The 1980 election of Seaga restored the Jamaican commitment to capitalism, with a distinctly pro-American edge. Whether it will fare better than Manley's experiment with "democratic socialism" remains to be seen.

NOTES

1. For a discussion of Caribbean Communism, with an emphasis on Jamaica, see Trevor Monroe, "Winds of Change in the Caribbean," *World Marxist Review* 23, no. 11 (November 1980), pp. 28-35.

2. The fifty-year-old Seaga took office on November 1, 1980, as Jamaica's fifth prime minister. He is a Harvard graduate and a financial specialist. (See *Jamaica Newsletter* 11, no. 4 [October 1980], p. 1.)

3. For a general description of Jamaica's economic, political, and social setting, see *Area Handbook for Jamaica* (Washington, D.C.: Government Printing Office, 1976); and Adam Kuper, *Changing Jamaica* (Kingston: Kingston Publishers, 1976).

4. Reports of these events may be found in radio broadcasts monitored by the Foreign Broadcast Information Service (FBIS). For example, see the report on anti-government demonstrations, FBIS, *Latin America and the Caribbean,* January 10, 1980; and on workers' strikes that disrupted health services, water supplies, transportation, and food supplies, ibid., January 22, 1980.

5. Gasoline sold at $2.65 a gallon in March 1980, bread was often unavailable, and wheat had to be imported. See James Nelson Goodsell, "Sunny Jamaica Losing Its Gloss," *Christian Science Monitor,* March 26, 1980, p. 16; and Tad Szulc, "Radical Winds in the Caribbean," *New York Times Magazine,* May 25, 1980, pp. 16 ff.

6. See *Latin America Weekly Report,* December 12, 1980, p. 4. Seaga's keynote address at the November 1980 conference of the Caribbean/Central American Action left no doubt about his determination to struggle against Cuban and Soviet influence in the Caribbean *(Caribbean Contact 8, no. 4* [December 1980], p. 9).

7. Soviet scholarly journals pay increasing attention to the Caribbean, an area depicted as hastening the weakening of imperialism and neo-colonialism. See L. Klochkovsky, "The Struggle for Economic Emancipation in Latin America," *International Affairs* (Moscow), 1979, no. 4 (April), pp. 39-47; and V. Yakubov, "Behind the Screen of the 'New Approach,'" *Pravda,* March 2, 1978, in FBIS, *U.S.S.R. International Affairs,* March 7, 1978. At the same time Moscow accused the United States of fomenting violence in Jamaica in late 1980 (*Pravda,* October 15, 1980).

8. For Michael Manley's sharp perception of Jamaica's dependency legacy, see his *The Politics of Change: A Jamaica Testament* (London: Tonbridge Printers, 1974), chap. 1; and *The Search for Solutions* (Ontario, Canada: Maple House Publishing Co., 1976), introduction.

9. See Wendell Bell and J. William Gibson, "Independent Jamaica Faces the Outside World," *International Studies Quarterly* 22, no. 1 (March 1978), pp. 5–45; and Wendell Bell, "Independent Jamaica Enters World Politics: Foreign Policy in a New State," *Political Science Quarterly* 92, no. 4 (Winter 1977-78), pp. 683-703.

10. See W. Raymond Duncan, "Caribbean Leftism," *Problems of Communism* 27 (May-June 1978), pp. 33-57.

11. "Neo-colonialism" refers to the high prices Caribbean countries pay for foreign goods, the lesser amounts they receive for their products, the high interest rates they frequently have to pay for loans, the profits that foreign investors expect to make, and the tendency for foreign investment to be capital- rather than labor-intensive (see *The Economic Crisis, Broadcast by the Prime Minister, Honorable Michael Manley*, January 5, 1977 [Kingston: Government of Jamaica, n.d.]).

12. Manley sees Jamaica as distinctly within the Third World. He advocates a common Third World economic strategy and strongly supports NIEO. (See Manley, *Politics of Change*, pp. 131-32.) Jamaica signed the 1974 declaration for NIEO, which calls for closer regulation of the activities of multinational corporations, active associations of producer nations, increased foreign aid from the developed countries, and other arrangements to establish a more equitable economic development strategy for the Third World. (See Guy F. Erb and Valeriana Kallab, eds., *Beyond Dependency: The Developing World Speaks Out* [Washington, D.C.: Overseas Development Council, 1975], pp. 165-202; Richard N. Cooper, "A New International Economic Order for Mutual Gain," *Foreign Policy*, Spring 1977, pp. 66-120; and Roger D. Hansen, *Beyond The North-South Stalemate* [New York: McGraw-Hill, 1980], chap. 1.)

13. U.S., Congress, House, Committee on Foreign Affairs, *Caribbean Nations: Assessment of Conditions and U.S. Influence: Report of a Special Study Mission to Jamaica, Cuba, the Dominican Republic, and the Guantanamo Naval Base, January 3-12, 1979* (Washington, D.C.: Government Printing Office, 1979), pp. 8-9.

14. U.S., Congress, House, Committee on Foreign Affairs, Subcommittee on Inter-American Affairs, *Economic and Political Future of the Caribbean: Hearings*, 96th Cong., 1st Sess., July 24, 26, and September 20, 1979 (Washington, D.C.: Government Printing Office, 1979), p. 41. See also *Keesing's Contemporary Archives*, July 27, 1979, pp. 29746-48.

15. On Jamaica's external debt and debt-servicing burden, see U.S., CIA, National Assessment Center, *Non-OPEC LDCs: External Debt Positions*, ER 80-10030 (Washington, D.C., 1980), p. 65.

16. Ibid., p. 13.

17. *Latin American Weekly Report*, April 4, 1980, pp. 4-5.

18. L. Alan Eyre, "Quasi-Urban Melange Settlement: Cases from St. Catherine and St. James, Jamaica," *Applied Geography* 69 (January 1979), p. 95.

19. J. Daniel O'Flaherty, "Finding Jamaica's Way," *Foreign Policy*, Summer 1978, p. 143.

20. *Latin American Weekly Report*, May 2, 1980, p. 6.

21. *Area Handbook for Jamaica*, p. 280.

22. The PNP did introduce, however, a five-year plan in 1978 (see *Keesing's Contemporary Archives*, July 27, 1979, p. 29747).

23. *Latin American Weekly Report,* April 4, 1980, p. 5.

24. Ibid.

25. House, Committee on Foreign Affairs, *Caribbean Nations,* p. 11.

26. *Latin American Weekly Report,* May 2, 1980, p. 6.

27. Ibid.

28. *Jamaica Newsletter* (a publication of the Jamaican Embassy in Washington, D.C.), January 1980, pp. 8-9.

29. The Manley government had previously suspended negotiations with the IMF in early 1977 and moved toward radical experimentation with the economy. By April 1977 this attempt had been discredited. (See O'Flaherty, "Finding Jamaica's Way," p. 148.)

30. See Richard F. Staar, ed., *Yearbook on International Communist Affairs, 1980* (Stanford: Hoover Institution Press, 1980), p. 486.

31. See House, Committee on Foreign Affairs, *Caribbean Nations,* pp. 10-11; and idem, *Economic and Political Future of the Caribbean,* pp. 32-33.

32. *Keesing's Contemporary Archives,* July 27, 1979, p. 29748.

33. Hansen, *North-South Stalemate,* chap. 1.

34. James Nelson Goodsell, "Cuba's Economic Report Card: 'F,'" *Christian Science Monitor,* May 9, 1980, p. 1.

35. See Graham Hovey, "Caribbean Nations Still in Focus," *New York Times,* February 3, 1980, p. 5; and James Nelson Goodsell, "Carter's Caribbean Sea of Confusion," *Christian Science Monitor,* February 11, 1980, p. 12.

36. The response included the establishment of the Caribbean Contingency Joint Task Force in Key West, Florida, plus the resumption of surveillance flights over Cuba (see Szulc, "Radical Winds in the Caribbean," p. 56).

37. See Goodsell, "Castro 'Loses' in U.S., Caribbean Elections," *Christian Science Monitor,* November 12, 1980, p. 1, which describes Washington's satisfaction over the Jamaican elections.

38. There are currently fourteen active World Bank loans totaling approximately $195 million, of which 71 per cent is undisbursed; and seventeen active Inter-American Development Bank loans amounting to about $123 million, of which one-half has been disbursed. Other loans are from Sweden, Holland, Algeria, West Germany, and Canada. The Jamaican government is working closely with Venezuela and Mexico on other projects. (Embassy of Jamaica news release.)

8. Grenada and the 'Moral High Ground'

By CHARLES KRAUTHAMMER

Focus Charles Krauthammer notes the cries coming from many quarters that the United States lost the "moral high ground" by its 1983 incursion into Grenada. But what most people seem to mean by "moral high ground," he says, is that we should stand by and watch while other countries commit immoral acts. We can then denounce the evildoers—on one condition, that we "do nothing real to help the victims. The denunciation must be impotent."

The U.S. action in Grenada, says Krauthammer, was an at least partly justifiable response to the behavior of a military junta that assassinated the prime minister, much of his cabinet, and a number of other citizens. That action cannot be equated, as many have asserted it can, with the 1979 Soviet invasion of Afghanistan. The Russians have been killing civilians with chemical weapons to prop up a subservient tyrant; in Grenada, the United States got rid of a "bunch of thugs" (to use President Reagan's words) so that the country could return to parliamentary democracy.

There are situations when vigorous action is the only responsible course. Mere expressions of outrage at brutal actions like the invasion of Afghanistan and the Soviet shooting down of an unarmed South Korean airliner in September 1983 are not a sufficient moral response, argues Krauthammer.

"Moral victories are things that saints, not statesmen, should covet, and in any case only for themselves," he concludes. Statesmen must be concerned primarily with the security and freedom of their people. In taking swift action in Grenada, the United States showed it can do more than merely *talk* about moral responsibility.

Charles Krauthammer is a senior editor of the *New Republic*.

THERE HAS BEEN A LOT of talk lately about the "moral high ground" (time is short: call it "mohgro"), that strategic territory the United States apparently ceded to Cuba and the Soviet Union in exchange for Grenada. The loss of this piece of real estate has provoked protests from quarters normally indifferent to the territorial exchanges of the cold war. From the gnashing of teeth and pointing of fingers occasioned by the loss of this former American province, one would imagine we'd lost another China.

Who lost mohgro? Ronald Reagan, of course. But how exactly did we acquire it in the first place? Robert Kaiser, of the *Washington Post,* explains. He criticizes the President for "squandering the moral high ground the Soviets had granted him by their bad behavior in Poland, Afghanistan, and the destruction of Flight 007." So mohgro was won because of "bad behavior" on the part of our adversaries. But wasn't there bad behavior in Grenada, too, shortly before the American invasion? Didn't the military junta assassinate the prime minister, much of his cabinet, and a still unknown number of civilians? Exactly. We were in veritable moral orbit then, with all those dead and dying to which we could point with satisfaction and say: "See, that's what happens when you mess with Marxists." Well then, how did we squander our advantage? Answer: By doing something about the thuggery that had granted our side the mohgro in the first place. To be precise, by ending it.

That's the point. When others are bad you can seize the mohgro with a pointed finger and a fine denunciation. On one condition: you do nothing real to help the victims. The denunciation must be impotent. That, after all, is what Afghanistan, Poland, and Flight 007 have in common. Not just bad behavior by the Russians, but bad behavior the victims of which we could variously mourn, applaud, or pray for, but do nothing to save. Raise a finger actually

Reprinted by permission from the December 12, 1983, issue of *The New Republic* (© 1983 by The New Republic, Incorporated).

to do something, and you forfeit your "moral" gains. Intervene to help the victim, and you run the risk of breaking a rule: for example, violating a frontier, or the OAS Charter, or the sensibilities of 106 members of the General Assembly or the editorial board of the *New York Times*. Then, presto! you become just like the Russians. "Simply put," the *Times* wrote, "the cost [of the Grenada operation] is loss of the moral high ground: a reverberating demonstration to the world that America has no more respect for laws and borders, for the codes of civilization, than the Soviet Union."

Really? Representative Thomas Downey says that in Grenada "we gave up the moral high ground we occupied after the Soviets invaded Afghanistan and shot down the South Korean airliner." Compare Grenada and Afghanistan. Both involved superpower intervention in a neighbor's affairs. The parallel begins and ends there. In Afghanistan the Russians have been killing people for four years (now with chemical weapons) to keep in power a despised tyrant (an old-fashioned word with the virtue of being acceptable to right and left). In Grenada the United States got rid of a bunch of thugs (not even the *Times* disputes that characterization) in a three-day operation. And it's not just means but ends that are different. We know what kind of government Babrak Karmal runs. And not even Tom Downey doubts that the United States aims to return Grenada to parliamentary democracy.

When Intervention Is Justified

My argument is not that because we are a democracy the ends of any American intervention are inherently justified. There are cases—U.S. intervention in Guatemala in 1954, for example—where intervention is undertaken for (correctly or incorrectly calculated) geopolitical advantage at the expense of democracy. However, there are cases where U.S. action serves both its own geopolitical interests and the interests of democracy. Grenada is such a case. The burden of proof is always on those who advocate intervention. But if an extremely limited operation to restore a country from gangsterism to democracy is not justified, then what proof will the critics ever accept? None, I suspect. If you believe that mohgro simply goes to the aggrieved, they you don't bother with moral calculations. You seek instead more grief. It makes for a curious foreign policy.

And it's not just the foreign policy of the mohgro theorists that is curious. So is their language. "Obviously the United States has strategic interests to defend," writes Tad Szulc in the *New York Times,* "but, just as importantly, it must defend its moral high ground." The metaphor is military. And far from being an embarrassment to those making a case against the use of force, it is an asset. The metaphor is pointed: high ground, after all, is not a place to be coveted solely for its pristine air, unobstructed view, and the opportunity it affords to bask serenely in the radiance of one's own goodness. It is a place from which to dominate and control. The implication is that occupying the moral high ground confers advantages; losing it is costly—"far more costly than the loss of a dozen soldiers," calculates the *New York Times.* The critics' point is this: staying out of Grenada would not only have been the more moral thing to do; it would have been shrewder. It would have advanced American interests more, left us further ahead than we are now. What we forfeited by going in was so important that whatever our gains, on balance we lost.

The Balance Sheet

Now, what precisely did we lose? Our moral superiority to the Russians in the eyes of world public opinion. Grenada, explains Walter Mondale, "undermines our ability to effectively criticize what the Soviets have done in their brutal intervention in Afghanistan, in Poland, and elsewhere." Assume that's true. Assume that the invasion of Grenada was, in fact, wrong (something which I—and Speaker of the House Tip O'Neill, Representative Michael Barnes, Senators Biden and Kennedy, among others—deny). And assume further that the three-day Grenada operation was as wrong as the Soviets' four years in Afghanistan and forty in Poland (where one doubts that 91 per cent of the people, as in Grenada, would tell a pollster that they support the armed intervention of their superpower neighbor). Assume all that and look at the balance sheet.

On the one hand, Cuba has been expelled from Grenada (and on the very next day, domino-style from Surinam), its Caribbean enterprises effectively foreclosed. On the other hand, we lose the ability to criticize the Soviets about Afghanistan and Poland and Flight 007. Now, there are people who think that criticizing the Soviets in areas where we can do absolutely nothing is what foreign policy is all about. For them, the balance sheet is negative. Presumably they also believe that our previous exchanges of moral for strategic territory were positive: the Soviets re-Stalinized Poland, captured Afghanistan (putting them two hundred miles from the Persian Gulf), and ensured that nobody in his right mind will violate their airspace. In return we got to denounce them at the United Nations (though not at all on Poland); and on the KAL disaster our (vetoed) Security Council resolution mustered the barest majority of nine votes. We also got a sixty-day partial ban on flights to the Soviet Union, except that it was called off after twenty-one. Nice bargain.

I am willing to grant that victimhood may be ennobling, but not that it is profitable. Moral victories are things that saints, not statesmen, should covet, and in any case only for themselves. Statesmen, who are entrusted with the safety and liberty of their people, should be concerned first with the strategic high ground. If, in addition, it affords a view of any nearby moral heights, so much the better.

9. *Views of the American Catholic Bishops*

By ARCHBISHOP JAMES HICKEY

Focus   "We are not confused by Marxist ideology or strategy. The Catholic Church knows full well how human liberty and the basic freedoms are suppressed under Marxist regimes even as they are often suppressed by governments of the extreme right." In this testimony before two congressional subcommittees on behalf of the United States Catholic Conference, James Hickey, archbishop of Washington, D.C., defends the role of the church in Latin America and the U.S. bishops' statements on that region. The church will denounce injustice and oppression whatever the source, he says.

The U.S. bishops recognize the international dimension of the problems in Central America, says Hickey, but they believe that the indigenous economic and social problems are the fundamental causes of the conflict. Consequently, the bishops call for a major shift in U.S. policy, to give primary emphasis to development aid and creative diplomatic solutions. While they oppose large increases in military aid to the area, they concede that if "the diplomatic option were truly pursued, . . . some military component may be required. We acknowledge this with regret, but we do not deny it." Such aid, however, should be strictly linked to efforts to achieve dialogue and a cease-fire.

In El Salvador, say the bishops, the United States carries a great deal of weight, and the right U.S.

144

initiatives could significantly change the situation there. The Sandinista regime in Nicaragua has serious shortcomings, but U.S. threats to the Sandinistas have contributed to the formation of a garrison-state mentality on top of already misguided policies.

Notable by its absence from this statement is any reference to the Sandinistas' insulting treatment of Pope John Paul II during his visit to Managua in March 1983, which occurred just three days before Archbishop Hickey gave this testimony. (For an account of the Sandinistas' behavior toward the church in Nicaragua and their attempt to exploit the Pope's visit, see Miguel Bolaños, selection 25.) The bishops deplore the militarization of El Salvador, but they specifically criticize military assistance from the United States while speaking only vaguely of aid to the opposition forces "from other sources."

James Hickey, archbishop of Washington, D.C., gave this testimony on behalf of the United States Catholic Conference, a non-canonical body that is under the direction of the National Conference of Catholic Bishops.

I APPRECIATE THE OPPORTUNITY to come before these two sub-committees on behalf of the U.S. Catholic Conference. The USCC is the public-policy agency of the Catholic bishops of the United States. I appeared before the subcommittee on inter-American affairs March 5, 1981, regarding the topic we discuss today: U.S. policy toward El Salvador.

In November 1981 the USCC adopted at its general meeting a policy statement on Central America which has served us well in the last two years. Much has happened in Central America since 1981. In order to review the situation and assess the USCC position, Archbishop John R. Roach, president of our episcopal conference, asked me to head a delegation of three bishops on an eight-day trip to El Salvador, Nicaragua, and Honduras. The other two bishops were Archbishop Peter L. Gerety of Newark, N.J., and Archbishop Patrick Flores of San Antonio, Texas. We were in Central America February 1-9, 1983. Archbishop Roach asked me to present the USCC's position in these hearings as a continuation of our participation in the public debate on El Salvador.

GENERAL OBSERVATIONS

Before addressing specific questions, I will make some general comments based on our brief but intensive visit. The dual purpose of the trip was to express solidarity with our brother bishops in each of the countries we visited and to consult with them and with other people, in both the church and the wider society. We arranged ten hours of meetings per day, including courtesy calls on the government of each country, appointments at the U.S. embassy in each country, and meetings with the papal nuncios for the three countries. We had conversations with priests, religious, and laity in each country, and we particularly tried to meet U.S. Catholic missionaries serving in each country. I should note that we made efforts when planning the trip to include a visit to Guatemala. It was not possible to work out the logistics. I will make four general observations about the three countries we visited.

First, in every country visited we found the Catholic Church fulfilling its pastoral ministry in a profoundly impressive manner. This ministry is exercised in the midst of the most trying circumstances of violence, poverty, and great human suffering. It is a ministry carried on with very sparse resources; yet there is an inspiring, indeed heroic, spirit of hope and faith at all levels of the church.

The church's exercise of a prophetic social ministry, guided by the Puebla conference [of Latin American bishops, 1979] theme of a preferential option for the poor and by a commitment to defend human rights, is the basic reason for tension between the church and governments in Central America. Precisely because of its defense of human dignity and human rights the church is described by many in Central America as a "subversive force."

A most recent and very disturbing development in this process is the emergence of sectarian churches called Protestant, but decidedly not representing the mainline Protestant churches. These sects are militantly anti-Catholic, are very conservative politically, and are welcomed and cultivated by right-wing elements—in and out of government—in El Salvador and Honduras as a counterweight to the Catholic Church's social witness. As Catholic bishops we were particularly concerned about the fact that much of the funding for these groups comes from the United States.

A *second* pervasive theme of our visit was the evidence we found of human rights violations in all three countries. The situation varies in each country, but significant restrictions on human rights or direct assaults on the dignity of the person were in evidence in each country visited. The killing of thousands of innocent civilians in El Salvador, the pervasive economic injustice in the region, censorship, and mistreatment of Miskito Indians in Nicaragua are just examples of the human rights problems. Human rights issues are a concern of the church in each of the three countries; they will continue to be a high priority for the USCC as we examine U.S. policy toward Central America.

A *third* reality which is vividly evident in all three countries is the effects of war. In El Salvador the daily devastation is manifested in large numbers of displaced persons. Since they are within their own country, they are not entitled to refugee status and aid; yet they are victims of a struggle which grinds on relentlessly. In Honduras one sees the results of war in the neighboring countries; there are thousands of refugees from El Salvador, Guatemala, and Nicaragua. The threat of war is evident in the military buildup along the Nicaraguan-Honduran border. The military exercises sponsored by the United States occurred while we were in Central America. In Nicaragua, the belief—almost tangible because it is so strongly held—that the United States is on a course of destabilization has partially contributed to the creation of a garrison-state mentality and atmosphere in a country which desperately needs to use scarce resources in other ways.

Fourth, the influence of U.S. policy on each of the countries we visited and on the region as a whole is profound and pervasive. We affect each country differently, but we are part of the fabric of daily life in all of Central America. It was evident to the three of us in the delegation that a distinct shift in U.S. policy toward the region is needed. While I will discuss some specific aspects of this below, here I will say only that we need to be more convincing in our willingness to support and foster political democracy, social and economic justice, and human rights in Central America.

In light of these general characteristics, I now wish to comment on U.S. policy toward El Salvador and how that must be correlated with U.S. policy toward the Central American region. Briefly, a more effective Salvador policy will require a more perceptive regional policy.

U.S. POLICY IN EL SALVADOR

When I appeared before the subcommittee on inter-American affairs in 1981, I began my analysis of the situation in El Salvador by emphasizing the value of a historical perspective on the conflict. Since I believe this today just as strongly as I did then, and since I think the point I tried to make still is not sufficiently evident in U.S. policy toward El Salvador, I repeat it:

"My point is that long before there were charges of outside intervention there was a struggle on behalf of large numbers in El

Salvador for social, political, and economic change. The conflict has been over land, wages, the right to organize, and the issue of political participation. To ignore this long struggle of a people for justice, dignity, and freedom is to misunderstand the nature of the conflict today in El Salvador."

I repeat this point not only for continuity and emphasis, but because it is the basic message the church has to carry into the public discussion on El Salvador. The message is to highlight the need for greater social justice and equity in the internal life of the country. This requires change that is directed to justice, to participation by the people in the life of their nation, and to protection of fundamental freedoms. These elements are a moral requirement and a precondition for stable peace in El Salvador. This was the message of John Paul II in his letter to the Salvadoran bishops in August of last year: "I am perfectly aware that the discords and divisions that still disturb your country and cause new conflicts and violence have their true and deep root in situations of social injustice: a problem that has erupted with force at the political level, but is above all ethical in nature."

Because we have been convinced that the war in El Salvador is fundamentally rooted in questions of social injustice and the persistent denial of fundamental human rights for large sectors of the population, the USCC has always opposed interpretations of the Salvadoran and Central American conflict which place primary emphasis on the superpower or East-West rivalry. Unfortunately this geopolitical conception of the conflict has reappeared with new emphasis in recent days. We believed such an interpretation was mistaken two years ago, and we believe it is mistaken today. We do not deny the existence of an international dimension to the conflict, but we do reject the idea that it is the fundamental issue at stake.

The People's Cry for Peace

In the two years since I testified there have been many changes in El Salvador politically, economically, even legally. One purpose of our recent visit there was to speak with a broad spectrum of people, inside the church and in the society as a whole, to assess the present situation. The dominant note of the country is the desire of the great majority of the people for peace; one way of understanding the truly significant outpouring of people voting in the election last spring [1982] is to see it as a cry for peace and a vote for an end to the war. Yet the war continues: it even has increased in intensity in certain regions. The human rights of the population, especially the poor who are caught and cannot move, are still brutally violated by security forces not under secure governmental control. In addition, the extreme left continues its campaign to damage fundamental services in the country with enormous cost. Long before any outside intervention made the situation worse, the vast majority of Salvadorans found their human dignity, human rights, and life itself assaulted by an unjust system of exploitation and deliberate violence. This tragic failure to control human rights abuses continues. On our trip we heard repeatedly from church leaders of more killings, disappearances, and other brutal violations of human rights.

Every human rights violation of right or left is significant because every person has unique dignity and worth. But the never-ending argument and public debate in the United States about comparisons of human rights abuses seems an insufficient response in light of the brutal and tragic violence which still pervades El Salvador. The principal need of the moment is for fundamental moves in the political order to stop the war and secure social justice.

The three archbishops in our delegation returned from El Salvador convinced that the dominant message we heard can be summarized in three words: dialogue, cease-fire, and negotiations to end the war. Each step is necessary to reverse the pattern of violence in El Salvador. The need for dialogue and reconciliation has been the principal call of the church in El Salvador. On July 15, 1982, all the bishops of El Salvador directed a pastoral message to the country in which they said:

> For this very reason we exhort all the parties involved in the conflict to abandon every obstinate attitude and be open to a dialogue that is sincere, open and true, animated by good will and a spirit of authentic patriotism, placing the unity of the Salvadoran family above individual or group interests. For its part, the church maintains its readiness to work tirelessly within its own proper sphere for peace and for reconciliation among Salvadorans who have been constrained to become enemies to one another.

Only a month later Pope John Paul II's letter to the Salvadoran bishops reiterated the theme of reconciliation and the cessation of violence:

> Such reconciliation must therefore be able to be realized at all levels, above all among brothers bearing arms, motivated by contrary interests and guided by ideologies that sacrifice the fundamental aspirations of the human person. For the one and for the other, an indispensable condition for reconciliation is the cessation of all hostilities and the renunciation of the use of arms, with the sure guarantee that no one will be the object of reprisals or vengeance after having given his or her own adherence to the noble aim of joining efforts and initiatives that may assure the nation renewed vitality and an ordered progress.

Both political dialogue and cease-fire are indispensable steps to the third requirement: serious negotiations among the parties to the conflict, building on the elections of 1982, but going beyond them to ending the state of war and beginning the political and economic reconstruction of the country.

None of these three objectives will be easily achieved. All of them depend primarily on the willingness of Salvadorans to "place the unity of the Salvadoran family above individual or group interest" (Salvadoran Bishops Conference, July 15, 1982). After acknowledging both of these points it is still crucial to recognize that movement toward any of these goals will require commitment to them on behalf of U.S. policy. Both the Salvadoran government and the opposition forces recognized the significance of U.S. policy. Without encouragement from the United States, no dialogue or lasting cease-fire will occur.

The Mistaken Military Approach

Precisely because the influence of U.S. policy is so important, I am profoundly disappointed in the direction I see us taking. Just as the Holy Father was about to embark on a pilgrimage of peace to Central America, raising hopes that he could initiate a break in the cycle of violence, the U.S. call was for an increase in military means and perhaps deeper direct involvement by us in the conflict.

Our delegation returned from El Salvador convinced of the need for a new, substantial, and vigorous commitment by the United States to begin the process of political dialogue rather than rely on the relentless military struggle which consumes thousands of Salvadoran lives each year with no end in sight.

The American bishops have consistently called for a non-military approach to the conflict. For two years we have opposed all military assistance from all sources to any party in El Salvador. We have not been successful; the aid continues from the United States to the Salvadoran government and from other sources to the opposition forces. We believe that U.S. policy faces a crucial choice in El Salvador over the next few weeks, a choice which the Congress can and should influence. On the basis of both previous USCC policy and our recent visit, I submit that the primary imperative of the moment is to stress the political course in El Salvador, not the military option. The United States should exercise the considerable diplomatic influence it has to help terminate the war. The American bishops have entered the public debate on El Salvador numerous times to stress what the United States should not do—send military aid. Today we come before the Congress to recommend a course of action: promote dialogue, insist on a cease-fire, and support a negotiated end to the conflict.

We have never believed that a military solution in El Salvador—victory by either side, which could only mean abject surrender and bitter defeat for a large number of Salvadorans on one side or the other—was in the interest of either El Salvador or the United States. A society divided into victors and vanquished is unlikely to result in either stable peace or justice. We have from the very beginning of the policy debate argued for a creative diplomatic role for the United States. The present direction of our policy, however, is neither creative nor diplomatic.

The United States has two years of extensive investment in a policy of military support for the government of El Salvador; it is not our position that the United States forsake that government. However, we are convinced that other choices exist for the United States than the ones being promoted by the Administration at present. These other choices mean that the United States should talk more about ending the violence and less about prosecuting the war with large increases in military assistance and more advisors.

These other choices are in the political order; they are based on the conviction that the primary issue in El Salvador is the domestic political and economic structure of the country, not the role of the Soviet Union or Cuba in Central America. The other choices must be understood and implemented in concert with key nations like Venezuela, Mexico, or our European allies. The diplomatic option means that the United States should not go it alone in Central America. If the diplomatic option were truly pursued, we recognize some military component may be required. We acknowledge this with regret, but we do not deny it. However, we strongly recommend that any military assistance provided be conditioned on stringent requirements linking it to a pursuit of dialogue and cease-fire.

We hope the Congress will very carefully examine the purposes and evidence supporting any proposal to increase arms to El Salvador. We are deeply concerned that recent U.S. proposals to escalate American military involvement by major increases in military aid and additional advisors will lead us further in the direction of a military rather than diplomatic solution. In fact, such proposals may block creative diplomatic and political measures. Talk of impending "crisis" should not push the Congress into ignoring the longer-term consequences of increased reliance on military rather than diplomatic options. We believe any proposal should be measured by whether it moves the parties toward cease-fire and responsible dialogue called for by the Salvadoran bishops or whether it strengthens the extremists on both the right and left who wish to continue the conflict on the battlefield with enormous human and economic costs. U.S. policy ought to support the forces of moderation in El Salvador in their search for justice, reconciliation, and peace. The United States must use its leadership to enhance the prospects for dialogue, rather than adding more and more weapons to the spiral of violence.

In summary, the USCC believes a major policy review and a significant policy shift are called for on the part of the United States. We should more clearly see the problem in political, not military, terms. We should use our acknowledged influence with the Salvadoran government to define their efforts in primarily political terms. We should signal friendly allies with access to the opposition forces in El Salvador to exert the leverage necessary to bring about a cease-fire and the opening of political dialogue. We should stop the fantasy of believing that one more year of military struggle in an already devastated nation will be in our interest or theirs.

I must speak also of the unique needs of the displaced persons in El Salvador. In many cases their villages have been burned or rendered unsafe by the war. They are not refugees in the technical sense of the U.N. definition and therefore cannot benefit from refugee programs. We urge, however, that the Congress consider favorably their needs and entertain concrete proposals for their relief. This humanitarian activity can surely help us clarify our traditional American concern for the suffering and oppressed.

We continue to be seriously concerned regarding the status of Salvadoran refugees in the United States. One can argue whether some are economic rather than political refugees, but the effect on the human rights of those repatriated to El Salvador is severe. It is our understanding that deportees on arrival in El Salvador are closely questioned by the security forces; their names are checked with lists of actual or alleged security risks. It is our understanding that those whose names appear on such lists, whether rightly or by vindictive denunciation, are in a position of great personal danger. For that reason we continue to urge the Congress of the United States that, if necessary, special legislation be introduced to grant a stay of deportation for such persons until peace is achieved in El Salvador. These refugees come to America, as did our own ancestors, to seek freedom from political fear and from the dehumanizing poverty of a country prostrated by war.

We continue also to press for justice in the cases of the murdered American churchwomen, labor advisors, and Archbishop Romero. We believe that strong representations must continue to be made by our government and that, where needed, authorization for continued technical assistance in discovering the guilty be provided by our government.

U.S. POLICY AND CENTRAL AMERICA

A political approach in El Salvador must be part of a diplomatic strategy for the region of Central America. The danger of the moment is that the full-scale war in El Salvador will coalesce with the threat of war on the Nicaraguan-Honduran border and the explosive internal situation in Guatemala to create a regional war. Because the danger is regional in scope, U.S. diplomacy must be regional in substance. The United States has long treated Central America as a region in its strategic military planning; today it must have a comprehensive diplomatic conception of the region, treating each nation distinctly but treating all nations as systematically related. Two regional problems influence U.S. policy in El Salvador: (1) United States–Nicaragua relations and (2) the situation on the Nicaraguan-Honduran border.

1. *United States–Nicaragua.* The defeat of the brutal and repressive Somoza regime by the Nicaraguan revolution in 1979 acted as a catalyst throughout Central America; since then political opposition increased within El Salvador and Guatemala. Many observers have noted the impact of the Nicaraguan case on U.S. policy toward El Salvador; our posture seems to be not so much directed to the specifics of El Salvador as dominated by the rule "no more Nicaraguas." Relations between the United States and Nicaragua have deteriorated precisely in step with the rise of insurgency in El Salvador.

Nicaragua's importance politically and ecclesiastically made it a central part of our trip. We returned from Nicaragua concerned about some developments within the country. We met not only with people from the church but with labor leaders, journalists, businessmen, and leaders of the revolution. We gained a perception that the Nicaraguan government under the direction of the Sandinistas is steadily expanding its influence and control of crucial areas of societal life.

This development, a concern in itself, is combined with evidence of human rights violations where the state is either responsible or bears responsibility for not restraining others. We cannot agree, for example, with the minister of the interior, who stated to the press shortly before our visit, "Education belongs exclusively to the state." We cannot overlook serious indications of the maltreatment of prisoners and persons suspected of actions hostile to the new regime. Nor can we condone the harsh response of the Nicaraguan government to the efforts and statements of the bishops in behalf of the Miskito Indians. Neither can we understand the extensive censorship restrictions on the press.

Obviously the situation is complex and capable of moving in a positive or negative direction. We cite our experience and identify our concerns publicly because we fervently hope that the drift away from the stated goals of the revolution—social justice, political pluralism, and a mixed economy—can be reversed.

U.S. Policy: A Continuous Provocation

The future direction of the revolution should be decided by Nicaraguans, but the United States remains a significant external force. Our delegation was repeatedly told of how pervasive U.S. influence is, and we were also told—by many who shared our concerns about the internal direction of the revolution—that present U.S. policy is misdirected and counterproductive. U.S. policy over the past two years has not been helpful to the moderate elements in Nicaraguan life. Rather it has served as a continuous provocation which has given a pretext for ever-increasing governmental attempts to control important elements of Nicaraguan life. The bishops of the United States called in November 1981 for a U.S. policy that would engage Nicaragua diplomatically, not isolate it. My recent experience in Nicaragua has convinced me that what we said in 1981 is ever more applicable today.

The consistently hostile public rhetoric of our government toward Nicaragua, the cutoff of bilateral economic aid, and the perception that the United States hinders Nicaraguan access to international sources of aid and credit, as well as U.S. support for a military buildup on the Honduran border and rumors of covert efforts to destabilize the government, all contribute to a state-of-siege mentality and policy in Nicaragua which reinforce misguided policies. U.S. actions do not determine internal Nicaraguan policy, but they exaggerate some of its most troubling aspects. The forces of political moderation in Nicaragua are being choked off and depicted as American ploys. The resolution of the El Salvador question is more difficult because the United States and Nicaragua act as if no common ground exists upon which we could shape a stable, moderate, regional system in Central America. My point is not that Nicaragua is without fault; it is that the United States reinforces Nicaraguan errors when our size, influence, and diplomatic perspective should allow for a more creative policy.

As a beginning of such a policy, the USCC makes two recommendations. We see no useful purpose served by a continuation of the present direction of U.S. policy. First, we repeat our advice of 1981: Either through direct talks or through the good offices of Mexico, Venezuela, or Panama, we urge diplomatic engagement with Nicaragua aimed at a regional political solution. Second, as a specific form of engagement, we urge the restoration of U.S. economic aid to Nicaragua. This aid should be given because the people of Nicaragua need it; and it should be given with a clear and appropriate monitoring of the human rights issues in Nicaragua.

2. *United States–Honduras.* At the very least the change in U.S. policy toward Nicaragua must include clear signs that we will not use exiles to overthrow the Nicaraguan government or to provoke a Nicaraguan-Honduran conflict. Let me state personally that as an American citizen and as a Catholic bishop I find any use of U.S. tax dollars for the purpose of covert destabilization of another government to be unwise, unjustified, and destructive of the very values a democratic nation should support in the world.

While our delegation was convinced that there are specific U.S.-Honduran issues which the United States should address, namely, economic assistance for refugees and economic aid for Honduras itself, the key immediate issue is the potential for war between Nicaragua and Honduras. Currently there is little evidence that the United States is playing a positive role to ensure peace in the region.

Our role in providing a major increase of military aid to Honduras and our suspected role of funding covert activities on the Nicaraguan border are hardly helpful to the promotion of a climate of peace. Such activities are precisely opposed to the creative diplomacy this testimony calls for. The diplomatic option in El Salvador should be joined to a new diplomatic initiative to reduce the danger of a Nicaraguan-Honduran war.

CONCLUSION

I conclude these extended remarks, Mr. Chairman, with a comment on the rationale and motivation of the Catholic Church's continued involvement in the Central American issues. We always desire that our posture as a faith community be properly understood when we speak on public policy. Questions have been raised in recent days by high officials of our government about the motivation, or at least the consequences, of the church's role in the events in Central America. We reject the innuendo suggesting that church policy in Central America serves Marxist interests. On the contrary, Catholic policy and pastoral activity are guided by a clear and consistent teaching based on the Gospels and committed to the defense of the human person.

Certainly the involvement of Pope John Paul II is so clear in its orientation and so beneficial in its impact that it is beyond the need for any defense. The outpouring of faith and human emotion which his visit to Central America this past week [March 1983] has produced is eloquent testimony to the meaning the church has for the people of the region.

We believe the Pope's courageous pastoral presence and his consistent call for dialogue, peace, and reconciliation, his strong defense of human rights, his eloquent appeals for social and economic justice, have created a new moment in Central America. We need to hear his voice clearly. "My word is one of peace, concord, and hope," he said as he arrived:

> An unleashed clamor has reverberated with an urgent ring in my spirit, a clamor that rises from these lands and that calls for peace, an end to war and violent deaths; that implores reconciliation, expelling divisions and hatred; that aspires to justice, long but so far fruitlessly awaited; that wants to be called to greater dignity without renouncing its Christian, religious essence. . . .
>
> Change is possible if we accept the voice of Christ, which calls us to respect and love each man as our brother, if we know how to renounce practices of blind egoism, if we learn to have more solidarity, if we apply with rigor the norms of social justice which the church proclaims, if those responsible for the peoples open the door to an increasing sense of distributive justice in the burdens and duties of the various sectors of society, and if each people can confront its problems in a climate of sincere dialogue, without foreign interference.

We are here today to urge that American policy toward the region respond to this new opportunity with a policy more respectful of human rights, more concerned with issues of basic justice, and more open to political rather than military responses.

As for the church in Central America, I have already described its pastoral witness as heroic. It is true that many complex and wrenching choices have to be made by bishops, priests, and laity each day. But the animating force of those choices is clear—it is the preferential option for the poor, reaffirmed at the Puebla conference, which shapes the life and ministry of the church in Central America. Any hint that the Catholic Church is linked to alien ideologies in its guiding pastoral vision is to be rejected out of hand. Both the Pope's visit and the daily witness of the church in Central America demonstrate beyond a shadow of a doubt that the church has eminently more credibility in the lives of the people of the region than any government, including our own.

Finally, I speak for my brother bishops in the United States. We are aware how visible our position on Central America has been for two years now. We are confident we should be in the midst of the debate about U.S. policy; we have something to say and we do not believe it has been sufficiently heeded. We speak both as bishops of a church with significant human and religious interests in Central America and indeed with personnel working there, and we speak as American citizens who want our image and impact in Central America to be understood in terms of compassion, justice, peace, and freedom. We do not believe our present policy conveys this message. Far from being moved by alien ideologies or wishing to foster their influence, we are moved by the needs of the people of Central America and a desire to make the United States a beacon of hope for the dispossessed of the region.

We are not confused by Marxist ideology or strategy. The Catholic Church knows full well how human liberty and the basic freedoms are suppressed under Marxist regimes even as they are often suppressed by governments of the extreme right.

We are clear about our Christian and our American heritage. Both move us to say that we cannot solve basic human problems of deprivation, poverty, and long-standing injustice with ideological slogans or with military measures. The voice of the church in the United States is a voice for moderation in Central America; we want stable, just, moderate governments. We believe they must be assisted by a sensible, balanced, moderate U.S. policy. We have spoken for such a policy; we will continue to do so. We are confident we act for the good not only of our church but of our nation as well.

10. We Should Talk With Castro

By WAYNE S. SMITH

Focus   The former head of the U.S. interests section in Havana disagrees with the Reagan administration's apparent intention not to negotiate with Cuban president Fidel Castro over the Central American situation. One negotiates with an adversary, explains Wayne S. Smith, "not because he is a fine fellow, but because one expects to gain something in the process." President Reagan is overlooking an opportunity because he fails to understand this fact, says Smith.

The United States has persistent and deep differences with Cuba, but our primary concern should be to diminish Soviet influence in the Caribbean. Smith believes we could progress in this direction "more through gradual engagement than through unrelenting hostility."

Furthermore, the only alternative to a military solution in El Salvador—probably requiring an invasion of that country by U.S. Marines—is negotiation. Smith asserts that "Cuba may not be, as the Administration claims, the principal villain in the piece, but it is to some degree involved in El Salvador and does have influence with the guerrillas." Negotiations leading to elections with broad participation by all parties would, in his view, put an end to the tragic and longstanding social division in El Salvador.

Smith's analysis and recommendations have some merit. In light of Castro's mistrust of the United States, however, and the significant Cuban military involvement in Nicaragua, in Grenada (prior to the 1983 liberation by U.S. forces), and in revolutionary movements elsewhere in the Caribbean and Latin America, there are enormous obstacles to the success of such negotiations. For another perspective on Cuban influence in the region, compare the testimony of ex-Sandinista intelligence officer Miguel Bolaños (selection 25) and the analysis of R. Bruce McColm (selection 4).

Wayne S. Smith was chief of the U.S. interests section in Havana from 1979 until 1982. He is now a senior associate at the Carnegie Endowment for International Peace.

I N JUNE 1983 THE CASTRO REGIME reiterated to a group of visiting American newsmen its willingness to negotiate with Washington and to contribute to peaceful solutions in Central America. In March, Fidel Castro had emphasized to Senator Lowell P. Weicker, Jr. (R-Conn.), that he was prepared to discuss all issues in disagreement between the United States and Cuba.

The Reagan administration dismissed these, as it had dismissed previous overtures, by saying that they "offered nothing new." Clearly negotiations with Castro are not part of the Administration game plan. This is unfortunate. True, Cuban interests often conflict with our own, and the United States has no more reason to feel affection for Fidel Castro than he has to feel it for us. But that is beside the point. One negotiates with an adversary not because he is a fine fellow but because one expects to gain something in the process.

How might negotiations with Cuba benefit this country? First, there are a number of pressing bilateral problems that need to be resolved. To begin with, we want to send back the criminals and other excludables dumped on us during the boatlift from the Cuban port of Mariel in 1980. The Cubans have said that they are willing to discuss the matter. We also want to make certain that there are no more Mariels. We could do this by agreeing on immigration patterns and securing Cuban guarantees to respect them. Then there are our $3 billion in claims resulting from the Cuban seizure of U.S. assets more than twenty years ago. The sum is not enough to balance the budget, but it is worth a round of negotiations.

Important as they are, however, bilateral issues are not our principal concern at this point. Rather, as Cuba's relationship with Moscow is our chief preoccupation, reduction of Soviet influence

Reprinted by permission of the author from the July 1, 1983, edition of the *Los Angeles Times*.

must be one of our primary objectives. The most elementary analysis suggests that we could further this objective more through gradual engagement than through unrelenting hostility. Indeed, the more aggressive our posture toward Cuba, the more solidly fused the Havana-Moscow axis becomes.

An even more immediate U.S. concern flows from the conflict in Central America. The war in El Salvador can be brought to an end only through the military victory of one side or the other, or through a negotiated settlement. It is most unlikely that the side that we back can win militarily—without, that is, the direct support of U.S. troops. Realistically, then, we should be exploring the possibilities for a negotiated solution. Cuba may not be, as the Administration claims, the principal villain in the piece, but it is to some degree involved in El Salvador and does have influence with the guerrillas. The United States should be insisting that Cuba discuss the Salvadoran conflict with us; yet Cuba is offering to talk and the United States is refusing. It makes no sense to complain of Cuban activities in Central America but then refuse to discuss the subject with Cuba.

Why would Cuba be willing to open a discussion and to accommodate our interests in Central America? Essentially because it would be in Cuba's interest to do so. The guerrillas in El Salvador can win, at best, a Pyrrhic victory—one that would almost certainly provoke full-scale U.S. intervention. Meanwhile, Castro understands that as the military situation deteriorates the United States, in its frustration, will probably blame it all on him and may take direct military action against Cuba and its ally, Nicaragua.

Rather than accepting such risks and uncertainties, the Cubans, and apparently the Salvadoran guerrillas themselves, would rather settle for half a loaf. Instead of insisting on full power through the barrel of a rifle, the guerrillas, encouraged by Cuba, are ready to sit down at the negotiating table. They will not agree to participate in the December elections [later rescheduled for March 1984] or in any other balloting process unless it is preceded by broad negotiations that are aimed at redressing the conditions that brought about the civil war in the first place. Dealing with these grievances, many of which are deep-seated, would not be easy, especially as a transitional government might be required before elections could be held. The guerrillas, however, are ready to begin discussions and, according to their representatives, to try their luck in the elections that could eventually result.

As one guerrilla representative commented to me recently: "Even if we did not win a plurality, we would make a good showing and have a significant bloc in the assembly. We would be a legitimate force, and the way would be open to the future. That would be enough."

A solution satisfactory to all sides, then, is not unattainable. Unfortunately, neither the Reagan administration nor the Salvadoran government seems inclined to enter the kind of negotiations or to make the kind of compromises that might achieve it. And the Administration remains adamantly opposed to the idea of involving the Cubans in the peace process. This is unrealistic. Clearly any political arrangement to end the civil war in El Salvador would have a better chance of working if it had Cuban support. We simply deceive ourselves if we fail to recognize that fact.

11. This Time We Know What's Happening

By JEANE J. KIRKPATRICK

Focus
"We *know* by now what the Sandinista government of Nicaragua is and what it intends—in El Salvador, Honduras, Costa Rica. We *know* who the guerrillas in El Salvador are, where they get their arms, what plans they have, who their friends are." And such knowledge carries with it grave responsibilities, argues Ambassador Kirkpatrick, U.S. representative to the United Nations.

In her view, there is a definite plan to create a Communist Central America. This plan is no secret: the public words and actions of the Sandinistas in Nicaragua and captured documents of the FMLN rebels in El Salvador confirm it all too clearly, she says.

Some critics have opposed further U.S. involvement in Central America as likely to lead to "another Vietnam." Kirkpatrick replies that our experience in Southeast Asia has not turned us into isolationists. Had we known during that war what we now know about the true nature of the Vietcong, perhaps we could better have resisted the criticism that made an imperfect democratic regime appear less desirable than the takeover of the country by Communist revolutionaries. This experience carries with it some lessons about how we should respond to threats in the Caribbean Basin.

In addition, Central America and the Caribbean, she says, have an intrinsic importance to the United

States, both because of their proximity and because of the strategic importance of the Panama Canal and nearby shipping lanes to the Western alliance.

For a different view of the military significance of the region, see Abraham Lowenthal (selection 5). Miguel Bolaños (selection 25) supports Kirkpatrick's contention that there are plans for a Marxist Central America. Guillermo Ungo, a Salvadoran rebel leader (selection 15), and Tomás Borge, a member of the Sandinista ruling directorate (selection 24), deny the existence of such plans.

Jeane J. Kirkpatrick is the U.S. permanent representative to the United Nations. She previously was a professor at Georgetown University and a resident scholar at the American Enterprise Institute.

THE WHOLE SCENARIO sounds like a grade-B movie from the 1950s, but that, alas, does not mean it is untrue. It's almost unbearably unfashionable to say so, but there is a plan to create a Communist Central America which, if successful, will have momentous consequences for our security and that of our European allies, and for the unfortunate people of Central America.

Even though a well-organized lobby works indefatigably to confuse the moral, political, and intellectual questions involved in U.S. policy toward Central America, there is growing clarity about the issues and the stakes. We *know* by now what the Sandinista government of Nicaragua is and what it intends—in El Salvador, Honduras, Costa Rica. We *know* who the guerrillas in El Salvador are, where they get their arms, what plans they have, who their friends are.

As recently as July 1979 it was possible for American policymakers of optimistic disposition to suppose that, if they acted wisely and generously, Nicaragua would emerge from its bloody civil war with an independent, pluralist, socialist government. To this end the United States rushed $24.6 million in emergency food, medical, and reconstruction assistance to the new Sandinista-led Nicaraguan government, provided $117 million in direct economic assistance during the subsequent eighteen months, and helped secure $262 million from multilateral lending institutions. But before the Carter administration left office in January 1981, the decision was made that Nicaragua—its pattern of internal repression and external aggression already clear—no longer met U.S. requirements for assistance.

Everyone who cares to know now understands that the government of Nicaragua has imposed a new dictatorship; that it has refused to hold the elections it promised and has attacked the

Reprinted by permission of the author from the July 1983 issue of *Reader's Digest* (original © 1983 by the Washington Post Company).

opposition; that it has seized control of all media except a lone newspaper that it subjects to heavy prior censorship; that it denied priests of the Roman Catholic Church the right to say Mass on television during Holy Week; that it insulted the Pope during his visit in March [1983], when the Mass he celebrated was interrupted by Sandinista hecklers; that it has stifled the private sector and independent trade unions; that it has driven the Miskito Indians out of their homelands—burning their villages, destroying their crops, forcing them into exile or into internment camps far from home.

Persons interested in such questions understand, too, that Nicaragua's rulers have introduced into the country many thousands of Cuban teachers, trainers, and supervisors, including at least 2,000 military advisors. The Sandinista rulers are hardly ambiguous about who their friends are and what convictions motivate them. "We guide ourselves by the scientific doctrines of the Revolution, by Marxism-Leninism," Minister of Defense Humberto Ortega explained to his army. "Marxism-Leninism is a fundamental part of the Sandinista ideology," said junta member Victor Tirado López. And another member of the junta announced that, if asked, his government would consider installing Soviet nuclear missiles in Nicaragua.

Nicaragua's leaders are done with dissembling. They are proud of their ideology; proud of their monopoly of power; proud of their huge new military force (which has no peer in the region); proud of their role in Central America's guerrilla war; proud of their friends, including Libya, the Palestine Liberation Organization (PLO), and Cuba, their constant companion.

Clarity in El Salvador

The character of El Salvador's guerrilla struggle is no more ambiguous than that of Nicaragua's government. Since the elections of March 1982—in which so many brave Salvadoran citizens risked death to vote for the government—nobody even pretends that the Soviet-supported guerrilla movement, the FMLN (Farabundo Martí National Liberation Front), enjoys popular support, or is really just "a bunch of agrarian reformers" who, if victorious, would usher in a more perfect democracy.

The fictions with which Communist insurgents have conventionally clothed their conquest of power are not available to the partisans of the FMLN. Largely abandoned, too, is the pretense that the FMLN is an indigenous movement without significant foreign support. Too many truckloads, planeloads, boatloads of arms from Cuba, Nicaragua, Libya, and the Eastern bloc have been found, too many documents captured, too many pictures taken, too many bold announcements made from Managua. The FMLN is a professional guerrilla operation directed from command and control centers in Nicaragua, armed with Soviet-bloc weapons, and bent on establishing in El Salvador the kind of one-party dictatorship linked to the Soviet Union that exists in Nicaragua.

There has, moreover, been so much discussion among these Communist insurgents of "revolution without frontiers," of "liberating and unifying" Central America, so many threats to Honduras, so much bullying of Costa Rica and guerrilla activity in Guatemala, that it is hardly possible to doubt the regional character of Soviet/Cuban/Nicaraguan goals.

Yet to be fully faced, however, is the relevance of these small, poor nations of the Central American isthmus to the United States, and the importance of Caribbean sea lanes to the Western alliance. Nor is the extent of the Soviet investment—military, economic, cultural—in this hemisphere fully appreciated.

Money: Key to Survival

Very reluctantly, however, most serious observers have come to acknowledge that, yes, the area's location gives it a certain irreducible relevance to our national interest. There is also a growing, if grudging, acknowledgment that money—in the form of economic and military assistance—is quite probably the key to the viability of the region's non-Communist governments. Recently two top aides of previous Democratic administrations wrote in the *New York Times Magazine* that "the area is of clear strategic and political importance to the United States" so that "to stop American aid would be to deliver—yes, deliver—El Salvador into the hands of a guerrilla movement that is ... allied with America's adversaries and capable itself of the greatest brutality," and advised that "abandonment is an option Democrats should reject."

Yet if few in or out of Congress have advocated outright abandonment, many have argued for aid on such niggardly terms that the effect is almost sure to be the same.

It is often suggested that a "Vietnam syndrome" explains the extraordinary reluctance of America's political class to provide urgently needed assistance to endangered friendly governments in an area of clear national interest. But what does that mean? Obviously, the Vietnam experience did not make us isolationist. The U.S. government pursues, with the full consent of Congress, a foreign policy that involves us in the affairs of six continents. We station troops in remote places, provide billions of dollars in economic and military assistance to governments of all sorts in Asia, Africa, and the Middle East.

Neither the moral nor the military misgivings expressed about Central America are evident with regard to these other regions. Nobody objects when we rush weapons to Thailand or trainers to Lebanon. Nobody talks about human rights when there is murder and mayhem in Zimbabwe. Why?

Why is Congress so much more reluctant to assist an imperfect democratic government clearly important to our national interest than to help much less perfect governments in more remote regions?

What is it that Central America has in common with Vietnam that so repels liberals? Is it the fact that, in both cases, well-financed Communist guerrilla movements have simultaneously targeted the existing governments and what is generally called "world public opinion"? Is it because lobbies of the left have managed to make the anti-Communist side seem unfashionable?

God knows, there are parallels enough. In both cases, well-orchestrated international campaigns have focused mercilessly on the political and moral failings of the government. In El Salvador, as in Vietnam, the introduction of elections and reforms, the reduction of human rights abuses and corruption, have proved not to have much effect on the drumbeat of criticism. In El Salvador, as in Vietnam, Congress calls the U.S. commitment into doubt, undermining the confidence of vulnerable allies in our reliability and their viability. And as with Vietnam, doubt is continuously voiced about whether the government of El Salvador is morally worthy of American approval or even of survival.

But there are crucial differences too, differences that involve what we know and when we knew it. We know *now* who El Salvador's FMLN is, and we know now who the Vietcong were (although we didn't know then). We know how the Vietcong came down from the north, how they were supplied, how Western public opinion was manipulated.

We know, too, about human rights under the Communists in Vietnam, about the labor camps and mass deportations. We know that the Vietcong did not establish a broad-based government or a socialist democracy. We know what happened—and is still happening—in Cambodia. We do not much enjoy thinking about these matters, but we know about them, just as surely as we know the character and the stakes of the contest in Central America.

The crucial difference between Vietnam and Central America is not the Pacific Ocean, although that is important. The crucial difference is that the Congress that cut off aid to Vietnam could say that it did not know what would follow.

Today's Congress cannot.

12. Blind Eye on Central America

By GEORGE F. WILL

Focus Since the formal codification of détente between the Soviet Union and the United States in 1973, says George Will, Moscow has been involved in a long list of nefarious schemes around the world, including an attempt on the life of the Pope, a brutal invasion of Afghanistan, the exporting of revolution to many other states, and support for international terrorism. Yet people blame President Reagan for a return to the Cold War because he "gave a speech referring to the Soviet Union as an evil empire," says Will.

The Kremlin has been supplying Cuba with arms and economic assistance totaling $4 billion a year. Soviet military assistance to Cuba alone is twenty times more than the military assistance the United States gives to all of Latin America. Cuban, Soviet, Bulgarian, and East German advisors are spread over Latin America. But what seems to worry the U.S. Congress the most, notes Will, is the presence of "fifty-five U.S. trainers in El Salvador."

Both Congress and leaders of American opinion must wake up to the serious threat in Central America, a threat that is "close, clear, and indisputably Communist." Failure to oppose the enemies of freedom who talk of power-sharing as a means to full power, says Will, can lead only to a

Communist Central America in which bitter foes of the United States are "just a wade across the Río Grande."

George F. Will is a syndicated columnist and a television public-affairs panelist. His most recent book is *Statecraft as Soulcraft.*

TO BEGIN, a two-question quiz.

First question. Since détente was codified at the Nixon-Brezhnev summit in 1973, the Soviet Union has forced a nuclear alert by threatening to intervene with troops in the October 1973 war in the Middle East (a war incited and financed by the Soviet Union); has organized and financed the destruction of the Paris accords and a U.S. ally; has intervened with Cubans and others in Angola, Ethiopia, Yemen, Cambodia, Nicaragua, and El Salvador; has invaded Afghanistan; has orchestrated the crushing of Poland; has made a mockery of the Helsinki agreements; has repeatedly violated the informally agreed-to threshold test-ban treaty (although we even changed the way we measure violations, in an effort to avoid the need to make protests that would dampen détente); has tried to murder the Pope; is violating the terms of SALT II (an amazing feat, considering that SALT II is a tissue of loopholes and ambiguities); is funding and organizing terrorism worldwide; and is continuing an arms buildup unambiguously designed for political intimidation and military aggression. The first quiz question is: Why is there a "return to the Cold War"?

Answer: President Reagan gave a speech referring to the Soviet Union as an evil empire.

Second question. The Soviet Union has an army brigade (2,600-3,000 men), 2,500 military advisors (increased 500 last year), and 6,000-8,000 civilian advisors in Cuba. It gave Cuba 66,000 metric tons of military supplies in 1981, 68,000 in 1982 (worth $1 billion). Moscow's annual economic aid to Cuba is $4 billion (more than one-quarter of Cuba's GNP). Cuba has 200 MiGs, including two squadrons of MiG-23 Floggers, at least 650 tanks, at least 90 helicopters, including Mi-24 attack helicopters, a Koni-class frigate, two Foxtrot attack submarines, at least 50 torpedo attack boats, two amphibious assault ships. A Grenada minister says Cuba will use Grenada's new airport when supplying Cubans in Africa. Cuba, with one-seventh of Mexico's population, has military forces twice the size of Mexico's. The Soviet Union is giving twenty times more military assistance to Cuba than the United States is giving to all of Latin America. In the newest Soviet satellite, Nicaragua, 39 per cent of all males over eighteen are in uniform, and the regime intends to build a 250,000-person armed force, so one in ten Nicaraguans will soon be in the military or militia. (All of Honduras's security forces total 20,000. El Salvador's total 32,000.) Nicaragua's regime has built thirty-six new military bases and garrisons (the previous regime had thirteen). Nicaraguan pilots and mechanics are being trained in Bulgaria. The regime has received, so far, 50 Soviet tanks, 1,000 East German trucks, 100 anti-aircraft guns, Soviet 152-millimeter howitzers with a range of seventeen miles. Cuba has 4,000 to 5,000 civilian advisors in Nicaragua, plus 2,000 military and security advisors. There also are East Germans, Bulgarians, North Koreans, Soviets, and members of the PLO. The second quiz question is: About what in Central America does Congress seem most worried?

Answer: Fifty-five U.S. trainers in El Salvador.

Events in Central America are spinning rapidly toward a decisive moment in U.S. history. None of the fictions that were used to rationalize acceptance of defeat in Vietnam can be used regarding Central America. The threat there is close, clear, and indisputably Communist. There the United States will show—will learn—whether it is any longer capable of asserting the will a great power requires, or whether the slide into paralysis is irreversible.

Governments such as Costa Rica's and Panama's are listening as congressional complaints mount. The complaints are against U.S. assistance to armed opponents of Nicaragua's Stalinists, and about even minimal aid for the democratically elected government of El Salvador that is under attack from forces that are extensions, through Nicaragua and Cuba, of the Soviet Union.

The conjunction of these complaints can mean, in effect, the extension of the Brezhnev doctrine in this hemisphere. That is, Communist attacks on a regime leech away the regime's legitimacy, and produce pressures for negotiations aimed at "power-sharing" with Stalinists who do not believe in sharing power. But a Communist regime, however freshly planted and dependent on foreign totalitarians, as in Nicaragua, must be treated as legitimate and irreversible.

There is a war raging, and if all the substantial, determined military assistance is one-way, there can be but one result. The result will be a Communist Central America, and an Iran just a wade across the Río Grande.

PART TWO

The Struggle in El Salvador

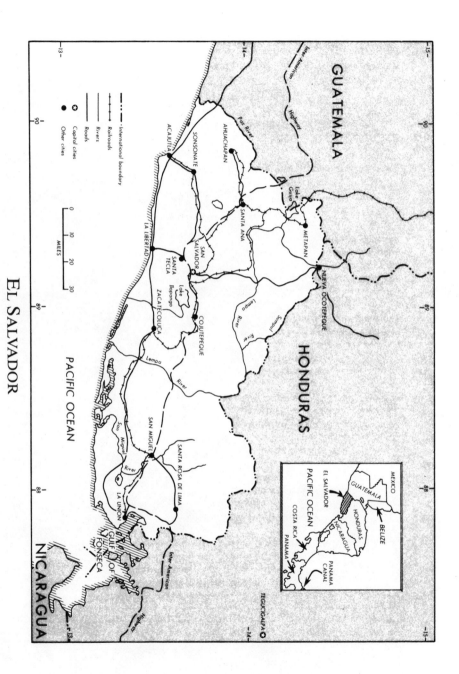

El Salvador Chronology

1932	Marxist-inspired uprising by peasants and Indians quelled by General Maximiliano Hernández Martínez. Approximately 20,000 peasants massacred in revolt against landed elite. Martínez continues repressive rule for over a decade. Military regimes follow until 1979.
1969	"Soccer War" over border tensions with Honduras. Honduran president Colonel Fidel Sánchez Hernández expels 300,000 illegal Salvadoran immigrants.
1972	Christian Democrat José Napoleón Duarte wins plurality in presidential election. Legislature, however, acting within constitution chooses Colonel Arturo Armando Molina as president. Duarte charges fraud, is arrested and exiled.
1979	Government of General Carlos Humberto Romero overthrown by young military officers in response to decade of rising demands for reform and escalating civil war.
1980	Land reform begun; banks nationalized.
	Archbishop Oscar Arnulfo Romero assassinated while saying Mass, by unknown gunmen.
	Revolutionary Democratic Front (FDR), a rebel political arm, formed. Guerrilla umbrella organization, Farabundo Martí National Liberation Front (FMLN), created with help of Fidel Castro. Three strikes called by rebels in summer fail.
	José Napoleón Duarte made president of four-man military-civilian junta directing government.
	Four American churchwomen in El Salvador murdered; in response, President Carter suspends economic aid to government.

1981 President Carter lifts arms embargo begun four years earlier.

Rebel forces launch "final offensive" to present U.S. president-elect Reagan with *fait accompli*; fails through lack of popular support.

U.S. Congress requires semi-annual certification of progress in human rights in El Salvador as condition for military aid.

1982 Elections held under Duarte for Constituent Assembly. Large voter turnout despite boycott, threats, and violence by rebels. Alvaro Magaña named provisional president; is first elected civilian head of government in fifty years.

13. A Culture of Violence

By JOHN KURZWEIL

Focus
According to John Kurzweil, the Salvadorans have only three choices: (1) to return to the old repressive military government, (2) to help the rebels install a Marxist dictatorship, or (3) to give elections and the moderate forces on both sides a chance.

To capitulate to terrorists of the right or the left would be to cave in to sheer power. Even worse, "it would be to carry on, newly ratified, the ideas of the past which disallow peace but are tailor-made for rationalizing war."

Kurzweil emphasizes the moral and political complexity of the Salvadoran conflict, in which all sides proclaim humanitarian goals. There are democratic and moderate elements both among the guerrillas and in the government. Among journalists and other observers, an all-too-typical response is despair. To react in this way, says the author, is to acquiesce in the hopelessness that makes people on both sides of the conflict embrace force as the only solution.

Kurzweil believes there is hope. The junta formed after the 1979 coup and the subsequently elected government have opened at least the possibility of a way out of the stalemate, he says. The "massive land-reform programs, bank nationalizations, and coffee-industry takeovers—projects ideal for making enemies of the wealthiest, most uncompromisingly anti-Communist elements in society" show that the government is no longer merely playing violent politics as usual. Reforms are going on, and the only constructive approach is to encourage them.

This article first appeared in March 1982; it was written during the Duarte presidency.

Robert E. White, U.S. ambassador to El Salvador under President Carter, presents a different analysis of the causes of the Salvadoran conflict (selection 14), and Shirley Christian (selections 16 and 17) describes the difficult divisions in the Salvadoran military and among the guerrillas that democratic elements on both sides face.

John Kurzweil was formerly a contributing editor of the *National Catholic Register* and the editor of *Policy Digest*.

AT THE BEGINNING OF Book III of *War and Peace,* Tolstoy describes Napoleon's invasion of Russia in 1812 as "an event ... counter to human reason and all human nature." What followed was "such an innumerable quantity of crimes, frauds, treacheries, robberies, forgeries, issues of counterfeit money, depredations, incendiarisms, and murders, as are not recorded in the annals of all the courts of justice in the world, but which, at the time, the men who were committing them did not regard as crimes." Tolstoy devoted the rest of that chapter and, for that matter, *War and Peace* in its entirety to answering the question why so many civilized men simultaneously took up so terrible a work of destruction. Indeed, the question should be asked about any war, particularly by peace-loving men *before* a conflagration actually begins.

The war raging in El Salvador is at least as mystifying as the invasion of Russia in its sheer unrelatedness to the humanitarian goals proclaimed by all involved. The left, filled with indignation over what they consider the "immoral" distribution of El Salvador's wealth and power, conclude that force alone will make the rich share, and so they fight. That such prescriptions as the "expropriation without right to indemnization [*sic*] of all properties in the hands of the oligarchy," their "subsequent redistribution as collective, communal, or state properties," and "management of the national economy on the basis of a system of national planning" embracing "all branches, sectors, and regions"—all demanded by El Salvador's guerrillas—have nowhere led to justice, morality, or peace can be confirmed by asking, among others, the nearest Pole. So why do the guerrillas continue to fight for an all-embracing socialism? It is not because the arguments for it have been irresistibly articulated. Rather, it is because the alternatives, freedom and democracy, have been defended so poorly, when they've been defended at all.

Reprinted by permission from the March 19, 1982, issue of *National Review* (© 1982 by National Review, Incorporated).

An Associated Press report from San Salvador dated January 25, 1932, read:

> The flower of Salvadoran aristocracy, heavily armed, roamed the streets of this capital city tonight to aid their government in stamping out the last vestiges of "Communist insurrection."
>
> On the suggestion of a prominent banker, Rodolfo Duke, adult citizens were equipped with rifles and revolvers and received carte blanche to shoot any Communist on sight. More than three hundred sons of the first families, both foreign and native, also were armed and turned loose to snare any radicals still at large.

The occasion for this nocturnal adventure was an uprising, primarily involving the country's Indian population, during the preceding four days or so led by the founder of the Salvadoran Communist Party, Farabundo Martí. Though Martí's Communists managed a fair show of carnage and terror around the countryside and even captured a few towns briefly, the revolt was thoroughly crushed in less than a week. Martí and a large number of his followers were executed.

First Free Election: 1931

The slaughter ended a decisive period in El Salvador's history which had begun optimistically only one year earlier. In January 1931, a liberal (in the nineteenth-century sense of the word) member of a wealthy Salvadoran family named Arturo Araujo was elected president in the nation's first free election. He had campaigned on a platform of education, better transportation and jobs for ordinary Salvadorans, and industrialization for the nation as a whole. Educated at Oxford, Araujo had seen the way in which the Industrial Revolution had promoted class fluidity and mass prosperity in England, and he wanted the same thing for his own country, then even more thoroughly agricultural than now. Using family money, he built El Salvador's first railroad and toured the land on it, campaigning along the way.

It must have made an interesting spectacle, Araujo's train chugging into town, probably festooned with banners and flags, and the candidate himself puffing away before crowds of illiterate Indians and peasants about competition and the rewards of hard work. It was regarded as somewhat less than edifying, however, by his own class of educated, well-off Salvadorans, who must have thought Araujo incredibly naïve. The poor, everyone knew, were capable of eating and of doing a little unskilled work, which was good because a certain amount of that had to be done. But that was it. Nothing but trouble could come from politicians' stirring the passions of the throngs with impossible dreams.

After he took office, Araujo legalized the Communist Party, and Farabundo Martí began trying to organize his revolution. On December 3, amid predictions that the Communists were about to overthrow the dreamer and seize power, the defense minister, Maximiliano Hernández Martínez, led a successful coup against the president and, with the financial backing of wealthy Salvadorans, took over the government. The United States and neighboring Central American countries, however, refused to recognize the new regime because it had taken power by force. "In this situation," the *New York Times* reported, "the Red elements felt encouraged to make a drive for power." Thus, instead of preempting the revolt, Hernández Martínez may have brought it on.

Martí may have been influenced by the anti-Araujo scare-talk into overestimating his strength. And Hernández Martínez himself, nearly as soon as the revolt began, started soft-pedaling the Red Menace which had loomed so large only two months earlier, before the coup.

"There are no revolutionary movements in El Salvador," Hernández Martínez's junta announced on January 25, 1932 (the same day the "flower of Salvadoran aristocracy" sallied forth to shoot Communists on sight). "What happened was that Communist groups in certain towns of the republic promoted disturbances which the government has energetically repressed. The capital city is undisturbed. The government is unanimously backed by all Salvadorans."

The following February, the *Panama Star and Herald* took up the theme in an editorial that described Martí's rebels as possessing too little fidelity or philosophy to claim membership in any party, and added that, had these "revolutionaries" turned up in Russia a few years earlier, Lenin would probably have had them "shot as thieves." If such opinions as these had turned up in print a few months earlier, democracy might have survived in El Salvador.

From the perspective of Hernández Martínez and his supporters, the real danger had never been from the masses' will to
revolt—that, they thought, was in any case unavoidable, like hurricanes or crop failures—but from what they considered Araujo's
naïveté and unwillingness to meet the rebels' challenge effectively:
which meant, of course, with bullets. Now that Araujo was out, the
real danger was past. As the present war in El Salvador shows,
however, it was Hernández Martínez, not Araujo, who was naïve.

What Araujo saw was the potential of the poor to learn and grow
and become productive. His enemies saw only a transparent plot to
take their land and dissipate the nation's wealth in a frenzy of
redistribution that would bring chaos and ruin to El Salvador. In
effect, the Hernández Martínez coup ratified the left's view of the
human predicament. With the overthrow of democracy, the new
government registered its tacit agreement with the revolutionaries
that the only way the poor could improve their lot was to take
wealth from the rich. And for the rich to retain what they had, the
poor would have to be kept poor. The distribution of political
power, not the production of wealth, was the key, and that distribution, both sides also now agreed, would be determined first and
foremost by brute force. Whatever silly notions about law or
authority or majority rule the people might have picked up from
Araujo, power was what mattered. The view is tailor-made to
justify and encourage violence, and that is exactly what it has done.

Sources of Social Friction

Over the years since Araujo's ouster, as the officer corps became
increasingly corrupt through the complex of political machinations, cliques, and bribery that replaced merit as the road to ad-
vancement, wealthy Salvadorans cooperated to protect their personal monopolies in land and industry by controlling the avenues
to wealth. Social, economic, and political distinctions based on
ancestry, education, nationality, or some other irrelevant characteristic, usually beyond the individual's control, provided endless
sources of friction. The present leader of the Communist Party in
El Salvador is a man named Shafik Handal, of Palestinian ancestry.
Arabs, who make up a small minority of the country's population,
have traditionally been excluded, along with most of the rest of the

people, from opportunities to improve their economic circumstances.

It should come as no surprise, therefore, that large numbers of people, reasoning that the sole road to prosperity is to take and keep it from someone else (and who has taught them otherwise?), now make war to accomplish that very thing. Handal is the man who personally arranged the import, through Cuba, of the Soviet-bloc weapons that have transformed a sporadic insurgency into a full-fledged civil war.

The 1972 Election Fraud

Over the years, the left and its opponents in the government—military men taught to govern in the Hernández Martínez tradition—have served to justify each other's ideas and violent methods. In 1972, for instance, Christian Democrat José Napoleón Duarte was elected president, beating the candidate of the National Conciliation Party (PCN), the political arm of El Salvador's military. The PCN had been ruling the country for nearly forty years at the time and was disinclined to relinquish power simply because of some unfavorable ballot totals. Duarte was picked up, beaten by police, and forced to flee the country. The presidency was then given instead to yet another reliable military man.

Each such "lesson" helps El Salvador's extreme, anti-democratic left convince more of its countrymen that war is the only answer. Each subsequent terrorist attack carried out by the left then convinces other Salvadorans that violence and fear alone will suffice to preserve order in the country. The guiding principle is thus passed to each succeeding generation that one's enemies are irrational brutes who must be done unto before they do.

"Some elements in the security forces," said Bishop Pedro Aparicio of San Vicente in an interview, "have become enraged at seeing the bodies of their mothers and sisters raped and mutilated just because they are their relatives. They have found the bodies of their younger teen-age brothers mutilated with the inscription on their chests: Traitor to the FPL [Popular Liberation Forces]. When they confront the guerrillas they are like wild stallions. They take matters into their own hands without authority."

1979: The 'Young Military' Coup

In 1979, with terrorist violence spreading out of control and even its staunchest allies abandoning the PCN, a group of young army officers ended the party's forty-five-year rule by overthrowing the presidency of the universally recognized incompetent Carlos Humberto Romero. The coup brought to power a junta composed of and backed by divergent factions, including moderate democrats, socialists, and Marxists of various shadings. In addition, a large number of powerful military men who had served under Romero survived the coup and stayed on.

The far left elements quit the government within a few months and, for the most part, joined or threw their support to the guerrillas who had been fighting since 1972 to establish a Marxist-Leninist regime. After a number of regroupings, a new governing coalition was formed, composed of ex-Romero officers interested in their own security and Christian Democrats who wanted elections and a mixed bag of economic reforms, including, in some cases, greater state control, and, in others, more freedom. Duarte, now back from exile, was made president.

Marxists, it should be recalled, really believe their own propaganda. When the new junta did not immediately begin dismantling Salvadoran society and rebuilding it on the Soviet and Cuban models, the only ideologically admissible explanation for the left was that the government was dominated either by the same old "oligarchs" or by some new manifestation of fascist repression. Both explanations have been used to reach the same conclusion: the junta is an inhuman, bloodthirsty beast which must be brought down and crushed before any hope of progress and justice is possible. This message is broadcast to American audiences through such left mouthpieces as T. D. Allman, writing in *Harper's* magazine.

"Anything they could find in their huts or fields," Allman reports (from "behind guerrilla lines, somewhere in El Salvador"), "or take from the forest that might be of use, the *campesinos* [peasants] had gathered together and attempted to interpose between themselves and the jeeps and armored cars of the soldiers who came, periodically, like blight on the coffee harvest or typhoons from the Pacific, to torture their lives at moments they could not predict, and for reasons of which they had no understanding."

During the Vietnam era, antiwar activists chided the U.S. military for projecting a "dehumanized" image of the Vietcong that blunted the American people's normally sympathetic reactions to the plight of the downtrodden rising in revolt. But Allman goes that one better. Not satisfied with obscuring the humanity of Duarte and the Salvadoran army, he transforms them into a blind, mindless force for evil. One doesn't *understand* or reason with the coffee blight or the typhoon, any more than one reasons with Christian Democrats. Suddenly, we're back on familiar ground: there is no solution but war. But if El Salvador's Marxists are barred by their ideology from seeing anything good in El Salvador's government, surely that is *their* problem. The problems of the Salvadoran people, meanwhile, are a good deal more complex than that. If thoughtful Americans wish to understand them, they'll require better information than is found in Allman's superficial melodrama, entitled "Rising to Rebellion."

In Support of Reform

To begin with, the Salvadoran tradition of political violence must be overcome, a job that won't be done by American journalists' writing about it as if it were an indigenous, permanent characteristic of the people. Nor will it be ended merely by overwhelming Castro's guns with more and better American guns. The situation might be helped, though, by seeking out and supporting those individuals and factions within El Salvador that favor elections and a free society.

No one, except the guerrillas, denies there are some such good people in the government—Duarte himself for one—and in the military, but genuine Salvadoran democrats are usually written off as too few and too weak to matter. The spirit of Hubert Humphrey would not recognize his liberal brethren today, so burdened with doubt and hopelessness have they become. Efforts toward reform *are* going forward in El Salvador, alongside the revolutionary and reactionary violence. These efforts should be supported if for no other reason than that to do otherwise is to become like the killers in their despair.

"We're not changing a system that goes back fifty years, but one that goes back five hundred years," said Salvadoran minister of education Carlos Aquilino Duarte (no relation to the [former] president). Duarte's nationally broadcast speech spelled out his ministry's plans for reforming the country's educational system. The changes to come in education, he said, would be integrated with those taking place throughout El Salvador, including the land-reform program and the scheduling of elections.

"As things have been done till now," he said, "if a lightbulb burns out in a school in San Miguel, that school's principal must request that the maintenance department of the Ministry of Education in San Salvador purchase a lightbulb and go to the school to change it. No more!"

The minister decried the inefficiency which used the country's schoolrooms at 20 per cent of capacity. (The educational TV channel that carried his speech was operating at only 30 per cent of its potential.) Duarte criticized the system's "pyramidal, centralized structure" which "kept teachers from developing," and outlined a program of "basic education for all adults and youth" that was of crucial importance, he said, because "a democracy is impossible with one and a half million illiterates—education will allow them to make intelligent choices in a democratic society."

Practicing Democracy

A good deal of rhetorical energy has been expended to deflate the hope that the junta's talk of democracy is more than window dressing. "Democracy, El Salvador style," Juan Vásquez wrote in the *Los Angeles Times,* "is a joke." But must it always be so? The Salvadoran education ministry has been sponsoring local elections of teacher representatives to a new national body which will advise the ministry on education policy. The country has been divided into four hundred school districts in which local teachers select three nominees for the national delegation. All adults then vote to elect their district's delegate.

"We wish to acquaint people with the way elections work, or fail to work, if that is the case," said José Interiano, an assistant to the education minister. "If irregularities occur, and some have, the election is done over." Why aren't such stories written up in the American press? Why are our journalists in love with gloom and despair?

The editorial blurb introducing Christopher Dickey's *Playboy* piece on El Salvador, "Death as a Way of Life," represents the triumph of a confidence game unusually transparent even for this age of credulity. "The reporter went down to El Salvador," it reads, "with the most absurd notion—he thought there would be *reasons* for all the killing." Though some editor at *Playboy,* and to a considerable extent Dickey himself, has succumbed to the "all life is absurdity" syndrome, the reporter actually did find the reason, which he duly relates:

"A goal of the terrorism all along had been to make the people cry out, *'¡Basta ya!'*—Enough—bring us peace, no matter what you have to do." The first, and ultimately the only, demand of the terrorists is that power replace authority as the legitimizing characteristic of government. Elections, the very symbol of government by invested authority, have no place. Now, the remarkable thing is that while the Salvadoran people have yet to cry, "Enough!" American liberals have been yelling *"¡Basta ya!"* to the terrorists in droves, declaring elections "unworkable" and democracy "a joke" at every opportunity. There are approximately five thousand leftist guerrillas operating in El Salvador. Suppose, to give a generous estimate, there are about the same number in the anti-Communist death squads. These ten thousand killers, then, amount to less than two-tenths of 1 per cent of the population. For every Salvadoran they've killed, by the most gruesome estimates, 275 remain alive. Shouldn't these more than five and a half million people be given the opportunity to repudiate terrorism by voting for a government of their own choice? Haven't enough died for the survivors to have earned the right to conduct free elections?

But the elections will be rigged, it is said, candidates shot, and the people deprived of opportunities to hear all sides. And for the first 132 years of our republic, half the citizens of the United States were denied the vote. Fourteen per cent were slaves until 1863, and after the Civil War the new freemen stood a good chance of being shot or hung if they tried to vote, much less run for office. To this day, several areas of the country have yet to turn in entirely valid ballot returns. Should we cancel all elections every time some such abuses turn up? The answer to electoral tampering, as to terrorism and blackmail, is to renounce and eliminate it, not to capitulate. It's a con game. The killers will never allow elections without a violent challenge, but there *are* ways to defeat them.

Under PCN [the military political party] governments, an intense animosity—at times resembling a state of war—developed between Salvadoran educators and the military government, a situation the left exploited to gain control of the nation's major teachers' union. Since the 1979 coup, however, government-educator relations have improved markedly, to the point where last summer [1981] a previously unthinkable meeting of university and government officials was broadcast over educational television. The two sides agreed on several compromises between the claims of educational autonomy and the government's legitimate prerogatives on campus. State intrusions onto campuses, even in pursuit of criminal suspects, had caused considerable friction in the past. Just by meeting with the ministry people, university officials tacitly recognized the junta's right to rule, itself a major breakthrough in a country where governing authority traditionally extends as far as the rulers' capacity to destroy their rivals and no further. And now a new, moderate teachers' union has formed to compete with the old left-dominated organization. Teacher strikes, previously endemic in El Salvador, are far fewer and less political than before.

"Lastly, and most important," the education minister told his countrymen after listing the various resources their nation possessed, "we have the people of El Salvador, who want to achieve through peaceful means the goals of the new society. Through education we must achieve a profound change."

What are we to make of all this? In the estimation of Cayetano Carpio, alias Commander Marcial of the general command of the Farabundo Martí National Liberation Front (FMLN), it's all part of the junta's "bloody reformist measures . . . used as a smokescreen to cover up genocidal practices."

Shafik Handal [head of the Salvadoran Communist Party] dismisses the whole affair as the work of the "murderous fascist military–Christian Democratic junta."

The question is why a regime which "is fighting the entire Salvadoran people," as Carpio revealed in April [1981] over Radio Moscow, would use precious broadcast time to attack the mass illiteracy which, if Carpio is right, is presumably one of its greatest allies. Why, if you are part of a regime characterized by "institutionalized criminality, exploitation, and oppression" (Commander Roberto Boca over the guerrillas' clandestine Radio Liberación), do you spend twice as much ($150 million in 1981) on education as on defense ($75 million)? Why institute massive land-reform programs, bank nationalizations, and coffee-industry takeovers—projects ideal for making enemies of the wealthiest, most uncompromisingly anti-Communist elements in society—when all you're interested in is crushing the revolutionaries? And why, on the other hand, would you undertake the mass slaughter of your own people, as Carpio claims, when that would alienate irrevocably the media and citizens of the one nation, the United States, upon whose support all your hopes depend?

Three Choices for Salvadorans

The Duarte government [was] not universally loved in El Salvador. Neither is the Reagan administration here. Nor was Carter, Ford, nor any other U.S. president ever. But as things stand, the people of El Salvador can choose either (1) to go back to the old PCN–Hernández Martínez style of government (a Maximiliano Hernández Martínez Brigade competes with the Farabundo Martí left in committing terrorist atrocities), (2) to fight with the FMLN to install a Marxist dictatorship, or (3) to give elections a try.

Virtually no one wants to return to the old way. In any event, a right-wing coup would mean a cutoff of U.S. aid and a fall to the left as inevitable as was Somoza's once Carter abandoned him. For the people of El Salvador, the only real choice, at least for the foreseeable future, is between elections and an imposed settlement giving some or all power to the left.

There is little support for the left among ordinary Salvadorans. Their resistance to the January 1981 "final offensive" was only one of the more dramatic instances of the people's repudiation of the guerrillas. Repeated calls for a general strike have been ignored. During the offensive, guerrillas hit towns and villages in fourteen areas of the country, aiming specifically at security posts and garrisons. In only one city—Santa Ana, the country's second largest—did government troops switch sides. But, though an army colonel and several commanding officers joined the insurrection there, the *townspeople*, armed with handguns, fought the rebels. They denied them control of the town until the army arrived to capture the rebellious officers and drive the guerrillas back to their hideouts in the hills.

The Cost of Resistance

The best chance the people have had to show their support for the left came when the revolutionaries were demanding a general strike. It was again ignored—or perhaps resisted is a better word, for failure to strike cost some Salvadorans dearly. For one example, a man—we'll call him Carlos (some of his relatives still live in El Salvador)—ran a coffee factory on the outskirts of San Salvador before the offensive. Carlos was thirty-two, had an attractive young wife and two small children. He stayed away from politics, had a good sense of humor, and was liked and respected by his employees, whom he had unionized in the mid-seventies.

In December 1980, a few days before those employees left for a two-week Christmas vacation, Carlos addressed them at a meeting. Leftists outside the factory had been distributing leaflets and turning up at employees' homes calling for worker participation in a national strike to be held in concert with a "final offensive" against El Salvador's government. Carlos told the workers—for whom the company had established pension and profit-sharing plans and scholarships for their children's higher education—that the strike, if successful, would hurt them more than anyone. Without production, he said, there would be no jobs and no pay.

A few days later, as he was driving to the factory, Carlos was stopped and dragged from his car. A telephone call informed his family he'd been made a "prisoner of war" by the "popular forces." There was no further word of Carlos's fate until the first week of January, when a "communiqué" was delivered to the San Salvador newspapers. It listed the names of several kidnapped businessmen, including Carlos, and threatened to kill those on the list and to take more such "POWs" should resistance to the general strike continue. One week later, a second "communiqué" told the factory workers they'd never see their boss again if they insisted on working after January 9. They went to work.

Within a week, Carlos's body, savagely beaten and shot once, was found on a country road leading to the port city of La Libertad. He'd been castrated and his testicles taped inside his mouth to prove—what? That Carlos was an "enemy of the people"? Or was the point to convince the workers that justice and mercy no longer existed and that war alone remained? It is no coincidence that El Salvador's terrorists chose the names of Maximiliano Hernández Martínez and Farabundo Martí. These men of violence, symbols of the past, lived by power and died by it. But the people of El Salvador have never wanted their country run that way.

In the course of solidifying their control over Russia, Aleksandr Solzhenitsyn told Americans in 1975, the Bolsheviks "reduced twenty provinces of our country to utter famine. This was in 1921, the infamous Volga famine. It was a typical Communist technique: to struggle for power without thinking of the fact that the productivity is collapsing, that the fields are not being sown, that the factories stand idle, that the country is sinking into poverty and famine. . . ."

The guerrillas' struggle for power in El Salvador has reproduced all of these classic traits. Since the collapse of the final offensive, they've concentrated on blowing up electrical power stations, periodically blacking out large sections of the country and shutting down industry and agriculture in the process. Without power, patients in hospitals cannot receive proper treatment. Some become more ill, others die. Fires set by leftists destroy the coffee crop. Sabotage, kidnappings, and million-dollar ransoms force businesses to close, drive foreign investment from the land, and provide the guerrillas ammunition for propaganda as they point to the misery they have caused and blame it on the junta. [For an estimate of war damage to the Salvadoran economy, see appendix C.] But then the aim was never to improve the lot of the people anyway. Power was all, from the beginning.

"Shortly before his assassination," said Bishop Aparicio, referring to Archbishop Oscar Romero, who was shot while saying Mass in March 1980, "he realized the Marxists' thirst for power was stronger than their desire for social justice."

The guerrillas, as Aparicio described them, are "well-trained terrorists. . . . We see that they have been active at night when we travel the highways early in the morning and find first the heads and then, further along, pieces of bodies blocking the road. . . .

"Ever since the leftist guerrillas lost the final offensive—because the people did not support them—they have turned their anger on the people, especially *campesinos*."

These are the people whom Mexico and France, among others, now proclaim have earned the right to govern their fellow citizens. They are to be included in a new government according to a "political solution" reached through negotiations, a course routinely advocated (at least since it became clear the left would lose the final offensive) in contrast to the evil of a "military solution." But a new government including any faction or party unable to win representation through free, fair elections would precisely constitute a military solution. The junta would have caved in to the guerrillas solely to avoid further violence and bloodshed. Their "right" to govern would be that of conquest. And for the left, any other road to power would be hypocritical anyway. If anyone remains unaware of the fact, let it be known that Marxists, deep down, are not democrats. Their ideology presupposes inevitable class warfare, and it would be absurd, according to every principle of Marxist-Leninist theory, to relinquish control of a country to the "genocidal fascist" enemy simply because a majority asked them to do so.

Their "right" to participate in running the country, the right endorsed by France and Mexico, is morally indistinguishable from that proclaimed by Maximiliano Hernández Martínez. To allow them to hold power simply because they've proven capable of mounting a creditable war effort—because they can endanger the lives of innocent Salvadorans day or night—would be to repudiate the very principles of legality, democracy, and freedom on which every opponent of the Salvadoran regime predicates his criticism. It would be to endorse the very political despotism and intolerance the left itself insists it is fighting to end.

Worst of all, it would be to carry on, newly ratified, the ideas of the past which disallow peace but are tailor-made for rationalizing war.

14. Turnabout in U.S. Policy

By ROBERT E. WHITE

Focus Former U.S. ambassador to El Salvador Robert White argues that President Reagan's policies in El Salvador have reversed the progress made during the Carter administration, under which he served. He believes that Carter's human rights emphasis was a major influence in encouraging the reform-minded "Young Military" to undertake the October 1979 coup that promised significant change for Salvadoran society. President Reagan's election and subsequent initiatives upset these fragile openings, leading to the resurgence of violent repressive forces, says White. "The men of peace, like President Duarte, have been swept aside; the right-wing fanatics have prospered."

White agrees with Reagan that we ought to deny Communism a new foothold in the Western Hemisphere—the President "is wrong only in his methods." According to the author, the United States has too often fought Communism with "huge CIA stations, swollen police-training programs, and oversized military missions." The result of all these has been to drive the moderates into the arms of the guerrillas, who see no hope for change other than revolution.

White tends to overlook the fact that the guerrillas were already decisively committed to relentless insurrection before they had even seen the program of the new junta following the 1979 coup. One of the rebel leaders, Joaquín Villalobos, has publicly acknowledged that they deliberately set out to prolong the period of disorder in order to keep the reform-minded leaders of the new regime from preempting their revolution. The guerrillas wanted to present President Reagan with a *fait accompli;* hence their January 1981 "final offensive."

Furthermore, the 1979 coup was at least partly inspired by the victory that year of the Sandinista forces in Nicaragua. Fear of a similar takeover probably spurred the reform effort much more than the Carter human rights stance.

White's view of Salvadoran history may be usefully compared with John Kurzweil's (selection 13). Appendix D is the fourth and final report presented by the U.S. State Department to the Congress as required by 1981 legislation making military aid to El Salvador contingent upon periodic certification of the government's progress in extending human rights.

Robert E. White spent most of his twenty-five-year diplomatic career in Latin America. His last post was that of U.S. ambassador to El Salvador, 1980-81. Currently he is Warburg Professor of International Relations at Simmons College, Boston, and senior fellow of the Center for Development Policy, Washington, D.C.

I WASN'T SURPRISED TO HEAR that the security forces of El Salvador's military rulers had kidnapped and assassinated six leaders of the opposition Democratic Revolutionary Front [November 1980]; the identity of the murderers had been openly discussed on the streets and in the markets for days. But to hear it confirmed by José Napoleón Duarte himself, as we sat together in the ornate halls of the Presidential Palace—that was a surprise. Duarte was then the top civilian member of the country's reform-minded junta; he was to become the junta's president within two weeks. In response to my remark—half question, half accusation—he nodded, and sadly admitted that certain elements of the armed forces were guilty of these brutal murders.

About a week earlier, on November 27, 1980, some forty armed men had seized a Jesuit high school a few blocks from the United States Embassy. Five oppositionists were forced at gunpoint out of the building and into waiting vehicles; the sixth was seized elsewhere at about the same time. The next day, their mutilated bodies were discovered dumped at various sites, including the edge of a nearby lake. The murdered men had been the most moderate among the leaders of the Democratic Revolutionary Front, a broad alliance linking the political groupings of the Salvadoran left with the guerrilla insurgency. The victims included the head of the organization, Enrique Alvarez Córdova, a wealthy coffee plantation owner and a former minister of agriculture. The men had met at the high school for a strategy conference. According to reports, they had planned to announce their readiness to enter into negotiations with the government.

In my numerous private conversations with Duarte since my appointment as United States ambassador to El Salvador in February 1980, he had never before admitted what we both knew to be

Reprinted by permission of the author from the July 18, 1982, issue of the *New York Times Magazine*.

203

true: elements of the dominant oligarchy, through the financing of shadowy "death squads" recruited from among active and former members of the armed forces, were continuing their deliberate policy of exterminating opposition leaders. Duarte's sadness was not only for the death of men he had known and respected; their removal was a serious setback for the cause of negotiated peace.

Nothing provides more poignant evidence of the failure of the Reagan administration's approach toward El Salvador than the change of fortunes since then. The men of peace, like President Duarte, have been swept aside; the right-wing fanatics have prospered. The terrorist group that took credit for the torture and execution of the six opposition leaders was the General Maximiliano Hernández Martínez Brigade. The group's reputed leader, the former Salvadoran army major Roberto d'Aubuisson, is now president of the Constituent Assembly and the new focus of power in the country.

The turnabout is symbolic of the tragic effect of President Reagan's ill-thought-out change of direction. Within the center-right coalition, power has been rearranged to the advantage of the extreme right, and to the detriment of our political interests. The opportunity to achieve peace through negotiation has diminished to the vanishing point. The civil war continues, with no prospect of victory for the Salvadoran regime, but now with sophisticated U.S. weapons in the military's hands.

Progress Through a Human Rights Policy

The situation, in short, is not what one had reason to hope for at the end of 1980. I, at that time, had little doubt that the United States, despite the change of administrations, would continue to press for a negotiated settlement. It was precisely because of our emphasis on human rights and the reconciliation of the Salvadoran family that popular support for the government had increased over the previous year and the revolutionary threat had thereby diminished. Ronald Reagan, it was true, had disparaged President Carter's human rights policy while running for the Presidency, but I had supposed that his campaign rhetoric would have to yield quickly to the responsibilities of power. Surely, I reasoned, any objective analysis of the situation in El Salvador would convince the new President and his foreign policy experts that to abandon our goals and revive the myth of a military solution would insure the resurgence of the weakened revolutionary forces.

On January 19, 1981, one day before Reagan's inauguration, Colonel Eldon Cummings, head of the Embassy's military advisory group, came into my office with a draft of a telegram he proposed to send to Washington over my name. The message requested the immediate dispatch of fifty-five American military advisors and huge quantities of military supplies. I asked Colonel Cummings what had possessed him to bring to me, out of the blue, a request amounting to a complete reversal of U.S. policy and all that we had worked together to accomplish. The loyal and competent Cummings appeared uncomfortable. He explained that the Pentagon had ordered him to prepare this telegram. "The Defense Department," he said, "is most anxious to receive this message today."

It was obvious to me that the Pentagon would not have violated normal channels on such an important subject without first consulting with the Reagan transition team. The Cummings telegram was not forwarded; I sent a message of my own. I said that on the eve of Reagan's inauguration, with the whole new foreign policy apparatus yet to be installed, certain people in Washington were trying to alter our policy toward El Salvador. With the failure of the guerrillas' January offensive, there was nothing, I said, to warrant emergency action, and the Embassy would make no policy recommendations until the new secretary of state indicated that he was ready to receive our advice.

My expectations were misplaced. Reagan's advisors, I was soon to learn, had every intention of acting on their campaign oratory. They chose El Salvador for their first foreign policy initiative because, in their view, there was no better place to dramatize the difference between the soft-headed, soft-hearted, human-rights-oriented Carter administration and the new no-nonsense, confrontational, anti-Communist Reagan team. A couple of weeks after Reagan was inaugurated, I was replaced as ambassador and forced out of the Foreign Service.

President Reagan is right to concern himself with denying Communism a new foothold in the Western Hemisphere. He is wrong only in his methods. His administration, like many of its predecessors, fears change in Latin America. It forgets that the first revolutionary message in the Americas was ours. Only when we deny our heritage and set our face against democratic change do people in Latin America lose faith in Western values and turn to revolution on the Cuban model, backed by the Soviet Union.

The Falkland Islands crisis should provide us with a lesson on the folly of tying our interests in Latin America to the right-wing military. The next time our chief delegate to the United Nations, Jeane J. Kirkpatrick, appeals for special understanding for her favorite anti-Communist dictator, we should recall the alacrity with which the representatives of the Argentine military junta flew to Cuba to embrace Fidel Castro and the threats of the then president, Leopoldo Galtieri, to accept weapons from the Soviet Union.

The lesson is particularly important now. Real revolutions, as distinct from coups, have been rare in Latin America. Authentic change, for good or bad, has occurred in only three countries—Mexico, Cuba, and Nicaragua. If, as it seems, we are now entering a more revolutionary era in that part of the world, the chances of our kind of revolution prevailing are not helped if we base our policies on brutal, military-dominated governments held in contempt by their own people.

Necessity of U.S. Involvement

At the same time, those who argue that the peoples of Latin America should be allowed to have their revolutions without any involvement on our part misunderstand both the nature of power and the struggle between democracy and Communism. If we do not do what we can to achieve our objectives in Latin America, others will fill the vacuum, and the outcome will be bad for the United States and bad for the people of the area.

All this is particularly true of Central America, a region enveloped by United States power. The issue is not whether to involve ourselves in the affairs of our Central American neighbors but the form and substance of that involvement. It is not surprising that when the watershed in our post-war relations with Latin America occurred nearly three decades ago, it took place in a Central American country.

Guatemala, a country of great natural beauty and ample resources, had been plagued by a succession of cruel and inept rulers. In 1954, the elected government of Jacobo Arbenz Guzmán was overthrown by an invasion of Guatemalan exiles, an operation engineered by the Central Intelligence Agency. The Arbenz government had offended Washington both by launching a reform program that expropriated some of the United Fruit Company's holdings and by requesting arms from the Soviet bloc after the United States cut off military assistance. In overthrowing Arbenz, the Eisenhower administration, in effect, announced to all of Latin America that we were forsaking the Good Neighbor policy of President Franklin D. Roosevelt, founded on respect for the sovereignty and juridical equality of the nations of the hemisphere, and were reverting to the Big Stick diplomacy of an earlier era.

No longer would political problems in Central America be dealt with through diplomatic influence and persuasion. From this point on, the preponderance of U.S. resources would go to fighting a vaguely defined Communism with huge CIA stations, swollen police-training programs, and oversized military missions. This counterrevolutionary approach actually insured the rise of an effective guerrilla movement. For as the corruption and repression increased and U.S. support of the reactionary forces continued, the moderates gave up hope of finding a constitutional alternative. In Guatemala, El Salvador, and Nicaragua, they united with the revolutionaries to achieve their overriding objective—oust the dictator and put an end to the oppression.

Under the Kennedy administration, a sense of vision was restored. President Kennedy grasped the essential truth that, in his own vivid phrase, "those who make peaceful evolution impossible make violent revolution inevitable." In 1961 he launched the Alliance for Progress, a far-reaching program of economic and social reform in Latin America underwritten by a pledge of $1 billion a year in United States economic assistance.

The Alliance for Progress released an explosion of energy and hope that transformed the entire concept of United States–Latin American relations. With Kennedy's death, however, the program lost momentum. Preoccupied with Vietnam, Kennedy's successors reverted to the policies of the 1950s, providing a feckless mix of economic and military assistance that did more to prop up military dictatorships than to improve the lives of the poor.

The Carter Strategy

Under the Carter administration, the emphasis shifted from a doctrine of counterinsurgency in the Third World to one of human rights. This change found particular resonance in Latin America, whose culture, despite the all too frequent violation of individual rights, gives special importance to the dignity of the human being. And it appeared to be particularly applicable to Central America, where a collision between popular rising expectations and immobile political and social structures had struck a revolutionary spark. President Carter's response was a strategy of selective use of our power and resources on behalf of the indigenous democratic institutions.

Costa Rica, with its half-century of representative government, was a haven of stability. Our hope was to nudge Honduras out of the grip of the military and back into the country's traditional pattern of civilian rule. While working to moderate the armed insurgency in Nicaragua, we put pressure on the new revolutionary junta in El Salvador to act promptly on its reform program. By persuading these countries, plus Panama, to join in a loose coalition of governments that were either democratic or tending toward democracy, we hoped to isolate the murderous military regime of Guatemala, the bitter fruit of the U.S.-sponsored 1954 coup. We had good reason to believe that the young officers of the Guatemalan army would eventually find this pariah status intolerable and throw out the generals in power.

The first test came in Panama. For years, the Panamanian National Guard and the small upper class had maintained an economic and political stranglehold on the country. After the populist leader Brigadier General Omar Torrijos Herrera became the effective ruler of Panama in 1969, he began the essential task of economic and social reform. But to secure his political base, he needed a Panama Canal treaty with the United States.

The object was to have done with the colonial vestige that removed a part of Panamanian territory—the Canal Zone—from Panamanian sovereignty. Fortunately, President Carter and the

Congress were not swayed by warnings at home that if we gave up the canal, it would end up under the control of Fidel Castro, whose triumph in 1959 had turned Cuba into an exporter of revolution. A treaty was concluded assuring the vital interests of the United States. This act of statesmanship made Panama a sturdy, tranquil, and increasingly democratic ally.

The next test came in Nicaragua. To his everlasting credit, Carter accepted the fall of General Anastasio Somoza Debayle in 1979 as a logical result of Washington's emphasis on human rights. His administration attempted to deal with the revolutionary Sandinista regime by renewing economic aid and seeking to moderate its policies (an effort abandoned, as we shall see, by the Reagan team). But the greatest threat to the Carter administration's plans for nonviolent reform came in El Salvador.

A small, coffee-rich but otherwise poor nation, El Salvador has one of the most skewed systems of income distribution in the hemisphere. The capital, San Salvador, is a juxtaposition of Calcutta and Beverly Hills; the countryside has been turned into a Latin version of Tobacco Road, with the *campesinos* (peasants) forced to move from place to place to find a few days' work.

There are four principal actors in the Salvadoran drama: the Roman Catholic Church, the rich, the poor, and the military. Traditionally, the rich controlled the country through the military; the church supported the system and counseled the poor to suffer in silence. But in 1968 came the rebirth of the Latin American church. Pope Paul VI, in an address at Bogotá, Colombia, during a visit to the hemisphere, said it was the obligation of the rich and powerful to "be sensitive to the voices crying out for bread, concern, justice, and a more active participation in the direction of society."

Awakening in El Salvador

The church in El Salvador began to preach to poor and rich alike the need for a common dedication to elementary social justice, wider political participation, and an end to institutionalized violence. The new message stirred and awakened the country's meek and humble. The peasants and workers responded by organizing community associations with objectives like land reform, better working conditions, and higher wages. They formed labor unions and *campesino* organizations.

The rich also heard the new voice of the church, but with alarm and horror. To the landed and industrial aristocracy, the transformation inside the church was tantamount to treason. They accused the church of Communist activity and condemned any movement toward reform as Marxist. With devastating effect, they sponsored the military death squads that targeted *campesino* leaders, union organizers, and priests.

The military had held the political reins in El Salvador since 1932 by making sure that their candidates always won the presidential elections. This uninterrupted exercise of power had terrible consequences: a slow accumulation of injustices and brutalities, of fraudulent elections and frustrated hopes, of suppressed reform movements and banned newspapers. Political institutions atrophied; the judiciary withered; civic organizations decayed.

In the 1972 presidential elections, the hard-line faction in the military prevented the civilian winner, José Napoleón Duarte, from taking office and had him arrested, tortured, and sent into exile. The Nixon administration, deaf to his appeals, gave its preference to Colonel Arturo Armando Molina, a corrupt nonentity who had finished a poor second. United States backing for the power structure drove the moderate democratic leaders to make common cause with Marxists who argued that the only answer lay in armed revolt. Cuba offered Marxist indoctrination, guerrilla training, and arms. The guerrilla movement, which had been simmering for years, began to gather force.

That was the situation when the Carter administration took over in 1977—and made clear its conviction that El Salvador could no longer be effectively governed under a rigid system of grave economic imbalances, a system incapable of accepting political or economic change. Partly because of this message from Washington, the young Salvadoran military took matters into their own hands. On October 15, 1979, junior officers overthrew the government and announced a program of radical change. After an unsuccessful attempt to cooperate with the more moderate revolutionary leaders, they invited Duarte and his Christian Democratic Party to join them in transforming Salvadoran society.

In March 1980, all land holdings over 1,250 acres were expropriated and turned into producer cooperatives. Another phase, under which 150,000 sharecroppers would be given title to the land they tilled, was begun six months later. Next on the agenda were plans to expropriate and redistribute the rich coffee lands of between 250 and 1,250 acres. The best evidence of the importance of these reforms was the oligarchy's reaction. During 1980, some of the rich land-owners and industrialists financed two attempted coups against the reform junta. Both attempts were led by Roberto d'Aubuisson.

A right-wing extremist, d'Aubuisson had been expelled from the army because of his shocking abuses against human rights. The moderate daily *La Crónica* called him a "psychopathic killer" and the "chief torturer" of the regime that had preceded the reformist junta. The Carter administration barred him from entering the United States as a terrorist. D'Aubuisson was arrested after the first abortive coup. Blaming the American Embassy for his jailing (which did not last more than a few days), his followers organized a siege of my official residence. Rightist demonstrators with guns and loudspeakers sealed off the exit for two days, until the deputy chief of mission, Mark Dion, and I crashed through the barricades in the embassy's armored Cadillac, while our Marine guards scattered a score of vigilantes with tear gas.

As firmly as we rejected a rightist solution to the problems of El Salvador, we remained unalterably opposed to a violent guerrilla takeover. We understood, of course, that the Salvadoran left constituted a vital and authentic popular force. But neither were we blind to evidence that many of the guerrilla leaders had fallen under Marxist-Leninist control. There was only one realistic way to deal with that: arrive at a negotiated solution that would prevent a guerrilla victory and augment the power of the democratic left.

The Reagan Reversal

On March 6, 1981, President Reagan said, "I didn't start the El Salvador thing, I inherited it." He inherited the problem, but he threw away the solution—a creative, innovative policy that maximized the chances of an acceptable compromise. The Salvadoran government had made an honest beginning on genuine agrarian reform. Pressure by the United States and the Christian Democrats had led to small but tangible corrective measures against human rights abuses by the military. In January 1981, the guerrillas failed in their highly touted "final offensive"; their leaders, once again, began to talk seriously of negotiating.

Within a few weeks, the Reagan administration cut the heart and soul out of the Salvadoran government's program. The policy reversal in Washington, with its insistence on a military victory, undercut Duarte's offer of political talks. Agrarian reform was slowed, and its most vital phase, the redistribution of rich coffee land, was indefinitely postponed. Then, as though in a broadcast to the world that we had learned nothing from Vietnam, we sent in military advisors and large amounts of military equipment.

The new message from Washington seemed to be that the United States would look the other way when the military used murder as a political weapon. This, the Salvadorans learned, would apply even when the victims were U.S. citizens of the "wrong" sort. Secretary of State Alexander M. Haig, Jr., sought to play down the December 2, 1980, murder of four American missionary women in El Salvador. Although our embassy reported unequivocally that the women were deliberately killed by the Salvadoran security forces, Haig responded to a congressional inquiry with the fiction that the women might have been killed in a crossfire while running a roadblock. Mrs. Kirkpatrick followed Haig's lead by falsely describing the women as "political activists." The exact opposite was true. These women, as I personally know, rejected any political role and saw themselves only as servants to the poor. But to some minds, identifying with the poor is the same as identifying with revolution.

As the massacre of young and poor Salvadorans by the rightist death squads reached sickening proportions—the count ran into the hundreds every month—Salvadoran moderates trying to contain the slaughter were demoralized by our abandonment of human rights. The hard-liners were encouraged in their opposition to peace talks; fighting increased in intensity. The last thing El Salvador needed, under these circumstances, was another flawed election. Yet an election was the device the Salvadoran military and the Reagan advisors chose in order to persuade the public and

Congress of the United States that the Salvadoran people rejected the revolutionary cause.

The 1982 Election

By voting in large numbers on March 28 [1982], the people of El Salvador demonstrated once again that they crave a political solution to the conflict: that much should be said for the election that took place in the midst of civil war. In other respects, it was a distortion of the democratic process. The ballots were numbered, the voters were handed their ballots upon presentation of their identity cards, and the urns that received the votes were made of transparent material. Numbered ballots have been the traditional means of making sure that Juan Pueblo votes as the authorities want him to. No power on earth can convince a poor, unlettered *campesino* with a numbered ballot in his hand that the military commandant of his district will not know for whom the vote was cast. Most important, the military would not give a place on the ballot to any candidate left of the centrist Christian Democrats. The surprise was not that the rightist candidates won 60 per cent of the vote but that they did not win even more.

The result was a political disaster. The Christian Democrats, the only participating party committed to reform, were effectively removed from the scene; Duarte was ousted as president. The oligarchy has been returned to its dominant position. Final authority has reverted to the hard-line military. Nothing is more symbolic of our current predicament in El Salvador than the Administration's bizarre attempt to recast d'Aubuisson in a more favorable light.

That, to be sure, had not been its original intention; at first, the Administration had recognized him for what he was. In a letter of May 12, 1981, to Democratic Representative Lee H. Hamilton, a member of the House Foreign Affairs Committee, Richard Fairbanks, then assistant secretary of state for congressional relations, wrote that "ex-Major Roberto d'Aubuisson reportedly leads a right-wing terrorist group called the General Maximilio Hernández Brigade." (The reference, of course, was to the General Maximiliano Hernández Martínez Brigade, whose death squads have executed hundreds of Salvadorans on the mere suspicion of sympathy for the left, as well as—by its own claim—the six opposition leaders murdered in November 1980.) However, after the Salvadoran election made d'Aubuisson the ascendant power in the country, President Reagan's advisors decided to let bygones be bygones. Administration representatives have been saying that d'Aubuisson may not be as bad as he was painted and that the pressures of office may have a salubrious effect.

Getting the Message

The people of El Salvador will draw the obvious conclusion. The workers and peasants will know that all they can now expect is a return to the old system of privilege for the few and misery for the many. Much as they may fear the upheaval and dislocation of a leftist victory, they will increasingly, if grudgingly, give their toleration and support to the guerrillas, feeling that only thus can they put an end to the atrocities routinely committed by the unfettered military.

Whether Cuba continues to support the revolution with arms and training is not going to make an important difference. Even if the Administration makes good on its threat to "go to the source" and eliminate Cuba as an agent of rebellion, the revolutionary movement will advance. The guerrillas' most important source of weapons has always been the international black market centered in the United States. It is not Russia, Cuba, or Nicaragua that makes the revolutions of Central America—it is injustice, brutality, and hunger.

A military victory for the Salvadoran government, on the other hand, is unattainable. In spite of all our military assistance thus far, there is no evidence that the guerrilla movement has been seriously hurt. When guerrillas have the advantage of exploiting a political status quo that has become unacceptable to most of the population, all they have to do to win in the end is endure. . . .

Last February [1982] the president of Mexico, José López Portillo, spoke in Managua, Nicaragua, of skies darkened by a foreign threat to the entire isthmus. To him, the threat came not so much from Havana as from Washington. He held the Reagan administration directly responsible for much of the current violence, and warned that further intervention of the present kind could provoke a resurgence of deep anti-U.S. sentiment throughout the hemisphere. The Mexican president then presented Washington with a foreign policy alternative. He offered to join other friends and allies in working out guarantees that any negotiated peace in El Salvador would protect the legitimate security interests of the United States. The offer, with its implied call for a reassessment in Washington, was predictably sidetracked by the White House.

The Reagan administration, on taking office, called the Salvadoran revolution "a textbook case of indirect armed aggression by Communist powers" against a Latin American state. It is nothing of the sort. The revolution is home-grown, and—as revolutions do—it got its arms and support wherever it could. One might, however, describe the Administration's approach to Central America as a textbook case of boldness, ignorance, and ideological certitude combining to weaken the region's defenses against Communist penetration.

The Administration's program for Central America is in deep trouble. The only way to rescue it is by returning to a policy of promoting a negotiated settlement, preferably with the help of our natural allies Mexico and Venezuela, which understand, better than we do, the history, culture, and motivations of those who fight and die in this neglected center of the hemisphere. President Reagan can still grasp the opportunity of backing the forces of freedom in Latin America. To do so, he would have to abandon his embrace of the region's most oppressive elements and put the United States back on the side of democratic change, where it rightfully belongs.

15. The People's Struggle

By GUILLERMO M. UNGO

Focus "It is not possible in El Salvador to aspire peacefully to human rights and political freedoms," says Guillermo Ungo, one of the more moderate spokesmen for the Salvadoran guerrillas. The pursuit of these values "is a reckless venture. This is the true cause of the present war." The repeated intervention of the U.S. government in Salvadoran affairs has made democracy "a cruel and painful deceit to Salvadorans," and "its practice is considered dangerous and subversive," he says.

Ungo argues that the guerrillas are a "people's army," and that a great majority of Salvadorans repudiate the government. He discounts the results of the 1982 Salvadoran elections, in which a large voter turnout gave heavy support to conservative parties.

Although many observers believe that the guerrilla umbrella organization FMLN-FDR was formed because of Fidel Castro's threat that he would withhold aid unless the guerrillas unified, Ungo denies that any aid has come from Cuba, from the Sandinistas in Nicaragua, or from other regimes.

He insists that the guerrillas regard negotiations as the answer to El Salvador's struggle, and he is critical of the Salvadoran oligarchy and the Reagan administration for what he regards as a refusal to negotiate. He glosses over the fact that the guerrillas began proposing negotiations only after their military and popular failure in the 1981 "final offensive."

Ungo's characterization of the guerrilla forces as a "people's army" is simplistic and self-serving. Shirley Christian (selection 16) gives a truer picture of the complex and often elitist nature of the guerrilla leaders. A former Sandinista, Miguel Bolaños (selection 25), contradicts Ungo's assertion that military support and direction have not arrived from external sources, and even Fidel Castro has publicly acknowledged such support.

Guillermo M. Ungo is president of the Democratic Revolutionary Front (FDR) and general secretary of the National Revolutionary Movement in El Salvador. The FDR is the political arm of the Farabundo Martí National Liberation Front (FMLN), an umbrella organization of the five major guerrilla groups that oppose the Salvadoran government.

THE STRUGGLE FOR democracy in El Salvador has a long history. Its fundamental causes are internal, but since the conflict's beginnings, its course has also been affected by a powerful external force, the government of the United States.

The oligarchic-military governments of El Salvador have long kept in place unjust institutions and policies that have excluded the majority of the people from real participation in the decision-making processes that affect their social, economic, and political life. Democracy has become a cruel and painful deceit to Salvadorans; its practice is considered dangerous and subversive. Any statement favoring social change provokes violent retribution as a matter of course. The social doctrine of the Roman Catholic Church and other churches, the exercise of trade-union rights and of freedom of thought, and criticism of the government are perceived to serve international Communism.

The consequences of this way of thinking are clear. Church leaders are persecuted, unions are destroyed, and opposition newspaper offices and radio stations are dynamited. More than 40,000 Salvadorans have been murdered since 1980, including reporters, teachers, students, professionals, political leaders, an archbishop, and priests, in addition to thousands of workers and peasants. Thus the practice of democracy in El Salvador has a history written in blood.

Making a mockery of Abraham Lincoln's ideals, El Salvador's rulers have created governments of the minority and for the minority whose survival has depended on institutionalized violence, on closing the channels of democratic participation, and on ever-increasing violations of human rights. Over the years, the dispossessed majority and the political, social, and religious leaders have faced a dilemma: to fight back and risk death in resistance, or to

Reprinted by permission from the Fall 1983 issue of *Foreign Policy* (© 1983 by the Carnegie Endowment for International Peace).

submit and risk death from hunger, poverty, or political repression. It is not possible in El Salvador to aspire peacefully to human rights and political freedoms; their pursuit is a reckless venture. This is the true cause of the present war.

Ruthless Anti-Communism

The anti-Communism of the oligarchy and of the army that serves it caused the murder of 30,000 peasants in 1932 and has fueled an even greater massacre today. This ruthless type of anti-Communism has been supported by successive U.S. administrations for several decades, chiefly in the form of training for army officers in military establishments in both the United States and the Panama Canal Zone. These efforts to teach officers to combat the so-called internal enemy have been based on an ominous theory of national security. This view of the problem and of its solution is essentially militaristic. And this approach has cost the lives of hundreds of thousands of men, women, and even children throughout Latin America. In the name of anti-Communism and of law and order, dictators such as Nicaragua's Anastasio Somoza Debayle, Paraguay's Alfredo Stroessner, and Chile's Augusto Pinochet Ugarte have brought only death, disorder, insecurity, and instability to the continent.

Successive U.S. administrations have followed the same dialectic of friend or enemy that Latin American dictators use, one that confuses friendship with submission and that was clearly rejected by Pope John Paul II during his March 1983 visit to San Salvador. The epithet of subversive or Communist is applied immediately to any who do not submit. The anti-Communist dictators, however, are not required to support pluralism or to hold elections, nor are sanctions imposed, credits withheld, or covert actions taken against them. They are considered friends and allies of the United States.

In spite of the unequal strengths of the two belligerents, the Salvadoran war is not being won by the Salvadoran government. Yet the aid sent to the Salvadoran government by the U.S. administration has not been modest or inadequate. It has reached nearly $1 billion in three years [since 1980]. In a small country such as El Salvador, where the great majority of the population has a per capita income of less than $250 per year and where in 1979 the government allocated $9 per person for health and $24 for education, maintaining each Salvadoran soldier costs U.S. taxpayers $10,000. The additional sums requested of Congress for 1983 and 1984 would double the cost. Put another way, accepting the Pentagon's own estimates that the guerrilla groups number no more than 7,000 combatants, the United States has spent more than $135,000 per insurgent.

These guerrilla forces are a people's army that operates in a small territory that lacks extensive mountain ranges, easy access to all corners of the country, and other geographic conditions favorable for guerrilla warfare. This people's army lacks airplanes, helicopters, trucks, tanks, and heavy artillery. It has nevertheless been able to resist, develop, and advance while fighting against a much larger and better-equipped force.

The ideological explanation given by those politicians preoccupied with Communism, who do not wish to face reality, attributes the guerrillas' success to external rather than internal causes—the support of Cuba, Nicaragua, and the Soviet Union. This explanation ignores many important aspects of the Salvadoran war. El Salvador does not have direct access to Cuba, Nicaragua, or the Soviet Union. It borders Guatemala and Honduras, which have military governments that submit to U.S. wishes and that oppose the guerrillas.

Since 1980 the U.S. government has tried to control the flow of arms into El Salvador, using helicopters, reconnaissance planes, radar, and modern ships, including a destroyer in the Gulf of Fonseca, as well as espionage and covert operations in El Salvador, Honduras, and Nicaragua. Until now [fall 1983], the Reagan administration has presented no significant evidence of this external support. This enormous array of technological and human resources has stopped the arms flow, revealed that the flow has always been minimal, or indicated that it does not exist. As Wayne Smith, a former State Department official, correctly observed recently, if U.S. claims concerning the extent of the guerrillas' logistical support were true, these forces would boast hundreds of thousands of armed men (Wayne S. Smith, "Dateline Havana: Myopic Diplomacy," *Foreign Policy* 48 [Fall 1982], p. 169).

Politically conservative analysts believe that dollars and arms alone can win the war. Although the Reagan administration continues to increase its aid, the Salvadoran government's army continues to deteriorate. Since 1982 the guerrillas have recovered from the army more than 3,000 automatic rifles and significant quantities of other weapons, as well as ammunition and supplies. More than 1,000 government soldiers have surrendered to the Farabundo Martí National Liberation Front (FMLN), a federation of guerrilla groups, and have been freed through the International Committee of the Red Cross.

Support at Home and From Abroad

The ideological perspective ignores two human realities. First, the struggle for democracy in El Salvador enjoys great popular support in all parts of the world. Even in the United States important sectors of the population have a better understanding of the situation of the Salvadoran people and the reason for their political and armed struggle than does the U.S. government. It is the people of many countries and not their governments who actively support the guerrillas and provide material aid such as money, medicine, and clothing.

Second, the Salvadoran war is a people's war, fought under adverse conditions, that can be sustained and advanced only with the support of the population. Some people in the United States demand proof of this support without realizing that current conditions in El Salvador make it impossible for the people to express themselves freely. More than 10 per cent of the population are refugees who have fled the army's massacres and repression. Moreover, unemployment is dreadful, and inflation is increasing. Because of the militarized social and political life, the people live in fear. They cannot express themselves publicly and openly in the streets, factories, and plazas without risking a massacre, as shown even at the funeral of Archbishop Oscar Arnulfo Romero. The exercise of the right of free assembly risks bloody reprisal.

Nonetheless, the great majority of the Salvadoran people repudiate the government. They support and sustain the struggle in many different ways, or wait for their moment. Thus despite dozens of killings every day and the appearance month after month of mutilated bodies displaying the marks of torture, the peace of the cemetery has not been achieved.

The simple fact that the struggle continues means the social base is not inactive. A popular war such as the one in El Salvador involves more than a confrontation of armies. It involves the incorporation of the broader population into diverse aspects of both the political and the military struggle. Moreover, conditions in El Salvador today prevent the expression of popular support for all opposition political groups, either in elections or in mass demonstrations. Nor can elections that are held under these conditions accurately reflect public desires.

In Zimbabwe-Rhodesia in 1979, for example, 67.3 per cent of the electorate voted for Bishop Abel Muzorewa, favored by the white minority, which then suggested that the Muzorewa victory proved the guerrilla forces had little popular support. Yet less than ten months later this interpretation was exposed as an illusion. Guerrilla leader Robert Mugabe won a new election; Muzorewa captured only 8 per cent of the vote. In a similar vein, should people conclude that the government in Poland enjoys popular support because there are no longer massive demonstrations or strikes involving millions of workers following the declaration of martial law in Poland? Strangely, some people reach such conclusions regarding the degree of support enjoyed by the government of El Salvador, a country where 40,000 people have been murdered and leaders of the Democratic Revolutionary Front (FDR), a coalition of political parties, have been kidnapped and murdered after suffering atrocious tortures.

If Outside Aid Stopped

But the best way to put the ideological, conservative arguments on trial is to pose the question: What would happen to the Salvadoran government if the United States stopped sending military aid? The Salvadoran government and the Reagan administration have already given a response: They cannot afford to risk such a cutoff. The opposite question, about the supposed Cuban, Nicaraguan, or Soviet aid to the guerrillas, could also be asked. The FDR-FMLN has already responded: That aid does not exist, and it is not necessary. The solidarity of groups and social and political forces from many parts of the world, as well as the aid they provide, is the only external assistance necessary. To dispel any doubt about this matter, the FDR-FMLN has advocated a negotiated solution to the conflict, sponsored by any governments, witnesses, or international mediators who not only possess respectable reputations but also are friendly to the United States.

The discussions and guarantees agreed upon during negotiations will allow Salvadorans to resolve the conflict without external interference. For two consecutive years the United Nations General Assembly has approved resolutions calling for the suspension of military aid to the contending parties. Failure to agree to this step will only prolong, deepen, and widen the war in which we Salvadorans provide the corpses. The Reagan administration's responsibility for the continuation, intensification, and regionalization of the war is undeniable. The Reagan administration's role contrasts with the position of the Contadora Group (Colombia, Mexico, Panama, and Venezuela), which has majority support in Latin America and which rejects a strategy of pacification through a war of extermination covered by a façade of elections.

The Reagan administration claims that if military aid to the Salvadoran government is terminated, the regime will collapse and El Salvador will fall into the hands of Communists. Consequently, since El Salvador is regarded as the back yard or the front yard of the United States, it is said to be necessary to step up the war and the massacres to save El Salvador. The same mentality was apparent during the Spanish Inquisition, when suspected heretics were burned alive to purify their souls. This rationale reveals a primitive imperialist anti-Communism. It destroys the basis for international coexistence, which rests upon a respect for political pluralism among states and upon the right to self-determination and nonintervention. This mentality is also used to justify covert operations intended to destabilize or overthrow foreign governments. Such operations constitute genuine acts of intervention and war and reflect an insolent pursuit of supremacy.

This rationale also reveals an implicit recognition that the Salvadoran government is losing the war despite U.S. military aid, which increases in geometric proportions. But above all, it betrays an analysis of Salvadoran politics that is totally ideological and has no base in reality.

The Reagan administration believes that its policies are paving the way for political pluralism in El Salvador. But this pluralism neither exists now nor has it ever existed in my homeland. Death, jail, exile, or silence is the price of opposition to the government or to the oligarchy. What the U.S. administration and its supporters fail to see is that pluralism has ideological, political, and sociological dimensions, all related to one another. The first refers to the components of the concept of democracy, the second to a democratic reality, and the third to a democratic possibility.

The Possibility of Pluralism

Real sociological data show that a wide variety of political organizations of different types exist in El Salvador both within the government and within the FDR-FMLN coalition. They are real political and social forces organized from different social bases, which have developed in spite of the repression that so many have suffered. This means the possibilities of constructing political pluralism in El Salvador through negotiations do exist. A military victory achieved by any of the parties in conflict will limit and reduce those possibilities.

The sources of political power are varied. Power stems not only from the force of arms, but even more important, from the legitimacy of a regime, from national consensus, and from popular support. Armed power, when it is illegitimate, enhances neither the security of a country—as opposed to the interests of dictators—nor the security of the hemisphere; nor does it assure stability and peace. The Salvadoran crisis in all of its intensity has persisted for more than ten years, and the armed power of the military has produced only death and destruction in El Salvador and turmoil throughout the region.

The FDR and the FMLN have been allied for more than three years. This alliance has provided concrete and practical experience in pluralism by requiring its members to discuss whatever differences arise and to reach decisions by which all will abide. So the question of who controls whom within the FDR-FMLN is irrelevant. Such pluralistic understanding and coordination take place not only in the military arena but also in the sphere of programs, positions, and political initiatives, particularly in relation to the questions of dialogue and negotiations with the government.

The alliance also recognizes that its policies must reflect the realities of international politics and power. El Salvador is not in Eastern Europe; it is a part of the Americas. Our big neighbor is not the Soviet Union; it is the other superpower, the United States. For reasons of survival the FDR-FMLN wants and needs to establish and to maintain dignified and collaborative relations with this big neighbor. The alliance is well aware of how difficult it has been to mobilize the country to oppose the oligarchy. It would be madness to add to this problem an absolute barrier, the hostility of the first superpower in the world.

The FDR-FMLN has certainly not tried to provoke U.S. hostility in its struggle. FDR-FMLN efforts have received the deepest international support from a broad range of countries in both the capitalist and the socialist worlds—from Cuba, France, Mexico, Nicaragua, Sweden, and Third World countries. The FDR-FMLN is not a social democratic movement seeking assistance only from the Socialist International, nor a Communist movement seeking support only from Cuba. The FDR-FMLN has sought broad-based support to guarantee its nationalist and nonaligned position. The FDR-FMLN understands very well that to reconstruct El Salvador, aid from many sources will be required, especially from the Western world. FDR-FMLN nonalignment is, consequently, a position of principle, of necessity, and of political convenience. The FDR-FMLN wants to have friends, not enemies or masters.

President Ronald Reagan says that the United States must safeguard its national security. The FDR-FMLN agrees, but it differs with the President's definition of threats to U.S. security and, above all, with the policies he has implemented to counter these threats. In reality, it is these policies that endanger the security of the hemisphere and consequently the security of his own country.

The Necessity of Dialogue

Nevertheless, the FDR-FMLN has always been willing to hold a dialogue with the government of the United States in order to discuss and agree upon concrete points that involve mutual security. The FDR-FMLN does not seek an ideological debate but a political agreement that would reflect its neutral and independent position on issues such as: the exclusion of military bases and facilities of other governments; the sources and appropriate levels of military aid to a future government; the security of navigable ocean routes; and the prohibition of military alliances. Certainly the FDR-FMLN does not pretend to be a factor in cold war or confrontation because the alliance does not want to contribute to the bipolarity of the world.

The FDR-FMLN is certain that all these points can be resolved on a plane of dignity and respect through a dialogue with the Reagan administration. It is a practical and efficient way to test each other before the international community. Contrary to the Reagan administration's views, the governments of Latin America, Europe, and the rest of the world believe that external military interference in El Salvador's affairs must cease and that it is urgent to open the door to a dialogue and negotiations.

U.S. military aid, however, serves only to strengthen the militarist sectors inside El Salvador that oppose dialogue and want to democratize the country by exterminating the opposition. Yet U.S. strategy must overcome an unresolvable contradiction: It seeks to construct an impossible populism, to create a centrist and reformist government in cooperation with the military, political, and economic right—that is, the senior officer corps and the oligarchy. Former president José Napoleón Duarte has repeatedly stated that a vacuum of power exists in the present regime. In fact, a crisis of power exists. His statements, however, imply a recognition that the political parties in the government, the civil political sector, count for almost nothing.

Building a National Consensus

The Salvadoran government contains weakened, but important, political and military sectors that are inclined toward a dialogue and negotiations as the only viable solution to the conflict. They do not dare to cross the bridge, however, for fear of the two sectors that oppose dialogue—the extreme right and the Reagan administration. The FDR-FMLN believes it is possible, and urgently necessary, to construct a national consensus through the dialogue.

Since the early 1970s there has been a national consciousness determined to create democracy through changes in the oligarchic structure of the country. It is quite possible that this anti-oligarchic, democratic national consensus could be transformed into a coalition containing the FDR-FMLN, certain sectors of the government, and other social and economic forces that have not yet chosen between the contending parties.

The Reagan administration insists upon pluralism, but the doors to negotiation, the instrument best able to guarantee this objective, are closed. The administration has repeatedly argued that FDR and FMLN efforts to negotiate power-sharing constitute attempts to obtain with bullets what they cannot achieve through ballots. This argument is false.

First, there are precedents for power-sharing. In October 1979 the Communists and Social Democrats entered the Salvadoran government with the formal acceptance of the U.S. government. In the beginning of 1980, the Christian Democrats publicly justified their pact with the army as a first step toward initiating a broad dialogue with all the political organizations of the left to build a government of broad participation.

Second, those who do not want to share power are not willing to hold free and democratic elections, much less to accept the results. It is also obvious that the FDR and FMLN have a broad popular base. Precisely how much representation the alliance is entitled to can be discussed, but it is undeniable that the FDR and the FMLN speak for important segments of the Salvadoran people.

Third, opposition to power-sharing flows from the premise that a democratic government exists in El Salvador and that it was produced by free elections. This is false. The people themselves never elected Provisional President Alvaro Alfredo Magaña; he was chosen as a result of palace intrigue between the high military command and the ambassador of the United States. The elections of March 1982 were held without FDR-FMLN participation because the armed forces—supposedly neutral and charged with guaranteeing impartiality and electoral integrity—publicly declared that as subversives and terrorists, alliance members were legitimate targets of persecution. A government that violates human rights on a genocidal scale cannot call itself democratic.

Somoza also held electoral events, and El Salvador's history is filled with examples of this type of fraudulent exercise. It must not be forgotten that voting is compulsory in El Salvador and that the regime used all of its propaganda resources to accuse those who would not vote of being subversives.

The truth is that the FDR-FMLN and the Salvadoran people do want free elections, but guaranteeing the security of the political leaders, or even of the FDR-FMLN rank and file, is not enough. The security of all the people must be guaranteed so that they can participate without fear in an election campaign. To insure such security, it is necessary to dissolve the death squads, to bring peace, to respect human rights, and to permit the exercise of political and trade-union rights. Finally, the objective of the FDR-FMLN is a negotiated political solution that modifies the present repressive power structure. In January 1982 José López Portillo, then president of Mexico, in a speech given in Managua, Nicaragua, put the problem in the proper framework when he rejected the false dilemma of negotiations without elections or elections without negotiations.

Six Issues to Negotiate

To establish a process of negotiation it is essential to begin with a dialogue without preconditions. Insisting upon preconditions can be seen only as a ploy to avoid dialogue. The FDR-FMLN opposes dialogue for the sake of dialogue, as a way to buy time for its military struggle. Doing so is not necessary, since the Reagan administration is already providing that time by rejecting the negotiations. The FDR-FMLN believes that a process of negotiation must resolve six fundamental issues: profound reforms that lead to economic and social progress; an international position of nonalignment; a cease-fire; the composition of a provisional government; the reorganization of the army; and the holding of elections. All six points are closely related. Negotiating the conditions of electoral participation requires addressing the problems caused by the repressive power structure, the status of the security forces and the death squads, as well as the issues of human rights violations, of access to the media, and of freedom of assembly.

As Eldon Kenworthy, who teaches Latin American politics at Cornell University, recently wrote: "The president [Reagan] talks about elections in El Salvador as if they were held in the United

States, where civilians control the military. The Salvadoran left, of course, knows only their own reality."

I was a member of the first civilian-military junta from October 1979 to January 1980. That meant I was formally commander-in-chief of the army. I cannot deny the lesson of that experience: The military has the final word in El Salvador today.

Not even the most powerful superpower in the world has been able to obtain punishment for the murderers of American churchwomen and agricultural advisors, despite the billions of dollars it has given the Salvadoran government. What are Salvadorans to think about the impunity of those who murdered Archbishop Romero, the leaders of the FDR, including its former president, Enrique Alvarez, and more than 40,000 others? Only one answer can be given: The murderers are in the government; they are in power.

16. *Rebel Factions*
17. *The Divided Military*

By SHIRLEY CHRISTIAN

Focus
Like John Kurzweil (selection 14), Shirley Christian in these two essays emphasizes the complexity of the struggle in El Salvador and the deep divisions that beset both the governmental and the rebel forces.

The Salvadoran army, says Christian, has been the real source of political power for much of the country's history. This does not mean that there has been only a succession of repressive military regimes. There is also a tradition of reform within the officer corps. The 1979 coup that swept the military dictator General Carlos Humberto Romero from power was one such attempt by the more enlightened military officers to respond to changing circumstances. Reforms were proposed, land expropriations begun, and elections held. The government set up as a result of the coup and subsequent elections continues to have its problems, however, in part because of persistent tensions within the army. Christian believes that "the Salvadoran military, in large measure, look to the United States to define what is necessary." A clear message from the U.S. side could help certain military leaders take the lead in effecting more far-reaching reforms and in controlling the right-wing death squads.

Serious ideological and personal splits also exist within the rebel bands, though the various factions have been united at least nominally under a man who is "apparently Castro's own choice," Joaquín Villalobos. The author urges Washington to consider carefully compromises that the guerrillas have proposed, even though they may be only tactics for gaining time or some other advantage.

But we must harbor no illusions, says Christian. She cautions: "All five guerrilla groups have in the past produced documents or made declarations calling for the creation of governing systems combining the philosophy of Marx and the methods of Lenin." Although in recent years these groups have toned down their ideology in favor of compromise and have proclaimed their desire to remain free from the East-West struggle and Soviet influence, Christian warns that "they still embrace the Leninist concept of internationalism, the worldwide solidarity in which one 'socialist' government or group helps another."

The complex situation analyzed here is often downplayed in proposals for power-sharing (see for example Piero Gleijeses, selection 19) or other suggestions for the establishment of a democratic center that will combat extremists. Guillermo Ungo (selection 15) gives the guerrillas' view of this question.

Shirley Christian is a journalist specializing in Central American affairs. She won the Pulitzer Prize for international reporting in 1981.

16. Rebel Factions

O NE EVENING last April [1983], Tomás Borge, a member of the nine-man Sandinista directorate [in Nicaragua], arrived at the suburban Managua home of Salvador Cayetano Carpio, the 63-year-old patriarch of El Salvador's guerrilla movement, with shattering news: security agents working under Borge in the Interior Ministry had gathered conclusive evidence implicating people close to Carpio in the murder the previous week of Mélida Anaya Montes. Anaya Montes had been Carpio's senior deputy in the Popular Liberation Forces (FPL); she had been seeking a negotiated end to the war in El Salvador over his objections. Sometime that evening, Carpio shot himself.

It was two weeks before the FPL revealed Carpio's suicide, saying he had done it out of "revolutionary pain" caused by the circumstances surrounding his comrade's death. But diplomats from several countries with intelligence sources in Managua say Carpio's death occurred "Rommel style," with Borge telling him the choice was between suicide and public revelation of all the names and facts in Anaya Montes's murder, including the possible implication of Carpio himself, and the accompanying damage to the guerrilla movement. If he chose suicide, Borge reportedly told Carpio, the circumstances surrounding the murder of Mélida Anaya Montes would remain an internal affair of the FPL.

Borge kept his promise. Although state security officials subsequently announced the arrest of Rogelio Bazzaglia, a young member of the FPL Central Command, and five others, no judicial procedures have been started against them, and it is not known whether they are still in prison or even alive.

The killers slipped into Anaya Montes's home south of Managua in the early morning hours of April 6. They stabbed her eighty-three times with an ice pick, then slit her jugular vein with a knife.

Reprinted by permission from the October 24, 1983, issue of *The New Republic* (© 1983 by The New Republic, Incorporated).

Carpio, who was in Libya, rushed home. He arrived on April 9, just in time to go directly to her state funeral, which was held in a hot, dusty market plaza on the outskirts of Managua. There were protestations of grief and anti-imperialist rhetoric, but they masked historic divisions in the Salvadoran left, divisions that had now become of concern to Fidel Castro and to the Sandinistas.

The deaths of Anaya Montes and Carpio grew out of efforts to attain unity, and support for negotiations, among and within the five guerrilla organizations that make up the Farabundo Martí National Liberation Front (FMLN). By the time Carpio went to his grave (in an unknown spot in Nicaragua, and without the public tributes given Anaya Montes), he had come to be viewed by his comrades as the chief obstacle to a negotiated settlement—as much or more so than the Reagan administration. The Sandinistas, themselves besieged by anti-Sandinista guerrillas who have the backing of the United States, had concluded that they would have a better chance to halting these pressures and consolidating their own power if they could promote a negotiated settlement in El Salvador. Along with Castro, they wanted Carpio to turn over the leadership of the guerrilla movement to a younger man more in their line of thinking.

The man chosen to succeed Carpio is Joaquín Villalobos, a thirty-two-year-old former economics student. His path to the top, first of his own guerrilla organization and now of the five-group coalition, has been marked by an expressed willingness to use violence to provoke repression and by the deaths of four guerrilla leaders under questionable circumstances. Despite this history, Villalobos is now attempting to show the outside world that he is a reasonable man, and that the guerrilla movement is eager to negotiate and willing to concede more than ever before in working out the kind of government and military structure that might emerge from negotiations. It may be a sincere move or it may be a feint. Given the confusing and bloody history of this movement, even the man who made the proposals may not know.

In many ways, the war in El Salvador is a product of the original split in the Salvadoran left, precipitated by Carpio's decision in 1970 to leave the Moscow-line Salvadoran Communist Party and form a guerrilla band. Since then, the left has been divided by a progression of issues. When Carpio quit the party, the issue was armed struggle versus what he disparagingly called bourgeois Communism. Then it became prolonged struggle, Mao-style, versus broad-based insurrection—the kind of quick kill in which all the elements unhappy with those in power are brought together, as in Nicaragua in 1979.

The success of the insurrection in Nicaragua was much noted by Marxist-Leninist revolutionary groups throughout Latin America, with their penchant for interminable analysis and self-criticism. Until 1979, they had only two examples to study of how Marxist-Leninists could come to power in the Western Hemisphere. One was Cuba, where Castro came to power at the head of a small guerrilla force and seemed destined to last forever. The other was Chile, where Salvador Allende's coalition of socialists and Communists came to power in 1970 through elections, only to be ousted by the military less than three years later. This convinced most Marxist revolutionaries in the region not to put their faith in electoral politics. On the other hand, for the two decades following Castro's rise, those who tried to emulate his methods failed—in Venezuela, Bolivia, Argentina, Uruguay, Guatemala. In Latin American guerrilla circles, Cuba had come to be viewed as an aberration. Then came 1979, when all the pieces fell into place for the Sandinistas and the dream was reborn.

In the years since 1979, however, the Salvadoran guerrillas have come to realize that El Salvador is not Nicaragua. There was only one Somoza family, the common evil against which it was so easy to unite a disparate opposition. In El Salvador, the struggle is against something faceless and diffused, a military institution and power structure in which good and bad, right and wrong are often inseparable. This realization created a new issue to divide the Salvadoran left: continued struggle versus negotiated settlement.

ORIGINS OF THE GUERRILLA GROUPS

Historically, the issues that have splintered the Salvadoran left have related to the means of reaching power, not what to do once in power. All five guerrilla groups have in the past produced documents or made declarations calling for the creation of governing systems combining the philosophy of Marx and the methods of Lenin, though such positions have been publicly tempered in recent years as the Marxist-Leninist groups have formed alliances with individuals and groups with Western democratic tendencies. In theory, the Salvadoran guerrillas reject Soviet hegemony, but they seem to do it primarily as a practical matter of survival in this hemisphere. Their argument is that they are a national liberation movement and therefore outside the framework of East-West confrontation or of any kind of accord in which the Soviet Union might promise to stay out of the U.S. neighborhood. However, they still embrace the Leninist concept of internationalism, the worldwide solidarity in which one "socialist" government or group helps another.

The Salvadoran Communist Party claims direct descent from Farabundo Martí, who rode with Sandino in Nicaragua, then returned home and organized the 1932 peasant revolt, to which the military reacted by massacring thousands of people and sending Martí to the firing squad. For the next four decades, the party, formally organized two years before the revolt, concentrated on staying alive. It functioned above ground and below ground, shifting as necessary to accommodate the electoral laws laid down by El Salvador's succession of military governments. The Salvadoran Communists followed Moscow's dictate of seeking power through legal means. They formed front groups, infiltrated labor and student organizations, and, though able to command only a few percentage points of the vote, joined electoral coalitions supporting centrist candidates such as José Napoleón Duarte and Guillermo Ungo. During tough periods, the national university provided them a secure refuge because the Salvadoran government usually (but not always) respected the Latin American tradition of university autonomy, which means the physical inviolability of the campus as much as academic freedom.

This complaisance, this unwritten pact with the establishment, guaranteed a certain anemic well-being. But it rankled some within the party, particularly Salvador Cayetano Carpio. A former bakery worker and union activist, he had joined the party in 1947 and risen to secretary-general by the mid-1960s. In the 1950s he had spent two-and-a-half years in Moscow at a school run by the

Central Committee of the Soviet Communist Party. By 1969, however, Carpio faced a dispute within the party over his desire to take up arms. He was challenged for the job of secretary-general by Jorge Shafik Handal, a son of wealthy Palestinian immigrants, who was then thirty-nine and showing signs of becoming a permanent law student.

The FPL, the ERP, the FARN

The Soviet party gave its backing to Handal and to a continued political approach, so Carpio left the party in early 1970 and formed the Popular Liberation Forces (FPL). The statutes of the new organization accused the Communist Party of being swept up in opportunism, revisionism, bourgeois reformism, bureaucracy, and other right-wing notions that ignored the needs of the people. Carpio once said that he began the FPL with seven people, including himself, and without any money or even a single pistol.

The People's Revolutionary Army, known by its Spanish acronym ERP, was born about a year after the FPL as the result of the coming together of university activists, among them Joaquín Villalobos, with some other people who left the Communist Party. In 1975, an internal struggle between the "military" and "political" factions of the ERP ended in a bloody purge and the creation of another guerrilla group by the surviving losers—the Armed Forces of National Resistance (FARN). In the process, two members of the losing faction, including its leader, Roque Dalton, were condemned by a guerrilla court-martial and executed. Death threats were made against other dissidents. Once Dalton was dead, the victorious faction claimed that he had been a Cuban agent, a CIA agent, and a revisionist. Five years later, in an interview with the Mexican news weekly *Proceso,* the man who became the leader of the FARN, Ernesto Jovel, accused Villalobos of having personally killed Dalton.

Before the interview was published, Jovel himself died in confusing circumstances. His light plane went down in the Pacific on September 17, 1980, as he flew to Panama for a meeting with friends who were arranging arms supplies for the FARN. Doubts about whether it was an accident were raised, however, by the first report from the FARN command saying he had died in a traffic accident in Salvador, followed by a statement saying the FARN did not blame any other revolutionary organization, then followed by the plane crash report.

Guerrilla Growth in the Seventies

The guerrilla groups made relatively little impact on El Salvador until the mid-1970s, when they began a series of kidnappings for ransom that netted an estimated $60 million, most of it going to the FPL and the ERP. They also specialized in occupying churches, factories, and government buildings, taking over unions, and manipulating contract bargaining for political gain. Much of this was accomplished through so-called mass organizations, which were created by the guerrilla groups for the street activities. Each of them sought affiliation with dozens of smaller groups, such as organizations of teachers, students, and peasants.

The Salvadoran military, governing through its own political party, played into the guerrillas' hands by its proclivity for repression and its suspicion of any kind of dissent, however peaceful. El Salvador's Marxist-Leninists might have been able to dream their dreams in a vacuum, but they could not have grown and prospered in one. External help aside, they were aided by two key factors inside El Salvador. One was the electoral fraud perpetrated by the military in 1972 and 1977 to prevent victories by the moderate opposition. This served to disillusion people about the prospects for Western democracy and to channel many of them, particularly the young, into the ranks of subversion. The guerrilla groups also benefited from the country's poverty and injustice, which produced uncritical international sympathy for whoever opposed the Salvadoran power structure.

Villalobos, in the foreword of a book written in 1978 by one of his ERP comrades, Ana Guadalupe Martínez, acknowledged the usefulness of these elements to the guerrillas and the need to exploit them. Martínez would not have been able to publish her story of torture and rape in a National Guard prison, Villalobos wrote, if she had not first been willing to take up arms and fight. Such actions revealed to the world the state of human rights in El Salvador, he said. Martínez, the ERP commander in eastern El

Salvador, was imprisoned in mid-1976 for the murder of a policeman, but the ERP kidnapped a wealthy industrialist seven months later and secured her freedom as part of the ransom. The industrialist died in guerrilla hands of wounds suffered in the kidnapping.

In April 1979, the Salvadoran Communist Party met secretly and decided to join the armed struggle, reportedly with the agreement of the Soviet Union. Handal has attributed the decision primarily to the Chilean example. However, Allende's downfall had occurred nearly six years earlier. It is more likely that the Salvadoran Communists saw the ranks of the guerrilla groups swelling while the party remained small and static. With the guerrillas and their mass organizations mounting so many antigovernment activities as to make people think an insurrection was imminent, the Communists ran the risk of having no role in the future government if they remained nonviolent. Even so, the Communists delayed in organizing a guerrilla force, because, says Handal, they did not know how to do it.

About the time the Communists were making their decision, a group of army officers was reaching the same conclusion, that insurrection was imminent. The officers moved against the government of General Carlos Humberto Romero, which they judged intransigent and incompetent. On October 15, 1979, they took power, with a promise to meet some of the demands of the left and to open a dialogue with it. This threw the revolutionary groups into disarray. Led by a junta of two colonels and three civilians, including the social democrat Guillermo Ungo, the new government was joined by Communists and members of other revolutionary groups at the cabinet level. But the major guerrilla groups didn't give an inch. The ERP and the Popular Revolutionary Bloc, the FPL's mass organization, mounted military assaults and takeovers of factories and government buildings in the first days of the new government. When the junta broke apart ten weeks later, it was not clear whether it was the result of disputes over excessive violence on the part of the military—as some of the civilians said—or of the pressures from outside by the revolutionary groups.

The FDR, the FMLN Umbrella

Almost everybody involved in the Salvadoran drama organized or formed new alignments in 1980. The military made a pact with the Christian Democrats, the largest opposition party, and formed a new government. The right, distrustful of the Christian Democrats and the army High Command, coalesced around Roberto d'Aubuisson, a former army major forced into retirement by the coup leaders. Disaffected center-left politicians who had left the previous government, led by Ungo and Enrique Alvarez Córdova, united with some of the mass organizations controlled by the guerrillas and formed the Democratic Revolutionary Front (FDR), a political group that concentrated on diplomacy in Western nations.

The guerrilla groups, now numbering four, met in Havana and formed a unified military directorate. They later took the name Farabundo Martí National Liberation Front (FMLN). In 1980, the FARN temporarily dropped out of the directorate because of its old dispute with the ERP, but after the death of FARN leader Jovel in September, it returned to the fold under Jovel's successor, Fermán Cienfuegos. At the end of 1980, a fifth guerrilla group came into the FMLN—the Revolutionary Party of Central American Workers, organized the year before with indirect ties to the Communist Party through one of its founders, Fabio Castillo.

Despite an awesome organizational structure, the tactics and strategies of the Salvadoran left have been as peppered with mistakes as those of the military and the government. First there were the differences over how to react to the 1979 coup. Then came the inability to capitalize on the assassination of Archbishop Oscar Romero in March 1980. The killing of the archbishop by an unknown gunman sent tremors through the government, which was convinced that it would produce an insurrection. Instead, the left appeared to lose face with the people after the largest of the mass organizations, the FPL's Popular Revolutionary Bloc, disrupted the funeral.

During the same period in 1980 that the guerrilla groups were forming their alliances and unified directorate, two of the four—the Communist Party and the FARN—were secretly, but unsuccessfully, appealing to one of the military officers on the junta,

Colonel Adolfo Majano, to stage a palace coup. (Elements on the right were simultaneously trying to convince other military officers to purge Majano.) The FPL, meanwhile, was preparing for a long war from its power base in the mountainous province of Chalatenango on the Honduran border, and the ERP was laying plans to seek victory through insurrection with Villalobos and his lieutenants as the revolutionary vanguard.

After sealing an agreement for Cuban and Sandinista support during meetings in Managua in mid-1980, the FMLN brought off a general offensive in January 1981. It was impressive, but it did not set off the hoped-for popular insurrection, and the Army was able to beat it back even before the resumption of U.S. military assistance. Since then, military initiatives have seemed oriented more toward political and diplomatic objectives than toward territorial conquest. Neither side has been able to turn the errors and losses of the other into significant victories for itself. The guerrilla forces have reached an estimated five to six thousand combatants. Until recent months the FPL was considered the largest single group, with at least two thousand. Villalobos's ERP is now thought to have become the largest and strongest, in part because of its easier access to weapons and training through Nicaragua and Cuba.

PROPOSALS FOR NEGOTIATION

Until the end of 1980, the ERP and the FPL both opposed any suggestion of talking to the other side, apparently convinced of the inevitability of victory. The first of many public calls for talks began in late 1980, with Ungo saying in Mexico that the left wanted to talk with the owner of the circus, not the acrobats—meaning the United States, not the Salvadoran government. The joint Diplomatic-Political Commission of the FMLN and the FDR wrote a "common platform" at the end of 1980 proposing a government based on nonalignment, self-determination, social reforms, democratic representation, a new armed force, continuation of some elements of private enterprise, and freedom of religion. These terms can mean whatever the user wants them to mean, but the platform contained no Marxist-Leninist rhetoric. Nobody ever denied that the guerrilla organizations still had their

Leninist programs in mind, backed by reams of documents floating around, some old, some not so old, but the argument was that those were just dreams for some distant future.

Preliminary contact with the United States was subsequently made through a Honduran politician, but the effort ran up against two concurrent events: the change of government in Washington and the big offensive in El Salvador. Since then, the question of negotiations has moved through numerous offers and proposals to today's two sets of contacts, one between the rebels and the special U.S. envoy, Richard Stone, the other between the rebels and a commission named by the Salvadoran government.

The moderates in the left, primarily Ungo and Rubén Zamora, have been arguing in meetings with U.S. congressional delegations that the logic—from a U.S. perspective—of reaching a political settlement to the war, meaning power-sharing or a transitional government in which the left would participate prior to elections, is to prevent Marxist-Leninist hard-liners from gaining the upper hand in the government. Conscious of the distaste with which the Sandinista government in Nicaragua is viewed by most U.S. politicians, from conservative Republicans to liberal Democrats, they contend that things have turned out the way they have in Nicaragua because the 1978-79 war against the Somoza dynasty was allowed to continue to the point of a military victory by the insurgents. To avoid this in El Salvador, they contend, it is necessary to reach a political settlement now to give the moderates more clout in a new government. There are some holes in this argument—including the ongoing debate in Nicaragua over whether the Sandinistas really defeated the National Guard or just conned the Western world with their democratic façade. It is also based on the debatable assumption that if the war continues the guerrillas will eventually win. But it is the argument they use.

Negotiation as a Tactic

U.S. diplomats and the Reagan administration have frequently claimed that these offers to talk are just tactics to help the guerrillas gain time or some other advantage that would contribute to total victory. At least in part, the experiences of the past three years confirm that point of view. For example, at the beginning of February 1981, right after the offensive in El Salvador, someone in the Nicaraguan government leaked a document of the joint Diplomatic-Political Commission of the FMLN and the FDR proposing that the left offer to negotiate with the Salvadoran junta if the United States would first terminate military assistance. The objectives of such a maneuver, it implied, were less to reach a settlement than to gain time in the war and improve the standing of the Salvadoran left with European and Latin American governments.

The Salvadoran military and the Christian Democrats used the document as proof of what they considered the endless treachery of the left, but it is also possible that the proposal, since it carried the names of Guillermo Ungo and some other moderates, was part of a maneuver within the left to try to bring the hard-liners into a pro-negotiations stance by whatever means. Six months later, in August 1981, an internal FPL document from Carpio spoke of using dialogue and negotiation as "an auxiliary but strategic factor in our struggle for power." Leftist sources say that during this period Carpio put his name to joint proposals for negotiations only very reluctantly, arguing that a lengthy war was necessary to allow time for the growth of the class consciousness of the masses.

Others in the left compared Carpio to a religious fanatic for his determination to see his method through, no matter how long it took or how much hardship it imposed on the revolutionary movement. But the other leaders were unable to prevail over a man who, at the age of fifty, had been willing to start a guerrilla war with seven people and no weapons. He resisted even the pressures of Castro and the Sandinistas until the bitter end. When Anaya Montes was killed, he was in Libya looking for the arms that would allow the FPL to continue the war on his own terms. Between the lines of the oration he delivered at her funeral was a pathetic plea for the Sandinistas not to abandon his cause. But the decision to make Villalobos the commander in chief of the guerrilla forces had been made.

A Proposal From Villalobos

Until now, Villalobos has been known primarily as a battlefield tactician, having translated a skill for kidnappings and urban violence into a talent for planning the guerrillas' larger military operations. He also developed a relatively sophisticated knowledge of weaponry. He had talked little about other matters until the beginning of September [1983], when he made a lengthy clandestine radio broadcast putting forward the guerrillas' most conciliatory proposal to date for a settlement of the war. Claiming to speak for the entire FMLN, he made four basic points: (1) a call for a new economic and social order but denying any intent to expropriate all private property; (2) a government of three branches that would carry out "truly free elections"; (3) a new national army formed by elements of the existing army and the guerrilla organizations; (4) a nonaligned foreign policy, but one recognizing the strategic necessity of good relations with the United States.

Given the ideological and tactical history of the Salvadoran guerrilla groups, much of what he said may be dismissed as a smokescreen. However, one point seems worth noting. By offering to form a new army made up of rebels and elements of the existing army, Villalobos is trying to address the primary weakness, from the standpoint of non-Marxists, that existed when the Sandinistas came to power in Nicaragua. The Carter administration, in the last days of Somoza, made a panicky effort to salvage part of the old National Guard to merge with the Sandinistas to form a new army in which the United States might retain some influence and which could serve to strengthen the hands of civilian moderates in the government. The effort failed for a variety of reasons still in dispute, not least of which was the shortage of time. Villalobos, who three years ago was predicting the "moral collapse" of the Salvadoran army, is suggesting that we talk about this now, when neither side appears on the verge of collapse or victory.

In many ways, Villalobos's army proposal is a major concession. He recognizes, for good or for bad, the importance of the army officer corps as a political institution, and seems to accept that it must be part of any settlement. By making the proposal, he is also revealing the left's basic insecurity about its own long-run military capabilities and the uncertainties of continuing supplies and training from Nicaragua and Cuba.

But there is still one major hedge in this—for the Salvadoran left, for the Sandinistas, and for Cuba. It is Villalobos himself. The decision to anoint one man, apparently Castro's own choice, to lead the Salvadoran left both militarily and politically reduces the likelihood of the other major weakness that showed up in Nicaragua after Somoza's downfall—the division of power in the Sandinista Directorate among nine theoretically equal men. Just as Nicaragua's non-Marxists found themselves hampered by a lack of influence in the new military structure, so the Sandinistas found their efforts to consolidate power restricted by their internal divisions and bickering. By putting Villalobos at the top now, the Salvadoran left is in a strong position to deal with whatever comes its way, whether it turns out to be total victory, a piece of the Army, or years more of inconclusive struggle.

17. The Divided Military

ONE EVENING IN MARCH of 1980, a slightly built man wearing glasses and the three gold stars of a full colonel in the Salvadoran army went on television and told the nation that more than 200 of the largest private farms in the country were being expropriated, as part of the military's commitment to bring social and economic justice to the downtrodden. The next morning, army troops led by officers waving the new decree moved onto the farms to begin setting up cooperatives run by peasants. During the coming weeks, in a temporary operations center at the High Command headquarters, an army major kept track of completed takeovers by placing pins on a large wall map showing most of the farms in the country. Because of the tense atmosphere caused by the brewing guerrilla war and bitter opposition from well-armed landowners, it was thought that only the Army enjoyed the power and security to set the agrarian reform in motion, a job that otherwise would have been given to a civilian agency.

One night a few months later, uniformed men pulled up to one of the newly created farm cooperatives in an armored vehicle, awakened a dozen or so men—including cooperative members and government specialists assisting them—and shot them to death. Two agronomists died while they were trying to show the troops their government identification cards.

Most of the outside world has come to look on the Salvadoran military as a murderous, repressive, monolithic institution—the problem, if you will. But there is also the other side of the Salvadoran military—the one that is looking for solutions to the country's social, economic, and political problems, and that is willing to break with the past to find them. It is a military that cannot be characterized only with a set of good-bad, black-white images.

Reprinted by permission of the author, Shirley Christian, from the June 1983 issue of *The Atlantic Monthly*.

When I try to think of episodes or circumstances that capture the essence of the Salvadoran army, it is neither the reforms nor the killings that come to mind. Rather, it is the night three years ago [in 1980] when a captain in his mid-thirties sat before me, a bandage on one shoulder visible through his freshly ironed yellow *guayabera* shirt. It was not a guerrilla-war wound that the bandage covered but a wound from the army's own internal warfare. Someone had shot the captain as he drove down the highway from Santa Ana, a provincial capital. He thought it was one of the supporters of Roberto d'Aubuisson, a vehement anti-Communist major who had been invited to leave the Army a few months earlier, because he had refused to turn over to the new military-civilian junta his files on leftist subversion and political prisoners.

D'Aubuisson and about a dozen of his army and civilian friends were being detained for allegedly plotting a *coup d'état* on behalf of rich men who had lost land to the agrarian reform. Troops loyal to Colonel Adolfo Majano, one of the two military officers in the ruling junta, had swooped down on an isolated farmhouse the night before and captured the alleged plotters. The wounded captain was in an agitated state. Majano, who was his colonel, might be in danger; there had been threats from members of the d'Aubuisson camp. The whole officer corps, about 700 men at the time, was in confusion as it began several days of debate on the crisis.

It was tempting to characterize the debate—as the captain did—in terms of Majano, a committed reformer, being under assault from a group of officers serving the interests of big money. But it was just as much, or more, a dispute over the undefined rules under which the officers of the Salvadoran army hold themselves together as the ruling elite. Majano had ordered the arrests without consulting Colonel Jaime Abdul Gutiérrez, the other army officer in the governing junta. Gutiérrez was angry. He too supported reforms, and was not fond of d'Aubuisson, but he thought the way to deal with the problem would be quietly to ship those involved abroad, instead of arresting them and running the unacceptable risk of army officers killing other army officers. The issue of what d'Aubuisson and his friends had, or had not, been plotting became entangled with what Gutiérrez thought of as Majano's questionable methodology.

Gutiérrez appointed a military judge to rule on the charges against d'Aubuisson. In a fence-straddling decision worthy of Salvadoran military tradition, Gutiérrez selected as judge a major who was strongly identified with the so-called Majanista, or reform, sector of the Army but who also had graduated from the military academy in the same class as d'Aubuisson. Gutiérrez hoped that a man with allegiances in both directions might somehow decide the case on its merits. To Gutiérrez that meant a decision avoiding a permanent rupture in the military institution.

Within the week, d'Aubuisson went free and fled to Guatemala, and his alleged co-conspirators were dispatched in various directions. Majano lost a subsequent vote of confidence to Gutiérrez but remained in the junta until he was thrown out of the government, though not the Army, at the end of 1980. My captain subsequently did the unbelievable and took to the hills with the guerrillas. D'Aubuisson returned to relative glory last year, by founding a political party and getting himself elected president of the Constituent Assembly. Gutiérrez saw the government through to those elections, then stepped out of the picture and watched in dismay as some civilian politicians tried to undo the social programs he had helped put in motion.

The Appeal of an Army Career

Where it begins for most of these men is at the Captain-General Gerardo Barrios Military School, a place of waxed tile floors, fresh paint, tropical flower beds, and polite cadets. The teachers talk of rewards that come with loyal service to the nation, and the cadets learn that the welfare of the Army and the welfare of the fatherland are indistinguishable. Most of the cadets come from lower-middle-class families who struggle to put their sons through high school in the hope that they will pass the entrance examinations for the military school, which provides four years of free education and living expenses. Becoming an officer is the most certain way to rise socially for an intelligent, earnest young man lacking family means. It will never put him on the same social level as those whose ancestors built the great coffee estates, but it offers the imprimatur of respectability in a country where that is denied to all but a few. It has traditionally led, at the very least, to influence; to moderate and sometimes great wealth; and to cabinet ministries and maybe the presidency.

Many enter the academy, few finish. Most officers now deciding the future of the country graduated in classes of twelve to twenty men in the late 1950s and the first half of the 1960s. They emerged from the academy with strong alliances and a sense of shared past and future; most received advanced training in the United States, Panama, Taiwan, Argentina, and Chile, and at the Army's own school of high command. By law, a professional military career lasts thirty years, beginning the day a young man enters the academy, which means that most officers retire before they are fifty. Though their paths may cross only occasionally in the years during which they move to seniority and power, no one forgets his classmates. Together they constitute what Salvadorans call a *tanda*. We might call it a caste, each graduating class a subcaste of the larger caste. If a member deviates too much from a line that nobody can define, he gets a stint abroad for re-education, drumming on a desk in a cubbyhole at a Salvadoran embassy in some country that hardly knows El Salvador exists. Seldom is a member of the caste turned out permanently.

The military in El Salvador is divided into two groups of armed bodies: those traditionally concerned with defense of the national territory and those concerned with keeping internal order. The first group includes the 22,400-man Army plus the Navy and the Air Force, each of which has only a few hundred men. The second group includes the National Guard, with 3,300 men; the National Police, with 3,500 men; and the Treasury Police, with 1,700 men.

The creation of the internal-security forces is generally linked by historians to the conversion of El Salvador's agricultural economy, in the second half of the last century, to coffee-growing and private ownership of land by *criollos,* Spaniards born in the New World. Such farms needed labor, so the emerging military forces were used to persuade Indians, who had previously farmed in an informal communal system, to work on the farms. When the National Guard was created, it was for the express purpose of carrying out a new law against vagabondism aimed at any Indians who did not want to work for the *criollos.* The Guardsmen also protected private property agains thieves or squatters. The Treasury Police was created after the turn of the century to combat trafficking in all kinds of contraband, on which the central treasury was being denied its tax revenue. Specifically, however, it was understood that the Treasury Police agents were to prevent Indians from getting drunk on *chicha,* the local version of corn liquor, and being unable to work. Treasury agents chased the *chicheros* who produced and sold the liquor to the Indians.

Of the three branches of the internal-security forces, only the National Police, which is assigned to handle police functions in the twenty largest urban areas, has dealt with anything remotely connected with protection of human life. Protection of the economic system was always the primary function of the security apparatus. By tradition, the toughest, meanest men in villages and rural townships were selected for the National Guard and Treasury Police, which offered lifetime careers that were attractive to men who had done their army draft duty and needed work. Because of the large size of many estates, groups of Guardsmen or Treasury Police were often based on the farms and worked virtually at the direction of the owner or his manager. No one ever told these men to use finesse in carrying out their assignments. The prevailing philosophy of the security forces was found in a phrase thought to have been brought to the New World by instructors from the Spanish Civil Guard and repeated often in the Salvadoran National Guard: "Authority that does not abuse loses its prestige."

In addition, the National Guard, too shorthanded to cover the entire country, organized canton patrols under the command of sergeants or retired sergeants and staffed by men who are not formally a part of the National Guard but are given uniforms and guns. As the war has developed, an additional paramilitary organization, called Civil Defense, has organized patrols in rural battle areas, with only loose connections with the nearest army base. The quality of the manpower, and the attitudes toward individual rights among these two groups, are, at best, on a par with those of the National Guard and the Treasury Police.

The Army developed as a garrison force, and until the war began, more than three years ago, its strength was held to only about a third of its present size. The young conscript soldiers, recruited among the peasants and urban poor for twelve to eighteen months of service, sat in barracks in the fourteen departmental capitals waiting for war with a foreign power, such as the hundred-hour war with Honduras, in 1969, while the academy-educated officers devoted themselves to building the only political party that mattered at the time.

To a large extent, the officers have been the only element connecting these various defense and security forces, and officers have traditionally come from that tight little network of graduates from the Army's military academy. In recent years, there has been some promotion from within the security forces, but the control and leadership of each force has remained with Army officers.

1932: The Martí Uprising

Newspaper stories often say that El Salvador has been ruled by the Army for half a century. In fact, since Central America became independent from Spain, in 1821, El Salvador has almost always been governed by men whose right to power is based on guns. But historians usually treat 1932 as the watershed year in Salvadoran history. That was the year of a peasant uprising led by Farabundo Martí, one of the first Communists in Central America and the man whose memory the present guerrilla movement invokes in calling itself the Martí National Liberation Front. A military dictator named General Maximiliano Hernández Martínez emerged to quell the uprising by killing a number of people, mostly peasants, put variously at between 7,000 and 30,000. He won for himself the designation of El Salvador's first modern military ruler. Before 1932, the rulers were men who commanded local armies or were combinations of landowners and warlords. After the bloodbath came a period of modernization. Highways were built, a communications system established, and a national currency created for the first time.

Even counting only from 1932, El Salvador has experienced the longest-running and most institutionalized military rule in Latin America. This rule has been centered in the military, in contrast to the personal dictatorships common in many other Latin American countries, where one man—a Somoza, a Trujillo, a Stroessner—ruled or rules through the military. In El Salvador during the past fifty years, no one individual has ever been allowed to place himself above the military, with the exception, to a certain extent, of General Hernández Martínez, who put the system in motion.

In the late 1940s, the Army organized a formal political party through which it governed the country, though other parties were not prohibited. At the beginning of the 1960s, the party was reorganized and named the National Conciliation Party, but the system of relying on senior army officers for leadership and for presidential candidates remained the same. The officers called elections every five years and established a national assembly. If the National Conciliation Party did not win the elections, the military stuffed the ballot boxes.

The National Conciliation Party and its predecessor were not ideological parties; they existed for the purpose of attaining and holding power behind a façade of legitimacy. An officer had to support the party. It was not something he learned in the academy but something he learned as he went along in his career. If he did not, he passed his days in dead-end hardship posts. The presidential candidate was always a military officer, though civilians were occasionally in the running for the nomination.

In 1966, General José Alberto Medrano, the head of the state intelligence agency (inspired, he says, by John F. Kennedy and the Alliance for Progress), founded a vast rural network called the Nationalist Democratic Organization, known by its Spanish acronym, ORDEN, to promote democratic virtues and to combat Communism. It served as the grass-roots structure for the party: white-collar civilians, particularly business and professional men, were also encouraged to support the party.

Corruption in the Army

The birth of institutionalized army rule in the 1930s came about in tacit agreement with the landed rich, usually referred to as the coffee oligarchy. It was not a hand-in-glove arrangement, in which the rich pulled the military strings, but an unwritten pact to use and abuse each other for mutual benefit. One coffee grower told me that the arrangement guaranteed an "accommodating" attitude by the military toward those with economic power. Another member of his class explained that the "productive sector" agreed to finance the government—i.e., pay taxes and close its eyes to the fact that army officers steal a substantial amount—in return for being left in peace to make money. The rich financed the electoral campaigns and were allowed to name their own kind to the ministries dealing with the economy and foreign affairs. They looked down upon their military partners, who, in turn, felt great social resentment toward those who bankrolled them.

Corruption is still extensive. Officers are routinely bought off or blackmailed by civilians seeking military influence. Some officers receive payoffs from men doing business in their territory; each provincial commander has the opportunity, for example, to make a profit on the monthly food budget for the 1,000 or so troops under his command. In some cases, it is difficult to draw the line between corruption and the granting of favors, such as the offering of bank directorships and jobs in private business after retirement from the military.

Some officers accept only what is dangled in front of them; others aggressively seek payoffs. In 1976, the chief of staff of the Army was convicted in U.S. federal court in New York and sentenced to prison for his part in a scheme to sell $2.5 million worth of submachine guns to American gangsters—guns he was intending to buy in the United States by submitting to the State Department a false certificate saying that the weapons would be shipped to his own army.

Corruption is so much a part of anything related to the Salvadoran military that any time an officer changes his position on any question, Salvadorans automatically assume that someone has bought him. Over the past four years, I have heard so many whispered charges and countercharges of corruption from officers and civilians that I conclude that the alleged corruption adds up to an impossible amount. Even the rare officer who joins the left or so much as proposes talking to the insurgents is likely to encounter the allegation that the guerrillas have offered him money. One theory of why U.S. military assistance is not more successful as a pressure device for ending human rights abuses is that it offers little prospect of individual rake-offs, because very little of it actually comes into El Salvador as money. Most comes as equipment and supplies or in the form of training Salvadoran soldiers in the United States and Panama.

Military Changes From Within

Despite the electoral framework created by the military and its pact with the rich, there have been periodic eruptions from within the military caused by various things: the desire for reform; individual officers' overstepping acceptable bounds of corruption; pressures from younger officers eager for their turn at the top; and external events. Each such eruption, however, has had some lasting effect, because each new group of officers has justified the assumption of power with promises to create a fair society and hold free elections, and has taken at least some steps toward keeping them. Two tumultuous periods of coups and government reorganizations, one in the mid-1940s and another at the beginning of the 1960s, resulted in substantial improvements, relatively speaking, in social and labor laws and the freedom to organize opposition political parties. This freedom led, in turn, to the birth and growth in the 1960s of the Christian Democratic Party, now the strongest single party in the country, though it lacks an outright majority. Some smaller opposition parties to the left of the Christian Democrats also developed, including a legal front organization for the Communist Party. Throughout the 1970s, the Communists participated in elections as part of the opposition coalition, but a split in their party spawned three of the present guerrilla groups, and the party itself opted to become a guerrilla force at the end of 1979.

It was obvious that this gradual opening up of the society would lead to a victory by the opposition, given free elections. When that came close to happening in 1972, the year the coalition led by José Napoleón Duarte got a plurality and possibly an outright majority of the popular vote, the Army went through another eruption. It announced false election results, giving the victory to its own candidate. A month later, several officers, dissatisfied with the fraud, attempted a rebellion. Perhaps because this rebellion raised the ultimate question—whether the military would actually give up power—the rest of the Army put it down with a hundred or more deaths and no significant change in the power structure. Duarte was arrested, beaten, and sent into exile, though he had played no role in organizing the rebellion. Today, many officers, as well as foreign analysts, believe that the failure to allow Duarte his victory contributed to the growth of guerrilla groups and social problems.

In May of 1979, a small group of officers began to meet. They saw a burgeoning leftist movement that not only was raising tens of millions of dollars by kidnapping wealthy Salvadorans or foreign businessmen but could put 200,000 demonstrators in the streets at one time. They looked at Nicaragua, where the Somoza dynasty was in its death throes, and saw that the United States was doing nothing to rescue the Nicaraguan National Guard, a military institution that had been, until recently, as strongly entrenched as that in El Salvador. Finally, they considered the occupant of the presidential palace, General Carlos Humberto Romero, who was isolated from many senior officers, deaf to the pleas of moderate civilians that he take drastic measures to correct national problems, and out of favor with the Carter administration because of the growing number of bodies turning up in trash cans and along the roads. The officers concluded that circumstances were such that the Marxist-Leninist guerrilla groups and their supporting organizations could carry out a successful insurrection by the end of the year. They decided to act before then.

The 1979 Coup

On the morning of October 15, the three senior men in the small group of officers—Colonel Gutiérrez, Lieutenant Colonel René Guerra y Guerra, and Major Alvaro Salazar Brenes—took command of San Carlos, the headquarters of the First Brigade in the capital. Junior officers working with them demanded the surrender of barracks commanders around the country. Gutiérrez telephoned President Romero to request that he leave the country.

Another shaking of the military tree was under way, and everyone involved thought that this one would turn out to be more momentous than any in the past. Salazar Brenes had said during the planning sessions that it would have to be the last military coup in El Salvador for at least twenty years. The political planning that went into it was even more careful than the logistical planning. A proclamation was written containing a heavy dose of theory about the redistribution of wealth—primarily through an agrarian reform—a vague promise to call elections, and a commitment to work to repair the divisions in Salvadoran society, presumably meaning an attempt to patch things up with insurgents. In a country desperately short of skill in political analysis and organization, the three officers represented a remarkably large amount of what skill there was. Gutiérrez, an engineer, had respected administrative and managerial talents. Salazar Brenes had earned a degree in political science at the Central American University after finishing military school, an unusual education for a military officer. Guerra y Guerra, more highly born than most military officers, consulted closely with a relative among the Jesuit priests, who dominate the teaching and administration of the university.

After much jockeying in the final days before the coup, Colonel Gutiérrez and Colonel Adolfo Majano were selected to represent the military in the new ruling junta, which was also to include three civilians. Guerra y Guerra wanted to be a member of the junta, but Gutiérrez insisted that only full colonels should serve, so Guerra y Guerra and the younger officers working with him asked Majano, then deputy director of the military academy, to represent them. He played no role in organizing the coup and apparently hesitated at the last moment, not arriving at the San Carlos barracks until late on the day of the coup.

Majano was then forty-one and Gutiérrez was forty-three; both were part of the small elite that full colonels constitute in a country where few make general. Like the U.S. Senate, the colonels form an exclusive club of people with great influence and status. After the coup, nearly sixty senior officers, including all the generals and the majority of the colonels, were retired or sent abroad. Only about a dozen full colonels were allowed to remain, all of them handpicked by Gutiérrez, though the number was allowed to rise with promotions made in the months after the coup.

A Continuing Military Shakedown

The 1979 coup was not the beginning and end of change in the military. The years since have brought an ongoing shakedown involving both power and ideas. The Salvadoran military has washed its linen in public as no other Latin American military institution has, providing a rare look inside a situation that would be reported with rumor and supposition in other countries. In part, this public display came about because the coup was followed by the assertion of a form of internal military democracy by the entire officer corps; for a while, everybody claimed the right to an opinion and a vote about every government policy. Gutiérrez thought that this was no way to fight a war, and set out to reassert the traditional top-to-bottom command structure. Eventually, some twenty-five commanders, all colonels or lieutenant colonels, assumed the power to make most military decisions, but the lingering effects of the democratization period have made it necessary for commanders to take into account the opinions of lower-ranking officers if they want their barracks to function. There was military unity when the coup was carried out in 1979, but within a few months it began to break down over various issues, and the consensus continues to be in debate today. Among the issues being debated are commitment or non-commitment to the promised reforms; past associations; corruption; relations with, and manipulations by, civilian groups; personal ambition; and, on occasion, conduct of the war.

Guerra y Guerra and many young officers, for example, viewed Gutiérrez as corrupt, because of his past position as head of the state communications corporation, a traditional source of rake-offs. The left regularly dropped the suggestion that Gutiérrez worked for the CIA. Guerra y Guerra was distrusted by Gutiérrez and his friends, who saw him as too personally ambitious and for that reason damaging to the agreed-upon goals. Gutiérrez, a somewhat retiring person, thought that Majano hogged the limelight too much for a man who had done nothing to bring off the coup. Majano, known to friends and detractors alike for honesty, intelligence, and naïveté, thought that as the elected representative of a group of younger officers he had the responsibility to improve the miserable human rights record of the armed forces. Robert E. White, the American ambassador, encouraged him in this role.

In all the allegations of coup attempts and purges during 1980, it was never clear who was trying to do what to whom. Some officers accused Majano of flirting with the guerrillas, whose political front groups were tempting him to make a grab for total power with statements to the effect that they knew him to be "recuperable, not bloodthirsty." At the same time, some officers, particularly those friendly to the ousted Major d'Aubuisson, were viewed as being in the pay of the extreme right.

When the many versions of civilian government that have shared power with the military since the 1979 coup are added to this equation, the machinations and interests involved in any policy decision are multiplied. The first junta, made up of the two colonels and three civilians and backed by a cabinet that ranged from businessmen to Communists, lasted through ten weeks of tears, shouting, and mutual accusations before the inevitable self-destruction. Most of the civilians in the junta and the cabinet wanted Majano to assert the power of the younger officers to remove three senior officers the civilians perceived to be blocking progress: Gutiérrez, Defense Minister José Guillermo García, and Carlos Eugenio Vides Casanova, the director of the National Guard. Those three colonels, on the other hand, claimed that the civilians were being manipulated by the extreme left. Majano was apparently swayed against attempting a takeover by the fear that he might be destroying the military.

When the first junta broke apart, the Christian Democrats joined the military in forming a government, and while they had more collective staying power than the first set of civilians, they were shaken by the unsolved killings of various party activists and the flight of others to exile and affiliation with the insurgents. Though close to Majano in social ideas, the Christian Democrats found him a difficult loner in day-to-day affairs, and decided that Gutiérrez was more realistic and effective.

At the end of 1980, Gutiérrez and Defense Minister García made a written pact with the Christian Democrats that led to restructuring the government in the form that lasted until the elections in March 1982 for the Assembly, which began writing a new constitution. The catalyst for the 1980 restructuring, aside from the power struggles involving Majano, was the murder of four American missionaries by a National Guard patrol. The idea was to give a respected civilian, Duarte, more power by making him president of the junta (there had been none since the coup), and to establish firmer authority lines in the Army and security forces. In the process, García, Gutiérrez, and Vides Casanova became generals. A month later, however, the Reagan administration came into office almost simultaneously with the first big guerrilla offensive. The question of how to fight the insurgency on the battlefield quickly became more important than abuse of authority.

A Tradition of Violence

El Salvador's convulsions of the past four years have drawn attention to the terrible violence that has existed seemingly forever but that has increased as part of the reaction and counterreaction to the insurgency. Somewhere along the line, the general principle that in wars people try to kill their enemies has been replaced in El Salvador with the notion that one kills whoever is easiest to kill. Usually, that has meant any young man between eighteen and twenty-four, families of government troops and of guerrillas, politicians who think it might be a good idea for the sides to negotiate, and nuns and other social activists who become involved with the intention of helping the poor.

The killings and abuses fall into several categories. One is crimes committed by so-called death squads or by individuals in them, which usually single out individual people or families, often those known nationally or in small towns for commitment to a particular cause, revolutionary or otherwise. It is accepted, among military officers and others, that the death squads are commanded by a few middle- or lower-level officers, who, in the pay of civilian groups, recruit gunmen, particularly enlisted men from the National Guard or Treasury Police, to carry out political assassinations. This theory is largely based on supposition, but there are some factual kernels that support it. Papers taken from the briefcase of a captain arrested with d'Aubuisson during the alleged farmhouse plotting three years ago revealed a list of last names of military officers suspected by other officers of receiving payoffs to run death squads.

Distinct from the death-squad killings are mass killings in rural battle zones. The circumstances of these killings are clouded by great confusion and lack of information, such as whether the victims were families of guerrillas and whether they were killed intentionally by government troops, caught in crossfire, or eliminated in a no-holds-barred cleanup sweep. Sometimes what the guerrillas describe as the site of a military massacre the Army will describe as a burial ground for guerrilla combat losses. A third category of killings is related to feuds in small towns and rural areas which are only nominally, if at all, related to any of the issues in the war. In the absence of legal and police authority, those who have guns—which seems to be almost everyone—resolve things in their own way.

Some analysts like to fix responsibility for this violence squarely at the top of the military structure, particularly on General García in his long reign as defense minister, beginning the day after the 1979 coup and ending with his resignation in April 1983, and a few other men in key positions, such as the heads of the National Guard and the Treasury Police. But the structure of the Salvadoran military is so diffuse that there is no such thing as a clear order. By tradition, the defense minister presides rather than directs. He is dependent on the willingness of the fourteen departmental commanders and of the heads of the three security forces to obey him. Even the link from the heads of the security forces to their troops is imprecise, because the security-force detachments in the fourteen departments are responsible first to the provincial army commander. When officers are inclined to clean up the units under their command, the old ways are often so imbedded as to prevent it. The two officers assigned to take over the National Guard and the National Police after the 1979 coup, General Vides Casanova and Colonel Carlos Reynaldo López Nuila, sought unsuccessfully in 1980 to be relieved of their posts, because they feared that it was impossible to get internal control of the organizations they were supposed to command. Further removed from the center of power and the command structure is the network of canton and civil-defense patrols in rural zones. These patrols, unpaid or badly paid, appear to take the brunt of guerrilla firepower and, in turn, to bear a large part of the responsibility in mass killings.

There have been efforts to deal with these problems, with mixed degrees of enthusiasm and success. The National Police, the National Guard, and the Treasury Police have dismissed several hundred men during the past three years as part of a campaign to weed out those who abuse their authority and to replace them with younger men who might carry out their assignments in a more humane way. Since the time when he wanted to throw up his hands in defeat in his effort to control the National Police, Colonel López Nuila, a lawyer who previously served on the army legal staff, has made some advances in teaching the police how to investigate crimes, particularly kidnappings, and in developing a code of conduct that includes keeping arrest records. Nevertheless, it is still routine for the police to beat up anyone they arrest. The Army High Command has held occasional meetings, which are well publicized, with the leaders of the canton and civil-defense patrols, to plead for better behavior.

A key element in the problems of violence, to which military leaders point as proof that they cannot bear the full responsibility, is the absence of a functioning judicial system. Many people concerned with achieving human rights progress in El Salvador, Americans as well as Salvadorans, believe that until the example of legal punishment is demonstrated, those who commit violent acts, whether they wear uniforms or not, will never change their ways. Some army officers speak bitterly of arresting people and turning them over to the civilian courts for investigation and prosecution, only to find them soon freed on technicalities. Salvadoran judges are known for being easy to buy off and easy to frighten. Bombs, threats, and terrorist attacks are the established methods used by people on all political sides to influence judges. A colonel told me about a large cocaine bust in which he played a significant role several years ago: the defendants, two Peruvian women arrested in a San Salvador hotel, went free after a large amount of money came into the country and, according to the colonel, was generously distributed among key people in the judicial system.

Finally, there is the matter of what José Napoleón Duarte calls the "culture of violence" that prevails in El Salvador. Most Salvadorans are as convinced that extreme violence is part of their national character as they are convinced that corruption is endemic to the military and those who surround it. Government in El Salvador has traditionally been based on the authority of terror, implied even when not exerted. Rumor, cruelty, and ignorance are also at play in many killings among the rural population, which is largely illiterate. Some argue that the issue of military abuse will be solved only as the entire society resolves its violence problem by a combination of education and legal punishment for the guilty.

The Complex Truth

"Each one has his own truth," a colonel commanding a post in eastern El Salvador once told me as he discussed the Army's degree of commitment or non-commitment to social change. Anyone trying to take an objective view will indeed find many truths about the Salvadoran military institution. A few truths are commendable, some are only barely palatable, and some are despicable. Some are simply facts that will not go away. Among them: the Salvadoran military has a lot of innocent blood on its hands, and admits it only reluctantly. It also has an ample historical sense of how its hands got bloody. It has reached a degree of consensus about the need to change the country's social and political attitudes, and to make the military put a high value on human life. But there are sectors in the armed forces not in agreement, men who believe that it is still possible to use the threat of a Communist takeover to justify oppression. There is also disagreement, even among the majority, about how to reach the national goals and how much internal change the military can absorb in time of war. Finally, as Salvadoran military history has shown, conflicts over ideas and policies often get deflected by personal ambition and greed. The error lies in believing only one of these truths about the Salvadoran military, whichever it may be, and ignoring the others. In the end, the military wants to survive, and its leadership wants to do what is necessary to ensure that.

Despite its own soul-searching of the past few years, the Salvadoran military, in large measure, looks to the United States to define what is necessary. The messages it gets are unclear at best, and often contradictory. Trying to interpret the demands coming from the many centers of power and influence in the United States—the White House, the National Security Council, the State Department, the Pentagon, Congress, the press, opinion polls, pressure groups, and demonstrators—leads some officers to conclude that it is enough merely to talk a reformist line, and others to see the disaster ahead if the military does not take the lead in effecting actual reforms. Without a clearer message from the United States, the officers may be unable to agree on what to do next. This is a military that is at war as much with itself as with the guerrillas.

18. Misconceptions About the Role of the Church

By KERRY PTACEK

Focus The American media give the impression that the Catholic Church in El Salvador supports the guerrillas and opposes the government. Kerry Ptacek argues that the Salvadoran hierarchy, the only official voice of the church in that country, criticizes immoral violence of both the right and the left. Archbishop Rivera y Damas of San Salvador, however, has made it clear that he considers the reforms planned by the government preferable to the violent solution of the guerrillas, which does not meet the Catholic criteria for a just war.

Confusion exists about the archbishop's clear position, says Ptacek, because some unofficial church organizations and individuals have used ecclesiastical authority for political purposes. One Salvadoran bishop has pointed out that members of the so-called People's Church ("base communities" that promote political revolution more than they follow church leadership) have "used Bishop Rivera y Damas's name without permission and have forged his signature on several pamphlets to convince people in other countries that the church in El Salvador was requesting their help."

Socorro Jurídico, the legal aid office of the Archdiocese of San Salvador, while enjoying some official status, has been repudiated by the archbishop for its political bias. Spokesmen for this office "give evidence only of the victims of the

263

security forces," the archbishop said. "They have yet to attribute a victim to the guerrilla forces, though the guerrillas claim some deaths themselves."

The archbishop considers the extreme right the "true cause of the political ills that are currently causing the crisis" in El Salvador, but he does not identify the extreme right with the government. He counsels patience in the difficult task of creating a viable alternative to the repression of the right and the Marxism-Leninism of the left.

This analysis of the church's political judgments in El Salvador, which first appeared in 1981, should be examined along with the claims of guerrilla leader Guillermo Ungo (selection 15).

Notes for this essay begin on page 277.

Kerry Ptacek is the director of research at the Institute on Religion and Democracy, a private, non-profit research center in Washington, D.C., that examines the relationship between religious values and democratic principles.

AMERICAN CHURCHGOERS WHO ARE concerned about the tragic conflict in El Salvador often hear assertions about the position of the Catholic Church in that country. These often are bewildering, because virtually all parties to that conflict try to enlist the church in their behalf. But we rarely hear directly from the Salvadoran church—either in our domestic polemics or in the press. Yet the Catholic Church in El Salvador has taken a clear stand on the crisis afflicting the country, though that stand may not be entirely satisfying to any of the U.S. partisans in the debate.

Much of the confusion stems not from ambiguity in official statements but from a misunderstanding about who—in the tradition and doctrine of the Catholic Church—actually speaks for the church. In these terms, the positions of the church must be taken principally from the statements of the [then acting] archbishop, Monsignor Arturo Rivera y Damas, and those who speak officially on his behalf. [Monsignor Rivera y Damas was installed as archbishop of San Salvador in the spring of 1983.] Those views are readily available in the archbishop's weekly homilies and in his interviews with the press. They are also reflected in the positions of the Salvadoran Conference of Bishops and its officers.

The personal opinions of individual clergy and the statements of unofficial organizations claiming to speak for Salvadoran Catholics do not represent, properly speaking, the positions of the church. There are a number of Catholics in El Salvador who represent themselves as the "true" voice of the Catholic Church, or who use church auspices to present views contrary to those of the Conference of Bishops and the archbishop. Views of this kind, though they sometimes warrant consideration, should not be taken as official.

Reprinted by permission of the author from a pamphlet published in 1981 by the Institute on Religion and Democracy (IRD).

Sources of Misinformation

There are three main sources of misinformation in El Salvador about the positions of that country's Catholic Church: the guerrillas of the Democratic Revolutionary Front/Unified Revolutionary Directorate (FDR/DRU); the People's Church; and Socorro Jurídico, the legal aid office of the Archbishopric of San Salvador.

The Guerrillas

At the time of their "final offensive" in January 1981, the guerrillas promoted the idea that the church supported the uprising. Hugo Navarrette, a leader of the Democratic Revolutionary Front, had declared that "the Salvadoran church continues to support the guerrilla struggle against the regime of President Duarte."[1]

Navarrette's statement forced the Social Communications Secretariat of the Archbishopric of San Salvador to issue a communiqué insisting that "the bishops have never done or said anything that might be honestly construed in terms used in Navarrette's affirmation."[2]

But only three days after the archbishop's office repudiated Navarrette's false assertion, Father Rogelio Poncel claimed on Radio Venceremos, the voice of the guerrilla movement, that Archbishop Rivera y Damas's criticisms of human rights violations "cannot be interpreted except as implicit condemnation" of the government. Father Poncel contended that the archbishop's statements "indirectly lend support" to the guerrillas.[3]

By the end of May, Radio Venceremos had changed its opinion of Archbishop Rivera y Damas. The guerrilla radio now characterized his statements as being "biased and dangerous." But Archbishop Rivera y Damas's positions had not changed radically. Instead, during the intervening weeks, the church had clarified its positions and acted to restrain those who misrepresented them.

The People's Church

In the communiqué that denounced Navarrette's falsification of the church's position, the Social Communications Secretariat referred to another source of confusion, the People's Church: "The fact that a small number of priests, nuns, and laymen in the so-called People's Church have followed a specific political option and have made a public commitment to the Democratic Revolutionary Front is no reason to assume that this phenomenon is representative of the Salvadoran Catholic Church."[4]

The People's Church is not an official organization of the Catholic Church in Salvador. Indeed, it might be considered something of a Marxist "Reformation," since it substitutes the authority of "the revolution" for the authority of the church. On January 7, 1981, the Salvadoran Conference of Bishops issued a communiqué that accused the People's Church of "promoting a schism within the Catholic Church" of El Salvador. Catholics were asked to withdraw from this organization because it had "sown division" within the church. Monsignor José Eduardo Alvarez, the president of the Salvadoran Conference of Bishops, called on the faithful to "recognize the authority of the bishops as representative of the Holy Father."[5]

Unmoved by such appeals, the People's Church responded by calling the attitudes of the prelates "tendentious" and characterized the communiqué of the Salvadoran Conference of Bishops as "a biased position that reduces their moral authority."[6] The People's Church also declared that several of the bishops had asked army units to end occupations of their churches by leftist protestors. Apparently, in the eyes of the People's Church, the authority of the bishops does not include the right to make use of their churches when the left deems political protest to be in order.

The People's Church played an active role in the guerrillas' abortive "final offensive" of January 1981. Radio Sandino in Managua, the voice of Nicaragua's ruling Sandinistas, reported on January 14 that Father Plácido, a member of the National Coordinating Board of the People's Church of El Salvador, had announced the previous day the formation of several "Christian" committees in solidarity with the guerrilla struggle. Only a few days before, the Salvadoran bishops had characterized the People's Church as "a politicized group which seeks to ally itself with the leftist organization to participate in a fratricidal war in this country."[7]

The People's Church is largely responsible for the widespread impression that Christians support the Democratic Revolutionary

Front. And yet, not only does the People's Church not legitimately speak for the Catholic Church in El Salvador; it does not even speak for a significant number of the clergy. Archbishop Rivera y Damas, in response to a question about the "split" in the clergy, said:

> The priests who are most politicized, so to speak, and clearly on the side of the left-wing front number about fifteen [out of some two hundred]. Three of them are with the guerrillas, others are propagandizing for the front all of the time, some from underground, while others are traveling abroad carrying out propaganda missions.[8]

Rivera y Damas has also accused the People's Church of distorting the position of the Salvadoran Catholic Church in other countries. In June 1981, Bishop Aparicio, the secretary of the Salvadoran Conference of Bishops, while traveling in the United States, said that the People's Church pretends "to speak for the church and for the poor and ... to be the only official church in the country."[9]

Bishop Aparicio also pointed to fund-raising activities by the People's Church in Venezuela, Mexico, Central America, and Europe in which it falsely claimed the authority of the archbishop. "They have used Bishop Rivera y Damas's name without permission and have forged his signature on several pamphlets to convince people in other countries that the church in El Salvador was requesting their help."[10] These pamphlets have been condemned by Rivera y Damas and the Salvadoran Conference of Bishops, but the People's Church is undeterred, apparently convinced that it can deceive Christians in other countries into believing that it acts with legitimate authority.

Catholics in the United States should know that, according to Bishop Aparicio, "the only official organizations authorized to collect and distribute aid to the refugees in El Salvador are the Apostolic Conference and Caritas."[11] The bishop asserted that funds raised by the People's Church are never seen by "the poor people who need these contributions" but go to "produce more propaganda for the left."[12]

Of course, there is the possibility that funds raised in behalf of the People's Church may aid refugees in areas controlled by the guerrillas. But they appear to be few, according to church spokesmen in El Salvador. Archbishop Rivera y Damas told *Washington Post* reporter Christopher Dickey in March 1981 that "the majority of refugees are fleeing not the government but the guerrillas."[13] Some fifty to sixty thousand refugees have fled from areas controlled by the guerrillas. Moreover, the church provides care for around six thousand refugees connected with the left.[14]

Socorro Jurídico

Another source of confusion regarding the Catholic Church in El Salvador is Socorro Jurídico, the legal aid office of the Archbishopric of San Salvador. Socorro Jurídico has often been quoted in the United States as though it spoke for the entire church. Some of its statements have had the archbishop's name affixed to them. Few people outside El Salvador are aware of the conflict between Rivera y Damas and Socorro Jurídico precisely over the legal aid office's propensity to issue statements opposed to the views of the church.

The controversy over Socorro Jurídico arises from its refusal to report any acts of violence committed by the left. According to Archbishop Rivera y Damas, "they give evidence only of the victims of the security forces," and "they have yet to attribute a victim to the guerrilla forces though the guerrillas claim some deaths themselves."[15] In fact, the left has boasted of killing four to six thousand people as of the spring of 1981.[16] Socorro Jurídico's practice of issuing press releases reporting the actions of only one side makes it seem to world public opinion as if a general massacre instead of a civil war is taking place in El Salvador.

Socorro Jurídico has also created a distorted picture of the very serious refugee problem in El Salvador. While in the United States, Rivera y Damas mentioned one case in which the legal aid office reported military searches and abuses in church refugee camps, without mentioning the discovery of guerrilla bombs.[17] The archbishop said that he "was very unhappy with the way they have been acting because it wasn't a service of the truth."[18]

On May 31, 1981, the archbishop, his patience exhausted, deprived Socorro Jurídico of its right to speak on behalf of the archibishopric. Monsignor Freddy Delgado, the information secretary, was made the sole official spokesman on these matters.

THE CHURCH AND THE LEFT

What, then, is the true attitude of the Catholic Church in El Salvador toward the Democratic Revolutionary Front and the leftist guerrillas? First, of all, the church opposes the left's recourse to violent insurrection. Months before the guerrillas' "final offensive in January 1981, Archbishop Rivera y Damas made clear in a Sunday homily that the church wanted peace, "but not a peace won by weapons."[20] On the very day that the attack broke out, January 11, 1981, he was delivering a homily appealing to the left not to carry out its projected general uprising. He called on the left to "respect" the will of the majority, which "for some time" had rejected this option.[21]

On January 14, in the midst of the guerrilla offensive, Archbishop Rivera y Damas reiterated his position by way of explaining why the people were not supporting the insurrection: "I believe that the people have failed to respond to the call for a general uprising because for a long time now the people have had the feeling that war is not the proper solution for the problems which this country is facing."[22]

The church, however, does not counsel an unconditional pacifism. Rather, its position is that, under current conditions, insurrection is not justified. In a homily January 18, Archbishop Rivera y Damas examined the leftist insurrection in the light of Catholic moral teaching:

> Insurrection is justified when four requirements are satisfied: There is a serious abuse of political power by those in power, all peaceful alternatives have failed, the ills that accompany an insurrection would not be greater than the present difficulties, and the people must truly believe that the insurrection shall win.[23]

The archbishop contended that only the first of these four requirements had been met. "In this country there have been serious abuses that are still occurring, despite the efforts of the young military men who seized power in 1979," he said. But the other three conditions have not been satisfied. He insisted that peaceful methods existed for solving the country's crisis. "Unfortunately, many of the members of the contending parties have dogmatically refused to search for peaceful solutions to the problem."[24]

The church does not oppose only the *methods* of the left. During the same homily Rivera y Damas went into the other reasons for the failure of the insurrection. He asserted that the leftist coalition was "inclined toward Communism" and that "the Salvadoran people are not certain that the installation of a socialist regime in El Salvador is preferable to a continuation of the present one."[25]

And while Salvadorans could understand the necessity of liberating themselves from foreign domination, they could not make sense of the leftists' exclusive concern about the role of the United States when the "general offensive was made with the help of the other great imperialism." Salvadorans saw that it "would serve no purpose to give one's life and blood to liberate themselves from the domination of the United States" only to replace it with "the domination of the Communist superpower."[26]

On February 3, when the guerrilla uprising had clearly failed, the archbishop sought to weigh the mixed feelings of the people toward the conflict. "We cannot affirm that the civilian population is with the government, but it is a fact that they are accepting it at least as the lesser of two evils, although a large part of the people admire the dedicated ideals and sacrifice of many left-wing youth. Still, it is obvious that the majority of the people do not support violent solutions which destroy families, risk their lives, and destroy marriages."[27]

Archbishop Rivera y Damas explicitly rejected the notion that government repression was the main factor in preventing the leftist insurrection from gaining popular support. "I don't think they lost it only because of government repression. They lost this support because the people saw that they tended toward the conquest of power for its own sake and not toward satisfying the hopes of the people."[28] Indeed, the archbishop has argued that government repression increased in response to violence by the guerrillas. "I have always denounced repression and will continue to denounce it, but much of it is a reaction to the violent opposition."[29]

THE CHURCH AND THE GOVERNMENT

The supporters of the Democratic Revolutionary Front/Unified Revolutionary Directorate (FDR/DRU) in the United States have attempted to create the impression that there are only two sides in the Salvadoran conflict: the "left" and the junta. The junta is thought of as the representative of the oligarchy and the extreme right, or as a sort of cover for the oligarchy. The "left," in this simplistic view, is considered to embrace all those who want change beneficial to the poor, and in particular the peasantry.

This simple division of the various and complex currents in El Salvador's turbulent politics into "good" and "evil" is not the perspective of the Catholic Church. The church views the Christian Democrats and the young military officers as proponents of changes that have already benefited the peasantry. What has most concerned the church about the present government has been its inability to eliminate elements of the extreme right from the security forces and the military.

In a very important homily on March 8, 1981, Rivera y Damas noted three critical developments in his country's civil conflict: the reappearance of the extreme right, "the leftists' obstinancy in taking up the weapons of terror," and the government's commitment to a "peaceful and democratic solution."[30]

By "extreme right" the church generally means those groups associated with the old landed oligarchy, sometimes referred to, inaccurately, as the "Fourteen Families." This oligarchy exercised its power through the National Guard and local security forces, which were often paid directly by large landowners.

The archbishop said the "extreme right" was "the true cause of all the social and political ills that are currently creating the crisis in our country."[31] Far from seeing the government as a creature of the right, Rivera y Damas feared that the extreme right would engineer a coup in order to abort the process of reform. But he remained confident that "the Salvadoran people, with the same firmness and assurance with which they have said No to violence and Marxism-Leninism, will say a resounding No to any plan by the extreme right to seize power."[32]

A coup by the extreme right would "make pointless the sacrifice of so many lives"[33] to eliminate the arbitrary power of the oligarchy. In Rivera y Damas's view, "with the coup by the young military officers on October 15, 1979," "the root of the evil was removed."[34] . . .

After the Christian Democrats joined the military in a coalition government in 1980, the reform process was more successful. The reforms of the coalition government were credited by the church as the principal cause of the left's loss of popular support. While many supported the coalition government as the "lesser evil" in response to the guerrillas, Rivera y Damas insisted that "one also has to take into account that the junta has also achieved substantial reforms, especially in the area of agrarian reform."[35]

The church became more favorable toward the government as the role of the Christian Democrats within it increased and in particular as the Christian Democratic leader José Napoleón Duarte gained prominence. In mid-December 1980, after the killing of four American women missionaries, Rivera y Damas commented favorably on the Christian Democrats' demand to the military that "as a condition for continuing to participate in the government it combat the structures which favor the violence of the extreme right just as it combats the extreme left."[36] Rivera y Damas was pleased by the appointment of Duarte to the presidency of the government in December 1980. He hoped that the rise of guerrilla political leader Guillermo Ungo to a large public role in the revolutionary coalition would increase the likelihood for a peaceful settlement. But Ungo's rise was soon followed by the guerrillas' general offensive.[37]

The continuing fear of the people that the right would step in and nullify the reforms has hindered the government's efforts to consolidate popular support. The church has called for action against the vestiges of the oligarchy within the government and the army as steps to guarantee the reforms. "More than once the church has raised her impartial voice to tell the government to purify its ranks of the administrative and military personnel who were impeding the progress of democracy and following practices that were inconsistent with human rights," said Rivera y Damas in a March 1981 homily.[38]

THE CHURCH AND MILITARY AID

The position of the Salvadoran Catholic Church on military aid should be seen in the context of the church's broader analysis of the crisis in El Salvador. In this light, its actual position is quite different from the one often ascribed to it.

The church is first of all concerned that military aid not be viewed as the principal answer to the country's problems. In the words of Archbishop Rivera y Damas: "The problems here are not military. The problems here are social and economic, and social and economic solutions have to be found, not military ones."[39]

The church has opposed military aid to El Salvador not because it opposes the coalition government or wants it to lose the civil war. On the contrary, the church is fairly confident of the government's ability to hold on, given its popular support. The archbishop has repeatedly expressed his opinion that "El Salvador could cope with its military needs with what it has now."[40] The church seems concerned that large-scale military aid from abroad might persuade the extreme right and wavering elements of the army that the guerrillas could be defeated without the reforms that won the people away from the left.

Those who wish to construe the church's opposition to military aid as opposition to the government have failed to consider, or reveal to the public, the church's stand against aid to the guerrillas. The church has repeatedly denounced aid from Marxist-Leninist regimes, Nicaragua in particular. And this is not a mere effort to appear even-handed. In a little noticed interview he gave while visiting New York in April 1981, Archbishop Rivera y Damas told a U.S. audience that "instead of sending arms, you could help put a cordon around our country to impede the arrival of arms from the Soviet bloc."[41] This suggestion is rarely cited by those who quote the church extensively with respect to other questions of military aid.

The failure to halt the flow of arms and personnel from the Soviet bloc into El Salvador evidently led the Salvadoran church to reevaluate its stand on U.S. military aid to the Salvadoran government. Bishop Aparicio, during a visit to California in the spring of 1981, reflected this new attitude when asked about the church's position on military aid:

> The Church in El Salvador does not want military aid from the United States if all Soviet aid to the guerrillas stops. While Russia is supplying the guerrillas with arms we need the United States to help to strengthen our own army.[42]

Bishop Aparicio insisted that he was speaking as a representative of El Salvador's Catholic Church on this matter. "Prior to my trip, I asked the Apostolic Conference to grant me permission not only to come, but also to speak on behalf of the church on matters of U.S. involvement in my country and on the suffering our country is enduring now. So, yes, I am speaking on behalf of the church in El Salvador."[43]

THE CHURCH AND A 'POLITICAL SOLUTION'

Although he does not consider a guerrilla military victory likely, Archbishop Rivera y Damas recognizes that the left still "has the power to continue its devastation for many long years." The Salvadoran military could not be expected to accomplish much against such a terrorist strategy. "Contemporary history," he explained in a March 1981 homily, "shows that in places where terrorism becomes established, the police force is unable to control it."[44] Developments in El Salvador suggest that the left, frustrated by its inability to enlist the people on its side, has turned to a new kind of terrorism, which aims to destroy the economy through attacks on communications, power and water supplies, warehoused crops, and factories. The church refers to this leftist strategy as the "empty table."

The church hopes to help the country break out of the deadlock of terror from right and left by promoting a dialogue between the government and those elements of the left willing to accept free elections. The archbishop continues to hold that "there are highly valuable elements within the ranks of the FDR which cannot simply be discarded but must be given the opportunity to dialogue, to participate in public affairs and in the pacification and in the moral and material reconstruction of the nation."[45]

However, Rivera y Damas believes that certain options are non-negotiable, including any "reversal of the political and social reforms that have been undertaken," and opposition to "the radical ideologies of both the right and the left."[46]

It would be an error to confuse the church's desire for "dialogue" with the kind of "negotiated settlement" that would place the left partly or wholly in power without holding a free election. Rivera y Damas made clear the church's understanding of the distinction between these terms in an interview in May 1981:

> The Salvadoran government has been making a clear-cut difference between negotiations, mediation, dialogue, and political solution. It opposes negotiations because this would mean acknowledging that the armed groups and the front have legal status and must be viewed as belligerent parties, which would lead to their obtaining international support. The government does believe that there must be a political solution—that is, elections. However, I have said that elections require the appropriate atmosphere, and for this it is not enough to set a day for elections. First there must be a dialogue between the antagonistic parties—that is, the government and the front.[47]

In September 1981 the Salvadoran Conference of Bishops expressed its "numb shock" at the French-Mexican communiqué recognizing the guerrilla front as a political force. The bishops affirmed that they were "witnesses that in El Salvador a small sector of the people sympathized with the Farabundo Martí National Liberation Front and the Democratic Revolutionary Front, which have lost popular support and are now dedicated to sowing terror among the population."[48] The bishops also pointed to "the damage to the national economy which has been caused by the destruction of the people's goods and services in order to gain political-military advantage and create the conditions to seize power and impose a Marxist-Leninist dictatorship."[49]

The Conference of Bishops characterized the French-Mexican designation of the FDR as "a representative of the Salvadoran people" as a form of "intervention."[50] The bishops feared that this action would lead to the "recrudesence of the prolonged war of attrition with the consequent deaths of more Salvadorans and greater destruction of goods, as well as the proliferation of the people's suffering."[51]

For the church, support for free elections is the prerequisite for a political solution. The left, unfortunately, has called instead for a provisional government exclusively composed of those groups that have "actively struggled against the junta." The church is utterly opposed to the official policy of the left but may believe that some elements within it can be persuaded to accept democratic elections.

In a May 1981 homily, Rivera y Damas openly appealed to "the leftists who do not accept democratic elections within their political and revolutionary plans to be less dogmatic. If the present rulers are making an effort to create a democratic climate and the moral basis for election, they [the left] should give the people the opportunity to go to the polls."[52]

The Catholic Church in El Salvador has taken a thoughtful and courageous stand for social reform and democracy and against the extremes of right and left. This commitment to a suffering people has probably placed the church's own fate in jeopardy in the event of a victory by either of the extremes. We in the United States owe the Salvadoran church a fair and honest hearing on the reasons for its choice. Whether we agree or disagree with it, we should not let the church's stand be misrepresented by those who, whatever their reasons, are siding with one or another of the political extremes that the church itself opposes.

NOTES

1. Radio ACAN, Panama City, Panama, January 30, 1981.
2. Ibid.
3. Radio Venceremos, February 3, 1981.
4. Radio ACAN, Panama City, Panama, January 3, 1981.
5. Agence France Presse, January 8, 1981.
6. Ibid.
7. Ibid.
8. *Clarín*, Buenos Aires, Argentina, May 10, 1981.
9. *National Catholic Register*, June 14, 1981.
10. Ibid.
11. Ibid.
12. Ibid.
13. *Washington Post*, March 9, 1981.
14. Ibid.
15. *Catholic Standard*, April 2, 1981.
16. Ibid.
17. *Washington Post*, March 7, 1981.
18. Ibid.
19. Radio ACAN, Panama City, Panama, May 31, 1981.
20. *El Diario de Hoy*, San Salvador, El Salvador, September 8, 1980.
21. Homily, Metropolitan Cathedral, San Salvador, El Salvador, January 11, 1981.

22. Radio Bandeirantes, São Paulo, Brazil, January 14, 1981.
23. Agence France Presse, January 18, 1981.
24. Ibid.
25. Ibid.
26. Ibid.
27. Radio ACAN, Panama City, Panama, February 8, 1981.
28. *Washington Post,* March 7, 1981.
29. National Catholic Reporter News Service, March 19, 1981.
30. Homily, Metropolitan Cathedral, San Salvador, El Salvador, March 8, 1981.
31. Ibid.
32. Ibid.
33. Ibid.
34. Ibid.
35. National Catholic Reporter News Service, March 19, 1981.
36. Homily, Metropolitan Cathedral, San Salvador, El Salvador, December 14, 1981.
37. Homily, Metropolitan Cathedral, San Salvador, El Salvador, January 11, 1981.
38. Homily, Metropolitan Cathedral, San Salvador, El Salvador, March 8, 1981.
39. National Catholic Reporter News Service, May 19, 1981.
40. *Catholic Standard,* May 21, 1981.
41. *Diario de las Americas,* Miami, April 7, 1981.
42. *National Catholic Register,* June 14, 1981.
43. Ibid.
44. Homily, Metropolitan Cathedral, San Salvador, El Salvador, March 8, 1981.
45. Ibid.
46. Ibid.
47. *Clarín,* Buenos Aires. Argentina, May 10, 1981.
48. *Diario de las Americas,* Miami, September 6, 1981.
49. Ibid.
50. Ibid.
51. Ibid.
52. Radio ACAN, Panama City, Panama, May 17, 1981.

19. The Case for Power-Sharing

By PIERO GLEIJESES

Focus The Reagan administration, says Professor Piero Gleijeses, has made El Salvador a test case for the reassertion of U.S. power. Entering office soon after the failed "final offensive" of the Salvadoran guerrillas, President Reagan anticipated that "victory would be swift and at little cost." These hopes proved illusory, he says, and we are now bogged down in a military nightmare.

Like many other observers, Gleijeses proposes power-sharing as the way out of the stalemate. First, the Salvadoran military must be reformed. Rightist extremists like Roberto d'Aubuisson and other leaders of his National Republican Alliance (ARENA) must be exiled. This can happen only if the United States puts credible pressure on the Salvadoran government: an immediate cutoff of military aid and a threatened cutoff of economic aid if the army is not purged of right-wing extremists.

The plan put forth by Gleijeses calls for the democratic elements within the guerrilla forces to purge extremists on the left, paving the way for them to enter into negotiations with the government. Agreement can thus be reached for power-sharing in a three-year government of transition that, perhaps with the help of a foreign peace-keeping force, can pacify the people and rebuild the nation. Truly democratic elections can then be held.

Gleijeses bases his hopes for such a process on the events of the immediate past. In his view, the threatened abandonment of the Salvadoran regime late in the Carter years spurred the army to cast out former dictator Carlos Humberto Romero. But then the Carter administration failed to support the moderates in the junta because it was wary of their openness to dialogue with the radical left and of the presence of Communist ministers in the cabinet. Consequently, the hard-liners won out over the moderate, reformist group.

Is the Gleijeses plan workable? The fragmented and deeply divided nature of both the Salvadoran army and the guerrilla forces (see Shirley Christian, selections 16 and 17) and the strong-arm tactics of Joaquín Villalobos, apparently Castro's personal choice to direct the Salvadoran insurrectionists, make the success of such proposals unlikely.

Notes for this essay are on page 299.

Piero Gleijeses is an adjunct professor of U.S. foreign policy and Latin American studies at the Johns Hopkins University School of Advanced International Studies, Washington, D.C.

THE REAGAN ADMINISTRATION came to power confident of its ability to impose Washington's will on Central America. El Salvador was the immediate focus of its attention—and optimism ran high. The ill-timed January 1981 "final offensive" of the Frente Farabundo Martí Liberación Nacional (FMLN) had already failed when Ronald Reagan entered the White House. To the eager eyes of the new Administration the FMLN's defeat appeared a rout. Victory would be swift and at little cost, Washington believed, with no need for U.S. assistance markedly above the levels reached by the outgoing Carter administration. The easy success would spark little controversy at home and abroad and sweep away any lingering remnants of the Vietnam syndrome in the United States.

The Reagan administration also emphasized, and has done so consistently ever since, that the course of U.S. policy in El Salvador would influence American prestige and credibility throughout the world. Indeed, if the United States were able to attain the defeat of the rebels without indiscriminate violence, U.S. prestige would be greatly enhanced. Even victory through extreme repression would demonstrate the credibility of the Administration's guarantees, however costly the success might appear in moral terms.

But the Salvadoran "test case" has turned into a nightmare. Recent Administration requests for vastly increased military aid confirm the evidence from the battlefield: the war is not going well. The record of the Salvadoran regime on human rights and social reforms appears dismal to all but the Administration's most devout supporters. At home, Reagan's Salvadoran policy is increasingly divisive; abroad it evokes little sympathy, even among those who do not wish an FMLN victory. Rather than projecting an image of strength and resolve, U.S. involvement in El Salvador increasingly

Reprinted by permission from the Summer 1983 issue of *Foreign Affairs* (© 1983 by the Council on Foreign Relations).

betrays weakness and lack of purpose. The Administration haggles with Congress over a few million dollars of military assistance and a few dozen military advisors but is unable to suggest a coherent strategy for victory. Meanwhile, inordinate concern is focused on that small country, deflecting U.S. attention from other pressing issues—to the point that South America, beset by dangerous economic and political tensions, appears as an appendage of Central America and, in particular, of El Salvador.

President Reagan has asked Congress to "stay the course" in El Salvador but offers only old prescriptions that have already failed. American-trained battalions have performed poorly; in view of the pervasive lack of morale that characterizes officers and troops alike, there is no reason to believe that additional training will produce more satisfactory results. An election is scheduled for late 1983 [later rescheduled for March 1984] — as one took place in the spring of 1982—but there is no present indication that the second will prove any more effective than the first in solidifying the domestic strength or international prestige of the regime. The Administration's search for a "center" will continue in a game of musical chairs: generals will replace generals and civilians will replace one another. Meanwhile U.S. officials will claim, as they have done throughout, that the "process" of democratization (that ritual expression that masks a paucity of evidence) is under way, and that time must be granted to the president or defense minister of the moment.

The quagmire will deepen. This is the lesson of the U.S. involvement in El Salvador and of the "process" under way since 1980. As U.S. officials have periodically acknowledged, the easy victory over the guerrillas predicted in January 1981 has become a stalemate, and this stalemate is slowly turning in favor of the FMLN. Yet President Reagan disclaims any intention of sending combat troops—and his sincerity need not be challenged. But he also stresses, with an emphasis that seems to grow with the deterioration of the situation in El Salvador, that an FMLN victory will threaten vital U.S. interests, and that the United States will never abandon the Salvadoran people. Thus two principles are set forth which appear increasingly contradictory—a gap in logic which words, or robust optimism, cannot bridge and which may eventually confront the United States with the agonizing choice between a humiliating last-minute withdrawal and a desperate recourse to military intervention.

Both direct U.S. military intervention and military victory by the FMLN appear unacceptable to a large majority of Americans. Many agree with the view recently stated by Representative Clarence Long, an outspoken critic of the Administration's policy: "We made a mistake by becoming involved. But we are involved and it would be a mistake to pull out."[1] With rare exceptions even those who do not believe that a military victory of the FMLN would threaten vital U.S. interests fear the intangible toll that such an outcome would exact on U.S. prestige and, above all, on American self-confidence: however ill conceived the U.S. involvement may have been, a great power cannot afford simply to withdraw and acknowledge its impotence, particularly in its own back yard.

NEED FOR A NEW U.S. POLICY

While criticism is growing within the United States—and in Congress a majority is clearly dissatisfied with the present policy—the Administration retains one major advantage: its opponents lack a coherent alternative. The fear that a victory of the FMLN would lead to another Cuba paralyzes real debate. The growing radicalization of the Sandinista regime in Nicaragua fuels such fears, adding welcome support to the Administration's admonitions. Nor are congressmen necessarily impervious to the Administration's thinly veiled warnings: were El Salvador to "fall," Reagan's critics would be saddled before the American people with the responsibility of defeat—an ominous threat for elected officials.

Trying to break out of this vicious circle, the most vocal critics of the Administration, particularly those of the liberal persuasion, seek to strengthen the political center in El Salvador. Extreme repression, corruption, and lack of social reforms, they note, only deepen the regime's isolation, weaken its war effort, and make it difficult for the United States to provide much needed military and economic assistance. They demand, therefore, that the United States exert much greater pressure to force the Salvadoran regime to respect human rights and implement social reforms. Finally, both the Administration and its critics profess to want meaningful elections.

The thesis of this article is that the Salvadoran military is indeed the real source of power on the government side, and that moving toward its reform is a first essential step. But sweeping or lasting reform cannot be achieved in a state of continued hostilities. Likewise, elections cannot be truly meaningful, or produce stability, so long as they are held under essentially wartime conditions.

Accordingly, what is proposed here is a sequence of steps: (1) achieving significant reform of the Salvadoran military by determined U.S. pressure; (2) the initiation of a dialogue between a partially reformed military, on the government side, and the leaders of the guerrilla opposition—looking toward a truce and leading, after such a truce, to (3) the formation of a Government of Transition in which power would be shared by the contending forces, and the introduction of outside peacekeeping forces. Such a transition government would then operate for a period of two or three years, leading finally to (4) the holding of nationwide elections.

In carrying out such a course of action, the United States would consult closely at every step with the governments of other interested countries in the area. In short, to the maximum possible extent this process should have the genuine force and appeal of a regional solution.

As the Administration has argued so convincingly, real power in the rebel camp belongs not to the "moderates"—the civilian politicians of the Frente Democratico Revolucionario (FDR)— but to those who have the guns, the leaders of the FMLN. The same consideration applies, however, to the government camp. Duarte was an ineffectual president, not because Reagan provided him with less support than Carter did (a highly dubious proposition), but because power rested, then as now, in the hands of an unreformed military. President Alvaro Magaña and the moderate civilian groups that support him have as little influence with the armed forces as Duarte and the Christian Democrats had in 1980 and 1981. Clearly, the United States will achieve little in El Salvador without a fundamental restructuring of the military—a task particularly difficult in the midst of civil war. Mere reshuffling among senior leaders of the present military establishment (as was the case with the recent replacement of General José Guillermo García as defense minister) represents cosmetic changes of marginal significance.

Apparently, however, the advocates of a more moderate course have won an important victory. The House Foreign Affairs Committee has overwhelmingly voted to suspend military aid to the Salvadoran government if unconditional negotiations do not begin within ninety days of the legislation's enactment—unless it is the insurgents who have refused to negotiate. What is more, the Administration, in a sharp reversal of its previous policy, has announced that it will accept this condition.

Two Imperatives for Negotiation

But the committee's resolution still shies away from the twin imperatives that alone can make possible a negotiated solution: a thorough restructuring of the armed forces, and power-sharing between the military and the FMLN *before* elections. The resolution offers no way out of the dilemma represented by an oppressive military, and demands only, as a condition for further aid, that the Salvadoran government begin negotiations. Under these circumstances, there is no incentive for the regime to seek a negotiated settlement. Negotiations will remain a sideshow that will drag on without results while the war continues. It is little wonder, therefore, that the Reagan administration has at last moved away from its previous rejection of unconditional negotiations. By a long overdue formal concession the Administration will mollify—for a time—its domestic critics. Behind the rhetoric, the Administration will persist in the policy that it has consistently followed from the start—the pursuit of military victory. There is no other option, so long as the United States refuses to accept either a military victory of the FMLN or the only feasible peaceful solution: one based not on unconditional negotiations, but on power-sharing.

Power-sharing may appear, however, an equally unrealistic formula. An exceptional dose of optimism is required to imagine peaceful coexistence between the FMLN and the Salvadoran armed forces as presently constituted. Moreover, even if negotiations toward power-sharing under the present conditions were to prove possible and lead to some form of transitional government, the truce would doubtless prove fleeting, with the two camps maneuvering to position themselves for the final onslaught. Civil wars seldom end through negotiations, and this dictum seems particularly appropriate to El Salvador, in view of the chasm separating the antagonists. Is the battlefield therefore the only solution?

I do not believe so. The situation in El Salvador has not yet deteriorated to such a degree. There is a reformist group within the armed forces that could bring about a restructuring of the military sufficient to justify an earnest attempt at power-sharing without, however, destroying the institution in the process (for otherwise power-sharing would merely mean a negotiated surrender to the FMLN). And this proposition can be better appreciated if one looks back at the events of October 1979, when the military deposed the then president, General Carlos Humberto Romero.

The 1979 Coup

By the end of the Romero regime, the officer corps shared one common belief: that the Carter administration was ready to abandon the regime, while the growing guerrilla threat made U.S. support imperative. Thus the army felt compelled to act against Romero. Beyond this, there was no unity within the 800-man-strong officer corps, except on one crucial point: the military institution must be preserved. A large number were apathetic toward social reform and would follow any group within the military which could best ensure the survival of the institution, particularly if this group enjoyed the blessing of the United States.

There were, however, two factions of roughly equal strength that held more precise views. The first was led by Colonel Adolfo Majano and Lieutenant Colonel René Guerra y Guerra, two men untainted by corruption. It included a core of about 200 officers, mostly lieutenants and second lieutenants, but also a number of captains and majors. These were moderates, who had come to accept the principle of social reform as both morally just and indispensable for the survival of the army, and who favored the principle of negotiations with the radical left.

The other faction was led by Colonels García, Jaime Abdul Gutiérrez, and Carlos Eugenio Vides Casanova (the current defense minister); it was smaller in numbers but stronger hierarchically, for it included a majority of senior officers. This faction opposed both social reform and any negotiations with the radical left, and offered to the fledgling insurgency only a choice between unconditional submission and war; it accepted corruption as a normal feature of military life, as Colonels García, Gutiérrez, and Vides Casanova had amply demonstrated in the course of a long and profitable career.

This division between moderates and hard-liners, with an apathetic group in between, was not new in Salvadoran military politics; it had already appeared on several occasions (in 1944, 1948, 1960, and 1972); on each occasion the conservative group eventually won out, usually with the benevolent neutrality or the active support of the United States. Each time, however, the moderate group represented only a minority of senior officers, while those of lower rank remained passive. But following the events of 1972—when presidential candidate Duarte was denied victory at the polls through brazen electoral fraud—a new process began to unfold. Confronted by mounting popular unrest and growing evidence of the bankruptcy of the system, junior officers began to question, in increasing numbers, the entire structure of Salvadoran society. The divisions within the armed forces that emerged between 1972 and 1979 differed from those of the past in at least two crucial respects. Instead of a small group of senior officers, it was now a question of a large number of junior officers; and instead of the constitutionalist demands and vague populist aspirations of the past, the disaffected officers now sought deeper social change.

Decline of the Moderates' Strength

By October 1979 the forces were balanced: the moderates were stronger numerically and held the initiative, while the conservatives had the advantage of rank. In the tenuous equilibrium that marked the first post-Romero junta (mid-October 1979 to early January 1980), U.S. support could have tipped the balance in favor of the moderate group. But the Carter administration, while clearly sympathetic to the principle of social reforms in El Salvador, feared losing control of events. Washington's suspicion of the obvious inclination of the reformist officers to establish a dialogue with the radical left and of the presence of Communist ministers in the cabinet was matched by the failure to appreciate the true repressive nature of the group led by Colonel García.

By the time the first junta collapsed in early January 1980, the balance of power was already shifting against the reformist group—a process of emasculation that continued in the following months. U.S. distrust helped to isolate the moderates, while the escalation of the civil war that followed the demise of the first junta created a context of violence that made moderation difficult for military officers. Lieutenant Colonel Guerra y Guerra was forced into exile in late January 1980; Majano held out longer, but his power steadily decreased. He was forced out in December 1980, after losing the last major confrontation in September.

Majano, Guerra y Guerra, and other leading moderates, like Lieutenant Colonel Leonel Alfaro, Major Román Barrera, and Lieutenant Colonel José Francisco Samayoa, are now in exile,[2] but the great majority of their former associates remain in the armed forces—in positions, however, of little influence. The captains and the majors have been shunted off to desk jobs. The lieutenants are at the front—but their low rank means that they lead only small units. They are under the command of more senior and "trusted" officers, making it impossible for them to acquire an independent power base. Furthermore, the dynamics of the war and their own code of loyalty lead them to fight for the survival of the military institution, however much they disagree with the policies of their commanders.

It is obvious that on their own the reformist officers can no longer play a critical role with the armed forces—except perhaps in the chaos of a military defeat, when all that they would be likely to achieve would be a negotiated surrender to a triumphant FMLN. But Washington, if it has the political will, possesses the leverage to repair the error of the Carter administration and enable the reformists to attain key positions within the armed forces as a precondition for power-sharing.

This proposition may appear incongruous when critics and supporters of the Administration alike bewail the lack of U.S. influence over the Salvadoran military. But at present the leverage of the United States suffers from a devastating weakness: a lack of credibility. The Reagan administration scolds its Salvadoran protégés—at times even publicly—and warns them that, should they fail to improve their behavior, Congress will stop aid, against the Administration's own wishes. But the perceptions of many Salvadorans, and particularly the military, are more straightforward. The Administration has pawned its prestige on the Salvadoran test case, stressing repeatedly that a guerrilla victory would threaten vital U.S. interests, even raising the specter of falling dominoes from Panama to Mexico. Time after time U.S. officials have stressed that a guerrilla victory cannot and will not be tolerated—while arguing, for domestic consumption, that the conduct of the Salvadoran allies is far better than the critics claim, and continues to improve. The United States will never turn its back on the Salvadoran people, Reagan has solemnly promised, and the Salvadoran military conclude—perhaps with the naïveté of unsophisticated foreigners—that, with only minimal concessions on their part, the Administration will effectively shield them from the wrath of Congress.

Congress's own behavior reinforces these perceptions. Congressmen complain, threaten, and reduce the size of the increases in aid demanded by the Administration; yet the vital flow of military and economic assistance to the Salvadoran government is not cut off. Congress, too, is not ready to risk an FMLN victory and is hostage to its own fears.

A SCENARIO FOR POWER-SHARING

The United States can reestablish an eroded credibility, and acquire the leverage that the importance of its aid warrants, only when reproaches and highly circumscribed sanctions give way to concrete and decisive actions. The unambiguous suspension of military assistance, accompanied by the firm threat to cancel economic aid within a given time period, would be the only effective weapon to force a restructuring of the military. Such action, aimed at creating the indispensable preconditions for a negotiated settlement of the war, would have to be placed within an effective framework of mutually reinforcing policies.

Before delivering any ultimatum to the Salvadoran military, the United States should ascertain whether the conditions exist for power-sharing. Concretely this would mean that Washington would seek the collaboration of Latin American and European governments particularly concerned with Salvadoran developments and able to provide useful assistance.[3] Regional powers such as Mexico, Venezuela, Colombia, and Panama (already associated in the Grupo de Contadora) and, in Europe, France and Spain, would be logical candidates. Washington would also confirm the willingness of Majano and others in the same group to participate. Similarly, the United States would establish contacts with the FMLN to gauge the rebels' reaction. The FMLN would be asked to agree in principle to a truce and other key elements of power-sharing.

Initial U.S. Requirements

If the results of these preliminary talks prove satisfactory, the United States will present its desiderata to the Salvadoran armed forces. It will announce that within the framework of a peace plan formulated with other governments, it is suspending military aid to El Salvador, and will halt economic aid in a specific and limited period of time unless its demands for restructuring of the armed forces are met.

The initial U.S. desiderata should be significant enough to have a real impact, but not so sweeping as immediately to threaten the stability of the Salvadoran armed forces. The United States could demand that Colonel Majano be made defense minister (such an appointment under the constitution is the prerogative of President Magaña), and that some other key military positions go to officers from the moderate group that emerged in October 1979. Concurrently, a few senior officers particularly notorious for their repressive practices or particularly hostile to a democratization of the military would be retired or sent abroad as military attachés.

At this stage a full-fledged restructuring of the armed forces would not yet be in order, only an effective beginning of the process. For its part, once the initial U.S. demands were met, the FMLN would be expected to honor the commitment made in the exploratory talks by accepting a truce for a set period. Thus would begin the formal negotiations on power-sharing.

Probable Salvadoran Response

One must ask, however, whether the United States would indeed possess the leverage to impose these initial changes on the Salvadoran armed forces.

From a purely military perspective, the Salvadoran army could continue to fight for many months without U.S. military assistance. Once economic aid was suspended as well, however, the ability of the regime to resist would be drastically curtailed. But the significance of U.S. aid goes well beyond narrow military and economic considerations. Aid is necessary as proof of Washington's commitment to prevent a collapse of the already shattered morale of the Salvadoran army. Some argue that if the "Yanquis" were to push them too far, the Salvadoran military would react in a spasm of nationalism, fighting with fierce pride to the bitter end. But the behavior of the Salvadoran officer corps—a consistent pattern to which U.S. military advisors have been at times blunt witnesses—leads to opposite and unflattering conclusions.

Confronted by a credible U.S. threat, and fully cognizant of their own military weakness, the Salvadoran officers would not react with suicidal pride and defy the "Yanquis." Rather, two deeply rooted and mutually supporting impulses would prevail: personal opportunism and the desire to save the military institution. Both require not defiance but acquiescence to U.S. will.

Once the initial U.S. demands on the Salvadoran High Command have been met and the FMLN has responded by accepting a truce, negotiations between the armed forces and the FMLN could begin.

The moderating participation of civilian associates on both sides and the inclusion of mutually acceptable foreign governments would ease the process of negotiations. The United States would play a vital role behind the scenes, using its leverage to force deeper changes in the Salvadoran military—an indispensable condition for a negotiated settlement. The security corps murder machine would have to be disbanded. Moderate members of the

1979 Majano group would occupy more senior positions, while a significant number of officers implicated deeply in the repression would be cashiered or sent abroad as military attachés; some, instead, might receive scholarships for foreign study (in this regard the precedent of the settlement imposed by the United States in the 1965 Dominican civil war provides valuable guidelines).

A Government of Transition

While any suggested plan should not attempt to be overly precise (for many points will evolve during the negotiations), the negotiating process should end with the establishment of a Government of Transition (GOT) that would lead to internationally supervised elections. The GOT should last two or possibly three years—so as to afford the country the benefits of a long enough respite before elections after the convulsions of the civil war. Within the GOT, as many cabinet positions and key bureaucratic posts as possible should go to representatives of the civilian groups: the FDR and the parties that supported the Magaña government. Above all, personalities who have broken with the current regime, without however joining the FMLN/FDR, should be included. Many with impeccable democratic credentials are now in exile in Mexico, Costa Rica, Honduras, and the United States.

On the other hand, it is unlikely that ARENA, which is controlled by elements of the most extreme right-wing fringe, could be allowed to continue in its present form. Some of its most dangerous leaders, such as Roberto d'Aubuisson, should be exiled. One should not exaggerate the difficulty of this task: with the support of the military, ARENA can orchestrate widespread terror; its own military strength, however, is marginal (as in the case of ARENA's Guatemalan counterpart, the Movimiento de Liberación Nacional, which the current Guatemalan military government has neutralized with little effort). In the final analysis, ARENA's influence on the Salvadoran armed forces would prove insignificant if counterbalanced by an effective U.S. pressure.

The GOT would institute social reforms according to a minimum program previously agreed upon in the negotiations. As the FMLN has hinted, such reforms could be those enacted (but not implemented) since October 1979—on paper, an impressive bit of legislation. The realization of the program would create a critical momentum for peace, giving to the population, regardless of political sympathy, a vested interest in the survival of the transitional government. By the same token, it would strengthen civilian organizations such as the large peasant confederation, Unión Comunal Salvadoreña, which cannot prosper in the midst of civil war.

Economic aid of roughly $400-500 million annually would flow into the country to sustain social reform and economic recovery. Of this sum, the United States could contribute the amount it now disburses in economic and military assistance (within the framework of a GOT, any further inflow of arms into El Salvador would be both unnecessary and destabilizing). The balance of necessary aid would come from international organizations, and from U.S. allies that now refuse to further a unilateral U.S. policy they oppose. This assistance would be an additional guarantee of peace, since El Salvador's economy, to a much greater degree than that of Nicaragua in 1979, is in desperate straits. Representatives of international organizations, and of donor governments neutral in the conflict, should monitor the use of the aid.

To hope for a swift integration of the military units of the FMLN with the army would be overly optimistic. If necessary, the two forces should be allowed to coexist under some appropriate formula throughout the tenure of the GOT, leaving the issue of integration to an eventual elected government; an effort should be made, however, to decrease the size of the two forces proportionally. Above all, it would be imperative to establish an international peacekeeping force of a few thousand—that is, strong enough to police the agreement. Probably no foreign governments would be eager to volunteer contingents (except perhaps those governments which are not neutral in the conflict and would therefore be unacceptable). But several countries that have forcefully expressed their dissatisfaction with current U.S. policy and their eagerness to contribute to a peaceful solution would find it hard to refuse their participation in so important an undertaking.

In the Western Hemisphere, likely candidates include Mexico, Panama, Ecuador, and Canada; European governments such as those of France and the Scandinavian countries could also participate. The force should remain in El Salvador throughout the two-

or three-year tenure of the GOT and in the first year of the elected government to help ensure compliance with the results of the elections.

OBJECTIONS TO POWER-SHARING

Power-sharing runs agains the grain of present U.S. policy and goes beyond the proposals of most critics of the Administration. It raises significant questions about the fairness of the plan, the risks it would entail of a violation by the FMLN, and the effect it would have on the prestige and credibility of the United States. Many, and in particular Administration supporters, will condemn power-sharing as undemocratic and unfair to the Salvadoran government, arguing that "we would be treating our allies as puppets" while allowing the FMLN "to shoot its way into power."

But these objections are hardly pertinent in the Salvadoran context. The present regime is neither democratic nor representative of the population, and the Salvadoran armed forces, the real holders of power, are repressive and corrupt, as the Congress of the United States is discovering. The Reagan administration, furthermore, interferes daily in the internal affairs of the Salvadoran government, at times successfully (as in the selection of a provisional president after the March 1982 elections), but more often ineffectually. The issue, therefore, is not the principle of U.S. interference, but rather the efficacy of such interference in protecting U.S. interests.

Principled opposition to violent seizure of power seems equally irrelevant. In the case of El Salvador, both the Carter and Reagan administrations lent their support to those who shot their way into power in October 1979 (the "legitimizing" elections took place only two and a half years later, in the midst of bitter civil war). At present, in neighboring Guatemala, President Reagan is eager to embrace another group that overthrew an elected government ("Rios Montt has received a bad rap from the press," the President proclaimed after a brief meeting with the highly controversial Guatemalan general in December 1982). In short, U.S. policy does not oppose on principle the violent seizure of power, and with good cause—such rigidity would justify the permanence of dictatorships. Instead, the principle is conditioned by an Administration's approval of those who do the shooting—a task at which, unfortunately for U.S. policy-makers, the FMLN is proving increasingly proficient.

But even if one accepts that power-sharing must be imposed on the Salvadoran government, wouldn't fairness and prudence require that extremists be purged not only in the armed forces but also within the FMLN?

In the case of the Salvadoran military it is possible to purge a group of extremists without destroying the effectiveness of the institution, for they would be replaced by moderates. Reciprocity would demand that the same principle be applied to the FMLN. It is evident that the United States cannot exert over an undefeated enemy the same leverage that it has over an ineffectual client— thus it would be naïve to expect that the State Department could select members of the leadership of the guerrillas, as it can do for the Salvadoran military High Command. The issue is further complicated by the lack of unambiguous criteria by which to identify the extremists within the FMLN.[4] Many U.S. observers considered the late Cayetano Carpio an extremist among the major FMLN leaders because he was the last to accept the principle of a negotiated settlement. If extremism were based on "pro-Sovietism," then the villain would be not Carpio but Shafik Handal, the secretary general of the Communist Party of El Salvador, a minuscule group that has distinguished itself, within the FMLN, both for its close ties to Moscow *and* for its willingness to negotiate.

In short, the principle is far more complicated as applied to the FMLN than in the case of the Salvadoran armed forces. Furthermore, reciprocity may be to a large extent a moot point. By replacing extremists within the armed forces with more moderate officers, the United States would be doing much more than granting a concession to the guerrillas: above all, it would be pursuing its own objectives. As presently constituted, the Salvadoran armed forces are a prime cause of U.S. failure in El Salvador. Moderate officers would help restructure the military in a direction that most Americans, including Administration officials, wish to see, but that cannot be attained through present policy. The concession to the

FMLN, in other words, would also be a major gain for the United States.

It might prove tempting, however, to implement the same program of military democratization and socioeconomic reform without power-sharing—presenting the FMLN, instead, with a *fait accompli*. Yet this course would ultimately prove self-defeating. The war would continue, for unilateral U.S. moves could hardly assuage the FMLN's deep distrust. A program of democratization in the midst of civil war would be extremely difficult to implement, however sensible the proposition might appear in theory. Moreover, the vital international component of the plan would be sacrificed, since third countries would be highly reluctant to join in what they would consider as one more cosmetic effort on the part of the United States. For this same reason, independent Salvadoran figures whose participation is vital would remain aloof, if not outright hostile.

Will the Rebels Negotiate?

Power-sharing, however, can succeed only if the FMLN is willing to join in the negotiations and the subsequent transitional government in good faith. There are no ironclad guarantees that the rebels will be serious negotiating partners; there exist, however, strong indications to that effect, and, above all, countervailing measures built into the power-sharing plan. The FMLN has repeatedly stated its willingness to negotiate, arguing that the price of military victory would be a protracted struggle that would not only entail a high cost in human lives but leave the economy in a shambles.

While skepticism may be the better part of wisdom, this is no reason to refuse even to explore the possibility. If the guerrillas were to break the negotiations or violate their premises, the United States would retain the option of resuming military aid, and the Reagan administration would be in a far better position, both at home and abroad, to justify support for the Salvadoran regime. If the FMLN were to resort to force once the GOT had been established, or to disregard the results of the elections, the presence of the international force would place the rebels at an extreme disadvantage. Nor is it inconsequential that the neutral countries that would participate in the power-sharing scheme cannot be accused of bias toward the FMLN. Even France and Mexico, which have expressed with particular force their sharp disagreement with Reagan's policy in El Salvador, do not support the rebels. Their mounting disappointment with Sandinista rule in Nicaragua would harden their opposition to FMLN attempts to subvert the negotiations or the GOT.

Probable U.S. Gains

U.S. prestige and credibility abroad are suffering—and the damage will increase as long as the present policy continues. In contrast, through power-sharing the United States would demonstrate both the pragmatism needed to abandon a counterproductive policy and the intellectual flexibility to devise coherent alternatives. Power-sharing may also influence developments elsewhere in Central America but would not require, as a precondition, a general political settlement for the region. A peaceful solution in El Salvador should not be held hostage to a more encompassing settlement that may occur too late, if at all. On the other hand, just as the Salvadoran conflict exacerbates regional tensions, its solution could have positive repercussions throughout the area. In particular, it could help defuse tensions between the United States and Nicaragua. An improved relationship would strengthen the hand of the pragmatic group within the Sandinista leadership, depriving hard-liners such as Tomás Borge and Bayardo Arce of the argument that U.S. aggression requires stricter social control at home and closer ties with the Soviet bloc.

By the same token, the end of U.S. "covert" actions against Nicaragua would free Washington from the need to support the military faction of General Alvarez in Honduras. This faction, through widespread corruption and repressive practices, poses an immediate threat to the feeble Honduran democracy and, by furthering a process of radicalization, endangers the long-term political stability there. Finally, there is a distant possibility that the American refusal to sustain the Salvadoran regime any longer might spur Guatemalan officers to support a reformist policy in their own country before it is too late, rather than relying on cosmetic changes and prospects of U.S. assistance, as the current military dictatorship does.

The plan outlined here provides a framework rather than a rigid structure. It allows room for flexibility and modifications—as long as the essence of power-sharing is not weakened. It emphasizes the figure of Majano, but in the end that role might be played by another moderate officer. It stresses the suspension of military aid as an instrument to restructure the armed forces, though there might be flexibility as to the timing. It makes no mention of Cuba, yet a degree of Cuban participation might help allay FMLN suspicions. Other formulas as well could be devised for particular aspects of the plan, but definite contours would emerge only through the process of negotiations.

Power-sharing offers a realistic chance of success. Yet it requires a willingness on the part of the United States to take one chance: if the Salvadoran officer corps rejects the U.S. demands, it must be left to its fate. For reasons already noted, this act of defiance would be most unlikely; but should it occur, it must be said that the United States would only be abandoning sooner rather than later a doomed enterprise.

Alternatives to Power-Sharing

In the final analysis, the virtues of power-sharing must be assessed against the alternatives. It holds no attraction for those who believe that current U.S. policy in El Salvador has a fair chance of success. It is addressed to those who have concluded that "staying the course" in El Salvador can slow but not reverse the deterioration of the situation. If this assessment is accurate, then the present policy will eventually confront Congress with a cruel dilemma: a direct military intervention, or military victory by the FMLN in circumstances humiliating for U.S. prestige and credibility, and hardly conducive to an eventual *modus vivendi* with the triumphant guerrillas.

Those who believe that Nicaragua is becoming a second Cuba, and fear that without U.S. aid the same fate might befall El Salvador, should remember that the Sandinistas came to power through a total military victory. Power-sharing would deprive the

FMLN of just such a victory—far more effectively, indeed, than Reagan's present policy can hope to do—and restrain the rebels within effective limits. The period of transition would permit the growth of other political groups and a softening of the polarization between contending military groups. In elections, held under far more dignified circumstances than those of March 1982, the Salvadoran people could at last express their preferences. The Christian Democrats, the political parties of the FDR, and other forces of the moderate left and right could profit from this opportunity, as could the Salvadoran people, at last afforded a realistic hope of democracy and reform.

NOTES

1. Martin Tolchin, "Working Profile: Rep. Clarence D. Long, Shaping a Response to the 'Mistake' in El Salvador," *New York Times,* April 22, 1983, p. A16.

2. Majano is in Mexico, travels frequently throughout the region, and maintains excellent contacts with the governments of Mexico and Panama; Guerra y Guerra, who had acquired a graduate degree in engineering in the United States, lives in California. Barrera is military attaché in Venezuela; Samayoa is consul general in San Francisco; Alfaro has been sent to study in the United States. Technically, Barrera, Samayoa, and Alfaro are not in exile.

3. Many studies, like the recent Sol Linowitz/Galo Plaza *The Americas at a Crossroads* (April 1983), argue that the United States should give a major role in El Salvador and Central America as a whole to the regional powers. The intention is laudable, but only the United States has the leverage to bring about a negotiated solution. Therefore the key role in effecting a peaceful settlement in El Salvador must belong to the United States.

4. The FMLN consists of five groups: the Popular Forces of Liberation (FPL), which were led by Carpio; the People's Revolutionary Army (ERP); the Armed Forces of National Resistance (FARN); the Communist Party of El Salvador (PCS); and the Central American Workers' Revolutionary Party (PRTC). The FPL, the ERP, and the FARN provide almost all of the FMLN's mass support and military strength. The [April 1983] deaths of Carpio, the FMLN's most prestigious guerrilla leader, and, a few days earlier, of his second-in-command, are likely to have two effects: a decrease in the relative importance of the FPL vis-à-vis ERP and FARN, which have shown more inclination toward negotiations; and an increase in the influence within the FPL of those who are more inclined to compromise than Carpio was. The FMLN should thus be more receptive to the possibility of a negotiated settlement.

20. First Kill the Guerrillas

By RICHARD HARWOOD

Focus

Washington tends to oversimplify complex international problems, but according to Richard Harwood, in El Salvador Washington has taken a relatively simple problem and "complexified it enormously." In spite of all the political and military activity, what we are talking about is a small country of 4.5 million people who are confronting probably five thousand guerrillas.

Harwood proposes a simple military solution. We cannot stop the flow of arms to El Salvador from other countries, nor can we reasonably expect to alter greatly the poverty, injustice, and other deeply entrenched social problems that underlie the current conflict. But since the great masses of Salvadorans have not embraced the revolutionary cause, it is still possible for the army to pacify the country. "No guerrilla war in modern times with the exception of Zimbabwe has had anything but a military solution," observes Harwood. He therefore calls for reliable military aid and improved training and deployment of Salvadoran forces.

To be sure, formidable obstacles stand in the way of this solution. The army must be reformed and brought under civilian control, and the right-wing death squads must be eliminated. Shirley Christian's analysis of the Salvadoran army (selection 17) shows just how difficult this would be.

Richard Harwood is a deputy managing editor of the *Washington Post.*

D ANIEL PATRICK MOYNIHAN sermonized a few years ago on the deplorable tendency in Washington to oversimplify every problem. What is needed, he said, are people who can "complexify."

In the case of Central America, he was wrong. This town is now full of men and women who have taken the relatively simple problem of El Salvador and complexified it outrageously. They have elevated an insurgency of moderate proportions into an international crisis, while baffling their countrymen and themselves. The fleet has sailed, Henry Kissinger has been recalled from his various business enterprises, the only televised "covert" war in history has been launched, and the End of the Earth cult has been revved up for yet another Armageddon: all this over a country of 4.5 million people confronted with five quarreling bands of guerrillas in the number of 5,000 to 7,000.

The problem for the government of El Salvador and its patron, the United States, is not Nicaragua or Cuba or the Soviet Union, which provide the guerrillas with arms, sympathy, and advice. That kind of assistance cannot be interdicted any more than the United States can interdict the flow of dope over our own borders. Furthermore, it can be offset by arms, sympathy, and advice flowing from Washington to San Salvador.

The guerrillas are the problem, and that problem, in all probability, can be solved only by the army of El Salvador. There is of course talk of a negotiated settlement based on "power-sharing," but that is no more likely in the short run than a "power-sharing" settlement between the Sandinistas in Nicaragua and the *contras* we have launched against them.

There is also idealistic talk in the American Congress about eliminating the "roots of war"—poverty, injustice, illiteracy, and so on. But our record of rebuilding and reforming countries in our own image is not good under the best of circumstances. And in the midst of a war, those goals are wishful thinking. One of the cardinal principles of guerrilla warfare is to destroy or severely damage the strategic assets and infrastructure of the society under attack, whether that be power plants and transmission lines, roads, bridges, crops, factories, police stations, courthouses, schools, or medical clinics. That is happening all over the world today, wherever guerrilla wars are being fought.

A military solution to such problems is ultimately possible if the masses of the people have not been "revolutionized" or disaffected to the point of popular uprisings, as occurred in Nicaragua and Cuba. From all the evidence, that point has not been reached in El Salvador. It is indeed a poor country; the per capita GNP is only $650 per year. But poverty is relative. Nearly fifty countries in the world are worse off—including China and India, where per capita GNP is about half that of El Salvador, which the World Bank classifies as "lower-middle income." This reinforces the demonstrable truth that there is no necessary correlation between revolution and economic deprivation. If it were otherwise, China would be in flames.

The El Salvador problem is a military problem. No guerrilla war in modern times with the exception of Zimbabwe has had anything but a military solution. If the United States would keep its eye on that mark instead of engaging in diversionary sideshows, a solution might be found.

The first requirement is to train the Salvadoran army in infantry and small-unit tactics. The task of the soldier is to find, kill, capture, or exhaust his enemy, and he needs to know how to do that if he is to succeed.

The second requirement is to get those soldiers into the bush and into the hills to find, engage, and otherwise harass the guerrillas. The Salvadoran soldiers are courageous and sometimes "valiant to a fault," according to an American officer who has observed them up close in combat. But they provide no useful service in barracks or on parade grounds.

A third requirement is to keep them in the army once they have been trained and have experienced combat. Today, too many of them leave the service after a two-year tour. The guerrillas, on the other hand, are in for the duration.

A fourth requirement is for the United States to provide its ally with the necessary tools of war on a consistent and reliable basis. The requirements are modest; no exotic weapons are needed.

Finally, two reforms must somehow be achieved internally or imposed by Washington. The officer corps must be overhauled to break up the old-boy networks that create political commanders. The institution of the army must be made subservient and responsive to civilian control. At the same time, the private armies and death squads must be eliminated or brought under control. That is a tall order, but it is essential to the army's ultimate success.

The recent adventurism of the Reagan administration in Central America has put all of these modest proposals at risk. By alienating public opinion and dividing the Congress, it has imperiled the entire assistance program to El Salvador.

That is the danger in overly complexifying problems.

21. The Machete of Injustice

By STEPHEN S. ROSENFELD

Focus The author of this essay records a foreigner's shock at the culture of violence in El Salvador, but observes that foreigners also learn quickly that "there are few shocked Salvadorans left in this sad, sad country." Violence has a long and widespread history in El Salvador, and Stephen Rosenfeld believes it is the central fact about that nation with which Americans must come to terms.

In his view, the traditional oligarchy and the extreme right bear the primary responsibility for the violence, even if "both sides" now commit murders. The traditional sources of power institutionalized an injustice so oppressive that the violent reaction must be viewed in the proper moral perspective. "There is no defense of an order that keeps peasants in line with machetes," says Rosenfeld.

Yet the civilian-military junta has a genuine impulse toward reform and given the time and political opportunity could make a great difference in El Salvador. The question is how to curtail the violence of the extreme right without permitting the guerrillas to disrupt reform efforts and thus risking the danger of a left-wing totalitarian state.

As painful as the U.S. moral position may be in El Salvador, we have no choice but to continue to provide economic and military support and simultaneously to press for further reform. The only people who can offer a realistic hope for the future are the moderates of the Salvadoran government.

Repudiating our commitment to this group, says Rosenfeld, would mean abandoning the Salvadorans "to a depth of savagery not known at this point even to pitiful El Salvador."

Stephen S. Rosenfeld is a political analyst and deputy editorial page editor of the *Washington Post*.

MEET DOMINGO. He used to live in a "Christian community," one adopted by socially minded priests who are anathema to the oligarchy. He lived there until his family was routed by OR-DEN, a right-wing paramilitary organization since, ostensibly, disbanded. Now he lives with his mother behind locked gates at one of ten teeming church-run refugee camps around the capital. His father and three brothers were killed in the attack on their village. Across his arms, neck, and face are immense, crudely stitched welts made by the machete that nearly dismembered him. He is smallish and brown, his cheeks still soft, and when he is asked whether he is angry at what happened to him two years ago, he pauses long and says, barely audibly, "Yes." He is now thirteen.

There is the war in a form that shocks a first-time foreign observer. But one learns quickly that there are few shocked Salvadorans left in this sad, sad country, conditioned as it is by decades, if not centuries, of experience similar to this direct personal exaction of "justice" and vengeance. "How can this happen?" I asked the priest who had escorted me to a camp of a thousand such victims of right-wing terror—a priest who, by the way, is regarded as something of an apologist for official violence by some of his liberal fellow churchmen in the United States. "I—I don't know." He had already said to me, "You Americans love the law. We play with it."

The violence—not the war but the violence, lavish and uncontrolled like the bougainvillea that spills over the barricaded walls of San Salvador—is the central fact with which we Americans have yet to come fully to terms. There is such a fantastic amount of misperception and cant in our collective contemplation of it. It is laid bare, I think, by two questions.

1. How do you think Domingo is going to respond to a suggestion from, say, an American churchman or legislator or president

---

or even a journalist to put aside his sense of personal grievance and bereavement when he grows up—if he did not grow up instantly as the machete swung—and to accept a responsibility to build a new Salvadoran society, a society of law?

2. But which of these people—the churchman, the legislator, the president, the journalist—is actually going to make such a suggestion?

The "evidence" telling who is committing the violence against civilians in El Salvador—30,000-plus have died in the last two years—is essentially uncollectable, circumstantial and fragmentary, hearsay and surmise. The United States, infinitely better equipped to cope with errant soldiers, found it so in Vietnam.

There is no comfort in the assertion, true as it literally is, that "both sides do it." That passes over the responsibility—let us say the 100 per cent responsibility—of the traditional oligarchy and the political extreme right in starting the violence. This is no chicken-and-egg situation. Domingo and his family and his class did not start it. ORDEN and the class it represents—the class it represents perhaps without realizing it does so—started it. Force was used to consolidate injustice. It is as simple as that.

The Communist Party stirred here first in the 1930s. Why so late?, one might ask. El Salvador was then, and largely still is today, a Marxist's dream, a place to make dogma look supple. In a way, it is a great pity that a Marxist solution was not applied decades ago, before the real question arose of the international connections and implications of a contemporary Marxist solution. There is no defense of an order that keeps peasants in line with machetes.

I was told here of a socially conscious woman, very liberal by local standards, who did 4-H work with rural kids. On her small coffee plantation, one of the hands started to "cause trouble" and was found bound and dead in a ditch the morning after the police had paid a call. A "subversive," she shrugged. Remember: she is a liberal.

A Strong Reform Impulse

I happen to think the current [in early March 1982] military-civilian junta has a genuine and strong reform impulse, and if it were allowed the requisite time and political space, it could do a great deal for the country. In that sense, one could argue that the guerrillas have "won": they have forced the necessity of change upon most of the elite. To hear [then] President José Napoleón Duarte and the other deeply committed officials of his government spelling out their hopes for their country is to be convinced, almost, that the process of modernization is under way.

Almost. It matters next to nothing that foreigners or even the good civilians in the establishment may feel reform is the wave of the future. Distrust is the undertow. Official violence is generating it, and it goes on.

I met three of the top military people and talked with them for a total of five hours—the minister of defense, who is acknowledged to be the country's strongman, and the heads of the city and rural police, both comers. Now that the violence of their organizations has become central to the debate over the terms of American aid, they have been coaxed to come out of their traditional barracks cocoon and to receive representative Americans. This stuns savvy Salvadoran civilians. When I visited one of the generals, a ministerial official happened to be dropping by for his first call. He was with the general's secretary, not the general, and he was shaking.

I liked the three officers. They are not, to the eye, killers. One, the minister of defense, is a Buddha, smiling reassurances, calm. The head of the city police (National Police), a lawyer as well as an academy graduate, was smart, well spoken, and efficient. The head of the rural police (National Guard), also an engineer, had an impressive analytical dimension. The latter two were surprisingly forthcoming with certain bookkeeper-type information on malfeasance in the ranks (murder of civilians and the like) and on the discipline (civilian trial, expulsion, and so on) meted out as a result. Keeping order for the oligarchs is one thing. But the atrocities incident to a guerrilla war are something else. I caught myself thinking—unfairly?—that the armed forces may be pursuing the latter more vigorously than we ever did in Vietnam. Given their caste tradition, it must be painful and humiliating for them. Do you ever get angry at the American nagging?, I asked the minister of defense. Buddha smiled: "No."

How many of the National Police have died in the line of duty since October 15, 1979, the date of this junta's coup and the date its bookkeeping commenced? "151." How many people have the police killed?" "We don't count—no more than ten." *No more than ten?* —in a country littered by an average of forty or fifty often torn, sometimes headless corpses every day for the last two years—*no more than ten?* Tell that to Domingo.

If U.S. Aid Were Halted

On the basis of my interviews, I would say that the United States has the full attention of the Salvadoran military command on the violence. The *threat* of an aid cutoff is a useful tool for those in the command who are prepared, no doubt for reasons of their own, to stand up to the hard fascist right. The American military advisors, the second and third American-trained battalions soon to come on line, the 500 American-trained officers: these will help some, though not enough to spare many future Domingos. We are pushing uphill against the culture.

I asked many people what would happen if the United States, unable to stomach the violence, cut Salvador off. The most credible answer, representing a consensus, came from Dr. Jorge Bustamante, the heroic fifty-nine-year-old doctor who is setting up the elections of March 28 [1982]. The right wing would immediately seize power and kill 300,000 people, he said, and then Salvador would become a left-wing totalitarian state, an outcome accompanied by its own fearful slaughter.

It seems to me absurd to suggest that cutting off aid is the humane solution, let the politics go hang. The melancholy reality is that we are riding a tiger. We got on for good reason—to support what seemed like the best bet available for centrist reform. If we get off, we do more than abandon what scant hope exists of a breakthrough. We abandon a country for which, by our intervention, we have accepted no small responsibility. We abandon it to a depth of savagery not known at this point even to pitiful El Salvador.

PART THREE

Nicaragua: What Kind of Revolution?

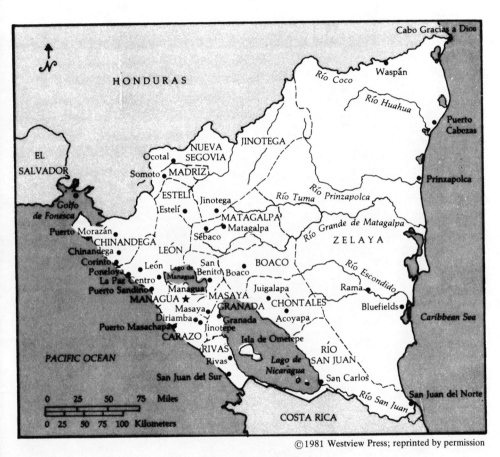

NICARAGUA

Nicaragua Chronology

1909 Dictator José Santos Zelaya overthrown. Chaos and instability follow, leading to U.S. financial and military intervention (1912-33).

1927 Peace accord among fighting factions provides basis for U.S. occupation and subsequent elections. General Augusto C. Sandino refuses to accept peace accord and leads guerrilla force against U.S. Marines.

1933 General Anastasio Somoza García named director of new "non-partisan" National Guard. U.S. Marines withdrawn.

1934 Sandino assassinated by National Guardsman; Somoza seizes power.

1937 Somoza officially becomes president.

1956 Somoza assassinated; sons Luis and Anastasio Jr. continue family domination.

1961 Sandinista National Liberation Front (FSLN) founded.

1967 Anastasio Somoza Debayle elected president.

1972 Earthquake devastates Managua; Somoza's mishandling of crisis and of international relief funds increases antipathy to regime.

1974 Election fraud ensures Somoza's reelection to six-year term.

1977 Popular unrest intensifies. U.S. suspends credits to Somoza government through votes at World Bank and Inter-American Development Bank.

1978 U.S. and Organization of American States fail in mediation attempts; U.S. suspends military aid to Somoza.

1979   Marxist FSLN (Sandinista National Liberation Front)
            supported by other opposition fronts overthrows
            Somoza.

1980   President Carter suspends economic aid to Sandinista
            government because of its arms shipments to rebels in El
            Salvador.

22. *Somoza, Sandino, and the United States*

By MARK FALCOFF

Focus   "If the history of U.S. relations with Nicaragua over the period 1912 to 1979 establishes anything, it is that even when it tried, Washington was unable to make that country behave like a democracy—even in the limited Latin American sense of the term." Mark Falcoff says that a careful study of U.S.-Nicaraguan relations over the past half century is called for. This research will not be helpful, however, if its main purpose "is to excuse the conduct of the present revolutionary regime in Nicaragua as a wholly justifiable reaction to past U.S. policies there."

In Falcoff's view, the main problem in Nicaragua has been not so much the exercise of U.S. power there as the lack of it. He traces the complex web of events in and outside Nicaragua and finds many American errors, but not as clear a pattern of U.S. behavior as is normally assumed. The United States supported the Somozas only fitfully, usually under the pressure of external events. The Somozas *claimed* strong American backing and were able to use the claim to their advantage. Against the accepted view, Falcoff maintains that "had Washington been able to fully control its putative 'alliance' with Managua, Nicaragua's political history would have been vastly happier . . . for the immense majority of its people."

According to the author, events developed as they did for the most part because America was much of the time preoccupied with weightier events: Nicaragua was only "a very small part of the international picture . . . and at best only a modest amount of foreign policy energy could be devoted to it." World War II gave the Somoza dynasty a chance to consolidate its power.

Americans have a strong desire to be fair in their foreign policy, and that is why many commentators on the current situation often refer to our past real or alleged misdeeds in Nicaragua. Falcoff argues that because of this tendency, "it is as much a matter of public policy as moral house-cleaning to set the record straight."

Mark Falcoff is a resident fellow at the Center for Hemispheric Studies, American Enterprise Institute for Public Policy Research.

THE EMERGENCE IN NICARAGUA of a regime hostile to the United States and allied to Cuba and the Soviet Union was bound to send many Americans to their history books. Yet two quite different purposes can and do motivate such exercises. One might hope to learn from past errors, with a view to preventing "other Nicaraguas" in the future. The scope of that effort is a very large one, with ample room for honest differences of opinion over precisely where U.S. policies went off track—and what might have been done to get them back on. No one can doubt that a careful, dispassionate examination of U.S.-Nicaraguan relations over the past half-century and more is in order.

The other "course of study" is quite different, in both spirit and substance. Its effect, if not intent, is to excuse the conduct of the present revolutionary regime in Nicaragua as a wholly justifiable reaction to past U.S. policies there. Some of what has been written under this rubric tries to pass itself off as history, when it is really nothing more than the manipulation of past events (or pseudo-events) in service of some very current agendas. Fragments of this approach can be found in declarations by academic caucuses, in the editorials of the prestige and religious press, and even in pronouncements by members of Congress. In its purest form, this line of argument was stated by Richard Fagen in *Foreign Policy* magazine:

> In 1912 after three years of unsuccessful attempts by Washington to stabilize Nicaragua by political and diplomatic means . . . the U.S. Marines were landed. At stake were the outstanding loans of U.S. and European creditors, . . . also the possibility of canal-building rights through southern Nicaragua. . . .
> Only in 1933 did the occupying troops finally depart, leaving in their stead the U.S.-created National Guard headed by General Anastasio Somoza García. For the next forty-six years the

---

Reprinted by permission of the author from the Fall 1983 issue of *This World*.

Somoza family never relinquished direct control of the Guard,
and seldom gave up the presidency. . . .

The senior Somoza ruled Nicaragua as a personal fiefdom,
with the Guard as his private army and enforcer and with the
continuing support and approval of the United States.

From the outset, the dynasty was welcomed in Washington as
a solid pillar of pro-American and anti-Communist strength in
an otherwise troubled area. . . . Until the early 1970s . . . the
Washington-Managua alliance seemed unshakable. . . .

So close was the identification of Washington's interest with
the continued rule of the Somozas, however, that little actually
changed . . . until the Carter administration took office.

On the other hand, the new administration also feared any
alternative to Somoza that would not be firmly controlled by the
most conservative of anti-Somoza forces. Meanwhile, Somoza's
powerful friends in the U.S. Congress and elsewhere were doing
everything in their power—in the name of anti-Communism
and hemispheric stability—to insure that the four-decades-old
policy of U.S. support for the dynasty continued.

It is hard to imagine a more indiscriminate indictment; it spares no
President since William Howard Taft, and very pointedly includes
Jimmy Carter. Admittedly, this is the way many Nicaraguans—by
no means all of them Sandinistas—have seen the history of their
country. However, insofar as the United States is concerned, it
happens to be quite false. The facts are these: The U.S. intervention in 1912 was *not* principally inspired by the motives offered;
Somoza did *not* rule with the "continuing support and approval of
the United States"; the dynasty was *not* welcomed by Washington
"from the outset . . . as a solid pillar of pro-American and anti-
Communist strength"; and the Carter administration did *not* insist
on restricting the alternatives to Somoza to "the most conservative
of anti-Somoza forces," unless, of course, one chooses to label
anyone who is not a Marxist a conservative, and an extreme conservative at that.

What Fagen rather disingenuously withholds from his
readers—and what many who repeat his argument in a watered-
down form simply do not know—is the vastly complicated
dynamics of Nicaraguan politics. This prevents us from reaching
the conclusion which typically overwhelms those who bother to
study the subject: that the problem in Nicaragua has not been U.S.

power so much as a lack of it—an inability to shape developments there according to our own values and preferences. For when all due tribute has been paid to Nicaraguan nationalism and the right of self-determination, it is still true that had Washington been able to fully control its putative "alliance" with Managua, Nicaragua's political history would have been vastly happier—for the immense majority of its people, if not precisely for the particular political sect of which Fagen happens to approve.

In the present context, the history of U.S.-Nicaraguan relations is more than a matter of mere academic interest. The reason is quite simple. Many countries are capable of formulating and executing foreign policy without excessive reference to their national conscience. The United States, however, is not one of them. If we conclude that we have inflicted a great wrong on a small and defenseless people, then we invariably ask ourselves, "Who are *we* to criticize the way its present leaders put things right?," or even assert, "We're just getting what we deserve." History thus used and abused leads to guilt, guilt to immobility. That is why on the subject of our present relations with Nicaragua some commentators make recurrent reference to the past—or to what they imagine the past to have been. That is also why it is as much a matter of public policy as moral house-cleaning to set the record straight.

PRE-1912: SEEKING STABILITY AND SOLVENCY

During the nineteenth century, U.S. interest in Nicaragua was dominated by a peculiar fact of geography—the existence of a huge volcanic lake comprehending approximately a quarter of the country's breadth—that made Nicaragua a logical site for an isthmus canal. A short trench incised from the lake's western shore to the Pacific, and a somewhat longer one in combination with the San Juan River to the Atlantic port of Greytown, would have produced an inter-oceanic route, and at a cost presumably far lower than at any other point of the isthmus, since elsewhere the requirement for excavation would be total. Moreover, long before the capital and technology necessary to produce this miracle were readily available, a shipping and passenger service across Nicaragua was in operation through a combination of steamer and stagecoach under the patronage of Commodore Cornelius Vanderbilt.

Vanderbilt's experiment was of short duration—begun in 1851, destroyed in 1855 by a flooding of the San Juan River, and supplanted by the Panama Railway the following year. The idea of a Nicaraguan canal nonetheless persisted into the early years of the present century. A commission created by the U.S. Congress reported in 1897 that it was technically feasible, and President McKinley even recommended its construction in his annual message to Congress in 1898. For reasons extraneous to the present narrative, the Congress decided in 1902 to build the canal in Panama instead. Construction began in 1904, and the facility opened ten years later. Thus in 1912, when Marines first landed in Nicaragua, the question of an inter-oceanic route had already been settled—elsewhere.

With the new route fully operational in Panama, U.S. policy in Nicaragua became virtually undistinguishable from that elsewhere in the region—to promote the basic stability and solvency of governments. Lacking both, these tiny nations (and therefore the approaches to the canal itself) might fall into the hands of some hostile power. Outright annexation was thought unlikely, but as Africa and China had recently demonstrated, there were other ways in which European powers could establish naval and strategic—not to say commercial—presences without the full encumbrances of formal colonialism.

In this connection the internal political life of the Central American republics (and Haiti and the Dominican Republic in the Caribbean) offered ample grounds for concern. Perennial outbreaks of revolution endangered the lives and property of European residents, whose home navies were wont to demand pecuniary damages in an extremely forceful fashion. On one occasion German gunboats even threatened to destroy an entire complex of government buildings in the Haitian capital of Port-au-Prince if $30,000 were not collected within a matter of hours. Political instability also provoked serious interruptions in economic life, making it impossible for the states to service their foreign debts. Default was an open invitation for European creditors to seize customs houses and port facilities, as prologue—many Americans and Central Americans feared—to a more permanent political presence.

Factions in Conflict

Thus at the heart of the region's international problems were an economic backwardness and a political backwardness that reinforced each other. Ostensibly, public life was a contest between "Liberal" and "Conservative" parties; in reality, it was a conflict among contending clans, families, and their retainers—typically organized along regional or provincial lines. Because the resources at stake were so scarce, the struggle was one in which quarter was neither asked nor given. No ruling party could afford the luxury of losing an election, and so its opponent was left with no other recourse than the crucible of civil war. "It too often resorted to savage reprisals when it came to power," diplomat-historian Dana C. Munro has written. "The cruelties practiced on political enemies engendered factional hatreds which were passed on from father to son and helped to keep the revolutionary spirit alive."

The State Department archives and also the published correspondence found in successive volumes of *Foreign Relations of the United States* for the years 1898 through at least 1914 unambiguously establish that in Central America and the Caribbean, U.S. statesmanship was obsessed with the search for policy instruments capable of breaking this vicious circle. All manner of devices were tried—"preventive intervention" under the Roosevelt Corollary to the Monroe Doctrine, customs receiverships, debt refundings. After World War I, the emphasis shifted to non-recognition of governments that had come to power by force, and an attempt to replace private, party armies with a non-partisan constabulary.

None of these mechanisms were warmly appreciated by the governments concerned. Nor were they particularly effective—at least in the middle and longer term. But they were not inspired by uniquely sordid or selfish motives. The United States did not land troops or seize customs houses principally to protect its investors and bankers, for the rather undramatic reason that before 1914 U.S. economic involvement in the area (apart from Cuba) was insignificant, and the major creditors remained to an overwhelming degree European. Doubtless such considerations existed in embryo, but they were unquestionably minor ones, Munro concludes, "compared with the desire to avert the danger that disorder would invite European intervention."

THE ERA OF INTERVENTION: 1912-33

Nicaragua was a particularly notable example of the failure of U.S. policy to achieve its announced goals—and for means and ends to stray rather farther from each other than proportion and good sense should have tolerated. Nonetheless, U.S. military intervention there must be divided conceptually into two quite distinct periods. The first began in 1912, when Marines were landed to stabilize a country torn by civil conflict (in the process, shoring up an incumbent Conservative government which was unpopular and probably unrepresentative even in the narrow terms of the day). It ends in 1927 with the Peace of Tipitapa, when the United States, in the person of Secretary of War Henry Stimson, negotiated a truce between Conservative and Liberal politico-military chieftains.

These years represent opposite ends of a learning curve for U.S. policy-makers and diplomats. At the beginning, reliance was indeed placed upon force alone. But by 1927 certain realities of Nicaraguan life managed to impose themselves, fostering a serious effort to address what today would be called the "structural" causes of instability. The first of these realities was that the Liberal party, supposedly less friendly to the United States than the Conservatives, could not be permanently denied access to power. Second, since no defeated party could ever accept the results of falsified elections, the Marines would have to remain for several years to assure the integrity of elections. And finally, since no victorious government could escape an armed challenge from its defeated rivals, private military and paramilitary forces would have to be disarmed and disbanded. In their place the Marines would train a non-partisan constabulary to preserve public order once the U.S. expeditionary force had departed. In effect, the United States proposed to give Nicaragua the national army it had never possessed.

From 1927 to 1933 the United States tried to put these hard-earned lessons into practice. The process turned out to be so nettlesome that even if the Depression had not eventually intervened to force a drastic reduction of overseas commitments, by 1933 Washington would in all likelihood have been ready to withdraw its troops from Nicaragua. One very large problem was the refusal of dissident elements of the Liberal party to recognize the Peace of Tipitapa. Led by General Augusto C. Sandino, they retained their arms to pursue a guerrilla campaign against U.S. and Nicaraguan forces for six years. Although Sandino's movement was centered largely in the mountain fastness of Nueva Segovia, in the northwestern part of the country, at several points it managed to threaten key cities, including toward the very end the capital, Managua.

The Sandino Legacy

Today Sandino is a brooding presence in Nicaragua—mutely peering down from dozens of walls, with others speaking on his behalf. But his real identity remains enshrouded in myth and misunderstanding. The Coolidge administration repeatedly referred to him and his followers as "bandits," which was patently untrue. But neither was he the Marxist social revolutionary depicted by U.S. Secretary of State Frank Kellogg, and many years later (in a curious coincidence of needs) by a Nicaraguan government bearing his name. In reality Sandino was an adventurer, a born leader of men, and a clever Nicaraguan politician much given to self-dramatization. But he was also what he often represented himself to be—a man of principle, forced to defend his country against what he regarded as a humiliation of its national sovereignty. From the very beginning he promised to lay down his arms the moment the last Marine departed Nicaragua—and he kept his word. Even more significantly, Sandino refused to be used by forces extraneous to his cause. Thus, although for a time in the late 1920s he received rhetorical (and some small material) support from both the U.S. and Mexican Communist parties, he steadfastly refused to follow Moscow's dictates, and even denied that a social revolution was necessary in Nicaragua. This eventually led him to sever personal and political relations with Farabundo Martí, a Salvadoran Communist who for a time served as the Comintern's envoy to the Sandinista forces.

Although Sandino "won" only a few of his encounters with the Marines, his constant hit-and-run tactics succeeded in making Washington's policy of pacification in Nicaragua very expensive—in blood and treasure, as well as in Latin American and even domestic U.S. opinion. This made all the more urgent the formation of a professional military force in Nicaragua to take over from the Marines, but that was the other large problem. For neither party in Nicaragua was particularly anxious to have a constabulary above politics—were such a thing even possible. Eventually Washington compromised with this reality as well, accepting a bipartisan officer corps in the hope of forestalling what it feared—and what eventually came to pass: a force led by politicians of the party in power.

The National Guard of Nicaragua was thus organized under the twin pressures of time and circumstance. At first the infant force had American Marines as officers, but by 1931 and 1932 most of these had been replaced by Nicaraguans quickly trained at the new La Loma Military Academy. Since most of the enlisted men were drawn from Nicaragua's underclass, there was no "training up" into the commissioned ranks. Instead, officer candidates were drawn from civilian life, which made their indoctrination into non-partisanship a rather quixotic exercise.

The frantic search for reliable professionals to direct the Guard led the Americans to Anastasio Somoza. A Liberal general and politician, Somoza had studied at business school in the United States, and though of undistinguished social origins, had managed to marry into an aristocratic Nicaraguan family. During the 1920s he had served as consul in Costa Rica, deputy minister of foreign affairs, and, finally, minister of foreign affairs. During the last phase of the Marine occupation he was named chief director-designate of the National Guard. "The last appointment was partly due to the patronage of the American minister in Nicaragua," Neil Macaulay writes in *The Sandino Affair*. "The minister and his wife were impressed by Somoza's absolute mastery of the American language, and were captivated by his effervescent personality." And, he adds in an acid afternote, "Mrs. Hanna thought Tacho Somoza a smooth tango and rumba dancer." Somoza was also, however, an experienced, disciplined public official who put in long hours, scrupulously kept appointments, and in general impressed the Americans with his industry and serious attention to detail. The decision to make him director of the National Guard was far from illogical.

SANDINO, SACASA, AND SOMOZA

When the last American Marine departed in 1933, the deeper realities of Nicaraguan politics rapidly floated to the surface, sweeping away what positive legacies remained of U.S. involvement. Things had begun well enough: the elections of 1932, supervised by the Marines, were the freest and fairest in the nation's history. And shortly after his inauguration on New Year's Day 1933, President Juan Sacasa received Sandino in Managua to work out the details of a peace accord. Sandino agreed to "morally support" Sacasa's administration, in exchange for which he was allowed to keep a small remnant of his private army, and his followers were assured of preferential employment on future public works projects. Disbandment of Sandino's main force then followed, and the rebel general himself returned home to Nueva Segovia.

Almost immediately it became clear that General Somoza and the National Guard constituted a new kind of threat to peace and order in Nicaragua. Relations between Somoza and Sandino— never good in the best of times—rapidly deteriorated as Guard units harassed the guerrilla leader's former followers. And as early as November 1933, the American Legation in Managua began to receive information that Somoza was planning a coup to oust President Sacasa. In February 1934, Sandino came to Managua to discuss his differences with both the government and the Guard; a few evenings later he was brutally murdered by Somoza minions shortly after leaving a dinner with Sacasa in the presidential compound. Two years later, Somoza deposed Sacasa and seized the presidency for himself.

No one can dispute that these exact events could never have taken place in Nicaragua without U.S. intervention in 1912. On the other hand, the record is clear also on this: there was no direct relationship between the United States and the murder of Sandino, the overthrow of Sacasa, or even the creation of the Somoza dictatorship. None of these events figured in U.S. plans or policies, nor—even more importantly—were these events greeted by the State Department with satisfaction or even tacit approval. What is true is that beginning with the murder of Sandino, Somoza and, later, his sons and political heirs habitually *represented* their actions as having prior U.S. assent. For different reasons, both opponents and supporters of the regime found it convenient to accept this explanation, and both tirelessly propagated it in various forms for four decades.

What many Nicaraguans failed to notice—and what Somoza quickly learned to exploit—was a decided shift in U.S. policy just about the time that these events were unfolding. Over a rather long period Washington gradually recognized that constitutional democracy of the Anglo-Saxon type was not exportable to Nicaragua, or, for that matter, to Haiti, the Dominican Republic, or Mexico; and further, that attempts to impose constitutional democracy in tropical lands were both costly and counterproductive. Despotism and military rule seemed the inevitable fruits of the Caribbean environment, and, U.S. officials reasoned, we had best stop attempting to contravene the experience of history. As Arthur Bliss Lane, U.S. minister to Nicaragua 1934-35, confided to a friend toward the end of his mission:

> The people who created the G.N. [National Guard] had no adequate understanding of the psychology of the people here. Otherwise they would not have bequeathed Nicaragua with an instrument to blast constitutional procedure off the map. Did it ever occur to the eminent statesmen who created the G.N. that personal ambition lurks in the human breast, even in Nicaragua? In my opinion, it is one of the sorriest examples on our part of our inability to understand that we should not meddle in other people's affairs.

Of course, it was far easier to reach such conclusions in 1935, informed not only by the wisdom of hindsight but also by the shift in economic and naval power in the area, than in 1912. For after World War I, the threat of European intervention in the Caribbean had virtually disappeared, and political instability—far from being, as it once had been, an "international" problem—could now be regarded simply as a local matter. Somoza was no improvement over what the United States had sought to replace, but by the time he seized power, Washington had virtually abandoned its attempts to reform the Nicaraguans. Having struggled so hard to get off the treadmill of intervention, the United States—beset by the manifold ills of the Depression—was not about to get back on it.

Somoza also benefited indirectly from a broader change in U.S. policy toward revolutionary governments, or more precisely, governments which emerged from the extra-constitutional use of force. Before about 1930 Washington had attempted to discourage violent political change in the area by withholding recognition from *de facto* regimes. In 1907 and again in 1923 it had even sponsored treaties—to which all Central American governments were signatories—to this effect.

Over time it became apparent that the punitive use of diplomatic recognition put the United States in a serious bind. As historian William Kamman puts it, "Washington had to do more than just decide which government was in control, it had to determine the letigimacy of [that] government." This meant, perforce, that if the only regimes worthy of recognition were those which issued from the ballot box, then to have diplomatic relations at all with many Central American republics, one would have to insure that elections occurred in the first place. This led almost unswervingly to military intervention, with all of the attendant unpleasantries. It also provoked much nationalist resentment throughout Latin America, where the United States was not acknowledged to have the right to determine the appropriate form of political change for its neighbors.

The Estrada Doctrine

On this subject the Mexicans were particularly vehement, and in 1930 that country's foreign minister Genaro Estrada went so far as to call grants of recognition "an insulting practice." According to what became known as the Estrada Doctrine, only *states* could be recognized; when a new government came to power—by whatever means—its *bona fides* were not subject to the value judgments of others. Of course, the Mexicans had in mind their own revolution of 1910, which was very different from the upheavals in Nicaragua, since it went far beyond a periodic shift in the fortunes of contending elites. That upheaval had swept away an entire host of social and economic institutions. and in the process inflicted serious damage—both physical and legal—upon foreign property and investment, much of it belonging to American nationals. For nearly a decade Washington attempted to influence events there by withholding (or granting) recognition to the various governments that succeeded the dictator Porfirio Díaz. Extrapolating from their own experience, the Mexicans declared conditional use of recognition an offense to sovereignty and the right of weaker peoples to self-determination.

Other Latin American nations picked up this theme, and it quickly became part of a package of demands for "non-intervention" thrust at the United States during the Havana Pan American Conference in 1928—the first such meeting at which American delegates were forced to confront a serious and unified opposition. The events of that meeting plunged senior State Department officials into a mood of sober reappraisal, and during the next four or five years there was a gradual reconsideration of U.S. policy. Matters were helped along by the coming of the Great Depression, which suddenly made the United States more attentive to its image in Latin America, whose markets—some New Deal planners imagined—held the key to domestic economic recovery.

In any event, under both the Hoover and Roosevelt administrations, there was a gradual turnaround generally associated with the Good Neighbor Policy. The Marines were withdrawn not only from Nicaragua but from Haiti as well, and at the Montevideo meeting of American states in 1933, and above all at the Buenos Aires Conference in 1936, the United States definitively renounced intervention as an instrument in its relations with other American states.

Meanwhile, in 1934 the Central American nations quietly abandoned their commitments under the 1923 accords to withhold recognition from *de facto* regimes and subscribed instead to the Estrada Doctrine. Between the Montevideo and Buenos Aires conferences, the United States followed suit; under the circumstances, it had no other choice. But in some quarters of the State Department, serious doubts persisted to the very end. One official pointed out, for example, that even if non-recognition had not succeeded in preventing revolutions, unconditional recognition would surely encourage them. It would also reinforce the temptation to back "any strong man who came along," with the attendant risk of identifying the United States too closely with a tyrant who would eventually fall. By 1935 or 1936, such apprehensions were overwhelmed by other considerations. The United States signed the Buenos Aires accords, tacitly accepted the Estrada Doctrine, won plaudits from "liberal" Latin American publicists and statesmen, and indirectly strengthened strongman regimes, such as that emerging in Nicaragua.

ANASTASIO SOMOZA: TWO DECADES OF DICTATORSHIP

Somoza seized the presidency of Nicaragua in 1936 and remained in office through successive "elections" in 1939 and 1947. He had just accepted his party's nomination for yet another term when he fell victim to an assassin's bullet in 1956. His tenure, by far the longest in Nicaraguan history, was made possible in the first instance by the National Guard. Unlike the Liberal and Conservative armies it replaced, the Guard was more or less professionally organized and equipped, and because it retained a monopoly of arms, there was no force in the country capable of challenging it. In this sense alone Somoza was Nicaragua's first "modern" president. What was striking and unique, however, was the way he adapted modern institutions—not just a professional constabulary, but eventually a rationalized administration, a central bank, public works, and economic development generally—to suit his dynastic needs.

The Somoza regime could thus be described as a patrimonial police state—but it was also something else: a peculiar kind of social revolution. Before 1936, Nicaraguan politicians tended to be gentlemen of property and refinement, recruited from the landowners and professional class of the country's two major provincial cities, León (for the Liberals) and Granada (for Conservatives). Their views on political and social issues were probably no larger or more responsible than Somoza's, but theirs was necessarily a more impersonal approach to the business of government. Then, too, precisely because Nicaragua had been so unstable before 1936, opportunities in public service or diplomacy had been passed around rather generously, if a bit sporadically. Now all the lines of political ascent ran directly through one man, his family, and their retainers. As the regime consolidated itself over decades, it absorbed an increasing share of the perquisites of power—bribes, kickbacks, and concessions. Corruption became less democratic—and therefore, more hateful.

This was a change; so indeed was the kind of man with whom the dons of León and Granada had to deal. Crude and brutal, Somoza possessed a sort of raffish charm which captivated some foreign admirers but represented for the more traditional political class in Nicaragua the triumph of *mala educación*. The people he brought into government with him—with rare exceptions—were of equally undistinguished antecedents or personal qualities. If the U.S. legation in Managua held a somewhat jaundiced view of the opposition during Somoza's early years of power, it was partly because memories of the old system were so fresh, and partly because it was too easy to evaluate the claims of displaced aristocrats at their true value. These men were not anxious to restore democracy to Nicaragua, merely to get back on the take (which was what *they* meant by democracy). The United States never accepted Somoza's charges that his opponents were agents of Nazism (before and during World War II) or Communism (thereafter). But it was not about to land Marines to return things to the *status quo ante* 1927.

U.S.-Somoza: Ups and Downs

Over the twenty-year dictatorship of the elder Somoza, relations between the United States and Nicaragua were far less cordial—or even consistent—than the term "Washington-Managua alliance" suggests. During the years 1936 to 1939, for example, U.S. diplomats maintained a discreet distance from the regime and repeatedly turned down its most frequent request—for military assistance. What suddenly brought Washington around was World War II. Somoza himself was invited to Washington, and eventually Nicaragua received $1.3 million in equipment under Lend-Lease. (In exchange, the United States obtained temporary rights to a naval base in Corinto.) Once the conflict ended, however, the United States pointedly refused Somoza's plea for allotments on a more continuing basis. One Pentagon official pointedly voiced the War Department's determination not to "burden the country with armaments," and added gratuitously that "military missions from foreign countries" in such places as Nicaragua "should be avoided at all costs." A further attempt by Somoza to purchase arms on a cash basis was blocked by the State Department. "Any arms which we might ship to him at this time," the relevant memorandum read, "could only be taken by him, the Nicaraguan public, and by the other republics of Central America and of the hemisphere as a demonstration of complete support for his plans." This impression "would not only be erroneous, but extremely embarrassing."

In 1947, when Somoza prepared to run for "re-election," Assistant Secretary of State Nelson Rockefeller called in Somoza's ambassador in Washington to impress upon him the Truman administration's acute displeasure, and warned that such an eventuality "might create difficulties . . . which would seriously affect relations between the two countries." To show that it meant business, the State Department once again blocked the sale of weapons to the regime, and even managed to pressure Canada and Great Britain into joining the embargo.

This was a nimble procedure, but Somoza was nimbler still. He withdrew from the race in favor of a puppet candidate, Dr. Leopoldo Argüello, who was "elected" in the usual fashion. Somoza, of course, retained control of the Guard. The opposition in Nicaragua tried to persuade the United States to refuse recognition to the new government, but Washington opted for a different course, partly because the new president had quietly assured the American ambassador that he intended to be his own man. Once in office Argüello did in fact make serious attempts to curb Somoza's power. The two men fell to quarreling over who was in charge—of the Guard and of the country. President Argüello eventually demanded Somoza's resignation and (in a fit of almost inconceivable daring) his departure from the country. Somoza's response was to overthrow his own putative puppet.

The United States, abruptly departing from its own recent adherence to the Estrada Doctrine, now withheld recognition.

Even a crude attempt by Somoza to exploit anti-Communism (in a new "constitution" which also made it easier for the United States to establish military bases in Nicaragua) left the State Department unmoved. But Washington changed course some months later, when other nations in the area either had recognized Somoza or were preparing to do so, and when it became clear that any sanctions short of actual military intervention were bound to prove ineffective. (For instance, having refused to sell the dictator warplanes, the United States found it impossible to block his acquisition of B-24 bombers from Brazil.)

The Guatemalan Question

Then, once again, international events converged to bring about a thaw in the diplomatic chill between Somoza and the United States. In 1944 a revolution in Guatemala had brought to power a generation of young officers and intellectuals imbued with vaguely leftist ideals. By 1952, however, under President Jacobo Arbenz, the principal prop of the Guatemalan regime had become the Communist-led Labor Federation. There is still considerable controversy over the exact nature of the relationship between the Arbenz government and the Soviet bloc. At the time, however, it was perceived by Washington as the opening wedge for Soviet penetration of the Caribbean, and operatives of the Central Intelligence Agency, working with right-wing Guatemalan exiles, staged a coup which overturned Arbenz in 1954.

By cooperating with the CIA in the Guatemalan affair—at least, to the extent of acting as a conduit of arms to exile forces—Somoza was able to neutralize some of the opposition to him in the State Department. On the other hand, he still could not obtain approval of his plans to purchase heavy military equipment from the United States; he circumvented the continued American embargo by turning to Sweden for P-51 fighters. Further, when he began to menace Costa Rica with his new weapons, Washington promptly dispatched Navy planes from the Canal Zone to convince Somoza that—whatever unpleasantries might have been necessary in the case of Guatemala—it would not tolerate his aggressive conduct against a democratic neighbor.

THE NEXT SOMOZA GENERATION

After Somoza's assassination in 1956, the regime moved into a qualitatively different phase. It was still undemocratic and dynastic, but it became more complex and even—at least to 1972—more popular. The fallen dictator's two sons, Luis and Anastasio Jr. (who was called "Tachito"), were forced to share power. Luis was elected by the Nicaraguan congress to fill out the unexpired portion of his father's term, and "re-elected" in 1957. Tachito, who had been sent to American military schools and West Point, assumed control of the National Guard.

Since the two Somozas had very different notions of how to discharge their legacy, they were continuously at odds until Luis's death in 1967 ended the rivalry and left Tachito in complete control. Unlike his brother, Luis Somoza was a man of some political imagination, who envisioned for Nicaragua a modified "Mexican" solution. The Somozas would retain, perhaps even increase, their power and wealth, but the formal leadership of the country would devolve into the hands of a succession of puppet presidents. In 1959 Luis even restored to the Nicaraguan constitution an earlier article prohibiting consecutive presidential terms and also succession to the presidency of any relative of the incumbent. In 1963 he selected Dr. René Schick to be the first of a new series of chief executives.

Luis also believed in governing with a somewhat less heavy hand than his father (or, as time would show, his brother). Restrictions on the press and on opposition political activity were loosened; the role of the Nicaraguan military was played down and its budget actually reduced. Some new programs of economic development—financed, to be sure, with foreign loans, and often subsidizing inefficient Somoza family industries—nonetheless created thousands of new jobs and therefore broadened the regime's base of support. These years also coincided with the rise of Castro in Cuba, the Bay of Pigs invasion (1961), and the missile crisis (1962), so that in addition to some marginal political improvement within Nicaragua, the Kennedy administration had other, more pressing reasons for dealing with the Somozas. It was just about this time that the United States began a serious program of military assistance to Nicaragua.

Even before the end of Schick's term, however, it was clear that a more impersonal form of Somocismo would not work. Schick attempted to rein in Tachito and the Guard as long as he dared; thereafter, he lapsed into impotence and alcohol. In 1966 Tachito finally arranged his own election to the presidency, and few observers doubted that he meant to remain in office for life. It was precisely this determination to withdraw his brother's modest concessions to pluralism that aroused so much resentment in the opposition, and even in the Liberal party, to which Somoza nominally belonged. At the same time, there was much resentment of the tendency to enlarge the family's financial holdings at the expense of the state and other entrepreneurs.

THE FALL OF SOMOZA

During Tachito's first term, a boom in international commodity prices and the ready availability of foreign credit muted some of the opposition to his rule, even to his fraudulent "re-election" in 1971. The real breaking point came in 1972, as the result of an earthquake which devastated the city of Managua. During the first critical days of the calamity, Guard discipline virtually disintegrated, and troops openly looted stores and warehouses. (Many of the stolen provisions later appeared on the Guard-dominated black market.) Somoza himself pocketed millions of dollars' worth of emergency relief from abroad; preferential allotment of what remained went to Guard families and government employees. The government's handling of this crisis created new centers of opposition in the church and the business community, and by 1974 or 1975 the regime had entered a decline from which it was never to recover.

It was in this first half of Tachito's presidency that the United States seemed most strongly to support the regime, largely because of the obsequious conduct of Ambassador Turner Shelton, whose excessive identification with the dictator created a scandal in Nicaragua and ripples of opposition within the State Department and his own embassy. Of course, many Nicaraguans could not be blamed for thinking that Somoza now had a blank check from the United States to do anything he wished, since this was the inevitable impression which the ambassador gave and which Somoza himself rebroadcast far and wide. Also, they were not privy to the relevant diplomatic correspondence, which told another story. But after Shelton's recall in 1975 and his replacement by James Theberge, Tachito began to note a decided shift in the political winds from Washington.

No doubt to the end of his days Somoza was mystified by the change, largely because his knowledge of this country was distant and dated. Although he was largely educated here, his English was never as good as he thought it was, and it did not improve with time. His picture of the United States was as dated as his contacts were unrepresentative of the U.S. mainstream: a 1940s collage of conservative Roman Catholic prelates, military officers, right-wing businessmen from Texas and Florida, and a handful of congressmen—the most vocal and active of whom was Congressman John Murphy, with whom Somoza had gone to private military school in New York (and who is now in federal prison following his conviction in one of the "Abscam" cases).

Further, Somoza's own diplomats and advisors in the United States were unrealistic and ill informed. His ambassador in Washington, Guillermo Sevilla-Sacasa, had been in place since 1943, and—though dean of the Washington diplomatic corps—had never managed to learn English. As to the dictator himself, with few exceptions his visits to Washington were fleeting and generally incognito. Thus he was never able to appreciate the degree to which he benefited from Americans' benign neglect and sheer ignorance of his country, which also explain the success for some years of the tiny "Somoza lobby" in the House of Representatives.

The Post-Earthquake Shift

After his fall, Somoza tried to credit the shift in U.S. policy to sinister forces in Washington. In fact, President Ford's instructions to Ambassador Theberge to distance himself from the dictator reflected nothing more than a sober awareness that since the earthquake in 1972, a dramatic shift had occurred in Nicaraguan politics. Opposition to the regime was more widespread than ever before and growing, and it was largely unrelated to the then-tiny Frente Sandinista de Liberación Nacional (FSLN, or "Sandinistas"). Rather, it embraced virtually every respectable interest outside the Somoza machine, including businessmen like Adolfo Calero and clerics like the archbishop of Managua, Monsignor Miguel Obando y Bravo. What Somoza never grasped was the degree to which such people (whose English was sometimes better than his own, and whose knowledge of American democracy was far more profound) were able to reach the State Department and Congress on their own.

From 1975 on, U.S. policy was clearly aimed at getting Somoza to restore some integrity to Nicaragua's political institutions, through dialogue with the opposition and free elections. When it became obvious that the dictator intended to do neither, Washington, in conjunction with other countries of the region, began to pressure him to resign. This telescopes, of course, a long and very complicated process. Over three years' time Somoza played cat-and-mouse with the opposition and the United States, in turn encouraging and then dashing hopes of a peaceful and negotiated solution.

During these tense and difficult months, relations between the United States and the Nicaraguan opposition became rather frayed. The opposition wanted Somoza out as expeditiously as possible, and at the beginning at least could not understand why the United States could not easily accomplish this, since in their view his regime was utterly dependent for its very existence upon Washington's good will. The State Department and the U.S. Embassy in Managua were equally anxious to see Somoza depart, at least after 1978, but also wished to avoid a power vacuum in which the radical elements in the revolution (that is, the Sandinistas) could seize power. That is why, for example, all of Washington's draft proposals included retention of the National Guard in some form or another. At the beginning the opposition largely shared these apprehensions; but as time wore on, it decided that even jumping into a void was preferable to continued rule by Somoza.

The State Department and the White House meanwhile debated to what degree it was possible or even proper to intervene in Nicaraguan events. This led, in the words of a former Carter administration official, to "policy paralysis." In the end, Washington's modest proposals were rejected by the opposition and voted down in the council of the Organization of American States (OAS), which had become involved in the mediation process. While the opposition quarreled among itself and with Washington, the FSLN closed ranks and projected an image of coherence and unity of purpose. After the last mediation effort in early 1979, it was obvious that in the event of Somoza's departure, the Sandinistas were bound to play a role in Nicaragua's future far out of proportion to their actual numbers. Fidel Castro himself recognized as much and, after having maintained a somewhat platonic relationship with the FSLN over its lean years, began to ship it vast supplies of arms.

Ironically, this was precisely the prospect favored by Somoza himself. By refusing to negotiate effectively with the mainstream of the opposition, over time he pushed them into an alliance with the Sandinistas. This was done very deliberately, so as to confront the United States with only two choices—Somoza's continuance in office, or a Marxist-dominated government in Nicaragua. To the very end, of course, Somoza was convinced that if the two alternatives were thus starkly posed, the United States would be forced to come down on his side. It apparently never occurred to the dictator that Washington might choose to interpret its own national interests differently, or even less, that it would be unable to decide one way or another and would thus lose what control of events it might have had. Somoza's own belief in his carefully cultivated image as Washington's ally may have proven the most critical element in his fall.

LESSONS FROM THE PAST

If the history of U.S. relations with Nicaragua over the period 1912 to 1979 establishes anything, it is that even when it tried, Washington was unable to make that country behave like a democracy—even in the limited Latin American sense of the term. Intervention could eliminate private armies but not the influence of the military in politics; it could assure honest elections at the bayonet point of a Marine—but not one moment beyond it. Moreover, even after renouncing its policy of intervention, the United States was held responsible for every untoward event which subsequently occurred in the history of Nicaragua, simply because at one point the United States had been present as an arbiter of events.

Both policies—intervention *and* nonintervention—were equally frustrating. Nonintervention won out because it was, quite simply, less expensive, and, at the beginning, more popular, if not with the Nicaraguan opposition, at least with other Latin American countries. In later years, the United States periodically vented its pique with the Somozas by resorting to milder forms of intervention—to no great effect. For example, U.S. arms embargoes tended largely to enrich other suppliers, and even the Carter administration's vote against Nicaraguan loans at the Inter-American Development Bank—while undoubtedly a psychological shock of major proportions—was not sufficient to force the regime to mend its ways.

The Limits of Power

The Nicaraguan experiment also demonstrates the way that vast asymmetries of power operate in international politics. Because the sheer physical and economic dimensions of U.S. power were so overwhelming to Nicaraguans, they simply could not accept the notion that Washington did not possess an equally unlimited capacity to arrange their political life—and this in the face of demonstrated failure. Rather, the outcome of every event in Nicaraguan political history was seen as part of a conscious policy in which the United States always got what it wanted. Understandably, but also unfortunately, Nicaraguans generally failed to recognize the role of inertia and drift in the foreign policy of great powers, much less the failure of political will—a failure which occurred more than once across the years, but most devastatingly in the final hours of the Somoza regime.

For the Somozas, it was precisely in the interstices of U.S. policy that they found their vital breathing space. Nicaragua was, after all, a very small part of the international picture of the United States, and at best only a modest amount of foreign policy energy could normally be devoted to it. For the Somozas, of course, it was 100 per cent of *their* energies, and they saw no reason to cooperate with Washington in any measure they viewed as detrimental to their own interests. When conflicts arose, they simply held their breath and waited for a change in the weather. In this they were uncommonly fortunate. World War II, the Guatemalan affair, the Cuban Revolution—each appeared at a critical juncture in the relationship, and each in turn forced the United States to bend in the Somozas' direction. U.S. motives were by no means dishonorable—Hitler, after all, was certainly a greater menace to humanity than the elder Somoza—but this could not prevent the impact of the larger policy from being felt negatively in Nicaragua.

Somoza's luck finally ran out when events in a tiny Asian country more than ten thousand miles from Nicaragua knocked the moral underpinnings out from under U.S. foreign policy. By 1976 or 1977 a new current was abroad in Washington and in the councils of its foreign policy establishment, one which emphasized "the ethics of clean hands" almost to the exclusion of "the ethics of consequences." Gone was the ice-cold pragmatism from which the Somozas had so often benefited in the past. This did not mean that Washington finally sympathized with the Sandinistas, but rather, that it concluded that the threat of Marxism in Nicaragua was no longer sufficient to counterbalance the brutality, the corruption, and above all, the sheer unpopularity of the Somoza regime. The Carter administration hoped to the very end that the FSLN would be swamped by moderates once the dictator was gone. They were, after all, more numerous and more broadly representative of the political forces in Nicaraguan society. It was a pious hope, and sincerely held, but poorly founded: Nicaragua was in the midst of a revolution, not a presidential primary. In the absence of the concrete application of its power, Washington's purposes remained ethereal, and ultimately irrelevant.

The Limits of Hindsight

No doubt there are other lessons to be learned from the Nicaraguan experience, and other historians will have plenty of time to offer them. But one point must be foreclosed: history does *not* tell us—and *cannot* tell us—precisely *when* the United States should have shifted its policy gears in Nicaragua, apart from never having landed the Marines in the first place. Intervention during the 1920s was resented, and understandably so, by Latin American publicists and American liberals alike, but so was nonintervention—equally—once the Somozas were in place. Washington should have seen that after 1936 the Somoza regime was moving Nicaragua into a qualitatively different kind of political system, one pernicious even by local standards, but the process of consolidation was slow, and by the time it was fully evident, World War II was upon the United States and indeed the entire world.

The State Department did attempt to rein in Somoza in the 1940s, but by that time the dictatorship was fully fleshed out, complete with U.S. journalistic, financial, and political connections. In the 1950s and 1960s other priorities in the region moderated Washington's zeal for political change in Nicaragua—and in one unfortunate ambassadorial case, made things much worse. Arguably, the biggest opportunity squandered by the United States was the assassination of the elder Somoza in 1956. Had Washington intervened at that point, the regime would have been unable to extend itself into the next generation. However, this would have required much more than an arms embargo or even an economic blockade, and there is no assurance that it would have worked. It also presupposes that it would have been possible to discard utterly our commitment to nonintervention, for a cause that—whatever one might think of the Somozas—was certainly not a pressing issue of U.S. security.

Ironically, time has proven that the hobgoblin to which Somoza so frequently pointed was real. Events *have* established that Marxism, if not Communism, was the final consequence of his fall. Perhaps it need not have been that way, and it will be left to earnest American liberals and sobered American conservatives to retrace the path which should have—and more importantly, could have—been taken. This is an exercise, however, in which sympathizers of the new Sandinista dictatorship need take no part; they got the outcome *they* prefer. The floor belongs, rather, to those who carry their past concern for the lack of freedom in Nicaragua firmly and consistently into the present—and, if need be, into the future as well.

23. The U.S. Obsession With Communism

By RICHARD H. ULLMAN

Focus
Professor Ullman recognizes that the Sandinista government has made some grave errors since taking power in 1979, but he believes that the Reagan administration's "obsession" with the threat of a second Communist government in the Caribbean Basin has been far more damaging to U.S.-Nicaraguan relations than the behavior of the Sandinistas. For him, President Reagan and his colleagues "are unlikely, unassisted, to find their way out of the web their paranoia has spun."

The Sandinistas' minister of defense, Humberto Ortega, did once assert "that Sandinismo and Marxism-Leninism are one and the same," but the actual makeup of the government and its methods of dealing with various sectors of Nicaraguan society are far from purely totalitarian, says Ullman. It is the relentlessly hostile Reagan administration and its military and economic threats to the revolutionary government that have driven the Nicaraguans closer to the Cubans and Soviets.

While Ullman's thesis contains some truth, he overlooks an important historical fact about our relations with Nicaragua: the Nicaraguans themselves, even when Jimmy Carter was still in the White House, rejected U.S. peace overtures (see the detailed account of this rejection by President Carter's USAID director in Nicaragua, Lawrence Harrison—selection 29).

Other sources such as former Sandinistas Edén Pastora (selection 26) and Miguel Bolaños (selection 25) show the current Nicaraguan regime to be far less benign than Ullman portrays it to be. Bolaños documents the political, military, and logistical support provided to the guerrillas in El Salvador—support whose existence Ullman denies. For another view of Nicaragua as exporter of revolution and the significance of that activity for U.S. relations with the Sandinistas, see Charles Krauthammer (selection 30).

Notes to this essay begin on page 368.

Richard H. Ullman is a professor of international affairs at Princeton University.

T HE REAGAN ADMINISTRATION IS AT WAR with Nicaragua. Like other wars the United States has fought since 1945 it is an undeclared war. It is also a small war. No U.S. serviceman has yet fired a shot, but American-made bullets from American-made guns are killing Nicaraguans, and the President of the United States has made the demise of the present Nicaraguan government an all-but-explicit aim of his foreign policy.

Indeed, the President and his closest advisors seem obsessed with Nicaragua, and their obsession has infected their government at all levels. There is ample evidence that no issue of foreign policy—not arms control negotiations with the Soviet Union, not the Middle East, not Poland or Afghanistan, not the spiraling economic tensions within the Western Alliance, not the Latin American debt crisis, not even the civil war in El Salvador—so preoccupies senior officials. Like the much larger war against North Vietnam half a generation ago, the war with Nicaragua touches every sphere of foreign relations. Armed with "talking points" prepared in Washington, American diplomats plead for support from friendly governments around the world, putting additional weight on alliances already sorely strained. Adducing implausible economic criteria, American representatives to international financial institutions use their blocking votes for the political purpose of denying Nicaragua access to funds, and in doing so make it easier for other governments to use the same institutions for purposes antithetic to long-term American interests.

In his speeches and press conferences, the President describes the Nicaraguan leaders the way he does the Russians and the Cubans: all are Marxist totalitarians implacably hostile to the United States and prepared to use terror and deceit to maintain their own power and to undermine their neighbors. But a special hostility is reserved for the Sandinista regime in Managua. Its very

Reprinted by permission from the Fall 1983 issue of *Foreign Affairs* (© 1983 by the Council on Foreign Relations).

existence seems to affront. How dare a nation of 2.5 million provoke a superpower 100 times larger, Mr. Reagan implies. His recent pronouncements on Nicaragua recall the question attributed to an English king obsessed with an overly independent archbishop of Canterbury: "Will no one rid me of this meddlesome priest?"

U.S. Saber-Rattling in Honduras

To rid Nicaragua of its meddlesome regime the Administration has chosen an exile army, backed by American military power. For nearly two years the Central Intelligence Agency has paid, supplied, and trained a force of counterrevolutionaries—*contras,* as they are universally called—based in Honduras just across the border from Nicaragua. That force now numbers about 10,000 men. The CIA is said to want to increase it to as many as 15,000. Simultaneously, the Department of Defense is pouring resources into Honduras's army (its air force is already the best in Central America) and into building additional air strips and perhaps also naval facilities to make it easier for the United States to bring in its own forces rapidly. And in early August [1983] U.S. army, marine, and air force units began preparing for an unprecedentedly long six months of training maneuvers with Honduran forces—including, for much of the period, 5,700 U.S. combat troops ashore—while two carrier task groups took up patrolling positions off Nicaragua's Atlantic and Pacific coasts.[1]

Nicaraguans are convinced that the Reagan administration would like nothing more than to provoke a full-scale war between themselves and the Hondurans, one that Nicaragua would appear to have started, as a pretext for taking direct military action. They are mindful that General Gustavo Alvarez Martínez, commander of the armed forces and politically the most powerful figure in Honduras, has said that no government in the region will be safe so long as the Sandinistas rule Nicaragua. "Everything you do to destroy a Marxist regime is moral," he told reporters in late July.

For their part, however, the Sandinistas are determined to avoid a provocation. They are therefore fighting with one hand tied behind their back, the hand that would strike the *contras* in their Honduran bases and training camps. Although widely accepted principles of international law would give them ample license to do so, the Nicaraguans have prudently elected not to make any incursions in force across the border so as not to give General Alvarez the excuse he seems to be seeking for a U.S.-backed holy war. Except for occasional short forays in pursuit, they have therefore elected to wait for their enemies to come over. Before the *contras* reach Nicaraguan territory, however, they disperse into small units much more difficult to locate and destroy. They are nevertheless numerous enough to do fearsome damage to the poorly armed communities that lie near the border.

The Administration has assured Congress that the counter-revolutionary "freedom fighters" strike at military targets. Reality is different. On a tour of rural development projects in August [1983] I saw farm buildings devastated by mortar fire or by the torch. And I heard many accounts of peasant families being kidnapped and taken across the border, often never to return, and of assassinated teachers, health workers, and agricultural technicians. The Nicaraguans claim that since March 1982, when the intensity of incursions substantially increased, the *contras* have killed more than 700 persons. Most of these victims have been unarmed civilians. A few have been civilians in uniform—hapless militiamen posted on isolated guard duty. Very few have been members of the regular armed forces. There is no reason to think that the Sandinistas have exaggerated these losses. They can scarcely gain by heightening the impression that they cannot protect their own supporters.

Spokesmen for the *contras* in Honduras—their political organization is the so-called Nicaraguan Democratic Front, or FDN—say that the purpose of their invasion is to furnish a rallying point for disaffected Nicaraguans who would like to join them in opposing the Sandinistas. Thus far the only group that has responded in any number to their appeal has been the Miskito Indians of Nicaragua's Atlantic coast, whom the Sandinistas alienated by insensitively harsh treatment at the beginning of their rule.[2] Among the majority *mestizo* population [persons of mixed Hispanic and Indian ancestry], particularly among the poor *campesinos* [peasants] who live in the mountainous territory near the border, the effect has been precisely the opposite. They are well aware that the *contra* forces in Honduras are led by, and contain within their ranks, many former members of the feared and hated National Guard, the instrument with which the Somoza family ruled Nicaragua for four decades. They see the *contras* as threatening the benefits that have come to them since the revolution—land, schools, health clinics, and an intangible but crucial sense that for the first time in their lives the state has *their* welfare in mind. In a dozen peasant communities I heard the same thing from scores of people: Nothing had rallied them to the Sandinista cause as much as the *contras* had done.[3]

Behind the *contras,* moreover, they see the United States. A page from a year-old copy of *Barricada,* the Sandinista party newspaper, tacked to the wall of a *campesino* hut in a new farming cooperative less than ten miles from the Honduran border, encapsulated the history of U.S.-Nicaraguan relations as most Nicaraguans see it. *A 126 años el enemigo es el mismo*—"After 126 years the enemy is the same"—the banner headline proclaimed. The accompanying text began with the murderous expedition of the freebooter William Walker in 1856. It ended with Ronald Reagan's embrace of the *contras*.[4]

REALITY AND U.S. MISCONCEPTIONS

For most of that dismal history, few Americans have had any interest in or concern for Nicaragua. But Nicaragua's agricultural and mineral resources (there were once flourishing gold mines) have been of intense concern to a small number of Americans, and it was the protection of those private interests that for so many years motivated official U.S. policy. That is no longer the case. In an era of burgeoning investments abroad, those in Nicaragua are barely of significance now.

Washington's earlier concern for the defense of private economic interests has been replaced by a preoccupation with Nicaragua as a pawn on the East-West chessboard. President Reagan and his advisors seem to regard as irrelevant ancient history the fact that many Nicaraguans feel that the Sandinistas liberated them as much from the interventionist hand of the United States as from a harsh dictatorship that exploited the entire country as its private plantation. They are unmoved by the efforts the new regime has made to put idle land at the disposal of peasants willing to work it, to teach vast numbers of illiterate adults to read, or to transform rural health conditions. And they are openly disbelieving of its assertion that the national elections it has planned for 1985—the first since "the triumph" (as it is called) of 1979—will be truly open and competitive.

The Administration's concern, instead, is with the Sandinistas as carriers of a revolutionary virus that came from the Soviet Union by way of Cuba, and with which they will surely attempt to infect the rest of Central America. They will do so, the President has said, because they are dogmatic Marxist-Leninists committed to monolithic totalitarian rule at home and to the propagation of violent revolution abroad. As such, they could not be believed even if they were to promise not to interfere in their neighbors' internal affairs. The clear implication—Mr. Reagan has stopped just short of saying so explicitly—is that it is fruitless to seek regional peace by means of negotiations, for the Sandinistas will break any agreement they sign.[5]

It is of course possible that the President—and the recently established "Outreach Working Group on Central America" in the White House Office of Communications, whose primary function seems to be to whip up domestic support for the Administration's Nicaragua policy—may be correctly characterizing Nicaraguan political reality. Despite their protests to the contrary, the Sandinistas may indeed be pursuing a planned process whose end result will be a state in which all dissenting views will be ruthlessly stifled and in which power will be every bit as centralized as it is in Cuba. Their insistence that they want a mixed economy, not a collectivized one, and their repeated appeals to the many Nicaraguan entrepreneurs and planters who were not Somocistas to stay and continue producing for the benefit of the nation (and themselves), may be intended simply to lull them into keeping their capital at home until the time is ripe for sudden and universal expropriation. Their efforts to incorporate the views of opposition parties into the three laws now being prepared to govern the 1985 election—one detailing the rights and obligations of parties, a second laying out electoral procedures, and a third establishing rules of access to mass media—may also be window dressing designed to cover a prepackaged Soviet-style landslide.

Disturbing Signs in Nicaragua

Certainly there are disturbing signs. Nicaragua's habitual voting with the Soviet bloc on major issues before the United Nations undermines the Sandinistas' claim to be following a foreign policy of nonalignment. So does the guiding role that Cubans evidently play in Nicaragua's armed forces and in its intelligence and internal security apparatus. While the Sandinistas may rationalize that role by pointing to the external threats that Nicaragua faces, they are likely to find that military and security services once grown fat and pervasive, as they surely will under Havana's tutelage, cannot easily be made to wane or to relax their grip.

It is dismaying, as well, that some leading early supporters of the revolution have felt that they had no alternative but to leave Nicaragua and go into exiled opposition.[6] And while the Sandinistas may be persuaded of the inherent justice of their decision, taken soon after they came to power, not to hold national elections until they had taught an illiterate peasantry to read and thereby to make informed political decisions (and, they also said, to assure that they themselves would not be swept into office by a tide of irrational enthusiasm), a visitor may be excused for being skeptical: by 1985 the peasantry will indeed be literate, but it is likely to be indoctrinated as well.

It may also be intimidated. There are many indications of a bullying zeal, particularly at the grass-roots level, that belie the earnest disquisitions on the crucial importance of pluralism that a visitor hears repeatedly from Sandinista leaders. Particularly jarring to North Americans are the neighborhood "Committees of Sandinista Defense" (CDS) that perform useful (and necessary) police functions but too often combine them with ideological vigilantism. Disconcerting also are the revolutionary slogans stenciled or (as it usually the case) scrawled like graffiti on every wall. They may be the more-or-less spontaneous products of youthful enthusiasm, but their effect cannot help being intimidating. There are, indeed, competing messages—usually staid appeals to support other political parties—but they are much less prevalent, and sometimes (unlike the Sandinista slogans) they are defaced.

Other indicators are less visible but equally unsettling. I heard accounts of a neighborhood medical dispensary sponsored by the Catholic Church and supplied with drugs by the Agency for International Development and other U.S. sources being vandalized by young members of a local CDS resentful of the fact that, owing to the critical shortage of foreign exchange, the regime's own dispensaries are much less adequately supplied. More disturbing, of course, are the prepublication censorship and occasional shutdowns of the press, which in practice affect only *La Prensa,* the most popular of Nicaragua's three daily newspapers and the only one that is an opponent of the regime. (The censorship of *La Prensa* is curiously ambivalent, however. Each day the newspaper is permitted to make photocopies of the material the censors delete and to distribute them to a list of subscribers that includes all foreign embassies. And it also posts a set of the photocopies on a bulletin board in front of its building, there to be read by any passers-by who choose to do so.)

Like other derogations from the rights and liberties promised by the Sandinistas in the Fundamental Statute they promulgated at the time of their victory in 1979, censorship is part of the State of Emergency declared in March 1982, after two important bridges were blown up by the *contras.* The other emergency measures include suspension of the right to liberty and *habeas corpus,* the right to freedom of travel, and the rights of association and peaceful assembly. Even the most critical domestic opponents of the Sandinista regime do not accuse it of being draconian in applying these restrictions, however. And they readily agree that the torture, summary execution, and other abuses of the person that are commonplace in a number of other Central and South American states are virtually unknown.[7]

A Bundle of Contradictions

Nicaragua in mid-1983 strikes a visitor as a bundle of contradictions. There are substantial departures from the civil and political liberties that North Americans take for granted, but the regime's opponents are not afraid to speak their minds. *La Prensa* is hobbled but not muzzled; its editors feel that it it still worth their while to continue publication. There is a functioning independent human rights commission (as well as a regime-sponsored commission) that copiously documents what it considers to be the regime's abuses. Opposition parties continue—warily—to critize the Sandinistas. An important part of the Catholic hierarchy (including the outspokenly confrontational Archbishop Obando y Bravo) openly opposes the Sandinistas; other influential churchmen (and women), including many of the Protestant pastors who work among the Miskitos and the English-speaking black population of the Atlantic coast, strongly support the regime.

Although the Sandinistas hold a majority of seats in the fifty-one-member Council of State that makes Nicaragua's laws, their practice is to legislate by a consensus that includes the representatives of the opposition parties and of the social and economic organizations (trade unions, chambers of commerce, farmers' organizations, and the like) that are not Sandinista. When draft legislation meets with opposition, it is modified until it gains general approval. Even severe critics of the Sandinistas concede that the Council (whose members are each elected by their particular organizations) has thus far functioned as a genuinely deliberative and pluralist legislative body. Finally, it should never be forgotten that Nicaragua under the Sandinistas is no longer a state in which the bulk of the population is terrorized by its own armed forces. In that respect it is nothing like as repressive as some of its neighbors.

If Nicaragua is less repressive than many other Latin American states, it is also far less repressive than the Soviet satellites in Eastern Europe to which the Reagan administration routinely compares it. The comparison with Eastern Europe is also on the minds of the Sandinista leaders themselves. In private conversations they indicate that they are fully aware of the danger that the so-called Patriotic Revolutionary Front, the governing coalition of parties including their own (itself confusingly bearing the label "front"—the Sandinista National Liberation Front, or FSLN), will degenerate into a fig-leaf organization in which the lesser parties play only token roles, like the patently bogus "fronts" that mask Communist power in Eastern Europe.

They are also well aware that, because they reject liberal standards for civil and political liberties, they may find themselves on a slippery slope in which increasing pressure from abroad will impel them to impose increasingly severe restrictions at home and thus alienate many who now support them. They insist that they want to escape this dilemma and to move in the direction of a more open and pluralistic society. At the same time, however, they say that while they welcome "constructive" dissent, their society is still too fragile to withstand the corrosive effects of criticism based on deliberate misinformation.

Pluralism vs. Efficiency

The message is familiar. It has been heard many times, and not only from the leaders of developing societies. Nearly all politicians welcome dissent—until they perceive it as undermining their personal position or otherwise making it more difficult for them to govern. Politicians professing democratic aims are most severely tested, of course, when the goals of pluralism and efficiency directly conflict. Many—particularly those who seek to transform their societies—fail the test and opt for efficiency at the expense of pluralism. They are especially prone to do so when they see themselves facing a severe external threat. Alas, there is no reason for optimism that the present leaders of Nicaragua will move in the direction of a more liberal society. Very few leaders of impoverished Third World countries (even those who lack any far-reaching social vision) have done so.

Yet that does not mean that Nicaragua will inevitably go the way of Cuba. There are, indeed, some Sandinistas who would like to move in that direction. Humberto Ortega, the minister of defense, who spent years in Cuba while exiled under Somoza, said in a speech to the armed forces in August 1981 (a speech to which U.S. officials constantly refer) that Sandinism and Marxism-Leninism are one and the same. But many other Sandinista leaders would disagree. They say that they are Marxists, but Christians as well—indeed, some are Catholic priests—and that while Marxism gives them a means of analyzing social forces, Christianity gives them a set of goals. They reject the coercion inherent in Leninist practice.[8]

Nicaragua today strikes a visitor as being no more easily comparable with Cuba or Czechoslovakia than with Mexico—whose revolution a generation and a half ago (we too often forget) also seemed profoundly frightening to North Americans and which is still today ruled by a single dominant party. And if there are no grounds for optimism that it will evolve in the direction of Western parliamentary democracy, there is no firmer basis for predicting that it will slide very much further down the slope that ends in a cruel and monolithic totalitarianism. Certainly Nicaragua now is not the repressive Communist dictatorship that figures in so many of President Reagan's speeches. North Americans and Western Europeans long resident there find simply bewildering the Administration's characterizations and the blatantly dual standard that it employs when it compares Nicaragua with other states of the region. Roberto Cardenal, one of the senior editors of *La Prensa,* might have had the Reagan administration in mind as well as the U.S. Congress when he told our visiting group: "When your senators and congressmen come down here, they are interested in their own politics, not in ours."

HARMFUL EFFECTS OF U.S. POLICY

The Administration's characterizations of Nicaragua's politics are not only inaccurate. They are also corrosive in their effect. "Marxist Nicaragua"—connoting a Soviet-style regime—is no more apposite today than "Marxist Portugal" was in 1975. Yet the phrase has become reality for most Americans, just as it has become a staple of the editorial writer's lexicon in even those newspapers that strongly oppose the Administration's not-so-covert war.

Similarly, the Administration's critics in Congress seem to feel an obligation to season their speeches opposing an increased U.S. military involvement with blanket denunciations of the Nicaraguan government. They do so, undoubtedly, for self-protection, so as not to appear naïve, or "soft on Communism." Surely, they reason, the importance of their central objective—halting a potentially disastrous military adventure—is justification enough for their uncritical acceptance of a caricature version of the complex and ambiguous Nicaraguan reality.

The tactic is doubly misguided. Leaving aside its intellectual shoddiness, it has two harmful political effects. First, characterizing the Sandinista regime as merely another Communist dictatorship and tool of Soviet policy does in fact make it easier for the

Administration to gain public and congressional acquiescence for escalating the scale of war against it. Second, it makes it more difficult for legislators to object to other policies the Administration has directed against the Managua government.

These are in the economic sphere. The Administration has denied Nicaragua access to credits available from U.S. official sources, and it has made a major and largely successful effort to cut off Nicaragua's access to funds it might otherwise receive from the three relevant international financial institutions—the World Bank, the International Monetary Fund, and the Inter-American Development Bank. The United States has traditionally been the principal market for virtually all of Nicaragua's exports. Last May the Administration reduced by 90 per cent Nicaragua's quota for sugar imports into the United States, severely crippling Managua's ability to earn foreign exchange. And over the past two years Nicaragua has found fewer U.S. customers for some of its other export products, another result of the general climate of hostility that the Reagan administration has engendered.

The combination of restrictions on its ability to borrow abroad and a diminished U.S. market for its exports has made Nicaragua critically short of hard currency. That has made it difficult to obtain spare parts and replacements for machinery made in the United States or in other Western countries. The result is that at all levels of Nicaragua's predominantly agricultural economy—on the many big estates still in private hands, on the very large numbers of smaller private farms, on the rural cooperatives, and on land once belonging to the Somoza family and now made into state farms (20 per cent of total farming land)—there are tractors, harvesters, cropdusting aircraft, and other machines standing idle rather than productively employed. Moreover, a principal tactic of the *contras* has been to destroy agricultural resources. They have leveled farm buildings and warehouses, killed livestock, and burnt many acres of coffee bushes (especially costly, since new ones require five years' growth before bearing fruit). All these factors have substantially diminished both Nicaragua's export earnings and its supplies of foodstuffs for domestic consumption. And the need to ration hard currency has led as well to shortages of medicines and petroleum products.

These shortages have made life in Sandinista Nicaragua more grim than it otherwise might be. They have led to grumbling and to disenchantment with the regime, especially among businessmen and the owners of large farms—undoubtedly the effects that the Reagan administration had hoped they would have.

Disenchanted But Not Disloyal

Yet the Administration would be ill advised to count these results a success. Almost certainly they will not be sufficient to undermine the regime. Unless conditions of life grow very much harder, the Sandinistas will retain the loyalty and the support of the large number of peasant smallholders and salaried rural and urban workers who still judge themselves to be net gainers from the economic, social, and psychological effects of the revolution. Indeed, for the short term, at least, the regime is likely to use these hardships, as it has the depredations of the *contras,* to win greater loyalty from them.

On the other hand, the disaffection of businessmen and wealthy farmers may lead them to abandon the country, thus giving over their property to state control and making both the economy and the political system just that much less pluralistic. In any event, the more militant members of the regime will see in these externally imposed hardships a justification for tightening discipline and increasing central control. And enforced isolation from the Western market economies will lead to greater dependence on the Soviet Union and its allies.

It is probable, therefore, that the policies now being pursued by the Administration will lead to exactly the outcome that will be most harmful to the long-term interests of the United States. The wars on the borders cannot succeed in toppling the Sandinista government without the direct involvement of U.S. armed forces. The *contras* are well trained and well armed, but they are far outnumbered by the Sandinistas, who have at their disposal 25,000 regular troops augmented by 55,000 reservists and militia personnel whose job it is to defend the districts where they live and work. Many of the later have only rudimentary training and inadequate weapons, but they have thus far borne most of the burden of the fighting for the Sandinista government, and they seem to have acquitted themselves reasonably well.

Despite the intense effort the Pentagon is now making to arm and train the Honduran army, it is unlikely that the impressed peasant boys who make up a high proportion of its ranks will sufficiently share General Alvarez's crusading zeal to fight bravely on Nicaraguan soil. The Hondurans would almost certainly not be able to launch an effective attack without substantial and highly visible U.S. assistance. Because their doing so—even in response to Nicaraguan border-crossing retaliatory blows against the *contras*—would be a clear violation of the charters of the Organization of American States and of the United Nations, they and their U.S. patrons would surely be branded as aggressors and ordered to desist. While it is conceivable that the Reagan administration might seek to evade such strictures, it is not likely that the Congress would long allow it. The Sandinistas would therefore survive, wounded but not killed, and more inclined to seek protection from Moscow and Havana.

The Administration's economic measures cannot fail to be similarly ineffective at exerting decisive pressure on Managua. Therefore the only conceivable result of American policies, if they continue on their present course, will be a Nicaragua domestically more militarized, more monolithic, and more repressive than today, and in its foreign policy more stridently anti-American, more dependent on the Soviet Union and on Cuba, and therefore more willing to do their bidding.

THE REAL RUB: EXPORTING REVOLUTION

In much of the discourse about Central America these days—in the off-the-record musings of senior American officials, in the editorials of newspapers that approve the Administration's policies, and in the speeches of congressmen and senators—the point is made that the United States has a right, even a duty, to control events "in its own backyard." That is how most of the world expects a superpower to behave, we are told, and it is how one should behave. A principal contention of the foreign policy section of the Republican Party's 1980 platform was that the Carter administration had critically weakened the United States by not acting like a superpower; among other derelictions it had allowed the "Marxist Sandinista takeover" of Nicaragua.

Those who advance arguments like these often go on to make an equation between Central America and Eastern Europe. Just as the Soviet Union should not be expected to tolerate a potentially hostile (because ideologically divergent) regime in any of the countries on its periphery, they assert, the United States should not be expected to do so in Central America. In each instance, the security of a superpower is at stake.

The implication of this equation is profoundly disturbing. It means that after nearly four decades of political combat, Americans are content to see their country equated with its principal adversary along two crucially important dimensions—the degree to which its security may be threatened by the very existence of ideologically divergent neighbors, and the amount of license it should have to bring pressure to bear upon them. If Americans indicate that they expect their government to behave the way the Soviet government behaves, and for the same reasons, why should foreigners expect more of it? There are many young and not-so-young persons in Western Europe and the Third World who profess not to be able meaningfully to distinguish between the United States and the Soviet Union. Both seek hegemony. Neither will tolerate political diversity within its sphere of influence. Neither deserves aid or comfort or political support.

Threat and No Threat

Yet the equation is not valid. The pressure that Moscow has applied against Poland, like its invasions of Czechoslovakia and Hungary earlier, has been universally condemned. Moscow reacted so harshly because political change within its sphere *does* threaten the Soviet Union—because the Soviet regime, like those of Eastern Europe, lacks ultimate political legitimacy among those it presumes to govern. If workers in Warsaw or Prague succeeded in changing their governmental structures, workers in Leningrad or Kiev or Tashkent would be likely to try to follow their example. Only by assuring that fundamental questions are never asked on its periphery can the Soviet regime assure its survival within its own homeland.

The threat to Soviet power is thus profound and primarily political. A Poland or Czechoslovakia whose population had enjoyed genuine self-determination would threaten Moscow whether or not it were armed. It is difficult to imagine a greater indictment of the Soviet regime two-thirds of a century after Lenin's seizure of power.

By contrast, political change in Central America poses no political threat to the United States, because the legitimacy of its governing structure is not in doubt. Revolutionaries who throw off a repressive regime in Nicaragua or Guatemala do not call North American institutions into question.

Nor do they pose a truly serious military threat. Even in the worst (and least probable) case—the establishment of Soviet bases on its territory—Nicaragua could not seriously harm the United States. The Soviets would be operating with long and vulnerable lines of supply. If they were ever to set up a base in Central America or the Caribbean for military actions against the United States, it allies (including other Latin American nations), or the strategic shipping lanes, the United States could deploy overwhelming power against it. Compared to the resources Moscow would have to devote to maintaining a base in the region, the cost to the United States of neutralizing it would be slight. Moreover, in an era of intercontinental missiles, firing nuclear weapons from nearby bases conveys no real benefit. And there are no plausible ways in which the Soviets could profit by attacking North America with conventional weapons.

The issue of Soviet (or even Cuban) bases is a straw man, however. Despite the U.S. administration's rhetoric, no one within it expects that bases will be established. A more probable development might be a Nicaraguan or other revolutionary Central American state without foreign bases but armed to the teeth with Soviet-supplied military equipment.[9] Such a state would not threaten the United States. Nor could it realistically threaten its neighbors. Under the Rio Treaty of 1947 the United States is committed to come to the aid of other American states under military attack. Does anyone doubt that it would do so if the aggressor were Nicaragua? U.S. officials complain about the quantity of Soviet-bloc arms Nicaragua is receiving—and then admit privately that in the absence of a full-scale invasion from Honduras there is not the slightest chance that the Sandinistas will risk their own downfall by using their new weapons to strike across the border.

They sometimes go on to argue, however, that even if the probability of an overt Nicaraguan attack on other Central American states is negligible, the very existence in their midst of a heavily armed, Soviet-supported Nicaragua would be profoundly unsettling and ultimately destabilizing. There may be substance to this fear. But their supposition points more to the underlying lack of legitimacy, and therefore the fragility, of the governments of Honduras, Guatemala, and El Salvador (Costa Rica, Panama, and Belize have no such problems) than it does to any logical chain of causation. Popular governments with the assurance of ample military support from the United States in the event they are the victims of aggression scarcely need fear Nicaragua.[10]

Arms to El Salvador

The real issue, of course, is not the political or military threat that Nicaragua poses to the United States, or even its potential military threat to its neighbors, but the political threat represented by its revolutionary ideology and its willingness to support insurgent movements elsewhere in Central America, most notably in El Salvador. I have called this a political rather than a military threat because no one has yet provided evidence that the flow of arms from Nicaragua has been of sufficient magnitude significantly to affect the course of the Salvadoran civil war. For their part, of course, the Sandinistas do not publicly acknowledge that they have supplied arms. If Washington had firm evidence of any shipments, they state, surely it would release it. Apparently good evidence does not exist. Knowledgeable U.S. officials admit that despite intensive intelligence collection efforts and reliable information that substantial quantities of Soviet-supplied light infantry weapons have reached Nicaragua, very few arms shipments to El Salvador have actually been observed, and that months go by when none at all are detected. They also concede that the Salvadoran guerrillas have had such easy access to arms from a range of other sources that at no time since 1981, and probably not before, have they been critically dependent on supplies that might have reached them from Nicaragua.

Administration officials insist, however, that the Sandinistas have nevertheless played an important role in the Salvadoran insurgency. Managua has been a safe haven where the civilian politicians and the military leaders of the insurgency can meet to plan and coordinate their strategies, from which they can send instructions to their fighting forces in the field, and where they can receive advice from Nicaraguan—and, no doubt, Cuban and Soviet—comrades. The Sandinistas acknowledge this role. They enjoyed a similar haven and similar facilities in Costa Rica during their revolution against Somoza. They say that by assisting the Salvadorans now they are repaying a debt. And they are well aware that they themselves provide models for the Salvadorans and for revolutionaries in other Central American countries—living proof that movements such as theirs can triumph over a government that, at least until its last months, enjoyed substantial support from the United States.

It is likely that this role and the way the Sandinistas insist upon playing it, more than any other factor, has made Nicaragua the object of the Reagan administration's outrage. But a visitor to Managua and to Washington during the late summer of 1983 must come away baffled by the Administration's obsession with Nicaragua. As supporters of the side that Washington opposes in the Salvadoran struggle, the Sandinistas are undoubtedly an annoyance and an impediment. But their contribution has scarcely been decisive. To behave as if it were, to assert that under their leadership Nicaragua poses a dire threat to the stability of the hemisphere and to the security of the United States, and on that basis to launch an unacknowledged but deadly war against them, evinces a frame of mind that future historians are likely to discuss more in terms of pathology than in those of logic.

It may be that the Administration is acting primarily from frustration born of the dreary war in El Salvador. "Our side" there has been guilty of atrocities that neutral observers feel far exceed in horror and in scale those of their opponents. Moreover, their forces have thus far exhibited considerably less zeal and fighting ability. How natural it is in conditions of moral, political, and military ambiguity to attribute one's failures to the malevolence of outsiders. And how much easier it must be to ratchet up the military and economic pressure on Nicaragua than to make real progress in the messy war on the other side of the Gulf of Fonseca.

WHAT A 'CONTRA' VICTORY WOULD MEAN

Public statements about the crisis in Central America by President Reagan and his principal advisors contain no hint that they have any clear notion of what sort of outcomes the United States can realistically hope to bring about, and what outcomes might prove truly harmful.

In considering this range of outcomes, they might usefully reflect on what it would mean if they were to win their war against the Sandinistas and the *contras* were to come to power. The *contras* would have done so only with considerable help from the Honduran armed forces, and almost certainly from our own as well. Few Nicaraguans would regard as liberators a mercenary army made up of many members of the same *Guardia Nacional* that had terrorized their country for Somoza. The rest of the world would surely consider them American puppets, and it would hold the United States accountable for their actions both at their moment of victory and afterward. Many Sandinistas would retain their arms and melt into the mountains to continue the war.

Meanwhile, the United States would have to prevent the Guard from committing excesses, no easy task. It would also have to hold the ring while some semblance of democratic politics was reestablished. Who could participate? What of the Sandinistas? What of the parties to their left? Would Somocistas flooding back from Miami be permitted to reclaim their estates from the thousands of peasants now farming them? Since they funded the *contras* until the CIA stepped in, would they not demand—and receive—a return on their investment? The United States would face a political dilemma like the one the Soviet Union faces in Afghanistan. Unlike in Afghanistan, however, there would be international journalists in every urban *barrio* [neighborhood] and rural community. (After all, we would not have overthrown the Sandinistas to have a closed society.) They would remind the Administration of its fine words about democracy. Could the United States acquit itself honorably? The odds are against it.

If the Administration has given no consideration to scenarios such as this, it is essential that it should do so, and that it should discuss them frankly with the Congress and with the American people. If it does, it is likely to conclude that the United States could well face far more difficult problems in Nicaragua than coexisting with the Sandinista regime.

It may be asking too much to expect such dispassionate reflection from Mr. Reagan and his colleagues, however. They are too committed. They are unlikely, unassisted, to find their way out of the web their paranoia has spun. If the United States is to be diverted from its present collision course with Nicaragua, the impetus for a change in direction must come from other sources— from the Congress, from the National Bipartisan Commission on Central America recently convened under the leadership of Henry Kissinger, and perhaps also from friendly governments, especially from U.S. allies in Europe and elsewhere in Latin America. [Excerpts from the Kissinger Commission report begin on page 33.]

Potentially the most important, of course, is the Congress, for only it has the power to do more than warn and cajole. It can if it wishes deny the Administration the resources it needs for the covert operations that constitute the core of its war against Nicaragua. There are many members of both houses of Congress—a majority among Democrats and a considerable minority among Republicans—who are known to feel that the Administration's policies are profoundly misguided.... In an atmosphere poisoned by allegations that those who oppose the President's policies are witting or unwitting appeasers, legislators fear being tarred with the brush of having "lost" Central America to Communism by tying the Administration's hands. Their inclination, therefore, is to have it both ways, by going on record with an expression of doubt but leaving the ultimate responsibility to the President. ...

THE NEED FOR NEGOTIATIONS

It is in the search for [constructive policy] alternatives that the Kissinger Commission can play a role. . . . Initially, its most important task will be to form its own perspective on the nature of

American interests—and threats to those interests—in the region. To do so it should seek the facts for itself, not receive them solely through the filters of the Administration: there is every reason to believe that reporting from Central America by both the Department of State and the Central Intelligence Agency has been biased by the all too familiar predilection of junior officers to send up the line what they know their seniors want to hear.

One thing their seniors have evidently not wanted to hear about is the existence of possibilities for diplomatic solutions. Indeed, one of the most striking characteristics of the Administration's policies toward Central America—and the Nicaraguan policy that has now become its core—is how small a role diplomacy seems to have played. The likelihood is that the White House does not want a diplomatic settlement with Managua. How could it justify concluding an agreement with a government that it has said cannot be trusted to keep one?

Mr. Kissinger has said that his commission will not get involved in negotiations; presumably it sees its tasks as primarily directed to the long-term political relationship between the United States and Central America and above all to what the United States might do with others to improve social and economic conditions there. Such a view may well be appropriate. But as a gifted negotiator Mr. Kissinger should not hesitate to point out where negotiations might lead.

Since 1981 the United States has approached the Sandinistas entirely with sticks, not with carrots. On several occasions the Nicaraguans have reportedly offered assurances that they would send no arms to El Salvador. But each time the Administration evidently decided not to take the steps—never very large ones—that the Nicaraguans had asked in return. On one such occasion, in March 1981, Managua requested a resumption of U.S. economic assistance and as a token of its good faith unilaterally suspended shipments to the Salvadoran insurgents. Inexplicably, the State Department acknowledged that the arms transfers had indeed stopped—and then went on to announce that the Administration had nevertheless decided to maintain, pending a later review if the "favorable trends" continued, its ban on economic aid. The ban remained and the shipments resumed.

This is not the place for reviewing the subsequent negotiating record with Nicaragua or for discussing the possibilities of a negotiated resolution of the essentially civil conflict in El Salvador.[11] Yet it may well be that progress can be made only if the two sets of negotiations are linked. It is obviously the case that a settlement in El Salvador would simplify the task of reaching a U.S.-Nicaraguan understanding, for Nicaragua's role in the Salvadoran conflict is the ostensible cause of the Reagan administration's hostility. But a negotiation between Washington and Managua could conceivable produce a reciprocal agreement, an explicit Nicaraguan undertaking to end all material support for the guerrillas in El Salvador in return for an explicit U.S. commitment not to assist armed groups opposing the Sandinista regime. Surely such an agreement could be adequately verified by a regional peacekeeping mechanism. It might in turn lead to a situation where neither side in El Salvador sought a military solution, and thus to an eventual compromise political settlement.

Really to heal the rifts of the region, however, there must ultimately be a multilateral negotiation, involving all the states of Central America. Such a negotiation is in fact already under way under the auspices of the so-called Contadora powers—Mexico, Venezuela, Colombia, and Panama. Their task is to work out ground rules for coexistence.

Those rules must be based upon two premises. One is that the export of armed revolution—or counterrevolution—is impermissible. The second is that it is realistically impossible to erect a barrier to the transmission of revolutionary ideas. With all its flaws, Sandinista Nicaragua is likely to remain a magnet and a model for men and women elsewhere in Central America who would transform repressive oligarchical societies. Those who fear the force of that model should be constrained to look to the inequities in their own societies, rather than—as would Honduras's General Alvarez—seek temporary safety in a holy war.

NOTES

1. The President himself has been singularly disingenuous in describing these maneuvers. In his press conference of July 26, he described them as simply like past maneuvers in the area—in effect routine—and expressed surprise that their announcement had aroused such worldwide attention (*New York Times,* July 27, 1983). But the largest previous land exercise in Honduras involved 900 U.S. troops and lasted only six days. One other maneuver to which Mr. Reagan made reference, in Panama for the defense of the Canal, was also of brief duration and involved 3,000 U.S. troops as part of a combined inter-American force. And there is no precedent for the scale or proximity, let alone the intent, of the naval deployments.

2. The Sandinistas now freely admit that their treatment of the Miskitos has been characterized by disastrous errors. On August 3, 1983, at a press conference announcing the release from detention of forty-six Miskitos and promising the early release of those still detained, Interior Minister Tomás Borge reviewed the record with a frankness that the Sandinistas' opponents would have found difficult to improve upon.

3. The *contras* operating from Honduras should be distinguished from the much smaller force of roughly 1,000 men now fighting the Sandinistas from positions along the border with Costa Rica in the south. This force is under the leadership of Edén Pastora Gómez—the famed "Commander Zero" of the revolution, who broke with his colleagues over what he considered to be their betrayal of the goals for which they had fought in common. Until recently, when he reportedly made an agreement for collaboration with the FDN, Pastora has eschewed association with former Somocistas, including members of the *Guardia* [National Guard]. But his force is so small, and the terrain to which it has access is so remote and sparsely populated, that it can be at most a nuisance, not a serious threat. Moreover, in contrast to the FDN *contras,* Pastora's force has received little, if any, U.S. support.

4. Other events that Nicaraguans invariably recall are the U.S.-backed overthrow of at least one president (José Santos Zelaya, in 1909), the frequent intervention of the Marines, including their almost continuous occupation of the country from 1912 to 1933, and the creation of the National Guard, making possible the Marines' withdrawal. Works to consult include, for the early period, Wilfred Hardy Calcott, *The Caribbean Policy of the United States, 1890–1920* (Baltimore: John Hopkins, 1942); and, for the later period, Richard Millett, *Guardians of the Dynasty: A History of the U.S.-Created Guardia Nacional de Nicaragua and the Somoza Family* (Maryknoll, N.Y.: Orbis Books, 1977).

5. The Administration has insisted that any commitment the Nicaraguan government might make not to supply arms to the insurgents fighting in El Salvador must be accompanied by air-tight verification provisions because in their absence the Sandinistas would surely cheat. Yet U.S. officials also say that they think it impossible that satisfactory verification mechanisms can be devised.

6. See the eloquent statement by one such figure, Arturo J. Cruz, "Nicaragua's Imperiled Revolution," *Foreign Affairs,* Summer 1983, 1031-47.

7. For a balanced and thorough account of the state of human rights in Nicaragua, compiled from a wide variety of sources including the U.S. Department of State and the Permanent Commission on Human Rights (a Nicaraguan organization avowedly in opposition to the regime), see *Nicaragua: Comments on the Nicaraguan Government's Report to the U.N. Human Rights Committee*, issued by The Lawyers Committee for International Human Rights, New York, March 1983.

8. One of the most bewildering aspects of revolutionary Nicaragua is its complex structure of government. The FSLN is not a party in the conventional (either Western or Soviet) sense. It is a loose collection of individuals and of associated popular organizations, with no prescribed set of ideological tenets. The nine *comandantes* who form the FSLN directorate are all professed Marxists, but many members of the Nicaraguan cabinet are not, and some are not members of the FSLN. The cabinets serves under the three-member "Junta of Government" (including two Sandinistas) which is the nearest thing Nicaragua has to a head of state. Laws are made by the Council of State. They are subject to veto, however, by the junta. On more than one occasion, when the two organs have been deadlocked, the junta has given way.

9. Nicaragua, it should be noted, is nowhere near this position. Its air force is still substantially weaker than that of Honduras. It would remain so even if it were to receive the ten Soviet MiG fighters that are allegedly waiting to be flown in from Cuba. And while its army may have received substantial quantities of tanks and other heavy military equipment from Moscow and its allies (the U.S. government alleges this to be the case, but has not specified the quantities), it still suffers from serious deficiencies. One notable deficiency is in the arming of the reservists and militiamen upon whom it relies for the bulk of the fighting on the Honduran border. Many of those I saw were armed only with antique World War II rifles that give them nothing like the firepower of the M-16-armed *contras*.

10. It is worth noting, incidentally, that all three of these countries that cause the Administration so much evident concern are considerably more populous than the Nicaragua whose military prowess will supposedly destabilize them. Their populations figure in the Administration's threat scenarios in yet another way, however. They will be the source of refugees—millions, the President has suggested—who will flood into the United States and sorely strain its social fabric. This projection seems more an effort to play upon racist fears than to depict reality. The refugees who fit the Administration's scenarios—those who flee revolutionary regimes—are likely to be relatively few and from the educated middle and upper classes; like their predecessors of the Cuban exodus of 1959, they would fit easily and productively into U.S. society. On the other hand, the military confrontation that the Administration seems intent on fostering would produce precisely the kind (although probably not the quantity) of refugees it presumes to fear: peasants fleeing repressive authoritarian regimes and a widening war.

11. For a review of the U.S.-Nicaraguan negotiating record since 1981, see Jay Peterzell, *Reagan's Secret Wars* (Washington: Center for National Security Studies, 1983), pp. 28–30. For a suggestive discussion of the possibilities for a negotiated solution to the Salvadoran conflict, see Piero Gleijeses, "The Case for Power Sharing in El Salvador," *Foreign Affairs*, Summer 1983, pp. 1048–63. [The Gleijeses article appears in this volume on pages 281-99.]

24. Washington's Lies and Half-Truths

By Tomás Borge Martínez

Focus This Sandinista leader sees the United States engaged in a two-fold aggression against Nicaragua: an obvious military aggression and "an aggression of constant lies, half-truths, accusations based on false premises, and interpretations motivated by bad faith." An example of the latter, he says, is the charge that the Nicaraguan revolution has betrayed its original principles and is heading toward totalitarianism.

Borge argues that it will take five years to "reorganize a country destroyed by war" but that in the meantime political pluralism exists. There is a strong private sector and a mixed economy. Illiteracy has been drastically reduced and health care improved. Religion flourishes.

The United States has justified its aggression against a poor and weak country, says Borge, under the cloak of an East-West confrontation. The Soviet Union did not help the revolutionaries take power, and the current junta is not dominated by Moscow or Havana.

Nor are the Sandinistas fueling revolution elsewhere in the region, according to Borge. These movements are indigenous and spontaneous in response to poverty, ignorance, and repression. "We want peace. We need peace in order to work, to study; in order to sing, to laugh; in order simply to live."

This official view of the Nicaraguan revolution should be carefully examined in the light of the further testimony provided by a defector from the regime, Miguel Bolaños (selection 25), and by a former comrade-in-arms of Borge who is now the leader of a group of anti-Sandinista *contras*, Edén Pastora (selection 26). Mark Falcoff (selection 22) provides a much different perspective on the role of the United States in Nicaraguan history.

Tomás Borge Martínez is a leader of the Sandinista National Liberation Front (FSLN) and a member of the Directorate of the Nicaraguan Revolutionary Government.

A GREAT NATION GAINS in honor and prestige by respecting the sovereignty of small, weak nations, rather than by oppressing those who fight to secure their rights." These are the words of General A. C. Sandino, who led the fight against U.S. Marine intervention in Nicaragua 1927-33 and served as inspiration for the Sandinista National Liberation Front.

It is recognized internationally that Nicaragua is the victim of an unjustified military aggression. This aggression is in violation of international laws and the very laws of the United States. As many facts concerning this aggression are well known by now, there is no need to enter into details about it.

There is another, less apparent form of aggression, an aggression of constant lies, half-truths, accusations based on false premises, and interpretations motivated by bad faith.

It is obvious that this latter form of aggression was planned months ago in order to justify to an uninformed public a later military aggression. This is an affront to the intelligence and good will of the people of the United States.

What is said of Nicaragua? That the revolution has altered its original program and that the present government has liquidated democratic liberties to establish a totalitarian regime.

Several political parties covering a broad span of the political spectrum are active in Nicaragua today. We distinguish clearly between legitimate opposition and counterrevolutionary opposition: the latter is based on anti-national premises that seek a return to dictatorship and the forfeiting of our people's needs to the interests of other nations.

We asked our people to give us five years to reorganize a country destroyed by war. Part of this reorganization is setting the institutional bases for elections to be held in 1985. Have the American people, after 200 years, forgotten that the United States required thirteen years of reorganization before the first national elections were held in 1789?

Today the process is moving forward. Our council of state is studying the political systems of other countries, including the United States, in order to see what aspects are pertinent to our reality, and to develop our own democracy.

A law of political parties, which guarantees political parties access to power through the electoral process, has been approved by our legislature.

Economic and Social Progress

Political pluralism is growing side by side with a strong mixed economy. In 1982, the private sector received 60.5 per cent of the credits approved by the banks. That sector also obtained 68.8 per cent of the authorized foreign exchange. More than 70 per cent of the land and 60 per cent of industrial activities are private. The agrarian reform is not based on whether the land is privately held or not; rather, it is founded on the productive use of the land.

Don't these facts disprove the statements made by the government of the United States concerning Nicaragua's political and economic reality?

In Nicaragua today there is a greater percentage of private enterprise than is the case in countries such as Venezuela, Mexico, and Brazil, to state a few examples.

In just four months in 1980 we reduced illiteracy from 51 per cent to 12 per cent, and we have developed programs to prevent relapse into illiteracy. The entire child population is incorporated into the school system. (Some of these schools have been attacked by the CIA-financed counterrevolutionary forces.) The number of children attending primary school has doubled, and there is an increase of 53 per cent at the secondary level. There has been a 92 per cent increase in university registration.

The achievements in health care during the last four years have been greater than the accomplishments during the previous 150 years. We have eliminated diseases such as poliomyelitis, reduced tuberculosis, virtually eradicated malaria, reduced infant mortality by about 50 per cent, and increased the number of vaccinations by

190 per cent. The entire population is incorporated into the program of preventive medicine. Nicaragua is recognized by international organizations to be at the forefront in public health care. Both education and health care are available to our people free of charge.

Is this not respect for human, economic, and social rights? Is the Reagan administration fighting against this? What other country in Latin America has accomplished so much in such a short period of time, in spite of sabotage and the opposition of the most powerful country of the planet?

Full Religious Freedom

We have been accused of religious persecution. Many religious organizations have stated the contrary.

Since 1979 full freedom of religious expression exists in Nicaragua for the first time in our history. There are 240 priests in the country, most of whom support the revolution. Sixty per cent are foreigners. They offer more than 300 masses daily in more than 350 churches located in 155 parishes. Catholic orders, including the Dominicans, Calazans, Jesuits, and Maryknolls, as well as dozens of Protestant churches, including the Moravians, are all represented in Nicaragua. The Protestant and evangelical churches have quadrupled their membership since 1979. Several Catholic priests serve as ministers of state, and a Jesuit priest, Father Fernando Cardenal, is one of the leaders of the Sandinista Youth Organization.

Is this reality consistent with the accusations leveled against us by the government of the United States? And if there are doubts as to whether we have freedom of religion, why don't they come to Nicaragua and see firsthand, as have so many honest and open-minded U.S. citizens who have changed their opinion after visiting our country?

Recently we have been accused of anti-Semitism. In Nicaragua no one is persecuted because of his religion, race, or political beliefs. Those who participated directly or indirectly in the genocide carried out against the people of Nicaragua by the Somoza dictatorship were punished. Two individuals of Jewish origin had their properties confiscated because of their involvement in the above-mentioned crimes. We are sending documentation to Rabbi Morton Rosenthal, who initiated these charges against us. Moreover, we have invited him to come to Nicaragua so he can see for himself how mistaken he has been.

If, in the process of reviewing the case of the alleged confiscation of a synagogue, the government finds sufficient grounds to consider that the building—though registered in the name of an individual very much linked to the Somoza regime—is in fact patrimony of the Jewish community, the government will facilitate its return.

No East-West Implications

To pose the issue of the Central American crisis as part of the East-West confrontation could be considered ridiculous if it did not have such dramatic consequences.

When we were fighting against Somoza, the Soviet Union gave neither arms nor advice to us Nicaraguans.

Following the revolutionary victory, Nicaragua has established diplomatic and commercial relations with the Soviet Union and other socialist countries, within the normal parameters that are the rights of all modern states that are fighting to keep from dying.

Our people are fighting to keep from dying of hunger. Our struggle is against hunger and backwardness. Hunger and backwardness create a conflict between the selfishness of bloody dictatorships and the people. What does the East-West conflict have to do with gastroenteritis, illiteracy, and the genocide of repressive military rulers?

I think that this argument is a brutal sophism to deceive the people of the United States, to justify the aggression of a powerful, rich country against a small, impoverished, weak country. This argument is a deliberate lie whose only force lies in its constant repetition.

Central America has been victimized by dictatorships, each of which might have provided chapter and verse for the apocalypse. It has been calculated that the National Guard, Somoza's army, in the course of nearly half a century, assassinated more than 300,000 Nicaraguans. Since 1954, more than 10,000 persons have been assassinated in Guatemala, and the Salvadorans since 1979 have offered more than 50,000 victims to the holocaust.

They accuse us of being dominated by the Cubans and the Soviets. All Nicaraguans remember that, in the evil hour of Somocismo, the maximum authority in our country was the ambassador of the United States. We overthrew Somoza, fundamentally, in order to be the masters of our own decisions. This is a Sandinista principle of elementary national pride.

I can affirm, with full knowledge of the facts, that neither the Cuban ambassador nor Fidel Castro, with whom we have frequently conversed, nor the Soviet leader, Yuri Andropov, with whom we have also spoken, has ever told us what we must do. To think the contrary would be to accept that we have no criteria of our own, that we are simply puppets. If we were nincompoops, if we were so dishonorable as to sell out to somebody, there can be no doubt whatever that it would be much easier and much more comfortable to sell ourselves to the government of the United States. We Sandinistas never have been, are not, and never will be anybody's satellites. The Manichean concept that a country which has stopped being a satellite of one country has to become a satellite of another country is simply inconceivable to us.

Our concept of nonalignment is not inconsistent with our right to establish relations with other countries based on the principle of mutual respect. What is more, it is our hope that the United States will become one of those countries. We are not to be blamed that there exist those who maliciously confuse the diversification of our relations with alignment.

No Threat to Any Other Country

Another accusation that has been launched against Nicaragua is that we are fomenting an arms race in Central America. Let us see what the real facts are:

Nicaragua was first threatened and then invaded. We have the right and the obligation to defend ourselves, as we also have the obligation not to attack other countries. We do not propose to invade Honduras, and neither do we propose—however unnecessary it be to mention this—to invade the United States. Nicaragua has clearly demonstrated over the past four years that it is not a threat to the national security of any country. It is not we who have constructed naval bases in the Gulf of Fonseca, military training bases outside our borders, military air bases from which C130s daily unload munitions. We do not violate the airspace of any country with espionage overflights, nor do we send against the coasts of any country powerful naval task forces, complete with aircraft carriers and missile cruisers.

Faced with the escalation of armaments in Central America, clearly directed against us, we have the elemental right of self-defense. In this regard, we are certain that we will receive aid from all around the world, including the American people.

The problem of Central America is not the supposed expansionism of Cuba or the Soviet Union in the region. It is not the aggressiveness of Nicaragua with respect to its neighbors. The problem is the philosophy of the big stick: the inconceivable concept that the United States believes it has the right to decide who should govern our countries, and to become irritable if other peoples determine styles and forms that fail to please whatever U.S. president happens to be in office.

Negotiations: Blocked by U.S.

We have made numerous proposals for dialogue, for negotiations. The response of the United States has always been either silence or an escalation of threats and aggression. It has responded similarily to proposals launched by such countries as Mexico and France. We always insist that our problems are with Honduras, whose territory is being used as a base of U.S. military operations and attacks against Nicaragua.

Because of that, negotiations must be of a bilateral nature with those two countries. The U.S. response, and consequently that of Honduras as well, is that the so-called regional problem that Nicaragua supposedly represents must be negotiated multilaterally.

Very well. In order to avoid pretexts, on July 19 [1983] we announced that we are disposed to negotiate multilaterally. We proposed a nonaggression pact with Honduras. We proposed the absolute end to all supplies of weapons by any country to the forces in conflict in El Salvador, so that the Salvadoran people may resolve their problems without foreign interference. We proposed an end to the militarization of the area and to the use of any territories to launch aggressions against any other country. We also proposed the noninstallation of military bases and respect for the self-determination of each country. Who can doubt that all of these are measures conducive to peace?

This has been recognized by personalities such as Bernardo Sepulveda, foreign minister of Mexico, who stated publicly that the six-point proposal presented by the government of Nicaragua "is a step forward in the process toward peace in the region."

And what has been the response? In the first instance, the dispatch of powerful naval fleets to "carry out maneuvers" along our Pacific and Atlantic coasts. At the same time, statements that the principal obstacle to peace was "the leftist government of Nicaragua."

But the international reaction remains on the side of reason and common sense. The presidents of Panama, Venezuela, Colombia, and Costa Rica have stated their opposition, as has the president of Mexico, who warned that a generalized war in Central America "would result in victory for neither side" and called on the international community to take steps "to stop the outbreak of an irrational war before it destroys the legitimate yearning for peace and development."

The foreign ministers of France and Japan have also made similar statements. The Social Democratic Party of Germany and the Labor Party of Great Britain have demanded that their respective governments expressly condemn the policy of the United States toward Central America.

It seems that the unanimous statements in favor of peace and against war have somewhat moderated the U.S. government's language a bit. In its most recent declarations it says that the United States "is not preparing a war" against Nicaragua, and it hopes peace can be achieved "without bloodshed."

But the facts contradict these affirmations. The aircraft carriers are there. U.S. troops are carrying out "prolonged maneuvers" in Honduras. The CIA continues financing the counterrevolution. The Green Berets continue training the Honduran army. And we continue contributing the dead.

We want peace. We need peace in order to work, to study; in order to sing, to laugh; in order to simply live.

We want peace. *Why don't they leave us in peace?*

What wrong have we done to the people of the United States? We have offered the hand of friendship. Why does their government respond with a clenched fist?

We want peace, but we are disposed to defend ourselves. Neither our petition for peace nor our determination to defend ourselves is rhetorical.

Our people, like Sandino, prefer "to die as rebels rather than to live as slaves."

George Washington, that apostle of truth, would have applauded this determination of our national hero and this heroic determination of the Nicaraguan people.

Perhaps the gravest error is to believe that the force of arms is superior to the force of truth, or to the force of peoples who have conquered their liberty.

25. *Nicaragua: A View From Within*

By MIGUEL BOLAÑOS HUNTER

Focus Several top officials have defected from the Sandinista regime, among them two Nicaraguan ambassadors to the United States, army commander Edén Pastora (see selection 26), and counterintelligence officer Miguel Bolaños. Bolaños here tells his story of a revolution betrayed.

The Sandinistas defeated Anastasio Somoza Debayle through the combined efforts of many sectors of Nicaraguan society. Since the revolution, these collaborators—the church, business and financial leaders, the press, and other political parties—have found themselves subject to repression comparable to what they suffered under the hated Somoza. Bolaños says that virtually every major sector of society is monitored by a special department in the government security apparatus.

In the churches, "divine mobs" are organized to pose as parishioners and stir up trouble for anti-Sandinista pastors. The Sandinistas orchestrated the heckling of John Paul II during his visit to Managua in March 1983 and made sure laymen less sympathetic to the revolutionary cause could not get close to him. Businessmen have been harassed, foreign diplomats set up to appear as spies. The press has been roughly censored, provoking some to claim there was more freedom of opinion under Somoza. Various Indian groups have been resettled in the hope that they will become more obedient to the wishes of the regime.

Much of this security activity, says Bolaños, has been conducted or ordered by the large numbers of Cuban, Soviet, and Eastern-bloc "advisors" now present in Nicaragua. These advisors have been overseeing aid to the rebels in El Salvador as well. During 1980-81, the Sandinistas delivered some 6,000-7,000 machine guns and rifles to El Salvador, says Bolaños. The Salvadoran guerrillas no longer need more arms, only ammunition. They have five times as many weapons as the Sandinistas had when they overthrew Somoza. Many of the leaders of the Salvadoran rebels live in and work out of Managua.

Bolaños believes that "if the United States refuses to aid the anti-Sandinista forces, who are growing stronger in internal support, it will be morally responsible for selling the Nicaraguan people into slavery. And in a few years, the United States will have to respond to Communist gains throughout the rest of the hemisphere."

Miguel Bolaños Hunter was a counterintelligence officer in the Nicaraguan Revolutionary Government until he defected and fled to Costa Rica in 1983.

BEFORE COMING TO POWER, the Sandinistas signed accords with the free enterprise sector, the Catholic Church, and the existing political parties, in order to unite the entire country against Somoza. Once that was accomplished, however, all these sectors were betrayed. Private enterprise has been virtually destroyed by state controls and nationalizations. Although freedom of expression was promised, it lasted no longer than three months after the triumph of the revolution. The church is now being attacked and maligned, as a result of disturbances provoked by the Sandinista front to discredit and neutralize its political power. Today, the church recognized by the Sandinistas as legitimate representative of the Catholic followers is the "Church of the Poor," previously known as the "People's Church." The new church is not recognized by Rome, and Archbishop Obando y Bravo of Managua has officially discredited its activities.

When the Sandinistas assumed control of the government in 1979, they had to share power with democratic forces, a situation which they never had any intention of maintaining. They consolidated their position by taking control of all the propaganda media, the army, the internal police, the prisons, and a very large part of what by then appeared to be a democratic political system. Thus, as the revolution developed, opposing political forces did not have any opportunity to argue their case against the changes imposed by the Marxist Sandinistas.

During the campaigns, the Sandinistas subtly discredited those opposition elements that the FSLN (Sandinista National Liberation Front) leadership wished to portray as aligned with the Somocista National Guard. Through the use of disinformation, front organizations, youth organizations, teacher organizations, and a barrage of Sandinista propaganda, the Marxists successfully

Reprinted by permission from Heritage Foundation *Backgrounder* #294, "Inside Communist Nicaragua: The Miguel Bolaños Transcripts," September 30, 1983.

prevented the opposition from becoming recognized as a viable alternative to Communism, thus assuring that no force within the opposition became a political threat to them.

After the triumph of the revolution, the Sandinista Front rejected democratic forces such as the MDN (Movimiento Democrático Nicaragüense) and the Conservative Party of Nicaragua, which played important roles in the revolution, claiming that the FSLN was the lone force that overthrew Somoza and remains the only alternative to Somoza. The Marxists scorned the role of the church and Archbishop Obando y Bravo, who sometimes acted as mediator between the FSLN and Somoza. The Sandinistas now claim that Archbishop Obando y Bravo performed this role solely for personal interests. This is part of the propaganda used today against him. Archbishop Obando y Bravo always maintained his neutrality; he criticized the Somoza regime as well as the Sandinista idea of a military victory.

NEUTRALIZING THE OPPOSITION

The line of governmental command to neutralize the opposition is extremely well organized in Nicaragua and is under the supervision of State Security. There are numerous sections charged with broad responsibilities. Section F-1 is responsible for interrogation and capture; F-2, for surveillance of foreign embassies; F-3, counter-revolutionaries; F-4, political parties, churches, and independent labor unions; F-5, economic control; F-6, operations, technology, telephone and mail interception, clandestine searching of diplomats, internal intelligence, and filming of events. Section F-7 has responsibility for the surrounding area, the suburbs, and mob control.

Section F-2 has a number of units, covering the CIA and the American Embassy (Unit A), Latin American embassies (Unit B), European and Asian embassies (Unit C), and hotel accommodations for the press (Unit D). There are about thirty to forty people in this section alone.

Lenin Cerna is the chief of security. This includes all intelligence and counterintelligence. All the F sections are counterintelligence units and come under the direct command of Cerna. Through the

State Security operations, the Sandinistas have been able to control virtually all aspects of Nicaraguan life, domestically and politically. With their counterintelligence surveillance they have infiltrated all levels of Nicaraguan society.

The Campaign Against the Church

The project to neutralize the church, the most powerful force opposing the Sandinistas, is directed toward denigrating the church hierarchy, associating it with the Somoza guard, and identifying it with the United States and the Nicaraguan wealthy classes.

The Sandinistas have used different types of operations to accomplish this. One is the use of government-organized mobs, called "divine mobs" by Comandante Tomás Borge. Such mobs are placed in parishes, where they pose as devout Catholics. They gradually gain power by supporting priests who back the revolution. The idea is to divide the church and to make it look as though the church establishment is the enemy and these "progressive" priests are for the people.

For example, it was an F-4 operation that discredited Father Carballo, who was dragged through the streets naked and appeared on the front page of local newspapers and on television, after supposedly having been caught by a jealous husband. The woman he was accused of having been caught with actually was a Sandinista prostitute considered to be the mistress of the High Command. She lived in the hills but was sent to Father Carballo's parish on the opposite side of town. This woman approached Father Carballo and said she was a Sandinista who wanted to repent and seek his counsel.

The incident was set up to discredit the priest because he is the manager of the Catholic radio station. The whole operation was so skillfully orchestrated that, prior to the priest's being accosted, mobs had been placed outside the house, TV cameras and newspaper photographers were ready, and an officer of the F-7 section was selected to play the role of the jealous husband (the woman was not married). In front of the house, a van from the F-1 section with dark colored windows was parked. It carried two important observers, Lenin Cerna and Tomás Borge, two governing directors of the Sandinista regime. The F-7 agent posing as the "husband" tore the clothes of the priest inside the house and hit him, dragging him to the front door, where the mobs were gathered. The woman, meanwhile, took her clothes off in accordance with the plan and was carried out to the police station, giving credibility to the story.

In a related incident, Archbishop Obando y Bravo removed a pro-Sandinista priest from a parish in Santa Rosa. In retaliation, the Sandinista mobs played the role of parishioners and created an uprising, taking over the church. The mob took away religious items and turned the building into a warehouse. The government filmed the "spontaneous" incident for propaganda purposes.

The mobs that heckled the Pope during his visit to Nicaragua were also organized by State Security. They prevented large numbers of Catholics who wanted to participate in the papal Mass from getting close to John Paul II.

Harassment of Business Leaders

Harassment of the business community began in 1980 with the assassination of business leader Jorge Salazar, head of the Nicaraguan Businessmen's Association (COSEP). I am personally aware of this incident; the head of all the F sections, Alejandro Royero, gave me details of all the players and how it was planned to send José Moncada, Cerna's assistant, as a double agent to induce Salazar to join an armed movement against the Sandinistas that Moncada supposedly led. Salazar was killed when they went to a gas station to pick up arms. Moncada was armed and Salazar was not. The security guards shot at Salazar only. Following the incident Moncada was sent to Cuba. He returned from Cuba in 1983 and holds a high position in State Security.

Business leaders have also been subjected to harassment. The jailing of nine businessmen in February 1982 was part of an operation to scare them into leaving the country and to make them aware that they were not immune from Sandinista repression. The idea is to make it so that those who remain will cooperate with the Sandinistas.

Press Manipulation

Since 1979 the Sandinistas have been working with the foreign press through F-2 Unit D. This security unit collects information about all the correspondents who come to Nicaragua, categorizing them as useful, manageable, or hostile. For example, on numerous occasions, whenever a network crew would arrive at their hotel, members of the F-2 D unit were secretly sent to their rooms to review videotapes made by groups such as CBS, NBC, or ABC. Sometimes the tapes were confiscated and replaced with blank tape. The crew's notes were read and cassette tapes listened to—all this while the crew was on assignment for a long period away from the hotel. The minister of tourism has assisted in creating a group for surveillance of the international press, which on a regular basis bugs reporters' rooms. Hotel clerks are in reality security agents, all coordinated by State Security. This process really begins at the airport, where passports of reporters are photographed and files are kept on them.

The more serious censorship of journalists is done upon their exiting the country at the airport. All information is reviewed without their knowledge while they await departure. All passports are checked against the files taken on their arrival.

During my last few months as a counterintelligence officer, I discovered a plan to keep even better control of journalists. This entailed the F-2 D unit's assigning colored ID cards to all journalists. The colors would show how favorable they had been to the Sandinistas. Those who had been favorable would have better access to all areas of importance, including the fighting in the north of the country.

Roberto Sánchez is the public relations man for the army and is in charge of taking journalists to the war zone. The security section decides who can go, and these are always the journalists judged the most flexible and favorable. There is an understanding that they are going out at their own risk, but F-2 D never really takes them to an area of combat. According to prior agreement, television crews have to give the Sandinistas copies of everything they film. The Sandinistas would prepare an area beforehand, taking the crews to an area where there is some fighting and where the Sandinistas control the anti-Sandinista groups. It is important to show that the Sandinistas are winning the war.

The Sandinistas have also worked on ways of manipulating international press representatives in an effort to control their activities. One correspondent in Managua for a widely respected American press organization has been working as an agent of the F-2 D unit since December 1982. Though he is not being paid, he is receiving direction from State Security. He is sometimes critical of the Sandinistas in his dispatches, but it is only to maintain credibility. For example, he will do interviews with leaders of democratic groups and then give the information to the Sandinistas. His employer does not know that he is working for the Sandinistas. However, he is not a full agent, because State Security believes that the CIA could have planted him and that he could be a double agent. There are many other journalists working like him.

Manipulating Missionaries

Journalists are not the only ones used to promote the image of the Sandinistas abroad. A number of religious representatives have been manipulated; one of the most prominent among them is the Catholic Maryknoll order of missionaries. The Sandinistas' foreign minister, Miguel D'Escoto, is a Maryknoll priest and the former editor of *Maryknoll* magazine, a Catholic publication which has printed stories favorable to the Sandinistas and very critical of the rest of the governments of Latin America. D'Escoto has used his influence in the Catholic Church in the United States to gain support for the Sandinistas.

The Maryknoll order represents a very influential Catholic force both in Latin America and in the United States. The Sandinistas have realized they need the promotion of a religious group to have a credible image in the United States. Maryknoll is only one of several religious organizations in support of the Sandinista regime that promote the FSLN abroad.

The Sandinistas have skillfully taken advantage of U.S. minority groups such as the American Indians to project an image of people oppressed by the United States. At one time, representatives of the American Indian caucus were taken to Managua, where the Sandinistas claimed they were together as oppressed victims of the United States. Following the Indian representatives' return to the United States, they spoke in solidarity with the Sandinistas. But the campaign failed to affect the whole American Indian community, as other members of it did not unanimously share the views of their visiting representatives.

Operation Spiderweb

This operation involved discrediting political leaders, the Catholic Church, the private sector, and independent labor unions, with the idea of painting American imperialism as the manipulator of these organizations. This propaganda scheme was organized in an effort to obtain control of them by 1985, making the FSLN the only legitimate political party in Nicaragua.

For the last two years, I had been assigned on various occasions to tape, follow, photograph, and bug political officers and other diplomats of the U.S. Embassy in conversations with different political, church, and independent union leaders in Managua. The idea for propaganda was to show the "links" between these officers and the different local leaders. In particular, I was in charge of following U.S. political officer Linda Pfeifel from June to December 1982. I was able to learn everything about her. We were ordered to do a number of films of her activities and edit the film to show a conspiracy against the revolution. We would provoke American double agents, telling the agents to lead the Americans into forming a group in opposition to the regime. In this manner we could frame diplomats and expose them as CIA agents, completing the internal propaganda campaign in efforts of getting support from the populace and proving their propaganda correct.

Upon my departure on May 7, 1983, the operation to discredit the Americans was temporarily halted. The original exposé was to have taken place in April, but because of lack of sufficient evidence it was postponed. Knowing that I would disclose the operation, they speeded it up and decided on criminal charges against Linda Pfeifel. The films that were shown to the international press implicating Miss Pfeifel were in reality a compilation of films that had been collected since January 1982.

All the plans for Operation Spiderweb were under the direct supervision of a Cuban. General Roberto (*nom de guerre*) was the former head of counterintelligence in Cuba and is now an advisor to the chief of security in Nicaragua. The Cuban advisor in section

F-2 who collected the information was called "Pancho." The incident with the Americans is only one of many planned for foreign diplomats of Western nations.

Human Rights Abuses

The Sandinista security forces systematically employ methods of interrogation against their opponents that deny their basic human rights. When the Sandinistas bring someone in for interrogation, they usually need only to confirm information or to obtain names they do not yet have. They apply the KGB method of psychological torture. Even the jails are constructed for psychological torture; their layouts have been brought from Cuba and are based on KGB models.

The F-1 interrogators are trained by Cubans, who themselves trained for five years in the Soviet Union. They have the ability to reduce anyone's resistance within two days. Outside Managua the methods are not so sophisticated. In the north, anti-Sandinista rebels are often brutally killed *en masse*. If fifteen are captured, two will be taken to Managua for debriefing, where they are put on TV, and the rest will be killed. Often they are killed by stabbing, but there is also the "vest cut." In this, the prisoner's arms and legs are cut off while he is alive, and he is left to bleed to death. It is an old technique used by Somoza and Sandino.

Stedman Fagoth, the leader of the Miskito Indians, was one of those who were psychologically tortured. He gave F-1 more information than he realized. Because of the interrogation, he negotiated with the Sandinistas. Later, however, we realized it was an intelligent move on his part, because it allowed him to get away. The Argentine Victor Frances was interrogated in this manner when he was kidnapped in Costa Rica and brought back to Managua. It was then that he was forced to make statements about U.S. and Argentine involvement in helping the anti-Sandinista rebels.

INVOLVEMENT BY THE COMMUNIST BLOC

Intervention by Cubans, Soviets, and other elements of the socialist bloc exists on a grand scale in all areas of Nicaraguan society today. There are Soviet and Cuban political advisors, and, as a consequence, there is rapid movement toward a Marxist economy. There is already a plan to establish firm economic ties with the Soviet Union.

Renán Montero (*nom de guerre*), commander of the Nicaraguan intelligence service, is a former colonel in Cuba's intelligence service who became a nationalized Nicaraguan citizen. He was ordered to work with the Sandinistas fifteen years ago, in efforts to help them seize power and set up Communism in Nicaragua. Sandinista leader Tomás Borge was so pleased with his work that he asked Fidel Castro to allow Montero to remain permanently in Nicaragua.

Today, Nicaragua has 3,000 Cuban soldiers (not counting high-level advisors) and a covert team of 2,000 soldiers working as technical advisors, building roads and handling heavy machinery. Their purpose is to help Nicaragua in case of an attack or emergency. There are 400 Cuban advisors to the army alone, and forty high-level officials on the staff of the regular army. There are 200 Soviet military advisors in Nicaragua, of whom fifty are high-level officials working with the army. There are also high-level Cuban and Soviet advisors working with intelligence and counterintelligence. The Cubans' role with the regular army involves military training of low-ranking Nicaraguan soldiers, as well as developing all aspects of army security and defense.

In the counterintelligence unit where I worked (F-2, Unit A), there are two Soviets and a Cuban advisor. There can be at least seven to ten Cubans at any given time; the Soviets only come occasionally to review and brief the F-2 section. In total there are seventy Soviet advisors involved in all aspects of Nicaraguan State Security, along with some 400 Cubans. There are forty to fifty East Germans and about twenty to twenty-five Bulgarians. The Bulgarians have a center of operation dealing with counterintelligence matters where they process information gathered by our office and then make recommendations on the operations. Bulgarians are expert analysts in matters of counterintelligence. The East Germans also get to see data we collect and will give their analysis of our findings. The F-2 section, which is responsible for the surveillance of foreign embassies, has several East German advisors. Their interest is mainly in operations directed against the West

German Embassy. East Germany has provided Nicaragua with its latest surveillance and bugging equipment. The Soviets have also given technical equipment for security and counterintelligence operations.

The State Security forces have hand guns which are the same as those the KGB uses (9 mm short Makarof), which were gifts from the Soviets. The whole structure of the security system, the methods and means of working, are from handbooks and studies given in Cuba and Bulgaria. The Soviets have already built a school for State Security in Nicaragua.

The PLO and Libyans have established headquarters in Nicaragua as a convenient Western Hemisphere base from which to work against Israel. Libya is also sending military and financial help, including light planes especially designed for anti-terrorist activities.

Soviet Arms in Nicaragua

Arms from the Communist bloc have flowed freely into Nicaragua. Today the army, the militia, and the police, including the security police, special troops, and commandos, are outfitted with Soviet arms. Armaments that have been sent by the Soviet Union to Nicaragua include bazookas, machine guns, mines, and hand guns, as well as "Katuska" rocket-launchers and .45 cal. recoil-less rifles.

There are 100 Soviet tanks in Nicaragua and, according to the head of the Nicaraguan air force, eighty Soviet MiGs are waiting in Cuba until Nicaraguan pilots return from training in Bulgaria. There are armored transport vehicles of Soviet manufacture and Soviet-made artillery. Nicaragua has also received radar-guided surface-to-air missiles [SAMs] and the heat-seeking SAM-7 missile. Two subterranean missile bases have been established. One is located in the Sandino International Airport; the other is in a restricted area near Managua, in a project called *Granja*.

The Soviets have rented the port of South San Juan. They are expected to repair and recondition it for receiving their large fishing vessels. But, while they need the port for economic reasons, international Communism also needs this port for arms delivery directly to Central America. Afterwards, of course, there is the possibility of submarine use.

Furthermore, the Soviets are building a channel through Nicaragua so they will not have to depend on the Panama Canal. If Panama breaks ties with Nicaragua, the Soviets will have to build much faster. Aside from the port they are building in San Juan del Sur, on the Pacific, they are also going to build two more ports— one on the Lake of Managua, close to the capital city, and another on the Lake of Nicaragua. It is the same route that Americans thought of using before deciding on the Panama route.

Exporting Revolution

Nicaragua has become the base of operations for the spread of international Communism in the Western Hemisphere. Cuba is an island and easily watched. However, Nicaragua has a commercial airport, and ships can leave Nicaragua more easily than Cuba.

Nicaragua has become the psychological center of support for revolutionary reawakening. The M-19 of Colombia, Montoneros of Argentina, FMLN of El Salvador, EGP of Guatemala, and the armed groups of Costa Rica and Argentina all have their centers of operations in Nicaragua. These are preparing for a new invasion of Argentina and Colombia.

Aid to Guerrillas in El Salvador

In El Salvador, the Sandinistas are offering total help, advice, and direction on how to manage both the war and international politics. Salvadoran guerrillas have been and continue to be trained in Nicaragua. The Sandinistas have helped the Salvadorans with their air force, army, and navy, in transporting arms into El Salvador. Some of the arms come from Cuba via Nicaragua.

The Salvadorans have two command centers in Nicaragua: one for communications and the other to meet with the Nicaraguan High Command. The Salvadoran High Command stay in Managua all the time, unless they go back to rally the troops. They are then flown in for a day and flown back. The political people have homes in Nicaragua.

The Salvadoran insurgents have all the positions in their "government" designated to certain individuals already. Everything has been carefully thought out: who will have a ministry, who will command the armed forces, and so on.

Many routes are used by the Sandinistas to transfer arms to the Salvadoran guerrillas. At one time, one of the routes was from Mexico, through Guatemala into El Salvador; trucks and mules were used for transport. There is an international arsenal of arms in Mexico where these weapons come from.

Other routes have been through Honduras, along the border with El Salvador and Nicaragua, and along the Pacific coast of El Salvador in fast speedboats that made landings on deserted beaches. The bulk of the arms were delivered in the early part of 1980 to 1981. This is when the Sandinistas delivered some 6,000 to 7,000 machine guns and rifles. At this time the Salvadorans do not need any more arms, only ammunition. They already have five times more arms than the Sandinistas had when they overthrew Somoza.

Recently, aircraft small enough to land on highways have been used, usually two planes a day. These planes drop thirty to forty rifles at a time, along with logistic supplies. Because of radar intervention, the Sandinistas use parachute drops to deliver their supplies when it is difficult to make a landing. This is one of the reasons why guerrillas in El Salvador hold on to areas of highways for several hours.

Destabilizing Honduras and Costa Rica

The guerrillas in Honduras, the Cinchoneros, were organized with international Communist help in 1980-81. They had been trained in Nicaragua since 1979. There are now 400 Cinchoneros.

The Sandinistas have a special interest in destabilizing the Honduran government—so much that they have created a special commando force to go into Honduran territory and attack. In 1982 they had a test run of attacks against anti-Sandinista rebels based in Honduras. They crossed into Honduran territory and wiped out a camp of two hundred rebels. These attacks have been repeated, though with fewer casualties.

But the ultimate target is Honduras, not the anti-Sandinista rebels. The Sandinistas want to test the Honduran military to see how far they will venture across the border, so that the battle will be on Nicaraguan territory and world opinion will be on the side of Nicaragua. I learned of this plan through interviews with other agents for counterintelligence operations.

I first became aware of the interest Nicaragua had in Honduras soon after the revolution in 1979. At that time there were five Soviet generals working as advisors to the Sandinistas. In one of their sessions, they displayed a map of Honduras with its military capabilities and next to it what was left militarily of Nicaragua. It was decided at that time that Nicaragua had to concentrate on a military buildup to fight against Honduras. Today, Nicaragua is capable of defeating Honduras militarily in a matter of days.

Since 1979, there has also been a plan to neutralize democracy in Costa Rica. The Sandinistas have been working covertly in Costa Rica, training guerrilla groups and infiltrating unions to cause agitation. The strategy is to cause internal struggle in Costa Rica between the labor unions and the government, and to challenge Costa Rica's police security, giving them a military image. When the economy gets worse, the Sandinistas will be able to organize popular forces aided by the guerrillas already there.

THE NEW PRIVILEGED CLASS

The slogan of the Sandinistas is, "Only workers and peasants will obtain power and last until the end." Why? Because workers and peasants are used to feeling inferior and are without high expectations. In transferring to a Marxist system, they cannot see the difference between the privileged classes under Somoza and the new privileged class under the Marxists.

In a few sectors, the poor do live better, but it is a limited standard preventing them from any achievements. The poor cannot become professionals and work for themselves; they will be controlled as they are in Cuba. And, as in Cuba, the people who belong to the ruling party will remain the privileged class, having good salaries and living in the best places.

Despite talk about the "new society of Nicaragua," the leaders who were going to construct this new society spend money on themselves. The *comandantes* feed themselves with the best food, while the people are reduced to rationing.

People want to join the party because that is where the good life is. The Sandinistas recently bought seventy new cars for their nine *comandantes*. All the *comandantes* have foreign bank accounts. It is called "money of the people."

When Cerna and Borge returned from a trip to the Soviet Union, they gathered 600 top government and party officials together to see all the things they had bought with the money that belonged to the ministry. Among their purchases were many cases of Bulgarian wine and caviar.

For party members, there are no waiting lines but a commissary well stocked with items which in the open market are heavily rationed and in great shortage. The Nicaraguan people have realized that the Sandinista directorate has become like the members of the Somoza family they fought so hard against.

RECOMMENDATIONS FOR U.S. POLICY

The Sandinista leaders were trained in Cuba from the early 1960s. Their training was ideologically, politically, and militarily supervised by Fidel Castro. To think that the model of the Nicaraguan revolution is unique, and to think that there exists the possibility that this revolution is different from others, is naïve. A revolution is never spontaneous, and in recent history, all revolutions have been motivated and created by one of two forces, capitalism or Communism.

International support was given to the revolution, not as a Communist revolution, but as a spontaneous revolution. The Sandinistas fabricated propaganda for domestic and international consumption portraying the Nicaraguan revolution and the FSLN as one and the same. Thus, little by little, world public opinion was led to believe that the radicalization of the revolution was actually a normal response to domestic conspiracy against the revolution.

The window which international Communism has opened in Nicaragua must be closed. This involves not only aiding the rebels but also playing "hard ball" with the international forces supporting the Sandinistas. They include the Socialist International and groups in Mexico, Venezuela, and France. The United States must persuade these international forces to cut the support they give the Sandinistas. This will pressure the Sandinistas into defining themselves and their revolution.

The United States has a moral responsibility to educate the Western world about the reality of the Sandinistas. Through a well organized propaganda campaign, the Sandinistas are viewed as democrats who will permit elections in 1985. The United States must warn the world about the Sandinistas as it warned about the Nazis in World War II. The Nazi strategy is the same as the Communist today, the ambition to conquer the world.

U.S. policy should give far more attention to Latin America. The United States must open up Latin export economies and increase its economic assistance to the region. The United States will reap the benefits of these actions.

The most direct assistance to the Salvadoran guerrillas is coming from the Sandinista Front, not the Cubans, in the same way in which the Cubans gave assistance to the Nicaraguan revolution. The practical experience needed to conquer El Salvador is based in Managua. The Salvadoran government must be helped, militarily and economically. Pressure must continue against Marxist rebels. The United States should not force the Salvadoran government to give the rebels the legitimacy they should earn only through the democratic process.

The United States should provide Honduras and Guatemala with military training and assistance. In the case of Honduras, it is a necessity to prepare the Honduran military to defend themselves from an attack by Nicaragua. Honduras has been a prime target of Nicaraguan military strategy. Costa Rica too is threatened by Nicaragua, but not militarily as much as politically. The democratic forces of the United States must realize that the Costa Rican democracy is now threatened by Nicaraguan triumph.

The Sandinistas have been fighting for twenty years to implant Communism. It is totally illogical to think that they would have friendly relations with the United States when they believe that it is their historic mission to export Communism to the rest of Latin America. Those Americans who naïvely think that negotiations will solve the problems don't know the Sandinistas. Negotiations serve only to buy time for the Sandinistas. This is something they tell you quite openly within the Sandinista organization: negotiation is used only to buy time to consolidate power.

Communism has come to this hemisphere because the area is of vital economic and strategic importance to the United States. The only option for the United States is to support those who are trying to defeat the Sandinista regime. If the United States refuses to aid the anti-Sandinista forces, which are growing stronger in internal support, it will be morally responsible for selling the Nicaraguan people into slavery. And in a few years, the United States will have to respond to Communist gains throughout the rest of the American hemisphere.

26. *A Revolution Betrayed*

By EDÉN PASTORA GÓMEZ

Focus
Edén Pastora Gómez, the famous "Commander Zero," was the most charismatic leader of the Nicaraguan revolutionary army that defeated Anastasio Somoza Debayle in 1979 and installed a revolutionary government. Almost immediately after the victory, however, Pastora felt that the Sandinista rulers were betraying the original aims of the revolution. He voiced his criticism, was ignored, and left the government to work quietly for a true Nicaraguan democracy. In April 1982 he made public his break with the Sandinistas and issued the statement below.

Eventually Pastora began an armed struggle against the Sandinistas. In 1983 his group of *contras*, whose bases are in southern Nicaragua near the Costa Rican border, joined forces with another army of freedom-fighters in northern Nicaragua. Later that year the two groups separated again over political differences.

Pastora's views, as this statement makes clear, are strongly nationalistic. Like Augusto César Sandino, the rebel leader for whom the Sandinista movement is named, Pastora is little attracted to ideology. His concern is for Nicaraguan freedom.

Nicaragua must be a truly nonaligned state, says Pastora. "Our Sandinismo cannot allow us to be dragged into the East-West conflict, since that is contrary to national interests." He denounces "U.S. imperialism" but also insists upon a withdrawal of the many Cuban and Eastern-bloc "advisors" from Nicaragua. "The time has come for those who are not engaged in activities strictly contributing to health and education to leave us alone."

Several serious internal deficiencies must be remedied as well, says Pastora. He calls for respect for the Nicaraguan Indian groups, a free economic system, political pluralism, free elections, "strict respect of individual rights and demands for workers' rights," true freedom of worship ("not just a mere declaration . . . a reality warranting the deepest respect"), and freedom of the press.

Pastora's views conflict strongly with those of the Sandinista leader Tomás Borge (selection 24).

Edén Pastora Gómez has spent over twenty years fighting for the freedom of the Nicaraguan people.

I WILL REMAIN ON GUARD so that the revolution will not be subordinated or betrayed." I said this back on that day of 20 July 1979 at the Plaza de la Revolución in Managua, Nicaragua.

Historical circumstances place responsibilities on men. Those circumstances oblige me to come and fulfill an obligation as a Nicaraguan Sandinista. It was my lot to have been born in the darkness with which Somocismo disgraced and degraded my fatherland, Nicaragua. When I was seven years old I lost my father, who was murdered by the oppressors of my people. As I grew up and learned, I realized that many other Nicaraguan families were enduring the same sorrow as mine. Later, thanks to the opportunities for education my mother provided for me, I discovered the sad reality that the sovereignty of my country had been injured many times by U.S. imperialism and that the vast majority of my fellow citizens were victims of the most degrading social injustice. In the course of my education I also learned that there was a patriot who deeply loved Nicaragua, and who gave up his life in the struggle for the liberation of the Nicaraguan people. That man, Augusto César Sandino, is the fundamental source of inspiration in my life as a citizen.

From the time I was very young I made the decision to be a revolutionary. I understood clearly that it was necessary to take up arms to overthrow the tyranny, and I gave up my medical studies in Guadalajara, Mexico. With the maturity acquired during years of struggle, I became increasingly convinced that a lasting peace could be achieved only by establishing democracy and by doing away with exploitation and with all kinds of injustice. Since I come from a family of working men, I alternated my periods of armed struggle in the mountains with periods of work in cattle-raising, farming, business, and fishing. It is possibly to that experience that I owe my firm conviction as to the need to establish guarantees and incentives for production and investment as the bases of economic development. The despotism of the system which reigned for more than forty years awoke in me a hatred for arbitrary command and a love for individual freedom. Those principles make up the foundations of my revolutionary ideals, and I would like to make it clear once and for all that I have never been concerned about doctrinaire labels.

Guided by those principles during my revolutionary struggle, in 1959 I became one of the founders of the Sandino Revolutionary Front, the first revolutionary movement to proclaim General Sandino as the immortal leader of our resurgence as a sovereign people. Subsequently, in 1961, I reaffirmed my Sandinista, anti-imperialist, democratic, and popular ideals by being one of the first to forge the Sandinista National Liberation Front, to which I have the high honor of having contributed twenty-one years as a disciplined and loyal member.

In 1976 I put an end to a peaceful break in my life, working side by side with my beloved wife and children, to begin yet another period of struggle in answer to another call from my Sandinista comrades. On this occasion I went to meet them on the battlefields, bursting with enthusiasm because it was the beginning of a transcendental crusade in the history of my people: the unification of all the national sectors in order to expel the dynastic tyranny from the fatherland forever and to establish a social system of complete revolution—an eminently just revolution, with participation by all, with hatred toward none, driven by justice and ready to defend national sovereignty. . . .

[In several paragraphs omitted here Pastora pays tribute to many "martyrs and heroes" who took part in the struggle to overthrow Somoza.]

At the moment of triumph, I went with enthusiasm to render my services to consolidate the revolution, filling any post that the national leadership of the Sandinista National Liberation Front ordered me to assume. However, from the first moment of triumph I noted with sorrow what in my opinion are deviations which endanger the revolutionary process and even the very security of the Nicaraguan state. Fulfilling my duty, I pointed out to my superiors the dangers to which those rash actions and errors might expose the country. I did so with a desire for rectification and with revolutionary loyalty. When I did not get a response, I thought it best to separate myself from the government and to channel my revolutionary ideals within Internationalism as a continuation of Sandinismo. I made that decision with deep sorrow and without resentment. My dissidence and my cooperation have been, are, and always will be within the framework of the revolution to which I am completely devoted. I have kept silent, confident that patriotism would prevail among the leaders of the revolution.

After I joined the Internationalist movement my exhortations were never heard, and in answer I was politically attacked by those whom I considered to be my brothers. Today, following ten months of prudent silence, I am obliged to break that silence to make public a statement of my attitude toward the governmental disaster and at the same time to express clearly my categorical repudiation of any aggression against my people and to say that I am ready and willing to fight from my trenches against any violation of the fatherland.

The Nicaraguans who truly love Nicaragua, and who wish for the good outcome of a fair revolutionary process, look upon Mexican president José López Portillo's peace initiative with satisfaction. I include myself among those Nicaraguans.

Nationalism and Nonalignment

Peace for our people is achievable to the extent that we are truly nonaligned. There can neither be contradictions nor ambiguities in Sandinismo: the invasion of Vietnam was as imperialist as the invasion of Afghanistan. Just as imperialist are those who support a fascist junta in El Salvador as those who support a totalitarian regime in Poland. Our Sandinismo cannot allow us to be dragged into the East-West conflict, since that is contrary to national interests. Within this nationalist policy, we know that injustice and class exploitation are the roots of the tragedy which Central America is experiencing, and we must combat these roots with determination. Today, as yesterday, the people have the obligation to free themselves from oppression and exploitation.

We must promote Central American brotherhood, respecting the right of each fraternal nation to seek social transformation by whatever means are most suited to its own realities and interests. In that context, we must aspire to our revolution's being truly

Nicaraguan, as the Mexican revolution is Mexican and the Cuban revolution Cuban. And I pay tribute to them. There are in both positive achievements which would enrich our revolution, while preserving its genuine and Nicaraguan character.

I am an Internationalist because I am a free man and I wish to contribute to the liberation of all men. The selflessness and total commitment of Commander Ernesto Ché Guevara are cause for inspiration to me. I am grateful, as I am sure most of my fellow citizens are, for the support which the International comrades of Panama, Costa Rica, Cuba, and other fraternal peoples have given us yesterday in war and today in peace, which is in danger. At this time I am interpreting the feeling—and the reason for that feeling—of that majority of Nicaraguans when I say that the time has come for those who are not engaged in activities strictly contributing to health and education to leave us alone. As a lover of my people, I will honor Sandino's ideas, calling on all Nicaraguans to put themselves on a war footing as long as there is one foreign soldier on our native soil. I know that the ranks of the Sandinista People's Army and the Sandinista People's Militia are made up of men and women of honor and love, and that they constitute the only guarantee that the revolution is irreversible. Today I am calling on that honor and love.

Necessary Freedoms

The national economy, vital to the revolution, will begin a process of free recovery only if we create a political climate which stimulates production and investment within a mixed economy system. A policy which generates both internal and external peace can only be one in which democracy enjoys the real attributes befitting it, without omitting political pluralism, the practice of free elections, strict respect of individual rights and demands for workers' rights. Freedom of worship is not just a mere declaration. It must be a reality warranting the deepest respect. The revolution does not need to limit freedom of the press, since, if it does, even the walls in the jails would be converted into newspapers.

The fundamental statute of the republic, the statute on the laws and rights of Nicaraguans, and the government's national reconstruction program are not being complied with when, in broad daylight or under the cover of night, the seizures, expropriations, and confiscations overwhelm Somocistas and anti-Somocistas, counterrevolutionaries and revolutionaries, guilty and innocent. In the jails the counterrevolutionaries rub elbows with the Marxist revolutionaries, the latter being punished for the grave offense of interpreting Marx by different criteria from those of their comrades with power. I have with sorrow seen that among my people there is anxiety, distress, fear, the bitterness of frustration and personal insecurity, when they see our Miskito, Sumo, and Rama Indians persecuted, jailed, or murdered, without a press or radio which might denounce to the world this reign of terror prevailing on the Atlantic coast and throughout Nicaragua by the already feared State Security.

By all that is stated here, I leave no doubt as to my disagreement with the way the national leadership is conducting the process. If it continues in the present fashion, the people will have to pay a very dear price, possibly even going back to the past unless the armed people expel from power those whom Sandino's condemning and accusing finger points to as traitors and murderers.

Long live the people's revolution.

Long live Nicaragua. Long live freedom, long live Sandino.

Free fatherland or death.

27. The Drift Toward Repression

By RONALD RADOSH

Focus Americans, says Ronald Radosh, generally hold one of two extreme opinions about Sandinista Nicaragua. They regard it either as a repressive Stalinist state or as a promising experiment in building democracy. During a visit to the country in 1983, Radosh encountered a considerably more complex situation. The new Nicaragua has not yet become completely totalitarian, according to Radosh, but there are disturbing signs of a "slow but clear movement toward a Cuban-style regime."

The Committees of Sandinista Defense (CDS), for example, are local block associations that keep order in their areas. Among other things, they organize militants "to spy on neighbors suspected of various deviations—shirking on the job, reading *La Prensa* [the only significant non-Sandinista newspaper], preferring to join the non-Sandinista trade unions." Since the CDS also control access to the ration cards needed to get basic necessities, non-cooperation can be both dangerous and costly.

The government claims that its censorship of *La Prensa* is necessary for reasons of wartime security, but many of the censors' deletions seem motivated more by ideology than by security. "Soviet action in Afghanistan," Russian submarines in Swedish waters, and "domestic happenings that might weaken appreciation for the Sandinistas" are among the forbidden topics. *La Prensa* is allowed to continue publishing primarily because the political cost abroad of shutting it down is deemed too high.

Various trade unions and other popular organizations still offer weak opposition to the government, but the looming danger of totalitarianism makes their existence precarious. A member of Nicaragua's Permanent Commission on Human Rights told Radosh: "The very concept of rights has disappeared in Nicaragua. Rights are now something conceived of as a gift from the authorities. In this sense, the human rights situation is worse than it was during the Somoza years."

Radosh's observations should be read along with those of ex-Sandinista intelligence officer Miguel Bolaños (selection 25) and should be compared with the claims of Nicaraguan minister of the interior Tomás Borge (selection 24).

Ronald Radosh, co-author with Joyce Milton of *The Rosenberg File,* is a co-editor of *El Salvador: Central America and the New Cold War* and the editor of *The New Cuba: Paradoxes and Potentials.*

A MERICANS SEEM TO HAVE two conflicting impressions of revolutionary Nicaragua. One impression—the one you get from
Ronald Reagan, or from books like Max Singer's *Nicaragua: The
Stolen Revolution*—is of a highly developed variant of Stalinism,
an all-powerful state run on pure terror. The other impression
comes from opponents of U.S. intervention in Central America,
such as the editors of the *Boston Globe*, who view Nicaragua as
a "serious, popular, mostly well-intentioned and frequently
competent national experiment not altogether unlike our own
revolution."

A visit reveals something more complex than either of these
skewed portraits. Nicaragua is a society increasingly militarized
and polarized, defined for the average person by the daily ration
lines for the most necessary commodities—soap, toilet paper,
gasoline. It is also a nation in which the heralded promises of the
Sandinista National Liberation Front (FSLN)—to build a revolution based on political pluralism, a mixed economy, and international nonalignment—have been replaced by a slow but clear
movement toward a Cuban-style regime.

Yet Nicaragua seems to be moving in two contradictory directions at once. A group of non-Sandinista Nicaraguan politicians,
supporters of the revolution but members of opposition parties,
recently traveled to Europe to draw up a report on the parliamentary system in France, Sweden, Spain, and Finland. The avowed
purpose was to report back on the parliamentary process so that
the revolution can create a meaningful democratic system. At the
same time, Sandinista leaders lash out at "bourgeois" democracy
and point to the supposedly higher democracy they are
building—symbolized by such institutions as the new revolutionary tribunals for detecting and trying counterrevolutionaries.

Reprinted from the October 24, 1983, issue of *The New Republic* (© 1983 by The
New Republic, Incorporated).

These leaders speak with evident pride of the work of the Committees of Sandinista Defense (CDS), local block associations that not only carry out administrative tasks but also organize militants to spy on neighbors suspected of various deviations—shirking on the job, reading *La Prensa,* preferring to join the non-Sandinista trade unions. Since access to ration cards—and therefore to state-controlled supplies—is a perk of belonging to the local CDS, even the stiffest opponent of the regime has to think twice before refusing to affiliate.

Democracy Sandinista Style

How Sandinista-style democracy works is most visible at the biweekly "face the people" sessions. At each such meeting, a few of the nine *comandantes* [members of the FSLN directorate], along with other government officials, appear in a different neighborhood to speak before the people and to hear their complaints. On one hot and humid night recently, Daniel Ortega, chief of state, and Sergio Ramírez, coordinator of the governing junta, led the list of prominent officials who presided at a meeting in a suburb of Managua. For two hours before they arrived, the crowd of several hundred was exhorted to chant revolutionary slogans by a small band of young militants, who at this particular session were not facing a receptive audience. They walked in front of nonparticipants with a megaphone, insisting that they join in. "Loud so the Pentagon will hear!" they admonished the audience.

Listening to their chants, I thought of the trenchant critique of the left-wing Honduran writer Rodolfo Pastor, who pointed out in *Dissent's* 1982 collection of essays on Central America that Nicaragua's armed-camp mentality creates an atmosphere "in which the highest civic virtue is submission to discipline and the worst sin is open political disagreement." This, Pastor writes, "is the antithesis to the revolutionary spirit of criticism, so that to defend it as revolutionary is contradictory nonsense." Pastor, I thought, would have found confirmation for his thesis in the words of the most popular chant: "National Directorate: Order us what to do!" Another chant celebrated the hooliganism of the *turbas,* the Sandinistas' quasi-legal goon squads that attack unwelcome dissenters. "We are mobs," the militants chanted; "so what?"

As the chanting subsided, Comandante Ortega opened with a brief talk. He began by attacking Alfonso Robelo and Edén Pastora—the ex-Sandinista officials who lead ARDE (Democratic Revolutionary Alliance), the Costa Rica-based rebels—as CIA stooges. This marked a tactical shift for the Directorate, which formerly responded to Pastora's threat by trying to forbid any mention of him. (*La Prensa* was even ordered to avoid the use of the word "zero," lest it be interpreted as an illusion to Pastora, whose *nom de guerre* was Comandante Cero.) But now that Pastora has decided to open a second front and to seek CIA aid, Ortega and his colleagues think they have an advantage in the propaganda war against him.

Ortega went on to blame the deaths of two American journalists, Richard Cross and Dial Torgerson, on Ronald Reagan. How, he asked, could the Hondurans, acting on behalf of the United States, have allowed them to travel on a border road without protection from their soldiers? When U.S. journalists went to the same area on the Nicaraguan side, he said, they got protection from the militia, some of whom died in the battle to save the journalists from an ambush. Then Ortega greeted the "North American journalists." There were four or five of us attending the meeting, and we shifted uneasily in our seats as he assured the audience we were "100 per cent in support of the revolution."

Finally it was the turn of "the people" to speak. A woman stood up. She began by reading a written statement: her community supported the revolution, she understood the need to have food and equipment for the boys at the front, it was her patriotic wish that the attempt of American imperialism to defeat the revolution be set back. With a brief pause for breath, she added: "So why can't we have cooking oil? We've gone five whole weeks without it." One of Ortega's aides, apparently the appropriate official, answered. The government, he assured her, would look into it. By the very next week, he promised, things were going to be better. Her neighborhood would get 60 per cent of what it requested. Sugar, rice, and soap would be made available, as well as cooking oil every eight to ten days.

The next questioner also knew that Nicaragua's problems were due to a war forced upon it from outside. She too favored resolute action to defeat the *contras,* and she praised the Directorate for its leadership. But the nearby primary school was so overcrowded. Couldn't the government build them a new one? A minister said he would look into it, and that she should form a committee and come to the Ministry of Education with a concrete proposal.

So it went. Later in the evening, when one man revealed a hostile tone, the militants began to chant: "Confiscate! Confiscate! Confiscate!" Daniel Ortega responded that the government functioned according to laws, that a person's property could not be taken away simply because the revolutionaries disapproved of his or her attitude.

More Feudal Than Revolutionary

The Nicaraguan people now have an institutionalized mechanism for talking directly to their top leaders. But the relationship between people and leaders was more feudal than revolutionary: the lord dispensing justice in return for loyalty. Nor did the intimidating atmosphere encourage dissent. The meetings are largely symbolic—theatrical productions designed to dramatize the government's concern for and closeness to the people. They are hardly a substitute for institutions of representative democracy, through which a people can freely debate and define their country's course.

Nevertheless, people find ways of expressing their feelings. One safe way is through the Catholic Church. Merely to support the traditional church has become per se an act critical of the regime. The Sandinistas, despite their own nominal devotion to Catholicism (Comandante Tomás Borge adorns his office with a personal collection of crucifixes), have created this situation. In response to the coolness toward the Sandinistas of Archbishop Obando y Bravo—who had supported the overthrow of Somoza—pro-Sandinista priests created the "People's Church," a minuscule sect seeking to blend Catholicism and Marxism along the lines of the new liberation theology. Pope John Paul II attacked these priests, two of whom hold major government posts, as "absurd and dangerous"—a comment that automatically turned defenders of the traditional church into critics of the government.

When the Pope was met with catcalls and revolutionary slogans, most Nicaraguans were offended by the reception afforded a religious leader they revered. The Sandinistas, for their part, were scandalized that the Pope refused to say Mass for the dead of the People's Militia, killed in the fight against the *contras*. Why, Father Arvello Argüello of the People's Church asked me, did the Pope refuse the pleas made to him by mothers of the dead? The archbishop, of course, sees the issue in a different light. The Pope, he argues, "prayed for all who died," and will not engage in propaganda for political reasons.

It is a perfect standoff. The archbishop proclaims that he and the Pope refuse to be politicians. The Sandinistas retort that the archbishop is indeed playing politics—using the church to create a center for a political opposition. The charge in fact does have some merit. To back the church in the context of the Nicaraguan revolution is to oppose the FSLN. Since this is the case, it is a shock to see the image of the Holy Father displayed throughout the country and pasted in storefronts, offices, and on the shacks of the poorest dwellers of Managua's *barrios*. Yet it is a relatively safe form of criticism. Having proclaimed themselves devout Catholics, the Sandinistas cannot afford to do anything but tolerate the outpouring of love for the Pope and the church.

The Survival of 'La Prensa'

For those who seek a window on a reality other than that defined by the Sandinistas, there is one remaining outlet, *La Prensa*. Under the stewardship of its martyred editor, Pedro Joaquín Chamorro, Sr., who was assassinated in 1978, it had become the focal point of opposition to Somoza—who had his National Guard bomb the newspaper's plant. The Sandinistas prefer to deal with *La Prensa*'s independence by censorship and by occasional closings—the latest occurring in August [1983] for publishing a story about the *turba* stoning of the home of Chamorro's widow. Pedro Joaquín Chamorro, Jr., the murdered editor's oldest son, exudes great warmth and charm. Exuberant and handsome, he manages to edit the paper and to survive each day's indignities with a keen sense of humor. For the time being, the paper is a symbol that the revolution can't afford to eliminate. And it continues to publish, within the constraints imposed by the Sandinistas, proudly proclaiming its slogan on each day's front page: "Without a Free Press, There Is No Freedom."

The government's spokesmen like to argue that censorship is a necessity imposed on them by the demands of national security in wartime. Chamorro responds with dozens of examples that undercut that claim. *La Prensa* was forbidden to run a story on rotted food on market shelves because the food was imported from Bulgaria. An article on the music of a noted Nicaraguan artist, who was attempting to create what he had called a "national" music, was censored on the grounds that it would harm the public's appreciation of Cuba, which happened to have musicians touring Nicaragua at that time. And *La Prensa* has been forbidden to run dispatches on Soviet action in Afghanistan, on Sweden's hostile reaction to Soviet subs in their waters, and on domestic happenings that might weaken appreciation for the Sandinistas.

Immediately before the Emergency Law of December 1981— the statute that among other things established the censor's bureau—*La Prensa* had printed the verbatim text of a letter, not intended for publication, that had been sent to the media by the communications minister, Frederico López. It described how the press should deal with what López termed a "delicate situation," his euphemism for the imposition of martial law in Poland. The directive stressed the need to neutralize "anti-Sovietism" and the appearance of any false analogies between Poland and Nicaragua. Clearly the regime worried about identification by the people with Solidarity—and with the concept of strikes and independent unionism. López asked that the issue be treated "dialectically," meaning that the only stories to be printed were those from the Cuban press agency Prensa Latina or from Tass, the official Soviet press agency.

The censorship is tight. Yet in another of the curious lacunae that mark the Sandinista system, the latest censored stories are tacked up on the bulletin board outside the paper's office, where the curious can read them.

La Prensa has not yet been closed, Chamorro says, "because the cost is too high to do so." How would it look, he asks, if they closed down a paper that they already censored? "Freedom means risk," Chamorro says. And he takes that risk, even though it has led at least once to the appearance at his own home in the middle of the night of *turbas*—who chanted and painted his house with slogans accusing him of being a CIA agent.

But the opposition to *La Prensa* is getting stronger, and one of the toughest advocates of suppression is Pedro Joaquín's younger brother, Carlos Fernando Chamorro, who, at age twenty-six, is editor of the official Sandinista paper, *Barricada*. Unlike Pedro, Carlos is introspective and shy. He seemed to me to be weighing each word, and to be more concerned with maintaining a correct political line than with engaging in anything approaching spontaneous conversation. *Barricada* is itself a poor imitation of Fidel Castro's *Granma*, which in turn is a Caribbean version of *Pravda*, albeit livelier. *Barricada*'s pages are filled with exhortations to serve the revolution, stories from the front or from the fields meant to build up patriotic fervor, and attacks on the provocations emanating from Honduras and Washington.

Sitting in his large, comfortable office, Carlos Chamorro defined for me what he saw as the role of the press in Nicaragua—that of a mechanism for forging a national identity needed to build the revolution. In a revolutionary state, he argued, the press cannot be "above society," holding a larger interest of its own. Any criticism must be of a "constructive" nature—not the kind that helps build counterrevolutionary sentiment.

'No Need to Hear the Other View'

But why press censorship? I asked. "We are not living in normal times," Chamorro responded, but are in the midst of a "cruel and dangerous war." He went on to argue for the necessity of closing down *La Prensa*. In Nicaragua, he told me, there is "no essential need to hear the other point of view." *La Prensa* "serves no purpose in the revolutionary process."

That *La Prensa* still publishes is testimony to the Sandinistas' need to retain sympathy in Western Europe. And not all Sandinista leaders share Carlos Chamorro's outlook. The new vice minister of the interior, Moisés Hassán, a former junta member and minister of construction, gave me his personal view that the existence of armed aggression should not in theory keep his country from developing pluralism. Hassán firmly declared that a democratic revolution needs an institutionalized voice of opposition. Only those who actively undertake to support counterrevolution, he said, should have their liberties curtailed.

The Political Opposition

Those liberties appear to be in growing jeopardy—perhaps, as former Ambassador Arturo Cruz puts it in the summer [1983] issue of *Foreign Affairs,* because so many "extreme leftist radicals consider dissent as treason." Yet dissent still does exist in Nicaragua. It centers around the Coordinadora Democrática—the formal coordinating body to which the opposition political parties belong, except for the Democratic Conservative Party, which wants no part of any Sandinista-approved structure. These parties—the Social Christian Party, the Social Democratic Party, and the Liberal Constitutionalist Party, along with the pro-government parties that belong to the Patriotic Front, are currently debating a new electoral law for Nicaragua, which allows the parties to "aspire to power," but only as long as they agree to accept "the basic principles of the Sandinista Revolution."

Adán Fletes, head of the Social Christian Party, sits in his party's ramshackle office in a lower-middle-class neighborhood of Managua. It is adorned with a giant photo of the Pope and posters of European and Latin American Christian Democratic leaders. Fletes says, "Nicaragua is not a totalitarian state. But it is not a democracy either." People are scared to join his party, which has been the victim of a few attacks by the *turbas.* Its goals, he says, are the same as during the Somoza era: free elections, better conditions, and democracy.

Fletes's party holds nine seats in the Council of State, a fifty-one-seat administrative body with no real political power, which reviews laws proposed by the junta. The governing junta and the *comandantes* are the real authority. Nevertheless the Christian Democrats try valiantly to participate in the electoral commission, despite false arrests and harassment of its members. Fletes insists he will stay and work in his country as a Nicaraguan patriot. "As long as we are here," he says, "the FSLN can't have total control. We occupy a space they cannot fill."

Others in the opposition are harsher. Miriam Argüello, a businesswoman, is now the head of the Democratic Conservative Party. Its previous chief, Adolfo Calero, fled to join the FDN (Nicaraguan Democratic Front) executive in Honduras. The party's headquarters are located in the very heart of Sandinista Managua, a few blocks from the security forces' new interrogation Center. The Conservatives have one distinct advantage. They are the repository of money from the old elite, and they can use those funds to purchase billboard space on the streets and highways. The result is unexpectedly jarring. Next to Sandinista billboards proclaiming "Arms to the People," one is likely to find the dictum "Nicaragua Is Diner's Club Country," and, most surprisingly, "Support Conservatives: For God, Order, and Liberty."

The Conservatives are the preferred party of the old established *burguesía.* Despite this, and despite the defection to the *contras* of their previous chief, the Sandinistas still allow them to publish and distribute their monthly newsletter, *La Marcha,* which routinely makes strong attacks on the government. A summer [1983] issue blazoned on its front page the headline "Conservative Party Denounces Persecution." The February issue condemned what it called the "sacrilege" committed by the Sandinista hecklers of the Pope.

'A Pretense of Pluralism'

Unlike Fletes, Miriam Argüello claims that Nicaragua is already "totalitarian." The electoral law debate is only a façade, she says, to allow the country to be dominated by Marxist-Leninists. Her party refuses to take part in the Council of State or to work in the electoral commission. The government, she says, confiscates private property, attacks the church, and teaches Marxism-Leninism to schoolchildren. "It has only a pretense of pluralism." Yet that pretense includes her freedom to sit in her party's office and expound her critical views forcefully to any and all who are willing to listen. Indeed, in August her party was allowed to hold its first political convention since the revolution.

Argüello insists that the Conservatives are patriots whose hopes for a decent future were dashed by the leftward course taken by the Sandinistas. Her role, Argüello says, is to lead the "struggle against totalitarianism," and to develop "civil resistance" to Sandinista policy—a position that gives some support to the government's charge that some of the opposition parties are close to advocating counterrevolution. Argüello argues that she seeks only to use "the last space of liberty available" to save her country from a new and disastrous civil war. But she answered a question about the *contras* by stating that all she knows about them is that they are composed of Nicaraguans who favor a "democratic alternative" to Marxism-Leninism. When asked if she did not think that the FDN leadership was composed of Somocistas and ex-*Guardia*, she responded: "We know only that they are Nicaraguans searching for the freedom of their country."

Other members of her party with whom I talked were neither as certain nor as hopeless. A prominent Conservative leader, who asked not to be named, saw real democracy in Central America as the only possible way to defeat the Sandinistas. An end to military rule in Guatemala, he argued, would hurt the propaganda of the Sandinistas more than anything else. Sitting on the man's bookshelf, I noticed, was a pamphlet I had previously spotted on sale at the Intercontinental Hotel's bookstand. It was a blistering critique of Marxism written by a Conservative intellectual, Dr. Emilio Alvarez Montalván. Updated for the recent centenary of Marx's birth, the booklet disputes the claim that Marxism is a science, and accuses Marxism of subordinating man to the state. I was told it was a key educational document used by the Conservatives to educate their young people. That such a pamphlet could still be printed and sold in Nicaragua said a great deal. The book, clearly, is not the kind of publication one could find in Castro's Cuba—to say nothing of any of the Eastern-bloc Communist countries.

The Sandinistas and Unions

Freedom to read is a key component of a democratic system. So is the political space allowed representative of the working class. The Sandinistas are worried that in a disintegrating economy in the midst of war, strikes for higher wages might exacerbate economic chaos, and even lead to a collapse of the government. To contain labor, the Sandinistas have moved to create their own trade union federation. That step has put them into immediate conflict with already established trade unions affiliated with the Christian Democrats, and even with one union led by the oldline Nicaraguan Communists.

The regime sees independent unions as potentially dangerous, and strikes as part of a CIA attempt to destabilize Nicaragua. The latter fear is not unfounded, given past CIA attempts to use American-backed unions in this manner. Legitimate grievances by Nicaraguan workers are almost automatically viewed as suspect, and patriotic union leaders find themselves considered potentially subversive. The Sandinista union federation attempts to deal with this by seeking bargaining rights previously held by unions such as the CTN (Confederation of Nicaraguan Workers) or the CUS (Trade Union Committee for Unification).

The minister of labor, Virgilio Godoy, denies charges of harassment, and claims that his ministry is "impartial and neutral." All workers complain about the sacrifices they have to make, he says, and he hopes that patriotism will lead them to understand that strikes can only worsen the economic situation. The real problem with the CUS and CTN, Godoy says, is that "sometimes they act as a union, but other times they act as a political party." Only then does the ministry have to move against them.

Union Goal: Social Democracy

That response makes union leaders bristle. Augustín Rodríguez, a CTN leader, explained to me how workers seeking representation from CTN are fired from their jobs, and how CDS block committees threaten neighbors who are known to favor CTN as their union. He also noted that their organizers have been arrested and are serving sentences ranging from six months to ten years— for the crime of trying to organize strikes.

The CTN's goal, he says, is Western-style social democracy. "We reject both capitalism and Marxism-Leninism." In Sandinista Nicaragua, despite Rodríguez' claim that his union is not political, that goal is of course a stance of political opposition. Rodríguez showed me a photo of Carlos Huembes, the union president, after he had been beaten up at the airport upon his return from a trip abroad. His head was bandaged and bloodied. Other photos Rodríguez displayed showed *turbas*—the Nicaraguan variant of 1930s American goon squads—using lead pipes to bash the heads of workers at a CTN demonstration.

It is not surprising that in the face of such provocation, the CTN has chosen to denounce Nicaragua's political course. Yet the Sandinistas allowed them to hold a national convention in 1982, at which the union passed a declaration accusing the government of "stealing the victory [over Somoza] from the people." While the CTN manifesto rejected attempts to "destabilize the current regime via armed struggle," thus rejecting the *contras,* it stressed that they would not let up in their opposition to the "harassment and violation of the rights and freedoms of those who pretend to replace the old Somocista dictatorship with a Marxist-Leninist dictatorship."

Bayardo López Pineder, secretary-general of the CUS, says pointedly that the workers, "not the FSLN, are the country." Yet he maintains that this view is not political, and he stresses that the CUS takes part in the Council of State—an official body—and that it is not opposed to the revolution. "Our only goal," he claims, is that "working people gain control of the political process."

That position, of course, implies that working people are not in control now—and the Sandinistas see their government as at one with all the workers. López goes on to cite common grievances of his membership. How can workers be expected to live, he asks me, when inflation is over 300 per cent? And he mocks the *comandantes* for living in the mansions of exiled *burguesía,* and for driving around in Mercedes Benzes. So far, the Sandinistas have not eliminated these unions—something Fidel Castro did at an early stage in Cuba's revolution. "Our presence and struggle here," López says, "keep Nicaragua from becoming totalitarian."

Uniting Against Yankee Intervention

The war has awakened fierce patriotism and nationalism. Many who might have been in opposition have come to the defense of their country against Yankee-sponsored invading forces—and all Nicaraguans know full well the sorry history of Yankee intervention here. Without doubt, CIA and Reagan administration support for the *contras* gives more internal leverage to the Sandinista hard-liners, who have all along favored a radicalizing of the country along Cuban lines.

The powerful minister of the interior, Tomás Borge, the sole remaining member of the original FSLN founders, is said to favor creation of a formal vanguard party, along with tight internal security measures to keep it permanently in control. It was Borge's ministry that closed down *La Prensa* in August [1983]. And the war undermines the position of those moderate Sandinistas who favor quick movement toward elections and the development of democratic institutions.

Moisés Hassán, again expressing his "personal view," emphasized to me that a veteran guerrilla fighter like himself did not battle "only to declare that we are turning our country over to some other power," which I took as a clear allusion to the Soviet Union. But Hassán argued that the closing off of economic aid from the West, and cuts in the sugar quota, put his revolution's "original plan to remain nonaligned in danger." Other Sandinista leaders seem less worried about this. "We will never compromise," Borge told me, adding that there is no difference between the revolution the Sandinistas promised and the one they're delivering. Unlike Hassán, Borge seems untroubled by his country's growing tilt toward the Soviets. "We are obliged to take help wherever it comes from," he told me curtly. He claims to be satisfied that his nation is one of the most democratic in Central America. "Our people have arms," he said. "This is the best proof that we are a democracy."

Human Rights Violations

But some people would say that the best proof that Nicaragua is *not* a democracy is the growing number of human rights violations. The situation is not as bleak as it is in Guatemala or El Salvador, where even moderate opponents of the regime are regularly gunned down en masse. Still, the files of Nicaragua's independent Permanent Commission on Human Rights are not encouraging. Xavier A. Cuadra, an editor of a literary-political journal who serves on the commission, claims that there were 540 political prisoners as of summer 1983, and about 90 "disappeared" persons. Most of those, he says, are workers and peasants from the

Atlantic coast, a remote area of the country where support for the government is especially thin. The work of the commission on behalf of political prisoners—an effort it describes as humanitarian and non-political—has led the Sandinistas to condemn it, and to attacks on its members by *turbas*. "When Tomás Borge was in jail and being tortured," Cuadra says with some irony, "we supported him. Now Borge calls us an agency of the CIA." But even Cuadra stresses that the Sandinistas do not torture or physically harm their prisoners. What Cuadra and others deplore is what they term "psychological torture"—an atmosphere of intimidation that works to inhibit dissent.

Nicaragua is not the totally closed society many Americans expect to find. For the time being, the opposition parties still exist and manage to function. Their effort to prevent the FSLN from emerging as a Communist vanguard party must be counted a success. Even fierce political opponents have a modicum of personal freedom, and can travel abroad regularly, though they may try to gather political support. Indeed, any Nicaraguan who wants to can leave his country for Miami or elsewhere—although such a decision means giving up his home and wealth in Nicaragua. And the revolution's friends are correct when they point to dramatic successes in the realms of literacy, health care, and agrarian reform.

Authoritarian or Totalitarian?

In some ways Nicaragua today is a good example of one of Jeane Kirkpatrick's "authoritarian" regimes. It is a reforming, modernizing military government that promises elections at some future date and permits the existence of institutions it does not control. The difference, though—and it is not a small one—is the totalitarian ambition of some its leaders. Xavier Cuadra put it this way to me: "The very concept of rights has disappeared in Nicaragua. Rights are now something conceived of as a gift from the authorities. In this sense, the human rights situation is worse than it was during the Somoza years."

"There *is* political space in Nicaragua," a knowledgeable senior Western diplomat here tells me. He notes that the internal tightening up pre-dates the stepped-up activity of the *contras*. But the war has "undoubtedly worked to pull the people together to defend the revolution," and American policy permits the Sandinistas "to pin the rap on the United States."

The drift toward repression serves to isolate the Sandinistas at home and to give their foreign enemies ammunition to be used against them. For its part, the Reagan administration claims that its goal is to get Nicaragua to restore democracy and to disentangle itself from the Soviet embrace. But the measures chosen ostensibly to achieve these aims—subsidizing the *contras'* war and economic strangulation—so far have worked to bolster support for the Sandinistas. Each time U.S. policy moves in a more confrontational direction, it damages the waning hopes of those brave Nicaraguans still here who consider themselves patriots and supporters of the revolution—but who reject the strident Marxism of the FSLN. Undermining these forces seems a strange way of promoting democracy in Nicaragua—but at present, for many reasons, the future of democracy in Sandinista Nicaragua seems bleak indeed.

28. *Foreign Christians Are a Problem*

By GERALDINE O'LEARY DE MACIAS

Focus "Imperialism can take many forms, but it is at its worst when it is combined with religious sanctimony," says the author, a former Maryknoll missionary in Nicaragua. In their eagerness to support the revolutionary cause, many American Christians ignore the protests of Christians in Nicaragua against such Sandinista practices as torture, disappearances, mass resettlement, and murder. Foreign Christians show the "worst kind of imperialism" when they claim intellectual superiority over those Nicaraguans who refuse to accept the Sandinista regime, she says.

Geraldine Macias is highly critical of foreign Christians who visit Nicaragua for a week or two and return home "convinced that they've seen all, learned all, and thus have the right and duty to pronounce on the situation there." Almost all of them know little about Nicaragua's history and misunderstand its current political reality. They tend to ignore the public statements and actions in which the Sandinista National Liberation Front (FSLN) confirms its commitment to a Marxist-Leninist view of the world. And they excuse FSLN excesses as "part of a process of political maturation."

For Macias, much of the problem stems from American sympathy with priests who have "carried their identification with Marxism to the point that it overwhelms their Christian identity." Such priests apparently accept "a partial revolution." But "man is more than advances in education and health. Man is also freedom of expression, freedom of organization, freedom to think, freedom to move," she says. The current Nicaraguan regime has shown very little inclination toward this larger understanding of freedom.

Mrs. Macias's views contradict the claims of Sandinista leader Tomás Borge (selection 24) that freedom of religion exists in Sandinista Nicaragua. Former Sandinista counterintelligence officer Miguel Bolaños (selection 25) describes explicit activities aimed at undermining the church and the Sandinistas' orchestration of the demonstrations that occurred during the Pope's visit to Managua in March 1983.

Geraldine O'Leary de Macias was a Maryknoll nun until 1974 and worked in a variety of church relief organizations in Nicaragua. Her husband, Edgard Macias, is a former vice minister of labor in the Nicaraguan Revolutionary Government.

DURING THE FOUR YEARS since the 1979 Nicaraguan Revolution, numerous groups have visited Nicaragua, among them many foreign Christians and church officials. The majority of these persons and groups stay seven to fifteen days. They return convinced that they've seen all, learned all, and thus have the right and duty to pronounce on the situation there.

Few realize or admit, however, that by doing so, and in the matter that they do so, they are demonstrating a new, even more devastating form of North American imperialism. They emphasize four areas in their defense of the Sandinista National Liberation Front (FSLN), and in all four—the revolution, Marxism-Leninism, the church, and U.S. foreign policy—they demonstrate a lack of knowledge of Nicaragua's history, its present political reality, and the country's internal events.

Misunderstanding 'Sandinista'

First, they talk about the "Sandinista revolution," using the term *Sandinista* interchangeably with *FSLN*. This is an error. The FSLN is an armed political party that claims Sandino as an inspiration. Nevertheless, almost all Nicaraguans are "Sandinistas" in that Sandino is a national hero and an inspiration because of his anti-imperialist stance. (He was also, by the way, anti-Communist.) In this sense the revolution *is* Sandinista, precisely because the majority of Nicaraguans participated in the overthrow of Somoza. But the majority of Nicaraguans were not, and are not now, members of the FSLN.

In 1974, seven political parties and two labor-union congresses formed UDEL, the first major political coalition that constituted a direct threat to the Somoza regime. The FSLN at this time was a minor guerrilla group, practically decimated by its own internal

---

Reprinted by permission from the October 16, 1983, issue of the *National Catholic Register* (© 1983 by Twin Circle Publishing Company).

problems and the systematic repression of the National Guard. The FSLN did not join UDEL but rather saw it as a threat to its own political viability. The death of Pedro Joaquín Chamorro, president of UDEL, in 1978 was the catalyst of the popular insurrection and was the prod, along with Fidel Castro, that led the FSLN to approach UDEL for collaboration. The popular support and the base organizations that UDEL had generated were needed by the FSLN. In return, the FSLN could offer UDEL arms and trained guerrillas.

It was an alliance of circumstance. The groups in UDEL had been politically active since the 1940s, although they had never obtained legal standing under Somoza and had suffered constant harassment and loss of members through exile, torture, and murder by the National Guard. They had also been almost totally ignored by U.S. foreign policy. Many of the members of the UDEL groups had, at different times, attempted to overthrow Somoza through armed movements. These groups, through their political and labor organizations, counted on tens of thousands of militants who turned out for demonstrations and who enforced nationwide strikes. The FSLN, on the other hand, founded in 1961, was constantly split into factions and never grew beyond isolated cell groups until the popular insurrections that began in 1977.

When North American Christians equate the Nicaraguan Revolution with the FSLN party, they ignore the role of the other groups that struggled, fought, and died for the revolution. And when they propagandize for the FSLN party they become accomplices in its treachery and the consequent betrayal of the Nicaraguan people.

Ignoring the Marxist-Leninist Tie

Secondly, these U.S. Christians state that Marxism-Leninism is not an official FSLN ideology. By doing so, they ignore the "72-hour document" published internally by the FSLN in November 1979, where its tactics for the eventual repression of all other political groups are detailed, its commitment to an alliance with the Soviet bloc is outlined (to be kept secret so that it could obtain financing from "bourgeois imperialists"), and its anti-North Americanism is stated. They also ignore the internal FSLN document of Christmas 1979, in which the gradual elimination of this Christian celebration is projected. They ignore the speeches given by members of the FSLN directorate in which *comandantes* state that Sandinismo is not revolutionary without Marxism-Leninism. These Christians apparently do not talk to members of the police and army, who have told me since 1979 that only Marxism-Leninism is taught in their weekly political indoctrination sessions and that any attempt to invite speakers from other political tendencies is refused. And these Christians ignore the fact that the cadres giving these political orientations are usually foreigners in Nicaragua—Cubans, PLO militants, East Germans, Marxist Chileans, and the like.

These visiting Christians apparently do not talk to those members of the CDS [Committees of Sandinista Defense] who are threatened with beatings if they do not do "vigilance duty" at night or join the militias. These members have their houses painted "CR" (counterrevolutionary) if they criticize the government or listen to rebel radio broadcasts, and they and their families are told that they will be the first killed if fighting breaks out.

The Nicaraguan Permanent Human Rights Commission has estimated that there are 10,000 to 12,000 political prisoners in jails in Nicaragua—not counting the tens of thousands of Indians held forcibly in resettlement camps. These same Indians, traditionally peace-loving and passive, have declared that they took up arms only after more than a year of submitting proof of FSLN human rights violations to international groups, where they were ignored. Thus, the present armed conflict is directly due, in many cases, to the refusal of U.S. Christians to recognize and denounce the systematic repression of dissent by the FSLN.

Misunderstanding the Christian Connection

Thirdly, these U.S. Christians point to the clergy working with the government as proof of the good will of the FSLN and the freedom of religion. As a Christian who has known and worked with these priests, I find myself dismayed by their identification with Marxism to the point that it overwhelms their Christian identity. I cannot accept, as they appear to do, a political ideology as the solution to mankind's ills. I cannot accept, as these priests do, a partial revolution. Man is more than advances in education and

health. Man is also freedom of expression, freedom of organization, freedom to think, freedom to move. I cannot accept that
Nicaraguans must give up basic human rights in order to have
literacy and vaccines. These are rights, long denied, that cannot be
the coin exchanged for other liberties.

These Christians from the United States also ignore the numerous systematic protests by Christians within Nicaragua against
tortures, disappearances, mass resettlements, and murders by the
FSLN. They ignore Managua's Archbishop Miguel Obando, who
has protested the FSLN's human rights violations and who, in a
case of almost unbelievable irony, has been called an "Antichrist"
by an FSLN commander. The presence of a few clergy in the FSLN
regime proves nothing when the words and actions of that regime
demonstrate the contrary, and it is a narrow vision that tries to use
such priests as an example of religious freedom. FSLN manipulation of these clergy is then successfully extended to being a manipulation of church groups and Christians in the United States as well.

Ignoring the Anti-FSLN Protest

Finally, these American Christians denounce U.S. government
intervention and the "CIA-supported invasion" of Nicaragua by
so-called *contras*. None so far have denounced the wider East-
West tensions created by the Soviet/Cuban infusion of military
advisors into Nicaragua, nor the militarization of the Nicaraguan
economy by the FSLN. None have denounced the wave of terrorism in Central America which uses Managua as its base. None
have recognized that there has been a steadily growing internal
protest in Nicaragua since 1979 that has been censored within the
country by the FSLN and externally by FSLN sympathizers. So it is
time that these foreign Christians admit that Nicaraguans are
capable of directing their own destiny and that tens of thousands of
Nicaraguans reject the present government.

The FSLN in 1979, at the height of the insurrection, had a
maximum of about 3,000 fighters and activists. The present anti-
FSLN guerrilla groups have a *minimum* of 15,000 fighters and a
calculated 20,000 active sympathizers. Many of these fighters are
ex-members of the FSLN, members of political parties that were in

alliance with the FSLN, and peasants and workers who actively fought with the FSLN during the insurrection; and these Nicaraguans also participated in the activation of the revolutionary process after the triumph. They fight because they have been betrayed. They fight because they want the same thing they wanted and fought for in 1979: a democratic revolution, a Nicaraguan revolution. They did not want, and they do not want, a Marxist-Leninist system in Nicaragua. They did not want, and do not want, a submission to the Soviet bloc. The present struggle is not between Sandinismo and Somocismo but between an FSLN dictatorship and a democratic revolution.

A Need for Humility

No one likes to admit that he has erred. But U.S. church groups seem especially resistant to admitting error. There is a need for humility. Nicaraguan Christians have shown this humility. They admit that they were used, that they were betrayed through their own good will and trust. By refusing to do the same, U.S. Christians demonstrate the worst kind of imperialism when they claim intellectual superiority over those Nicaraguans who have refused to accept the FSLN. U.S. Christians expect Nicaraguans to be grateful that there was a literacy campaign and a vaccination campaign, when in fact these were long overdue, and when the majority of those who participated in these campaigns were not members of the FSLN. U.S. Christians excuse FSLN excesses as part of a process of political maturation, again underrating the capacities of Nicaraguans to understand basic human freedoms and political options. Nicaraguans are not willing to accept a life of lesser freedoms, and it is colonialist and imperialist arrogance when U.S. Christians expect them to do so.

Too many foreign Christians and church groups have made the Nicaraguan Revolution, and thus the lives of many Nicaraguans, a matter of political party football. In their eagerness to be anti-Reagan they impose their own vision of history and revolutionary process on a country that strives to define its own future. They do this after lightning visits, conversations with FSLN officials and groups, and dialogues with U.S. missioners. Like all imperialists, they ignore the fact that when their "experiment" in revolution goes wrong, it is the poor of Nicaragua who will have to endure the consequences, while they and U.S. missioners return to live in the United States.

There is a need now for honest analysis, a need for true listening, and a need for humility on the part of U.S. Christians. Imperialism can take many forms, but it is at its worst when it is combined with religious sanctimony.

29. The Need for a 'Yankee Oppressor'

By LAWRENCE E. HARRISON

Focus From 1979—the year of the Sandinista victory—to 1981, Lawrence Harrison was responsible for administering U.S. assistance to the new revolutionary government in Nicaragua. The Carter administration sought to forge better relations with Nicaragua, he says, providing $120 million in aid that included 100,000 tons of food. "We tried very hard to build that new relationship. But the effort failed, principally, I believe, because the Sandinistas could not live with a positive image of the U.S. government. . . . And many in the United States cheered them on."

Harrison paints a picture of repeated rebuffs of gestures made in good faith and friendship toward the new regime, whose anthem includes the lines "we shall fight against the Yankee, enemy of humanity." Yet, upon his return to the United States, audiences at debates often jeered Harrison for his comments while applauding virtually anything said by representatives of the Sandinistas. Ironically, several of these spokesmen have since defected from the regime.

Harrison's view of U.S. behavior toward the revolutionary government immediately after the revolution should be compared with the criticisms of Tomás Borge (selection 24) and the account of events presented by Richard Ullman (selection 23).

Lawrence E. Harrison was director of the USAID mission in Nicaragua from 1979 to 1981.

433

T HE SANDINISTA GOVERNMENT of National Reconstruction was installed four years ago, on July 19, 1979. Three days later, I arrived in Nicaragua in a Flying Tigers DC-8 stretch jet loaded with food—the first of many such flights—to take charge of U.S. assistance programs, the most tangible evidence of our commitment to build a new relationship with Nicaragua.

I left Nicaragua two years later, on July 1, 1981. During those two years, the U.S. government was the most important source of food aid and one of the most important sources of financial aid to revolutionary Nicaragua. We provided assistance valued at $120 million, including 100,000 tons of food. We had tried very hard to build that new relationship. But the effort failed, principally, I believe, because the Sandinistas could not live with a positive image of the U.S. government. They did not try at all. And many in the United States cheered them on.

• Within a few months of the installation of the Government of National Reconstruction, an article appeared in the Sandinista newspaper *Barricada* announcing the imminent arrival of 600 Cuban teachers. I called on the minister of education, with whom I had been working to reactivate an old school construction loan, to express concern that so large a number of Cuban teachers would be interpreted in the United States as a Cuban takeover of the Nicaraguan education system. The minister replied that the government would welcome qualified teachers from any country.

I told him that the United States would certainly be interested in sending teachers, possibly through the Peace Corps. He responded, somewhat apologetically, "You know, we Latin Americans have a view of the Peace Corps which would make it an

Reprinted by permission from the June 30, 1983, edition of the *Washington Post* (© by the Washington Post Company).

inappropriate vehicle." (He meant, "We Latin Americans of the Left." What he had in mind was symbolized by the movie *Blood of the Condor,* which depicts Aryan-looking Peace Corps volunteers engaging in genocidal sterilization programs in Bolivia.)

At the end of 1979, as a result of the intervention of then junta member Alfonso Robelo (who is now allied with ex-Sandinista Edén Pastora's guerrilla movement), we received Sandinista approval in principle to start a Peace Corps program. After a lengthy study, the Peace Corps sent in a husband-wife team as co-directors. Both were experienced in Latin America, altruistic, and totally committed to building a new relationship with Nicaragua. After six months of being fobbed off by the Sandinistas, they left. Not one Peace Corps volunteer was accepted.

• We often expressed our concern to Sandinista officials about the line in the Sandinista anthem, "We shall fight against the Yankee, enemy of humanity." In November 1979, Jaime Wheelock, one of the most influential *comandantes* [the nine-member Sandinista ruling directorate] and a person with whom I sustained a very frank dialogue throughout my two years in Managua, told me that the word "poverty" was going to be substituted for "the Yankee." Soon thereafter, I was told the same thing by then economic czar (and Stanford MBA) Alfredo César, who has since defected. The change was never made.

• At about the same time, a U.S. congressional delegation, led by Rep. Dante Fascell (D-Fla.), visited Managua at Ambassador Larry Pezzullo's initiative. Fascell was extremely effective, as were his colleagues, Lee Hamilton (D-Ind.), Matthew McHugh (D-N.Y.), and David Obey (D-Wis.). They pressed hard on the issues of political pluralism and nonalignment in very intense meetings with both the junta, which was increasingly becoming a figurehead, and the Sandinista National Directorate, which is where the real power resides. The congressional group was particularly forceful on the question of elections. In each session they were told that national reconstruction had to be the first priority but that the Sandinistas were committed to elections.

• When Alfonso Robelo resigned from the junta in April 1980 and went into opposition, he was promptly labeled a traitor by the Sandinistas. In a conversation with Jaime Wheelock, I tried to explain our concept of dissent. I got nowhere—there is no Spanish word that accurately captures the nuances of "dissent." A day or two later I experienced similar frustration in a conversation about dissent with a young U.S.-trained cabinet minister who had on his desk a bottle of Cuban rum and a copy of *Das Kapital.* At one point, he suddenly beamed and said, in English, "Now I know what you're talking about—civil disobedience!"

He has since defected.

• A few months later, Larry Pezzullo and I were in Washington to lobby in Congress for the much delayed $75 million special appropriation for Nicaragua. The Sandinista minister of health, with whom I was working on several programs, was also in Washington, and we had dinner together. During the conversation I complained about inaccuracies and distortions in *Barricada,* the official Sandinista newspaper, and *El Nuevo Diario,* which closely followed the Sandinista line. Both sounded very much like Cuba's official newspaper, *Granma,* particularly in their treatment of the United States. The minister's response: "You don't understand revolutionary truth. What is true is what serves the ends of the revolution."

• The August 1980 ceremony to celebrate completion of the literacy campaign was a chilling experience. I had been invited to sit with the *comandantes* and the cabinet because AID had contributed food and some vehicles to the campaign. The ambassador sat in nearby stands with the diplomatic corps.

The Plaza of the Revolution was mobbed with kids in uniform shouting slogans in response to the urgings of leaders on the platform. I was reminded of films I had seen of Nuremberg in the 1930s.

Comandante Humberto Ortega gave the principal address. In the midst of a series of attacks on the United States, he announced that elections would not be held until 1985, thereby reneging on a commitment to opposition groups for early elections. Moreover, he assured his audience, the elections of 1985 would be nothing like the corrupted elections held in the United States. Larry Pezzullo and I both walked out.

• My youngest daughter, Amy, then sixteen years old, worked during the summer of 1980 as a volunteer with a Nicaraguan organization, Genesis II, which promoted breast-feeding and provided help to orphanages. The head of the organization was Geraldine Macias, a former American Maryknoll nun married to Edgard Macias, vice minister of labor. [See selection 28.] At the end of the summer (shortly after the completion of the literacy campaign), we had a get-together at our house for Amy and her co-workers. The evening was a little strained because some of the Genesis II people were totally committed to the Sandinista cause and doubtless felt uncomfortable being in the USAID director's house. The Maciases may have felt that way.

Two years later, after the Sandinista security police threatened his life, Edgard sought asylum in the Venezuelan embassy. The Maciases and their children arrived in Washington soon thereafter. They were treated as lepers by many left-leaning church people in the Washington area. The Maciases have found it very difficult to get work and have been living on a shoestring ever since. In a recent letter to friends they said:

> Since leaving Nicaragua we have had access to documentation of [the Sandinistas] and some of [their] former members that proves beyond a doubt that their plans for 1979 on were to deny political and religious freedom. Documents that also show how their methods resemble Somoza to the point they appear as a mirror image: rapes, torture, disappearances, murders, threats, and control of unions and community groups through the formation of the "elite" political party.

• During the last part of 1980, the Partners of the Americas program between the state of Wisconsin and Nicaragua, which had endured for some fifteen years, ran into trouble. Most of the activities were focused on the Atlantic coast. Among other problems, the Sandinistas attempted to take over the Partners' educational radio station (they subsequently did take it over); two Wisconsin plastic surgeons were harassed during a visit to Puerto Cabezas, where they did some highly complicated surgery free; and the Sandinistas circulated the word that Partners personnel were CIA agents.

The ambassador sent a letter to the junta expressing his concern, and I called on the *comandante* responsible for the Atlantic coast. After I ran down the litany of problems, the *comandante* said, "You have to understand, Mr. Harrison, that Americans are not very popular in this country." I replied that I had lived in Nicaragua for eighteen months, traveled extensively, and had the impression that, notwithstanding Sandinista efforts to paint us as devils, most Nicaraguans liked Americans. I added that this seemed to be particularly true on the Atlantic coast.

He paused for a few moments, then broke into a broad grin and said, "You're right."

• Norma Pineda, an accountant, was the senior Nicaraguan employee of the USAID mission, an admirable professional and human being. Her husband, Byron, had been a lieutenant colonel in a noncombatant unit of the National Guard. Just prior to their triumphal entry into Managua, the Sandinistas announced that National Guard members who had committed no crimes had nothing to fear. Despite the pleadings of family and friends to seek asylum in a nearby embassy, Byron Pineda chose to stay in his house because, as he told his wife, "I have done nothing wrong."

About two weeks after the installation of the Sandinista government, Pineda was arrested and much of his property was confiscated. He was tried some six months later and sentenced to eleven years in jail. As in thousands of other cases, all that was proven by the prosecution was that he had been a member of the Guard.

A few months later, the Sandinistas told Pineda that he would be freed if his wife would provide information on USAID activities to the government. She refused. He was, however, released to house arrest toward the end of 1980, perhaps because of representations the ambassador and I made at high levels of government. Shortly after, he was told that he would be returned to prison if he failed to persuade his wife to become a spy and if he refused to engage in spying activities himself.

A few weeks after that, Norma Pineda left Nicaragua. Byron Pineda sought asylum in the Peruvian embassy in Managua, where he has lived for more than two years.

• Late in 1980, the Latin American Studies Association, an organization of U.S. intellectuals interested in Latin America, held its annual meeting in Bloomington, Indiana. Junta member Sergio Ramírez and Foreign Minister Miguel d'Escoto attended and were given a hero's ovation. James Cheek, then deputy assistant secretary of state for Latin America, was jeered and heckled. (Cheek, one of the Foreign Service's most distinguished and enlightened specialists on Latin America, had played a crucial role in U.S. disengagement from Somoza as far back as 1974.)

In a subsequent Latin American Studies Association newsletter, Harvard professor and Association president Jorge Dominguez described the Bloomington meeting as "one of the darkest moments of my professional life . . . appalling . . . scandalous . . . damnable."

I returned to the United States on July 1, 1981, and retired from AID early in 1982. I have been at Harvard working on a book on the relationship between culture and development. In December 1982, I was asked to appear on a panel at the John F. Kennedy School of Government at Harvard. The principal speaker was Francisco Fiallos, then Nicaraguan ambassador to the United States. Despite a subdued speech on Nicaragua's economic problems, Fiallos was given a hero's ovation by the 300 people in attendance. My comments focused on Sandinista human rights abuses and, in particular, Sandinista reneging on commitments to pluralism and nonalignment. I was booed and jeered repeatedly.

One week later, Fiallos defected.

30. What's Wrong With Overthrowing the Sandinistas?

By CHARLES KRAUTHAMMER

Focus In light of what we know about the Nicaraguan regime, Charles Krauthammer asks, "Why *not* overthrow the Sandinistas?" The debate in Congress has revolved around the legality of seeking to subvert a foreign government or of supporting guerrilla groups, *contras* who believe the revolution in Nicaragua has been betrayed (see, for example, former Sandinista Edén Pastora's comments, selection 26). The Boland Amendment, adopted by Congress in 1982, prohibits the United States from supporting rebel groups intending to overthrow the Nicaraguan government, but this has led to haggling over what the rebels' intentions are and what President Reagan hopes to gain by supporting them.

Krauthammer directs our attention instead to what the Sandinistas have done: "In foreign policy, the Sandinistas have worked to destabilize Honduras and Costa Rica and to help guerrillas in El Salvador overthrow the government, which for all its weakness and brutality has a claim to legitimacy that the Sandinistas will never have: it was elected." Furthermore, the Sandinistas have hinted that they might accept Soviet missiles; this makes them potentially a direct threat to U.S. security.

Some observers have argued that since the *contras* are Somocistas—former Somoza loyalists— they are unworthy of our support. Krauthammer replies that at best this charge applies to the rebels in the north, not Edén Pastora's group. Furthermore, though the northern group does contain some Somocistas, if it were made up primarily of them the rebel cause would be "doomed from the beginning" because of the widespread and continuing hatred of Somoza in Nicaragua.

Others argue that we should not intervene in the internal affairs of other countries because various treaties and simple international ethics forbid it. Advocates of this position should logically drop support of the Boland Amendment and embrace the proposed Harkin Amendment, which would simply prohibit all aid to the *contras,* whatever their intentions. Krauthammer believes that the principle of nonintervention would apply only if we could stop Nicaragua from destabilizing other countries by hauling it "into the World Court at the Hague." This is not likely to happen.

The situation therefore presents us with a dilemma: either intervention is moral in this instance, or we prefer "the diplomatic equivalent of pacifism, namely isolationism."

Charles Krauthammer is a senior editor of the *New Republic.*

WHY *NOT* OVERTHROW the Sandinistas? The Boland Amendment, passed by Congress in 1982, prohibits the United States from directly or indirectly helping forces trying to overthrow the government of Nicaragua. The Reagan administration claims that its support for guerrillas fighting the Sandinistas conforms to the requirements of the Boland Amendment. The claim rests on the plausible assumption that two thousand or so lightly armed guerrillas are unlikely, in the near future at least, to overthrow a regime with the biggest army in Central America, backed by Cuban advisors and equipped with sophisticated Soviet- and Libyan-supplied arms.

While the Boland Amendment has not prevented the Administration from carrying on its not-so-secret war, the whole does-he-or doesn't-he question it raises has succeeded in distorting the debate over Nicaragua. Instead of asking, Should we help the guerrillas and to what end? the question has become, What does Ronald Reagan in his heart intend by helping the guerrillas? (Some in the U.S. press, including CBS News, have used the Sandinista pejorative "counterrevolutionary"—can you name a single good counterrevolutionary in human history?—in referring to the anti-government guerrillas; unlike the official press in Nicaragua, we are not obliged to use government-sanctioned nouns.)

This has led to a rather sterile debate between those who suspect the President of harboring hopes of overthrowing the Sandinistas, and those who say that his aims are more limited—to harass them, to divert their resources to an intractable guerrilla war, to make it harder for Nicaragua to supply arms to the guerrillas in El Salvador, and to pressure Nicaragua to negotiate a general settlement in Central America favorable to the United States and its allies.

But since Mr. Reagan says that it is not his intention to overthrow the Sandinistas, and since it is unlikely that anyone will produce empirical evidence to contradict him (unless, of course, he is indiscreet enough to tell King Hussein, which is as good as placing an ad in the *Wall Street Journal*), all that critics can do is call the President a liar. The charge is serious—because while every government sends diplomats abroad to lie for their country, the President would be lying at home, to Congress and his people—but since the charge is almost inherently unprovable, it prevents rather than promotes debate on the critical question of what the United States ought to be doing in Central America.

The Sandinista Record

It helps to start by asking what the Sandinistas are doing. They have reneged on promises to bring democracy to Nicaragua, methodically centralized power, suppressed the opposition, and militarized society. In short, they have betrayed their own revolution. That is the view not so much of Mr. Reagan, who was never much enamored of the revolution to begin with, but of many of Mr. Reagan's congressional critics, like Senator Patrick Leahy, who oppose efforts to overthrow the Sandinistas. More important, it is the view of Sandinista heroes like Edén Pastora (Commander Zero) and former junta leader and defense minister Alfonso Robelo, who fought Somoza and have now declared a new "war of liberation" against what they convincingly argue is a successor despotism.

In foreign policy, the Sandinistas have worked to destabilize Honduras and Costa Rica and to help guerrillas in El Salvador overthrow the government, which for all its weakness and brutality has a claim to legitimacy that the Sandinistas will never have: it was elected. The Sandinista regime threatens the United States not only by undermining American friends in the region, but more directly: defense minister Ortega has indicated that Nicaragua might accept Soviet nuclear missiles aimed at the United States. Tyranny at home, subversion abroad, and Soviet-backed threats against the United States: it might seem justification enough for American support to expatriate Nicaraguans who want to get rid of the Sandinista junta, and have no democratic means of doing so.

Critics make two principal counterarguments. First, that the guerrillas are not worthy of our support; they are Somocistas. The charge is not easily refuted, since reliable facts are scarce, but it is hard to believe that if the guerrillas were Somocistas they would be able to operate in, and draw recruits from, the countryside. Press reports indicate that they are able to do both. Press reports also indicate that the CIA, for reasons of logic if not of morality, took pains to weed out hard-line Somoza loyalists. The logic is simple: as the Sandinistas and the Vietnamese showed in victory, and as Ché Guevara in Bolivia and the Communist insurgency in Thailand showed in defeat, guerrilla war without a popular base cannot succeed. The memory of Somoza's regime is universally despised in Nicaragua. If the guerrillas are in fact Somocistas bent on restoration (and willing to overlook the fact that Somoza is dead), their war is doomed from the beginning. Even the CIA knows that. And if they are in fact not Somocistas, but instead represent many segments of Nicaraguan society, including Miskito Indians, the rural peasantry, and betrayed urban democrats, why not support them? Furthermore, the charge of Somocista control cannot be made at all against a second anti-Sandinista group, the Democratic Revolutionary Alliance, headed by Pastora and Robelo, which has just opened a second front (their undisguised aim, contra Boland, is to overthrow the Sandinistas) inside Nicaragua. Why deny *them* support?

Because, goes the alternative argument, we are bound by honor and by treaties like the OAS charter not to interfere in the internal affairs of other countries. There is a certain naïveté in this position. We are dealing here not with adversaries who play cricket; they promote revolution. For them that is not a breach of any code; on the contrary, it is a historic responsibility. If the United States could get Nicaragua to stop its efforts to destabilize El Salvador (no paradigm of democracy) and Costa Rica (a paradigm of democracy) by hauling Nicaragua into the World Court at The Hague, there would be no need to convince it by means of an exile army.

There is also a certain inconsistency in the critics' case. After all, we give arms, and are wholly justified in giving arms, to anti-government guerrillas in Afghanistan; and we support two non-Communist guerrilla factions in Cambodia. It would be hard to imagine the grounds for opposing American support to, say, anti-Qaddafi Libyan elements or Iranian factions less barbaric than the current regime.

Never an Abstract Choice

The question in foreign policy is never an abstract choice between interference and noninterference; it's a moral and prudential calculation of what circumstances justify interference. If the Sandinistas just wanted to run a domestic tyranny, that, in my view, would not be sufficient justification for American efforts to overthrow them: there are simply too many tyrannies in the world for that to be the criterion for American action. But they choose, in addition, to be an exporting tyranny, and a Soviet base. If that is not justification for the United States to interfere, then what is?

If the answer to that question is "nothing," then what we have is not a debate on the merits of intervention in Nicaragua, but a debate over the diplomatic equivalent of pacifism, namely isolationism (indeed a super-isolationism: the isolationists of the '20s and '30s sought only to keep us out of European entanglements). If Nicaragua, and not isolationism, is the issue, then it is time to clarify the debate. We might begin by repealing the Boland Amendment. Those who believe that the United States has no business in Nicaragua should instead insist on the adoption of the Harkin Amendment, which bans any aid to those fighting the government in Nicaragua. Those who believe that the fall of the Sandinistas is a consummation devoutly to be wished should stop quibbling about the terms of the Boland Amendment, and demand instead that the Administration make its secret war open and thus subject to honest debate.

Removing the secrecy surrounding the war would enable ordinary Americans and Congress to make an informed judgment as to whether this insurgency has any chance of success. If it does not, then we have the strongest possible argument against current policy: prudence dictates that the United States not embark on support for another doomed cause. The perversity of the present situation is that under the Boland Amendment, support for the guerrillas is permitted, but *only* if they cannot—or if we will not permit them to—succeed. That is no way to run a foreign policy.

Caribbean Basin Initiative

President Ronald Reagan introduced his plan for economic recovery of the Caribbean and Central American countries in the following address to the Organization of American States in Washington, D.C., February 24, 1982.

The principles which are embodied by the Organization of American States —democracy, self-determination, economic development, and collective security—are at the heart of U.S. foreign policy. The United States of America is a proud member of this organization. What happens anywhere in the Americas affects us in this country. In that very real sense, we share a common destiny. We, the peoples of the Americas, have much more in common than geographical proximity. For over 400 years our peoples have shared the dangers and dreams of building a new world. From colonialism to nationhood, our common quest has been for freedom.

Most of our forebears came to this hemisphere seeking a better life for themselves. They came in search of opportunity and, yes, in search of God. Virtually all descendants of the land and immigrants alike have had to fight for independence. Having gained it, they've had to fight to retain it. There were times when we even fought each other.

Gradually, however, the nations of this hemisphere developed a set of common principles and institutions that provided the basis for mutual protection. Some twenty years ago, John F. Kennedy caught the essence of our unique mission when he said it was up to the New World "to demonstrate . . . that man's unsatisfied aspiration for economic progress and social justice can best be achieved by free men working within a framework of democratic institutions."

In the commitment to freedom and independence, the peoples of this hemisphere are one. In this profound sense, we are all Americans. Our principles are rooted in self-government and nonintervention. We believe in the rule of law. We know that a nation cannot be liberated by depriving its people of liberty. We know that a state cannot be free when its independence is subordinated to a foreign power. And we know that a government cannot be democratic if it refuses to take the test of a free election.

We have not always lived up to these ideals. All of us at one time or another in our history have been politically weak, economically backward, socially unjust, or unable to solve our problems through peaceful means. My own country, too, has suffered internal strife including a tragic civil war. We have known economic misery and once tolerated racial and social injustice. And, yes, at times we have

447

behaved arrogantly and impatiently toward our neighbors. These experiences have left their scars, but they also help us today to identify with the struggle for political and economic development in the other countries of this hemisphere.

Out of the crucible of our common past, the Americas have emerged as more equal and more understanding partners. Our hemisphere has an unlimited potential for economic development and human fulfillment. We have a combined population of more than 600 million people; our continents and our islands boast vast reservoirs of food and raw materials; and the markets of the Americas have already produced the highest standard of living among the advanced as well as the developing countries of the world. The example that we could offer to the world would not only discourage foes, it would project like a beacon of hope to all of the oppressed and impoverished nations of the world. We are the New World, a world of sovereign and independent states that today stand shoulder to shoulder with a common respect for one another and a greater tolerance of one another's shortcomings.

Some two years ago when I announced as a candidate for the Presidency, I spoke of an ambition I had to bring about an accord with our two neighbors here on the North American continent. Now, I was not suggesting a common market or any kind of formal arrangement. "Accord" was the only word that seemed to fit what I had in mind. I was aware that the United States has long enjoyed friendly relations with Mexico and Canada, that our borders have no fortifications. Yet it seemed to me that there was a potential for a closer relationship than had yet been achieved. Three great nations share the North American continent with all its human and natural resources. Have we done all we can to create a relationship in which each country can realize its potential to the fullest?

Now, I know in the past the United States has proposed policies that we declared would be mutually beneficial not only for North America but also for the nations of the Caribbean and Central and South America. But there was often a problem. No matter how good our intentions were, our very size may have made it seem that we were exercising a kind of paternalism.

At the time I suggested a new North American accord, I said I wanted to approach our neighbors not as someone with yet another plan but as a friend seeking their ideas, their suggestions as to how we would become better neighbors. I met with President López Portillo in Mexico before my inauguration and with Prime Minister Trudeau in Canada shortly after I had taken office. We have all met several times since—in the United States, in Mexico, and in Canada. And I believe that we have established a relationship better than any our three countries have ever known before.

Economic Health of the Caribbean Basin

Today I would like to talk about our other neighbors—neighbors by the sea—some two dozen countries of the Caribbean and Central America. These countries are not unfamiliar names from some isolated corner of the world far from home. They're very close to home. The country of El Salvador, for example, is nearer to Texas than Texas is to Massachusetts. The Caribbean region is a vital strategic and commercial artery for the United States. Nearly half of our trade, two-thirds of our imported oil, and over half of our imported strategic minerals pass through the Panama Canal or the Gulf of Mexico. Make no mistake: The well-being and security of our neighbors in this region are in our own vital interest.

Economic health is one of the keys to a secure future for the Caribbean Basin and our neighbors there. I'm happy to say that Mexico, Canada, and Venezuela have joined in this search for ways to help these countries realize their economic potential. Each of our four nations has its own unique position and approach. Mexico and Venezuela are helping to offset energy costs to Caribbean Basin countries by means of an oil facility that is already in operation. Canada is doubling its already significant economic assistance.

We all seek to insure that the peoples of this area have the right to preserve their own national identities, to improve their economic lot, and to develop their

POTENTIAL BENEFICIARIES OF THE CARIBBEAN BASIN INITIATIVE

Total Population: 39 million
Total GDP (Gross Domestic Product): $45 billion

Country	Population (millions of persons)	GDP ($ millions)	Exports to U.S. ($ millions)	Imports from U.S. (% of total)
Bahamas	.22	1,267	1,382	51
Barbados	.25	815	96	28
Belize	.15	165	60	40
Cayman Islands	.15	—	3	—
Costa Rica	2.24	4,847	356	36
Dominican Republic	5.43	6,733	786	55
Eastern Caribbean (Anguilla, Antigua and Barbuda, British Virgin Islands, Dominica, Grenada, Montserrat, Saint Christopher-Nevis, Saint Lucia, Saint Vincent and the Grenadines)	.65	500	37	45
El Salvador	4.50	3,484	427	30
Jamaica	2.19	2,402	383	29
Guatemala	7.26	7,852	435	38
Guyana	.79	524	120	25
Haiti	5.01	1,453	252	89
Honduras	3.69	2,538	419	40
Netherlands Antilles	.27	—	2,564	—
Nicaragua	2.70	1,566	211	28
Panama	1.94	3,511	330	48
Surinam	.39	109	1,030	30
Trinidad and Tobago	1.14	6,708	2,378	39
Turks and Caicos Islands	.07	—	3	—

political institutions to suit their own unique social and historical needs. The Central American and Caribbean countries differ widely in culture, personality, and needs. Like America itself, the Caribbean Basin is an extraordinary mosaic of Hispanics, Africans, Asians, and Europeans, as well as native Americans.

At the moment, however, these countries are under economic siege. In 1977, one barrel of oil was worth 5 pounds of coffee or 155 pounds of sugar. To buy that same barrel of oil today, these small countries must provide five times as much coffee (nearly 26 pounds) or almost twice as much sugar (283 pounds). This economic disaster is consuming our neighbors' money, reserves, and credit, forcing thousands of people to leave for other countries—for the United States, often illegally—and shaking even the most established democracies. And economic disaster has provided a fresh opening to the enemies of freedom, national independence, and peaceful development.

Proposed Economic Program

We've taken the time to consult closely with other governments in the region, both sponsors and beneficiaries, to ask them what they need and what they think will work. And we've labored long to develop an economic program that integrates trade, aid, and investment—a program that represents a long-term commitment to the countries of the Caribbean and Central America to make use of the magic of the marketplace, the market of the Americas, and to earn their own way toward self-sustaining growth.

At the Cancún summit last October, I presented a fresh view of a development which stressed more than aid and government intervention. As I pointed out then, nearly all of the countries that have succeeded in their development over the past thirty years have done so on the strength of market-oriented policies and vigorous participation in the international economy. Aid must be complemented by trade and investment.

The program I'm proposing today puts these principles into practice. It is an integrated program that helps our neighbors help themselves, a program that will create conditions under which creativity and private entrepreneurship and self-help can flourish. Aid is an important part of this program because many of our neighbors need it to put themselves in a starting position from which they can begin to earn their own way. But this aid will encourage private sector activities, not displace them.

First. The centerpiece of the program that I am sending to the Congress is free trade for Caribbean Basin products exported to the United States. Currently, some 87 per cent of Caribbean exports already enter U.S. markets duty free under the generalized system of preferences. These exports, however, cover only the limited range of existing products, not the wide variety of potential products these talented and industrious peoples are capable of producing under the free trade arrangement that I am proposing. Exports from the area will receive duty-free treatment for twelve years. Thus, new investors will be able to enter the market knowing that their products will receive duty-free treatment for at least the payoff lifetime of their investments. Before granting duty-free treatment, we will discuss with each country its own self-help measures.

The only exception to the free trade concept will be textile and apparel products because these products are covered now by other international agreements. However, we will make sure that our immediate neighbors have more liberal quota arrangements.

This economic proposal is as unprecedented as today's crisis in the Caribbean. Never before has the United States offered a preferential trading arrangement to any region. This commitment makes unmistakably clear our determination to help our neighbors grow strong. The impact of this free trade approach will develop slowly. The economies that we seek to help are small. Even as they grow, all the protections now available to U.S. industry, agriculture, and labor against disruptive imports will remain. And growth in the Caribbean will benefit everyone with American exports finding new markets.

Second. To further attract investment, I will ask the Congress to provide significant tax incentives for investment in the Caribbean Basin. We also stand ready to negotiate bilateral investment treaties with interested basin countries.

Third. I'm asking for a supplemental fiscal year 1982 appropriation of $350 million to assist those countries which are particularly hard hit economically. Much of this aid will be concentrated on the private sector. These steps will help foster the spirit of enterprise necessary to take advantage of the trade and investment portions of the program.

Fourth. We will offer technical assistance and training to assist the private sector in the basin countries to benefit from the opportunities of this program. This will include investment promotion, export marketing, and technology transfer efforts, as well as programs to facilitate adjustments to greater competition and production in agriculture and industry. I intend to seek the active participation of the business community in this joint undertaking. The Peace Corps already has 861 volunteers in Caribbean Basin countries and will give special emphasis to recruiting volunteers with skills in developing local enterprise.

Fifth. We will work closely with Mexico, Canada, and Venezuela, all of whom have already begun substantial and innovative programs of their own to encourage stronger international efforts, to coordinate our own development measures with their vital contributions, and with those of other potential donors like Colombia. We will also encourage our European, Japanese, and other Asian allies as well as multilateral development institutions to increase their assistance in the region.

Sixth. Given our special valued relationship with Puerto Rico and the U.S. Virgin Islands, we will propose special measures to insure that they also will benefit and prosper from this program. With their strong traditions of democracy and free enterprise, they can play leading roles in the development of the area.

This program has been carefully prepared. It represents a farsighted act by our own people at a time of considerable economic difficulty at home. I wouldn't propose it if I were not convinced that it is vital to the security interests of this nation and of this hemisphere. The energy, the time, and the treasure we dedicate to assisting the development of our neighbors now can help to prevent the much larger expenditures of treasure as well as human lives which would flow from their collapse.

One early sign is positive. After a decade of falling income and exceptionally high unemployment, Jamaica's new leadership is reducing bureaucracy, dismantling unworkable controls, and attracting new investment. Continued outside assistance will be needed to tide Jamaica over until market forces generate large increases in output and employment, but Jamaica is making freedom work.

Threats to Security

I've spoken up to now mainly of the economic and social challenges to development. But there are also other dangers. A new kind of colonialism stalks the world today and threatens our independence. It is brutal and totalitarian. It is not of our hemisphere, but it threatens our hemisphere and has established footholds on American soil for the expansion of its colonialist ambitions.

The events of the last several years dramatize two different futures which are possible for the Caribbean area: either the establishment or restoration of moderate, constitutional governments with economic growth and improved living standards; or further expansion of political violence from the extreme left and the extreme right resulting in the imposition of dictatorships and inevitably more economic decline and human suffering.

The positive opportunity is illustrated by the two-thirds of the nations in the area which have democratic governments. The dark future is foreshadowed by the poverty and repression of Castro's Cuba, the tightening grip of the totalitarian left in Grenada and Nicaragua, and the expansion of Soviet-backed, Cuban-managed support for violent revolution in Central America.

The record is clear. Nowhere in its whole sordid history have the promises of Communism been redeemed. Everywhere it has exploited and aggravated temporary economic suffering to seize power and then to institutionalize economic deprivation and suppress human rights. Right now, six million people worldwide are refugees from Communist systems. Already, more than a million Cubans alone have fled Communist tyranny.

Our economic and social program cannot work if our neighbors cannot pursue their own economic and political future in peace but must divert their resources, instead, to fight imported terrorism and armed attack. Economic progress cannot be made while guerrillas systematically burn, bomb, and destroy bridges, farms, and power and transportation systems—all with the deliberate intention of worsening economic and social problems in hopes of radicalizing already suffering people.

Our Caribbean neighbors' peaceful attempts to develop are feared by the foes of freedom because their success will make the radical message a hollow one. Cuba and its Soviet backers know this. Since 1978, Havana has trained, armed, and directed extremists in guerrilla warfare and economic sabotage as part of a campaign to exploit troubles in Central America and the Caribbean. Their goal is to establish Cuban-style Marxist-Leninist dictatorships. Last year, Cuba received 66,000 tons of war supplies from the Soviet Union—more than in any year since the 1962 missile crisis. Last month, the arrival of additional high-performance MiG-23/Floggers gave Cuba an arsenal of more than 200 Soviet warplanes—far more than the military aircraft inventories of all other Caribbean Basin countries combined.

For almost two years, Nicaragua has served as a platform for covert military action. Through Nicaragua, arms are being smuggled to guerrillas in El Salvador and Guatemala. The Nicaraguan government even admits the forced relocation of about 8,500 Miskito Indians. And we have clear evidence that since late 1981, many Indian communities have been burned to the ground and men, women, and children killed.

The Nicaraguan junta cabled written assurances to the OAS in 1979 that it intended to respect human rights and hold free elections. Two years later, these commitments can be measured by the postponement of elections until 1985; by repression against free trade unions, against the media and minorities; and—in defiance of all international civility—by the continued export of arms and subversion to neighboring countries.

Two years ago, in contrast, the government of El Salvador began an unprecedented land reform. It has repeatedly urged the guerrillas to renounce violence, to join in the democratic process—an election in which the people of El Salvador could determine the government they prefer. Our own country and other American nations through the OAS have urged such a course. The guerrillas have refused. More than that, they now threaten violence and death to those who participate in such an election.

Can anything make more clear the nature of those who pretend to be supporters of so-called wars of liberation? A determined propaganda campaign has sought to mislead many in Europe and certainly many in the United States as to the true nature of the conflict in El Salvador. Very simply, guerrillas, armed and supported by and through Cuba, are attempting to impose a Marxist-Leninist dictatorship on the people of El Salvador as part of a larger imperialistic plan. If we do not act promptly and decisively in defense of freedom, new Cubas will arise from the ruins of today's conflicts. We will face more totalitarian regimes tied militarily to the Soviet Union; more regimes exporting subversion; more regimes so incompetent yet so totalitarian that their citizens' only hope becomes that of one day migrating to other American nations, as in recent years they have come to the United States.

I believe free and peaceful development of our hemisphere requires us to help governments confronted with aggression from outside their borders to defend themselves. For this reason, I will ask the Congress to provide increased security assistance to help friendly countries hold off those who would destroy their chances for economic and social progress and political democracy. Since 1947, the Rio Treaty has established reciprocal defense responsibilities linked to our common democratic ideals. Meeting these responsibilities is all the more important when an outside power supports terrorism and insurgency to destroy any possibility of freedom and democracy. Let our friends and our adversaries understand that we will do whatever is prudent and necessary to insure the peace and security of the Caribbean area.

In the face of outside threats, security for the countries of the Caribbean and

Central American area is not an end in itself but a means to an end. It is a means toward building representative and responsive institutions, toward strengthening pluralism and free private institutions—churches, free trade unions, and an independent press. It is a means for nurturing the basic human rights that freedom's foes would stamp out. In the Caribbean we above all seek to protect those values and principles that shape the proud heritage of this hemisphere. I have already expressed our support for the coming election in El Salvador. We also strongly support the Central American Democratic Community formed this January by Costa Rica, Honduras, and El Salvador. The United States will work closely with other concerned democracies inside and outside the area to preserve and enhance our common democratic values.

We will not, however, follow Cuba's lead in attempting to resolve human problems by brute force. Our economic assistance, including the additions that are part of the program I've just outlined, is more than five times the amount of our security assistance. The thrust of our aid is to help our neighbors realize freedom, justice, and economic progress.

We seek to exclude no one. Some, however, have turned from their American neighbors and their heritage. Let them return to the traditions and common values of this hemisphere, and we all will welcome them. The choice is theirs.

The Need for Assistance

As I have talked these problems over with friends and fellow citizens here in the United States, I'm often asked, "Why bother? Why should we try to help?" I tell them we must help because the people of the Caribbean and Central America are in a fundamental sense fellow Americans. Freedom is our common destiny. And freedom cannot survive if our neighbors live in misery and oppression. In short, we must do it because we're doing it for each other.

Our neighbors' call for help is addressed to us all here in this country—to the Administration, to the Congress, to millions of Americans from Miami to Chicago, from New York to Los Angeles. This is not Washington's problem; it is the problem of all the people of this great land and of all the other Americas—the great and sovereign republics of North America, the Caribbean Basin, and South America. The Western Hemisphere does not belong to any one of us—we belong to the Western Hemisphere. We are brothers historically as well as geographically.

Now, I'm aware that the United States has pursued good neighbor policies in the past. These policies did some good, but they're inadequate for today. I believe that my country is now ready to go beyond being a good neighbor to being a true friend and brother in the community that belongs as much to others as to us. That, not guns, is the ultimate key to peace and security for us all.

We have to ask ourselves why has it taken so long for us to realize the God-given opportunity that is ours. These two great land masses north and south, so rich in virtually everything we need—together our more than 600 million people can develop what is undeveloped, can eliminate want and poverty, can show the world that our many nations can live in peace, each with its own customs and language and culture but sharing a love for freedom and a determination to resist outside ideologies that would take us back to colonialism.

We return to a common vision. Nearly a century ago a great citizen of the Caribbean and the Americas, José Martí, warned that "mankind is composed of two sorts of men—those who love and create and those who hate and destroy." Today more than ever the compassionate, creative peoples of the Americas have an opportunity to stand together; to overcome injustice, hatred, and oppression; and to build a better life for all the Americas.

I have always believed that this hemisphere was a special place with a special destiny. I believe we are destined to be the beacon of hope for all mankind. With God's help, we can make it so. We can create a peaceful, free, and prospering hemisphere based on our shared ideals and reaching from pole to pole of what we proudly call the New World.

Contadora Proposals
For Peace in Central America

The following "document of objectives" adopted by the Contadora group (Mexico, Venezuela, Colombia, and Panama) was presented to the secretary general of the United Nations on October 6, 1983, by the foreign secretary of Mexico, Bernardo Sepulveda.

WHEREAS:

The prevailing situation in Central America, characterized by an atmosphere of tension which threatens security and peaceful coexistence in the region, requires for its solution the observance of the **principles of international law** that regulate relations among states, particularly:

- The free determination of the peoples.
- The nonintervention.
- The equal sovereignty of states.
- The peaceful settlement of controversies.
- The abstention from resorting to threats or the use of force.
- The respect for territorial integrity of states.
- The pluralism in its various manifestations.
- The enforcement of democratic institutions.
- The promotion of social justice.
- The international cooperation for development.
- The observance and encouragement of human rights.
- The proscription of terrorism and subversion.
- The eagerness to reconstruct the Central American fatherland through the progressive integration of its economic, legal, and social institutions.
- The need for economic cooperation among the Central American states, in order to fundamentally contribute to the development of their peoples and strengthen their autonomy.
- The commitment to create, promote, and strengthen democratic systems in all countries of the region.
- The unjust economic, political, and social structures that intensify the conflicts in Central America.
- The need to stop the tensions and establish the bases for understanding and solidarity among countries in the area.

457

- The arms race and the increasing traffic of arms in Central America, which deteriorate political relations in the region and divert economic resources which could be used for development.
- The presence of foreign advisors and other forms of foreign military interference in the zone.
- The risk of using the territory of the Central American states to undertake armed and political destabilizing actions against others.
- The need for political compromise to facilitate dialogue and understanding in Central America, to dismiss the danger of generalized conflicts and set into motion mechanisms which can ensure harmonic coexistence and security for its people.

HENCE:

They express their intention to achieve the following **objectives:**

- To reduce tension and end situations of conflict in the area, abstaining from any action which may endanger political confidence or jeopardize peace, security, and stability in the region.
- To ensure strict compliance with the principles of international law previously outlined, since nonobservance will determine responsibilities.
- To respect and guarantee the observance of human, political, civil, economic, social, religious, and cultural rights.
- To adopt measures conducive to the establishment and, in some cases, the improvement of democratic, representative, and pluralistic systems, which would guarantee effective popular participation in decision-making and ensure free access of the different currents of opinion to honest and periodic electoral processes, which should be based on a total respect for citizens' rights.
- To promote national actions towards reconciliation in cases of deep social divisions, allowing participation in democratic political procedures according to the law.
- To create political conditions directed to guarantee international security and the integrity and sovereignty of the states of the region.
- To halt the arms race in all its manifestations and to initiate negotiations on the subject of control and reduction of the current arms inventory and actual number of arms.
- To forbid the establishment in the region of foreign military bases or any other form of foreign military interference.
- To concert agreements to reduce, and eventually eliminate, the presence of foreign military advisors and other forms of foreign military and security actions.
- To establish internal mechanisms of control for the prevention of the traffic of arms from the territory of one country of the region to another.
- To eliminate the traffic of arms, within the region or from abroad, forwarded to persons, organizations, or groups attempting to undermine Central American governments.
- To prevent the use of their own territory by, and neither to lend nor to allow military or logistic support to, persons, organizations, or groups attempting to destabilize Central American governments.

• To abstain from promoting or supporting acts of terrorism, subversion, or sabotage in the countries of the area.

• To create mechanisms and coordinate systems of direct communication aimed to prevent or, if necessary, to resolve incidents among states of the region.

• To continue with the humanitarian aid directed to help Central American refugees who have been displaced from their country of origin, providing also conditions suitable for their voluntary repatriation, in consultation or cooperation with the high commissioner of the United Nations—UNHC—and other interested international organizations.

• To undertake economic and social development programs with the purpose of achieving a higher standard of living and a more equitable distribution of wealth.

• To revitalize and normalize the mechanisms of economic integration in order to achieve a continuous economic development based on solidarity and mutual benefit.

• To negotiate the acquisition of external monetary resources which will guarantee additional means to finance the reactivation of intraregional commerce, overcome the severe difficulties in the balance of payments, secure working capital funds, support programs for the expansion and restructuration of the systems of production, and promote short- and long-term investment projects.

• To search for a greater and wider access to international markets in order to expand the commercial flow between Central American countries and the rest of the world, in particular with industrialized countries, through a revision of commercial practices and elimination of tariffs and non-tariff barriers, and while assuring profitable and fair prices for the products exported by countries of the region.

• To promote mechanisms of technical cooperation to plan, program, and execute multi-sectorial projects of investment and promotion of commerce.

The ministers of foreign relations of the Central American countries initiated, with the participation of the Contadora group countries, consultations with the purpose of preparing the conclusion of agreements and adopting the mechanisms necessary to formalize and develop the objectives contained in this document, and to ensure the establishment of appropriate systems of control and verification. To that effect, the initiatives presented will be taken into account in the meetings summoned by the Contadora group.

APPENDIX C

War Damage to the Salvadoran Economy, 1979-82

This assessment of war-related damage was produced by the United States embassy in San Salvador in March 1983. Its "provisional and to some extent conjectural nature" is acknowledged in the document.

By almost any measure, the Salvadoran economy has been in a three-year tailspin. Since 1979 real GDP [gross domestic product] declined by about 25 per cent; export earnings dropped by 33 per cent from 1979 to 1982—from $1,113.2 million to $738 million. Real per capita income fell by an estimated 30 per cent from $670 in 1979 to $470 in 1982.

There is an obvious connection between the decline of the Salvadoran economy and the war. Although not all the decline can be attributed to the violence, the guerrillas have publicly stated that the economy is the principal target of their military strategy. USAID [U.S. Agency for International Development] recently funded a study to determine the extent of physical damage to the public-sector economic infrastructure. But the war's effects on the economy go beyond the destruction of this infrastructure and include a myriad of direct and indirect costs to the private as well as the public sector.

So far as we are aware, no one has yet aggregated the overall damage to the economy from the war, probably because data are at best scanty and unreliable. However, given the clear relationship between the economic costs of the war and the Salvadoran people's ability to continue their struggle, we have attempted to quantify the economic damage. We have divided our assessment into two parts—*direct costs of the war* (lost agricultural and industrial production and capital; direct physical damage and lost revenues in the commercial sector; payments of war taxes; increased security/protection costs; physical damage to the economic infrastructure; increased budgetary outlays for the military; and the cost to the government of El Salvador of caring for citizens displaced by the violence) and *indirect costs of the war* (balance-of-payments effects such as lost foreign-exchange earnings owing to declining agricultural production, capital flight, and increased food and oil imports; the drying up of foreign-source commercial credits; budget revenue losses owing to the contraction of economic activity; the decline in budgetary expenditures for social programs; and the increase in unemployment).

461

Because of the scarcity of data, most of our assessment of the direct costs of the war is based on our own estimates and our own assumptions as to what might have happened had there been no war. Obviously this exercise in estimating has its pitfalls and should not be taken as the final word on the economic costs of the war. We did not attempt to put an overall figure on the more nebulous category of indirect costs because in some cases we would be comparing apples and oranges; in others there would be double counting with direct costs (e.g., losses of export receipts resulting from reduced production of export crops); for some, costs were not measurable, or we were unable to make reasonable assumptions about conditions in the absence of war. However, we have outlined what we perceive to be the fundamental dimensions of the economic loss within each category of indirect costs, and the impact on the economy.

DIRECT COSTS OF THE WAR

A. Agricultural Sector

1. *Lost Production.* In the absence of good crop statistics broken down geo-graphically, which might provide a more direct measure of production lost to guerrilla activity, we have had to devise proxy measures to get a dollar figure for lost production either because fields were idled by guerrilla activity or because crops were destroyed. We measured actual production during the war years (1979-82) against a three-year average production prior to the war (the averaging intended to even out annual fluctuations due to climatic conditions, for example). The total of the differences is the "production lost" itemized below. We then used a four-year average of domestic retail prices to determine the hypothetical value of lost production of basic grains, and world market prices for export crops. Finally, based on our knowledge of conditions (weather, economic, geography, political) affecting each crop during the 1979-82 period, we assigned a proportion or percentage of the damage we felt could reasonably be attributed to violence.

Basic-grains production has suffered relatively less than export crops, in part because prices for human-consumption grains paid by the Salvadoran govern-

Crop	Production Lost (thousands of pounds)	Value of Loss (millions)	Loss Attributable to Violence
Corn	0	$ 0	0%
Beans	2,927.4	0.9	80
Sorghum	151,071.0	12.2	80
Rice	0	0	0
Cotton	234,601.2	86.3	50
Sugar	777,710.2	65.7	50
Coffee	47,800.0	14.0	20
Milk (bottles)	96,098.0	23.4	80
Beef	27,230.0	32.7	80

ment supply agency remain high. Production of sorghum, which is almost entirely consumed by livestock, dropped precipitously largely because of a decline in the herd size, in turn indirectly related to widespread violence in the countryside and the ease with which cattle can be "rustled." In all basic grains, the geographic distribution of production appears to have shifted noticeably away from the most conflictive three regions, indicating a close relationship between declines in production and violence. We have therefore conservatively attributed 80 per cent of the decline in basic grains to violence. For export crops, economic factors such as low international prices and uncertainty about the land reform explain a significant portion of the decline. In the case of coffee, exports rather than production is the operative constraint owing to international quotas and large surplus stocks. Therefore, while damage to farms has adversely affected individual growers, the damage to the economy as a whole has probably not been great, and we have therefore assigned only one-fifth of the decline in production to the war. The bulk of the coffee produced in El Salvador is grown in the relatively safe westernmost region 1 (Ahuachapán, Sonsonate, and Santa Ana).

2. *Protection and War Taxes*. These constitute a significant cost to agricultural producers, particularly the larger farms (including Phase 1 co-ops) which generally produce for export and are forced by the guerrillas either to take costly security measures or to pay war taxes. Smaller farmers who produce basic grains generally pay no taxes or protection because of guerrilla efforts to win *campesinos'* favor, and because of lack of resources. According to recent observations of the protection/war tax situation among Phase 1 co-ops, large farms are required to employ as many as five full-time guards each. Each costs about $215 per month, including salary, uniform, meals, transport, shelter. We have not attempted to estimate total protection/war taxes; however, this cost probably runs into the tens of millions of dollars.

3. *Processing Plants and Warehouses*. Costs of the war to processing plants and warehouses include (a) damage to the physical infrastructure from direct attacks by guerrilla forces and (b) costs of extra protection. None of our contacts in sugar, coffee, and cotton sectors admitted paying war taxes. Processors seem to realize that the mills are attractive targets and have thus allocated the resources necessary to defend them.

a. *Damage from direct attacks*

Coffee	$0.8 million
Cotton	0.5
Sugar	0.1
	$1.4 million

b. *Extra protection costs per year*

Coffee	$1.5 million
Cotton	1.6
Sugar	0.6
	$3.7 × 4 years = $14.8 million

4. *Agricultural Machinery Damaged or Destroyed.* We have been unable to obtain information on the value of farm machinery damaged or abandoned as a result of the conflict, but this has been considerable. The director of civil aviation has estimated damage to crop-dusting aircraft from terrorist actions at $363,000 between 1979 and the present (a total of fourteen aircraft lost or damaged).

B. Industrial and Commercial Sectors

The principal components of war damage to the commercial and manufacturing sectors are direct destruction of plant and equipment, lost production in the case of manufacturers, and for commercial firms, the loss in salary payments (this last a rough proxy for value added in commercial activities). Our estimates of lost production are conservative and are based on 1978 figures adjusted only for inflation.

Total capital destroyed	$ 1.7 million
Manufacturing production lost	90.1
Salaries lost in commercial and service enterprises	6.0
	$97.8 million

The figures cover the period January 1, 1979, through March 31, 1982, and include only those firms which were attacked so severely that they did not reopen. Our estimates do not include partial damage, of which there has been considerable. Lost production of commercial enterprises was estimated by multiplying the average wage in the commercial sector by the number of employees in the enterprises which have been closed; actual payrolls are not available. Conditions of industry suggest most of these workers remain unemployed. Guerrilla violence has proven a greater threat to small businesses than to large firms. This may be because small businesses do not have sufficient resources to pay for protection. Most of our contacts in industry and commerce claim not to pay "war taxes."

C. Economic Infrastructure

Costs to the economic infrastructure, including added service and maintenance costs, is largely based on an extensive study completed on December 6, 1982, by an AID contractor. The bus damage figure is derived from Ministry of Planning estimates.

Electrical system	$39.6 million
Rail system	5.5
Telephone system	15.0
Bridges and public works equipment	16.4
Water	0.8
Government buildings and vehicles	7.5
Buses (242 totally and 362 partially destroyed)	12.8
Petroleum refinery	0.5
	$98.1 million

Damage estimates include extra protection and above-normal maintenance costs to repair damage from subversive attacks. Maintenance costs are particularly high for electrical and telephone systems, which have significant investments in plant and equipment located in areas and of a type quite susceptible to guerrilla violence. Estimate also includes $20.44 million in diesel-fuel costs to fuel steam and turbine generators required to back up the frequently attacked hydro/geothermal stations and lines. Damage to the refinery resulted from a rocket attack in October 1982; while less effective than the guerrillas apparently intended, the cost of repairs is significant.

D. Budgetary Outlays

1. *Care of Desplazados* [displaced persons]. As of January 31, 1983, protracted violence in the countryside had created about 250,000 displaced persons. Private voluntary organizations, both domestic and foreign, and USAID have done much to relieve the financial burden to the government of El Salvador of caring for the war's displaced. Since 1980, however, the Salvadoran government has contributed approximately $2 million per year toward assistance for the *desplazados*. During 1980-82, using the $2 million per year estimate, the government spent $6 million which could otherwise have been used for public investment or other programs.

2. *Defense Budget.* From 1975 to 1978, the Salvadoran government spent an average of 7.5 per cent of its budget resources on defense. In 1979 this jumped to 12.7 per cent; by 1982, the government was spending about 17 per cent of its resources on defense and national security.

We estimate that even in the absence of the war, military expenditures would have increased moderately above the 1975-78 average because of the change in government in Nicaragua. If we thus assume a moderate increase of 2.5 per cent above the 1975-78 average, this would mean that in the absence of war military expenditures would have been 10 per cent of the budget. To simplify the calculation further, we have assumed that there would have been no change in the size of the budget.

The increase in defense expenditures that is due to the war is shown here, in millions of U.S. dollars:

	1979	1980	1981	1982
Actual total budget	581.3	658.0	795.4	844.4
Actual defense expenditures	74.0	94.6	120.3	143.4
10 per cent of total budget	58.1	65.8	79.5	84.4
DIFFERENCE	15.9	28.8	40.8	59.0

The total four-year difference between actual expenditures and a 10 per cent level of expenditures is $144.5 million.

E. Total Direct Costs

Keeping in mind that the above accounting is incomplete and includes some rough estimations, we can estimate the total of the war-related direct costs to the economy as follows:

Lost agricultural production	$235.2 million
Processing plants/warehouses	14.8
Industrial and commercial sectors	97.8
Infrastructure	98.1
Budgetary outlays (care of *desplazados,* defense)	150.5
Damage to crop dusters	0.4
	$596.8 million

INDIRECT COSTS OF THE WAR

The total cost of the war to the Salvadoran economy includes many side effects which, while not directly affecting the means of production, have nevertheless contributed to the slide in the GDP [gross domestic product]. These indirect costs often are the result of direct damage to the economy, such as the reduction in foreign-exchange earnings resulting from the precipitous decline in export-crop production, or in tourism; or the reduction in foreign-source credit availability owing to loss of confidence.

A. Balance-of-Payments Effects

The war has affected the balance of payments negatively in five major ways: an increase in food imports; a decline in foreign-exchange earnings, particularly from tourism, cotton, and sugar; an increase in diesel-fuel imports for back-up electrical power; a decrease in the availability of private foreign commercial credit; and capital flight. Certainly the war has had other negative effects on the balance of payments—for example, some part of the decrease in manufactured exports to the CACM [Central American Common Market] or the need to import other products which were previously produced here. But the five areas listed above make up the bulk of the balance-of-payments costs of the war.

1. *Increase in Food Imports.* Between 1971 and 1979, food imports as a percentage of total imports hovered in a narrow range of 8.7 to 11. In 1980 this proportion increased to 15.2 per cent, and in 1981 to 16.3. Some of the principal products showing increases included corn, milk, rice, vegetables, and processed meats. While these increases are not due entirely to the violence, the production declines noted above have played an important role in increasing reliance on food imports, along with the growing numbers of refugees displaced from the lands. Imports of wheat, corn, and rice under PL-480 have eased the balance-of-payments effects somewhat; but El Salvador will continue to rely heavily on imports of milk, vegetables, fruits, and meats until the security situation in the countryside improves.

2. *Decrease in Foreign-Exchange Earnings.* Foreign-exchange earnings from the three major export crops declined by 41 per cent between 1979 and 1982, from $786.6 million in 1979 to $463.7 million in 1982. Most of the decline which is attributable to violence is in cotton and sugar exports rather than coffee. The drop in coffee-exports receipts is in large part explainable by economic factors, including restrictions on overall export levels under the ICO [International Cof-

fee Organization] and low world prices. Unlike cotton and sugar exports, which are grown in the most conflictive areas, coffee is grown mainly in the westernmost provinces, which have been relatively peaceful.

Prior to the war, tourism was one of the fastest-growing industries in El Salvador. By 1979, tourism was the third-largest foreign-exchange earner, at $36.7 million, after coffee and cotton. By the end of 1981 this had dropped to $16.2 million. Some tourist hotels have been closed, and others are operating at low levels of occupancy.

3. *Increase in Diesel Imports.* Despite stable petroleum prices since the sharp OPEC increase of 1979, and despite normal decline in demand because of the sharp contraction in economic activity, El Salvador's petroleum imports have increased significantly since 1979.

Prior to the outbreak of the war, little petroleum was imported for electricity generation, since El Salvador produced most of its needs by geothermal and hydroelectric plants. In 1979, petroleum imports were $122.4 million or 11.9 per cent of total imports. By 1981 petroleum imports had increased to $180 million or 18.4 per cent of total imports. CEL (the state electricity-production company— Comisión Ejecutiva Hidroeléctrica del Río Lempa) alone reports that its extra diesel needs have increased by some $20 million since 1979 (the figure is included in the calculation of direct costs to infrastructure above). Most of the recent demand for diesel is explained by CEL's need to back up existing long-haul transmission systems from Cerrón Grande and the geothermal plant, which are frequent guerrilla targets, with steam or turbine generators. This increased burden on scarce foreign exchange has reduced the government's ability to import raw materials to maintain industrial production.

4. *Decrease in the Availability of Foreign Private Credit.* At the same time that pressures on the balance of payments were building because of declining exports and the need to import items on an emergency basis, foreign private credit contracted sharply. In the past most of these credits were short-term debts of the Salvadoran private sector to finance imports. In 1978, total private-sector short-term debt was $295.9 million. By 1981 total short-term debt had shrunk to $67.7 million. By their own admission, private foreign bankers' willingness to lend to El Salvador is highly dependent on political stability. The contraction in foreign private lending has had a depressing effect particularly on imports of spare parts, machinery, and raw materials for industry, which had previously been financed almost exclusively through the private banking network.

5. *Capital Flight.* It has been estimated that private capital flight occasioned by the violence has totaled as much as $1 billion, although no accurate figures are available.

B. Declining Budget Revenues

Nominal revenues declined by 4 per cent 1979-82, while expenditures were up by 52 per cent in the same period. The war has been a principal factor in the overall revenue drop. The major war-related reductions are in collections of income taxes owing to the contraction of economic activity; in the level of import taxes owing to a 10.2 per cent decline in the nominal value of imports; and in revenues from public enterprises such as the state-owned telephone and electricity companies. Coffee export taxes have also dropped precipitously but more as a response to economic factors than because of the war. El Salvador's overall budget situation has deteriorated since the war heated up in early 1979. The overall balance changed from a surplus of $39.1 million in 1979 to a deficit of $241 million in 1982, most of which was financed by Central Bank credit.

C. Socio-Economic Factors

This set of war-related costs is perhaps the most difficult to measure, but perhaps the most damaging to the economy over the long run. Of particular importance are severe real reductions in government spending for education, health, and other social programs. In 1979 health and education expenditures were 30 per cent of the budget; by 1982 this portion had dropped to 25 per cent. Two hundred forty-seven schools were closed because of violence in 1980, 877 in 1981, and 826 in 1982. In 1981-82 100,000 students and 1,500 teachers were affected by the violence. The campus of the National University has been closed since 1979 because of political violence. Increased unemployment, the separation of families by military service and emigration, the increasing number of refugees, and the proliferation of violence have further eroded the fragile stability of the Salvadoran socio-economic system. These are costs which society will be repaying long after the war finally ends. For example, the interruptions in electricity bring on a high public health cost. Potable water systems in El Salvador use electric pumps. When the guerrillas cut the electricity, potable water is not available for days at a time in some areas. This does not mean people stop drinking water; it means they drink dirty water. They contract gastrointestinal diseases, which affects their ability to work and increases demands on public health facilities. We understand that gastrointestinal diseases in the eastern "conflictive" departments are endemic. The cost is incalculable, but nonetheless real. And finally, there is no way to put a price on the lives which have been lost or the suffering to the families of the victims of violence.

D. Future Growth

There has been a substantial decline in investment in recent years, as gross domestic capital formation in 1982 was only 34 per cent of the 1978 level in real terms. The drop would have been even greater had it not been for continued government investment made possible by foreign assistance. It is impossible to estimate the value of the loss of future economic growth which this lack of new investment will entail, but it is undoubtedly considerable.

* * * * *

We emphasize again the provisional and to some extent conjectural nature of our estimates; readers should note carefully the procedural limitations we have described. We have omitted a number of factors. Not included, for example, are such things as outflows of goods from the system to supply guerrillas (i.e., confiscated foods, medicines, and the like); ransom paid for release of kidnap victims, especially in 1979/1980; partial damage to property; and the cost of increased security to persons and property in urban areas in recent years. Nevertheless, we hope we have been able to give some impressions of the nature and magnitude of the economic costs of the political instability since 1978.

Human Rights Progress in El Salvador: Fourth Certification

In 1981 the U.S. Congress passed legislation making military aid to El Salvador contingent upon periodic certification by the U.S. Department of State that the government of El Salvador had made progress in extending human rights. The following statement was presented to subcommittees of the House Foreign Affairs Committee on August 3, 1983, by two State Department officials: Langhorne A. Motley, assistant secretary for inter-American affairs, and Elliott Abrams, assistant secretary for human rights and humanitarian affairs.

ASSISTANT SECRETARY LANGHORNE A. MOTLEY

On July 20 Secretary Shultz, acting on authority delegated to him by the President, certified to the Congress that El Salvador meets the criteria set forth in Section 728 of the International Security and Cooperation Act of 1981, as amended.

I am pleased to have this opportunity to review this fourth certification with you and, since this will be the last such certification under the 1981 act, to offer some comments about the certification process as a whole.

As you know, section 728(d) requires periodic certification to the Congress that the government of El Salvador:

(1) is making a concerted and significant effort to comply with internationally recognized human rights;

(2) is achieving substantial control over all elements of its own armed forces, so as to bring to an end the indiscriminate torture and murder of Salvadoran citizens by these forces;

(3) is making continued progress in implementing essential economic and political reforms, including the land reform program;

(4) is committed to the holding of free elections at an early date and to that end has demonstrated its good faith efforts to begin discussions with all major political factions in El Salvador which have declared their willingness to find and implement an equitable political solution to the conflict, with such solution to involve a commitment to—

(a) a renouncement of further military or paramilitary activity; and

(b) the electoral process with internationally recognized observers.

The July 1983 amendment of section 728(e) of the act requires a determination in the fourth certification that the government of El Salvador:

(1) has made good faith efforts both to investigate the murders of the seven United States citizens in El Salvador in December 1980 and in January 1981, and to bring to justice all those responsible for those murders, and

(2) has taken all reasonable steps to investigate the killing of Michael Kline in El Salvador in October 1982.[1]

Certification Findings

El Salvador is in its fourth year under governments committed to building a lasting democratic order. Despite major handicaps, including a long history of military rule and dominance by a small elite and the violence of a struggle against armed guerrillas supported from outside, a hard-fought and evolutionary democratic process is under way.

Specifically, the certification report finds that at this time the Salvadoran government is working to increase respect for human rights and to reduce abuses by its security forces. It has strengthened institutions, repeatedly and forcefully emphasized the importance of human rights at all levels, and generally followed a democratic, reformist policy. Through the amnesty program more than 300 individual guerrillas and guerrilla supporters have laid down their arms and more than 500 political prisoners have been released from detention.

Nevertheless, convictions for serious crimes, especially those with political overtones, have been virtually unobtainable because of intimidation and corruption of judges, lawyers, witnesses, and jurors. In order to rectify this basic impediment to the effective rule of law, since the last certification the Salvadoran government has begun efforts to reform its criminal justice system. This long-term program seeks to upgrade the capacity and independence of the system at investigatory, prosecutorial, and judicial levels—a program essential to ensuring that no one's actions are above the law and that none may act outside the law without fear of lawful retribution.

There has been only slow progress thus far by the Salvadoran authorities in bringing to justice the murders of U.S. citizens. The prosecution of the security force personnel accused of murdering four American churchwomen is slowly proceeding through the Salvadoran court system. The case of the two National Guardsmen accused of the murder of American labor consultants has been raised to the trial stage, but others who may have been involved in the crime have not been arrested. The positive identification in the United States of the remains of John Sullivan is permitting a full investigation in El Salvador.[2] Three members of the Salvadoran army are under detention for the murder of Michael Kline, and the case is before the courts. There has been no progress in discovering the whereabouts of Patricia Cuellar or in resolving her disappearance.[3] We are receiving full Salvadoran cooperation in the investigation of the death of an American citizen killed since the last certification—Lt. Commander Albert Schaufelberger— victim of a political assassination for which a far-left guerrilla death squad has claimed credit.

---

1. Michael Kline was a young U.S. citizen traveling in El Salvador.
2. John Sullivan was a U.S. reporter who disappeared in El Salvador in December 1980. His body was identified in February 1983.
3. Patricia Cuellar is a dual Salvadoran-U.S. citizen who disappeared in El Salvador on July 18, 1982.

The major economic reforms of 1980—redistribution of farmland, nationalization of the banking system, and government control of coffee and sugar marketing—remain in force, and the agrarian reform has continued to move ahead, making more Salvadorans the owners of the land they work. A major promotion campaign earlier this year resulted in a sharp increase in applicants and beneficiaries under the land-to-the-tiller phase of the agrarian reform. Salvadoran efforts to restore illegally evicted beneficiaries have increased. The need for these steps is underscored by a study, compiled by the Salvadoran Agrarian Reform Planning and Evaluation Office as part of this effort and just received in Washington, which indicates that illegal evictions of beneficiaries may be higher than we believed at the time of certification.

Progress in developing democratic institutions is evidenced by:

• Continued functioning of the elected Government of National Unity;

• Completion of the draft constitution on which formal debate in the Constituent Assembly will begin August 8;

• Ongoing preparations for elections, coupled with repeated invitations by the Salvadoran Government's Peace Commission to guerrilla-associated parties to participate in them; and

• Increased activity by democratic political parties and labor unions.

The Constituent Assembly has become a forum in which competition among political factions is conducted in a democratic manner and in which a number of difficult decisions have been made. It is also functioning effectively as the national legislature.

The Salvadoran Peace Commission has made repeated calls, backed by President Magaña and the multiparty Political Commission which created it, for meetings with the guerrilla left to find ways they could participate in the coming elections. This effort to continue to broaden the democratic process begun in March 1982 is at the heart of the Salvadoran solution. Power-sharing based on the relative capacity of each side to destroy the adherents of the other is no solution. Only a democratic system, in which each side contends for ballots fairly and is confident that if it loses today it may try again and prevail tomorrow, can bring lasting peace to El Salvador and ensure responsive, just government there in the future.

In view of the foregoing, Secretary Shultz concluded that "the statutory criteria for certification are met." However, he also noted in his letter of transmittal that

... it is evident that the record falls short of the broad and sustained progress which both the Congress and the Administration believe is necessary for the evolution of a just and democratic society in El Salvador.

The development of democracy can be a long and difficult process, even under the best of circumstances. The situation in El Salvador today is anything but the "best of circumstances." What we are trying to accomplish in El Salvador by supporting democratic elements is nothing less than to help a society change the way its social, political, and economic affairs traditionally have been conducted. We are doing this in the face of a campaign of violence and terrorism supported and encouraged from outside the country.

Despite the efforts of the government of El Salvador, violations of human rights continue to occur. Rightist terrorists bear responsibility for many deaths attributable to political violence. Elements of the government security forces are believed to have been involved in or responsible for many of these violations of the rights of the person.

During the last six months, the number of press-reported civilian deaths attributed to political violence rose, and disappearances continued at about the same rate as during the last half of 1982. (There are differences among the Salvadoran organizations which monitor human rights developments over whether civilian deaths actually rose or fell slightly in this period.)

Major abuses, such as the February slaying of eighteen persons at Las Hojas, have gone unpunished. All of those involved in the murder of the two American labor consultants have not been brought to justice. Though the Salvadoran government is working to increase respect for human rights, it has not managed to punish those responsible for continuing abuses.

As Secretary Shultz's letter of transmittal stated:

> . . . our disappointment over the pace of change should not obscure the fact that change is occurring. The people of El Salvador deserve our support in their effort to achieve a truly democratic society, which will provide the best and most lasting safeguard of human rights.

The Certification Process

The certification process has assisted us to support those Salvadoran sectors who favor democracy, moderation, and progress by underscoring those issues of greatest concern to us and by ensuring that the entire U.S. government speaks with one voice on these key issues. The clarity and firmness of the certification process has been its great virtue.

But existing certification procedures also have numerous defects. Best known of these is the tendency of the certification date—essentially a legal event—to induce the far left to greater violence, either to inspire an overreaction by the Salvadoran defense forces or to take advantage of their temporary paralysis. This has produced so-called certification offensives.

Equally important, the certification has a "made-in-the-U.S." aspect which may place it out of synchronization with the realities and pressures in El Salvador. For instance, in this certification there is a criterion on Salvadoran elections—elections already held with great success. Though another round of elections is also in the works, these were not the elections contemplated in the original legislation. On the other hand, it is clear that Salvadoran political realities and the pressures and hatreds of so brutal an internal conflict have greatly impeded the effort to establish firm civilian control over the Salvadoran military and security forces. Progress has been further impeded during the past six months by leadership changes in the Salvadoran armed forces. As Secretary Shultz emphasized in his transmittal letter to Congress, much more needs to be done.

Perhaps most importantly, the certification process attempts to depict the process of change in El Salvador in a series of "snapshots" at six-month intervals.

On the basis of these frozen moments, a go/no-go decision must be made on U.S. military assistance. This methodology clearly overemphasizes high profile events and understates the longer term evolutionary processes. The land reform is a good example. It has now benefited more than 500,000 Salvadorans. But the "snapshot" taken at this time, on the heels of the bad news of the recent survey of evictions, obscures the fact that a developing Salvadoran institution conducted the survey and produced the report in order to monitor and further a key reform program.

In attempting political and economic reforms of the scope of those in El Salvador, developments must frequently accumulate to a critical mass before visible change occurs. When it does, it can occur quite rapidly—as in the will of the parties and people to make the March 1982 elections a success; as in the land reform; as in the amnesty program; as in the call for dialogue on elections with the far left. Yet as presently constituted, the certification process creates expectations of a continuing incremental progress on all fronts which is not likely to be achieved.

Last is the stick behind the certification process. At 180-day intervals, certification determines, immediately, whether the United States will provide military assistance and trainers to El Salvador on the basis of the "snapshot" mentioned earlier. As a result, Salvadoran commanders in the midst of a major war effort must plan on the basis of a supply line in constant danger of being shut off. This is neither conducive to good military tactics nor good for building the political will to sustain the development of democracy. The tendency will be to husband resources against an uncertain future, as occurred between October and January, and, potentially, even to encourage a return to traditional, more savage means of settling political disputes and dividing the economic pie. The repeated, periodic threat of discontinuity can undermine U.S. influence with those whose long-term commitment to profound change must be maintained.

We need to continue in close consultations with the Congress to see if we can construct an oversight mechanism which will retain the strengths of the present certification process while ameliorating some of its defects; a mechanism by which we can arrive at mutually agreed upon, practical goals toward which the Salvadorans can work with their own plans; a mechanism which also permits sound military planning; one which does not inspire synchronized violence by the far left or right; one which does not freeze the action into short intervals that obscure long-term trends; but a mechanism which also shows clearly and forcefully our expectations of an ally and a friend.

ASSISTANT SECRETARY ELLIOTT ABRAMS

I am grateful for the opportunity to appear before you once again to discuss the human rights aspects of American policy in El Salvador and more broadly in Central America. The advance of human rights in Central America remains a key goal of the U.S. government. We pursue this goal in two ways, and both are essential. One is to press governments for the rectification of specific abuses, and we work at this energetically. But it is not enough. Both the Reagan administration and its critics know how frustrating this effort is if it is all we are doing. It is frustrating because it deals basically with symptoms—symptoms of the utmost importance for people's lives—but not with causes.

Therefore, we are also trying to deal with the underlying situation that produces the massive violations of human rights in El Salvador. We are addressing it in several ways. First, by economic assistance and economic reform we hope to keep the Salvadoran people from the edge of desperation, to spread land ownership to larger groups, and to help build the basis for economic stability and growth which will contribute to political progress. Second, by military training we are transforming the Salvadoran security forces into a professional army. This process of professionalization, we believe, will produce higher discipline and more exacting standards toward civilians. Third and most important, we are encouraging the development of a secure democratic system in El Salvador. As elsewhere in the world, only democracy will be a real guarantee of respect for human rights.

So we have been extremely active on human rights. As you know, we used such influence as we had to press for a free election and a civilian government in Honduras. We have spent a very great deal of time supporting human rights improvements in El Salvador. These have been slow in coming, but as Secretary Shultz said in his letter of transmittal of our certification, "our disappointment over the pace of change should not obscure the fact that change is occurring." We have pressed the government of Guatemala on the subject of its secret courts— which have now stopped issuing death sentences and which the government of Guatemala is moving to reform or eliminate—and on setting a firm date for an election, which has now been done. We have supported the government and people of Costa Rica in their efforts to maintain their democracy, which is a model for all Central America.

Many of us are disappointed by the pace of progress on human rights in Central America. That pace is, of course, the product of many factors, including the weight of history. But there is one particular current factor of which we should take note—namely, the role of Nicaragua. I would, therefore, pose the question, What would the human rights situation in Central America be like today if the government of Nicaragua were a peaceful, democratic one?

I think that it would be markedly improved. First of all, the desire for democracy in Nicaragua, which led to the overthrow of Somoza, would be satisfied rather than repressed. The government of Nicaragua would be protecting the human rights of all Nicaraguans and would as well be providing a model for its neighbors, perhaps in the fashion that Costa Rica does today. In addition, Nicaragua would not be supporting Leninist guerrillas in El Salvador and thereby setting back he struggle for human rights in that country, just as it would not be engaging in subversion in Honduras.

I do not believe it to be accidental that the vast increase in violence in El Salvador has occurred since 1979, precisely the period of Sandinista rule in Nicaragua. Nor is it coincidental that the armies of El Salvador and Honduras have grown in this period: in El Salvador partly in response to increased internal guerrilla strength, and in Honduras in response to the Nicaraguan military build-up. How easy is it to proceed with economic reforms when these economies are forced into large-scale military spending and hammered by guerrilla attacks? How easy is it to increase the control of democratic civilian institutions over the military when subversion requires a society to concentrate such massive efforts on defending itself? Were Nicaragua to pursue the path of pluralism and to stop subverting its neighbors, I believe that not only the chance for democracy but the actual achievement of democracy and respect for human rights would be far more advanced in Central America than we find it today.

The defense of human rights often requires more than diplomatic pressure, more than economic assistance, more than training programs. Sometimes it requires a military shield behind which democracy can develop, In postwar Europe, we must remember, the Marshall Plan was not our sole effort to help Europeans achieve stability and democracy. The other pillar of our policy was NATO—the military shield behind which the European democracies could reestablish themselves, secure against outside aggression or subversion. This policy has succeeded, and Western Europe has seen nearly four decades of peace, economic growth, and democracy, extending most recently, and after decades of dictatorship, to Spain and Portugal. Of course, Central America is not Europe, for Europe had deep democratic roots to tap in the postwar period. Reestablishing democracy is a difficult task, but building democratic institutions for the very first time is a more difficult task, especially when a region is in conflict.

The transition to democracy is an extremely difficult undertaking for any country, and to achieve it in a time of conflict is even more challenging a task. Our efforts to achieve peace in Central America and our promotion of human rights there go hand in hand, for we know that respect for human rights and democratic institutions will be difficult to achieve while conflict is ranging. We are convinced that our support for economic and social reform, our pressure for advances in the cause of human rights and the building of democratic institutions, and our efforts to achieve an end to regional conflict in Central America together provide the most hopeful path for the people of Central America toward a peaceful and democratic future.

Bibliography

SOURCES OF RECORD

Hoover Institution on War, Revolution, and Peace. *Yearbook on International Communist Affairs* (annual).

Hopkins, Jack, W., ed. *Latin America and the Caribbean Contemporary Record* (annual).

UCLA Latin American Center. *Statistical Abstract of Latin America* (annual).

PERIODICALS

America (weekly); *Caribbean Review,* Florida International University, Miami (quarterly); *Christian Century* (weekly); *Christianity and Crisis* (weekly); *Commentary* (monthly); *Diario de las Americas,* Miami (daily); *Foreign Affairs* (quarterly); *Foreign Policy* (quarterly); *Inter-American Economic Affairs* (quarterly); *Journal of Inter-American Studies and World Affairs* (quarterly); National Catholic News Service: *Origins* and *Catholic Trends; National Catholic Register* (weekly); *National Catholic Reporter* (weekly); *Sojourners* (monthly); *Strategic Review* (quarterly); *Times of the Americas* (weekly).

U.S. GOVERNMENT DOCUMENTS

U.S. Department of State, Bureau of Public Affairs: *Current Policy, Department of State Bulletin, Gist,* and *Special Report.*

Part One: Regional Perspectives

Anderson, Thomas. *Central America.* New York: Praeger, 1982.

Erisman, H. Michael, and Martz, John D., eds. *Colossus Challenged: The Caribbean Struggle for Influence.* Boulder, Colo.: Westview Press, 1982.

Feinberg, Richard E., ed. *Central America: International Dimensions of the Crisis.* New York: Holmes and Meier, 1982.

Leiken, Robert S., ed. *Central America: Anatomy of Conflict.* New York: Pergamon Press, 1984.

Levine, Barry B., ed. *The New Cuban Presence in the Caribbean.* Boulder, Colo.: Westview Press, 1983.

Moorer, Thomas H., and Fauriol, Georges. *Caribbean Basin Security.* Washington, D.C.: Center for Strategic and International Studies, 1984.

Munro, Dana C. *Intervention and Dollar Diplomacy in the Caribbean*. Princeton, N.J.: Princeton University Press, 1964.

Wesson, Robert E., ed. *Communism in Central America and the Caribbean*. Stanford, Calif.: Hoover Institution Press, 1982.

Wiarda, Howard J., ed. *Rift and Revolution: The Central American Imbroglio*. Washington, D.C.: American Enterprise Institute for Public Policy Research, 1984.

Williams, Eric. *From Columbus to Castro: The History of the Caribbean, 1492-1969*. New York: Random House, 1983.

Wood, Bryce. *The Making of the Good Neighbor Policy*. New York: Columbia University Press, 1961.

Woodward, Ralph Lee. *Central America: A Nation Divided*. New York: Oxford University Press, 1976.

Part Two: El Salvador

Anderson, Thomas P. *War of the Dispossessed*. Lincoln, Neb.: University of Nebraska Press, 1981.

Baloyra, Enrique. *El Salvador in Transition*. Chapel Hill, N.C.: University of North Carolina Press, 1982.

Gettleman, Marvin, *et al.*, eds. *El Salvador: Central America in the New Cold War*. New York: Grove Press, 1981.

McColm, R. Bruce. *El Salvador: Peaceful Revolution or Armed Struggle?* New York: Freedom House, 1982.

Montgomery, T. S. *Revolution in El Salvador: Origins and Evolution*. Boulder, Colo.: Westview Press, 1982.

Webre, Stephen. *José Napoleón Duarte and the Christian Democratic Party in Salvadoran Politics, 1960-72*. Baton Rouge, La: Louisiana State University Press, 1979.

Part Three: Nicaragua

Booth, John A. *An End and a Beginning: The Nicaraguan Revolution*. Boulder, Colo.: Westview Press, 1983.

Crawley, Eduardo. *Dictators Never Die: A Portrait of Nicaragua and the Somoza Dynasty*. New York: St. Martin's Press, 1979.

Diedrich, Bernard. *Somoza and the Legacy of U.S. Involvement in Central America*. New York: E. P. Dutton, 1981.

Goldwert, Marvin. *The Constabulary in the Dominican Republic and Nicaragua: Progeny and Legacy of U.S. Intervention.* Gainesville, Fla.: University of Florida Press, 1962.

Kammen, William. *A Search for Stability: U.S. Diplomacy Toward Nicaragua, 1925-33.* Notre Dame, Ind.: University of Notre Dame Press, 1968.

Macaulay, Neill. *The Sandino Affair.* Chicago: Quadrangle Books. 1967.

Millett, Richard. *Guardians of the Dynasty: A History of the U.S.-Created National Guard and the Somoza Family.* Maryknoll, N.Y.: Orbis Books, 1977.

Munro, Dana G. *The United States and the Caribbean Republics, 1921-33.* Princeton, N.J., Princeton University Press, 1974.

Ptacek, Kerry. *Nicaragua: A Revolution Against the Church?* Washington, D.C.: Institute for Religion and Democracy, 1981.

Somoza, Anastasio (with Jack Cox). *Nicaragua Betrayed.* Belmont, Mass.: Western Islands, 1980.

Tierney, John J. *Somozas and Sandinistas: The U.S. and Nicaragua in the Twentieth Century.* Washington, D.C.: Council for Inter-American Security, 1982.

Walker, Thomas, ed. *Nicaragua in Revolution.* New York: Praeger, 1982.

Index of Names

481

CENTER ESSAYS

CENTER ESSAYS
(continued)

18. **Alienation and U.S. Foreign Policy,** *Paul Craig Roberts*
Excessive self-criticism in America and a sense of guilt about our shortcomings erode our capacity to respond effectively to the Soviet military and ideological challenge.

19. **The Cost of America's Retreat,** *Ben J. Wattenberg*
In the wake of Vietnam, America's power and influence have dangerously receded. We must defend freedom and peace through economic and military strength.

20. **The Soul of Man Under Socialism,** *Vladimir Bukovsky*
An exile who spent twelve years in Soviet prisons, work camps, and psychiatric hospitals vividly portrays the impact of a totalitarian system on human dignity and self-respect.

21. **What It Means to Be Number Two**
Fred Charles Iklé, with a response by Radomir Bogdanov and Lev Semeiko
A former top SALT negotiator says American weakness, bordering on inferiority, encourages Soviet expansion. Two Soviet officials dispute his claims.

22. **Dictatorships and Double Standards: A Critique of U.S. Policy**
Jeane Kirkpatrick
A carefully documented indictment of the Carter Administration's selective indignation toward allied and friendly Third World regimes.

23. **Taiwan: Pawn or Pivot?,** *Parris H. Chang, Gerald McBeath, and Ralph N. Clough*
Two professors and a former diplomat analyze Taiwan's past, present, and future prospects.

24. **Crusade Against the Corporation: Church Militants on the March,** *Herman Nickel*
Church activists, working through the Interfaith Center on Corporate Responsibility, are leading a campaign to curb the power of multinational corporations. A major objective is to control the sale of infant formula in the Third World; their major tactic is to boycott Nestlé products.

25. **America the Enemy: Profile of a Revolutionary Think Tank,** *Rael Jean Isaac*
A thorough examination of the Institute for Policy Studies suggests that it is the hub of a revolutionary political network masquerading as an authentic "think tank."

26. **Washington vs. the Public Schools,** *J. Myron Atkin*
Examines the increasing penetration of elementary and secondary education by the federal government to achieve social goals or to advance the interests of politically powerful minorities.

27. **Washington vs. the Universities,** *Daniel Patrick Moynihan*
The senator asserts that the government has the power "to shut down any university" in America by withholding funds if it fails to comply with regulations tied to federal grants.

28. **Christian Schools, Racial Quotas, and the IRS,** *Peter Skerry*
The author concludes that the recent Christian-school movement is a reaction to "creeping humanism" and moral relativism in the public schools, not to racial problems.

29. **Solzhenitsyn and American Democracy,** *George F. Will and Michael Novak*
Two respected political commentators admire Solzhenitsyn's insistence that an enduring society must have deep spiritual roots but find he expects too much from democracy.

30. **Religious Freedom and the Supreme Court,** *Dallin H. Oaks*
A law professor says that in applying the First Amendment the Supreme Court tends to define religion broadly in relation to the "free exercise" provision and narrowly for "non-establishment."

31. **Sanctifying Revolution: Mainline Churchmen Turn Radical**
Rael Jean Isaac and Erich Isaac
In pursuing justice and "liberation," mainline church leaders have increasingly supported revolutionary, sometimes even violent, means.

32. **Education, Character, and American Schools,** *Gerald Grant*
Students must once again be taught to respect a common code of behavior even if it is a "provisional morality" that they may later revise.

33. **The New Defenders of Capitalism,** *Norman Podhoretz*
The traditional hostility of intellectuals toward market enterprise shows signs of reversal; many now argue that capitalism is the most productive system and increases freedom of choice.

CENTER ESSAYS
(continued)

34. **Moral Implications of Energy**
    William G. Pollard, Frederick S. Carney, and Thomas J. Reese, S.J.
    A nuclear physicist (and Episcopal priest), a professor of Christian ethics, and an editor of *America* reflect on the moral and theological implications of nuclear energy.

35. **How to Lose a War: The Press and Viet Nam,** *Robert Elegant*
    A veteran Asia correspondent says the Viet Nam war was lost not on the battlefield but in the minds of Western liberals whose views dominated the prestige press in the United States.

36. **Why Latin America Is Poor,** *Michael Novak*
    Latin American poverty is caused not by North American wealth or multinational corporations but by domestic social and cultural forces rooted in the political and economic institutions and world view of the Spanish conquerors.

37. **On the Brink: The Myth of German Anti-Americanism,** *Uwe Siemon-Netto*
    The German left wing's "long march" through the courts, schools, churches, media, and other institutions has had considerable success, but the great majority of the German people do not support the radical demand for the withdrawal of U.S. troops.

38. **The Media Elite and American Values,** *S. Robert Lichter and Stanley Rothman*
    From interviews with 240 journalists and broadcasters the authors conclude that the views of the media elite on major social, economic, and political questions are substantially to the left of those of middle America.

39. **Risk and Nuclear Power: Scientists, Journalists, and the Public**
    S. Robert Lichter and Stanley Rothman
    A careful survey of nuclear specialists and other scientists shows that those who know most about nuclear power are its strongest supporters.

40. **Nuclear Weapons and the Peace Movement,** *Henry A. Kissinger*
    Combining a firm grasp of political realities with the wisdom of experience, the former secretary of state examines all major facets of the nuclear arms debate.

41. **Private Virtues, Public Vices,** *Jeane J. Kirkpatrick*
    The U.S. representative to the United Nations distinguishes between private and public morality and argues that compromise and consensus-building are essential and desirable in the American political system.

42. **Constitutional Democracy vs. Utopian Democracy,** *Raymond English*
    Constitutional democracy, based on a realistic view of human nature and on moral discipline, endures; utopian democracy, based on sentimental illusions, is ephemeral and often leads to tyranny.

43. **Crime and American Culture,** *James Q. Wilson*
    In tracing the relations between crime and civic virtue in America over the past century, a distinguished Harvard professor affirms that the family, church, and school can play a significant role in reducing criminal behavior.

44. **Moscow and the European Peace Movement,** *J. A. Emerson Vermaat*
    The peace movements of several Western European nations draw significant support from Moscow. Their activities have the effect of weakening Western military commitment relative to that of the Soviet Union, thus making nuclear war more likely.

45. **Revolution, Terrorism, and U.S. Policy,** *Ernest W. Lefever*
    Terrorism, increasingly used by leftist revolutionaries who seek power by the bullet rather than by the ballot, is a serious threat to democratic government and to the U.S. interest in stability and peaceful development.

46. **Reducing Risk by Restoring Strength: Reflections on Nuclear War**
    W. Scott Thompson
    The risk of nuclear war decreases when U.S. and Soviet forces are approximately equal and when we have confidence in the quality of our deterrent, says the author. He deals also with the morality of self-defense, the myth of overkill, and the pacifist temptation.

CENTER ESSAYS
(continued)

47. **Global Paternalism: The U.N. and the New International Class Struggle**
Jeane J. Kirkpatrick
Many U.N. representatives and staff members view its institutions as instruments to achieve the "new international economic order" by regulation, redistribution, and socialization of the world's wealth.

48. **Who Speaks for American Judaism? Competing Approaches to Public Issues**
Seymour Siegel, Marshall J. Breger, Joshua O. Haberman, and David Saperstein
Rabbi Siegel asserts that political liberalism, prevalent in the Jewish community, is true neither to Jewish interests nor to Jewish teachings; he sees signs of a turn toward conservatism. Responses to his theses are offered by a law professor, a leading Reform rabbi, and a religious activist.

49. **Advancing Democratic Principles: A European Examines a Neglected American Asset,** *Stephen Haseler*
To complete successfully with adversaries of the West in the battle of ideas, Americans should build more effectively on the near universal recognition that the United States is democratic, free, and dynamic, while the Soviet Union is "repressive, bureaucratic, and boring."

50. **Speaking to the World: Four Protestant Perspectives**
Richard John Neuhaus, Earl G. Hunt, Jr., Paul Ramsey, and Philip R. Cousin
Lutheran theologian Neuhaus asserts that the current crisis in Christian social ethics is fundamentally a crisis of faith, and that a thorough theological renewal is called for. Responses by a Methodist bishop, a professor of religion, and an African Methodist Episcopal bishop follow.

51. **We and They: Understanding Ourselves and Our Adversary,** *Jeane J. Kirkpatrick*
An incisive analysis of the worldwide Soviet threat to freedom and a call for the United States to defend itself and Western civilization by military and other necessary measures.

52. **A Tribute to Lech Walsea,** *Ernest W. Lefever, ed.*
Statements honoring the Polish patriot by President Reagan, Ambassador Jeane Kirkpatrick, Ambassador Max Kampelman, Dr. Zbigniew Brzezinski, Mayor Edward Koch, Governor Thomas Kean, and others, with a message from Walesa.

53. **If East Europeans Could Vote: A Survey,** *Henry O. Hart*
Opinion research by Radio Free Europe among Eastern Europeans finds a widespread antipathy to Communist regimes (only 4 to 7% of responding Czechs, Hungarians, and Poles support the party) and a strong preference for Democratic Socialist and Christian Democratic systems.

54. **Central America in U.S. Domestic Politics,** *Mark Falcoff*
The debate over U.S. policies in Central America is more often a reflection of domestic political differences than a realistic appraisal of the region. A Latin American scholar identifies the sources of common errors and points out the real problems we face there.

55. **The Grenada Mission: Crisis Editorializing in the** *New York Times,* **Wall Street Journal, Washington Post, and Washington Times**
Foreword by Edwin M. Yoder, Jr.; edited by Raymond English
The fourteen editorials reprinted here, from the two weeks following the landing of U.S. forces on Grenada in October 1983, show a diversity of response, from cheers to unremitting hostility. Veteran journalist Edwin Yoder gives an overview, and an appendix chronicles events on Grenada that led to the U.S. action.

56. **Nuclear Arms and Soviet Aims**
Ronald Reagan, Pierre Gallois and John Train, Eugene V. Rostow, and Paul H. Nitze
President Reagan discusses U.S.-Soviet relations; French general Gallois and American writer Train analyze the new trend toward low-yield, high-precision weapons; Yale professor Rostow examines Moscow's nuclear objectives; and chief U.S. medium-range arms negotiator Nitze describes what Moscow means by "peace."

Essays are $2 each.
Postpaid if payment accompanies order.
Orders of $25 or more, 10 per cent discount.